DOUBT AND DOGMATISM

DOUBT AND DOGMATISM

Studies in Hellenistic Epistemology

Edited by

MALCOLM SCHOFIELD
MYLES BURNYEAT
JONATHAN BARNES

CLARENDON PRESS, OXFORD
1980

Oxford University Press, Walton Street, Oxford OX2 6DP

OXFORD   LONDON   GLASGOW
NEW YORK   TORONTO   MELBOURNE   WELLINGTON
KUALA LUMPUR   SINGAPORE   JAKARTA   HONG KONG   TOKYO
DELHI   BOMBAY   CALCUTTA   MADRAS   KARACHI
NAIROBI   DAR ES SALAAM   CAPE TOWN

Published in the United States
by Oxford University Press
New York

British Library Cataloguing in Publication Data

Doubt and dogmatism.
  1. Knowledge, Theory of—Congresses
  2. Philosophy, Ancient—Congresses
  I. Schofield, Malcolm   II. Burnyeat, Myles
  III. Barnes, Jonathan
  121'.0938   BD161   79-41044

  ISBN 0-19-824601-3

*Printed and bound in Great Britain by
Morrison & Gibb Ltd., London and Edinburgh*

PREFACE

The conference whose records and results compose this volume was wholly timely and wholly successful. There have been other innovative meetings of this kind—I recall the first Symposium Aristotelicum in 1957—but I believe this matched all competition in friendly and argumentative collaboration. A field too often tilled by clever but isolated husbandmen is now opened to philosophers and scholars of philosophy who might otherwise have supposed that epistemology went lackadaisical after Aristotle and revived only with Descartes. The record is enhanced, to the benefit of both research and teaching, by a first chapter placing and characterizing the major philosophers to be discussed. Here, then, is a joint breakthrough.

G. E. L. O.

ACKNOWLEDGEMENTS

This book owes its origin to a conference on Hellenistic philosopy held at Oriel College, Oxford, in March 1978. The conference was attended by: Julia Annas, Jonathan Barnes, Jacques Brunschwig, Myles Burnyeat, Theodor Ebert, Troels Engberg-Pedersen, Michael Frede, Claude Imbert, Anthony Kenny, Christopher Kirwan, Geoffrey Lloyd, Tony Long, Mario Mignucci, Martha Nussbaum, Gwil Owen, Pierre Pachet, Malcolm Schofield, David Sedley, Bob Sharples, Richard Sorabji, Gisela Striker, and Christopher Taylor.

The individual chapters, with the exception of Chapter I, began life as papers read to the conference; and the authors wish to acknowledge the invaluable help they received from all participants in the discussion—indeed, the book itself is, in a real sense, a collaborative production.

The conference was generously supported by grants from the British Academy, the British Council, the Jowett Trust, the Literae Humaniores Board of Oxford University, Oriel College, and the parent Universities of the participants: we are most grateful to those Institutions.

M. S.
M. F. B.
J. B.

CONTENTS

TO THE READER

It is the hope of all who collaborated in the conference that this book will be of interest both to students of Greek philosophy and to a wider circle of philosophical readers. The Hellenistic philosophers are not as well known to the general philosophical community as Plato and Aristotle, nor have they been studied by scholars with the intensity they deserve. Yet the achievement of Hellenistic philosophy was considerable in itself and, historically, it had a formative influence on the development of modern philosophy: the problems and debates under discussion in the present volume marked out for philosophy some of its central concerns. Readers new to Hellenistic philosophy will find in Chapter I an introduction to the chief figures of the period and their philosophical standpoint, together with a chronological table showing their dates and affiliations. It remains to add a word about sources.

There is no doubt that one reason for the neglect suffered by Hellenistic philosophy is that the source material is, or appears to be, less readily accessible than the works of Plato and Aristotle. In fact, the situation is not nearly as bad as it may seem. The reader will find that the bulk of the material discussed in the following chapters derives from a handful of main sources, all readily available in English translation from the Loeb Classical Library series, with facing Greek or Latin text.

The works concerned, introduced by the abbreviations which will be used in referring to them, are as follows:

DL: Diogenes Laertius, *Lives of the Philosophers*
PH: Sextus Empiricus, *Outlines of Pyrrhonism*
M: Sextus Empiricus, *Adversus mathematicos*
Acad: Cicero, *Academica*

To which may be added some of the essays in Plutarch's *Moralia,* in particular *Adversus Colotem* (Plu. *Col.*) and *De Stoicorum repugnantiis* (Plu. *Stoic. rep*).

For the minority of references which fall outside this list, the abbreviations are based on those in Liddell–Scott–Jones, *A Greek-English Lexicon* (9th edn., Oxford, 1940) and the *Oxford*

Latin Dictionary (Oxford, 1968–). Many of the texts bearing on Stoicism are collected in H. von Arnim, *Stoicorum Veterum Fragmenta* (Leipzig, 1903–24), references to which are by volume, page, and line number (e.g. *SVF* II, p. 252, 7) or by volume and passage number (e.g. *SVF* II 109); but von Arnim does not translate his texts, and *SVF* is not a convenient work to use. We cite it only for passages which are not readily available elsewhere.

Further guidance may be found in the select bibliography and the index locorum at the end of the volume.

THE PROTAGONISTS

David Sedley

I

The primary object of this historical introduction[1] is to enable a reader encountering Hellenistic philosophy for the first time to familiarize himself with the leading philosophers of the period. But at the same time I have tried to show what influences shaped their approach to philosophy in general, and, more particularly, to epistemology.

The Hellenistic age officially runs from the death of Alexander the Great in 323 B.C. to that of Cleopatra in 30 B.C. Before it had even been going a year Aristotle was dead. Hence Epicureanism, Stoicism, and scepticism, the characteristic philosophies of the age, have frequently been called 'post-Aristotelian', a label which, if chronologically impeccable, has had a curiously dampening effect on their reputation. It has fostered the impression that, since Aristotle marks the zenith of Greek philosophy, after him there was nothing for it to do but decline. As recently as 1935 F. M. Cornford could write:[2]

> After Aristotle we have the letters of Epicurus, and then not a single writing by an original thinker of the first rank till we come to Plotinus. There is a much larger mass of fragments, but of greatly inferior value; because the succeeding eight centuries produced very few men worthy to stand beside that constellation of men of genius, the Presocratics. If the excavators of Herculaneum should bring to light the 750 books of Chrysippus—which Heaven forbid—any student would cheerfully exchange them for a single roll of Heracleitus.

The truth is that the leading Hellenistic philosophers lived neither in Aristotle's nor in anyone else's shadow. Certainly Socrates, Plato, and Aristotle, together with a whole range of

---

[1] To quote chapter and verse for all the statements made here would require annotation on a massive scale. Given the primarily introductory nature of these pages, I have chosen instead to restrict annotation chiefly to what I expect to be the most controversial or unfamiliar claims made in them.

[2] F. M. Cornford, 'The Unwritten Philosophy', in *The Unwritten Philosophy and Other Essays* (1950).

other thinkers, were integral to the intellectual background from which the new generation emerged, and not infrequently their work was, either consciously or unconsciously, taken into account. But in the vital first half-century of Hellenistic philosophy it was contemporary debates, issues, and theories that set the keynote. The result was one of the most exciting and prolific periods of ancient thought, in which some of the fundamental problems of philosophy were put on the map for the first time.

In the Hellenistic age, as in the entire preceeding century, Athens served as the great melting pot of Greek philosophy. Its public places were frequented by teachers in search of an audience and by young men (and, once in a while, women) in search of enlightenment. The most popular locations were the public gymnasia outside the city walls, including the Academy and the Lyceum, and the area around the central agora. A philosophical school needed no private premises, and in principle might be established in any spot where gatherings could easily take place.[3] With nearly all the leading philosophical movements of the day publicly offering their wares within a two-mile radius of central Athens, the city was a great public arena in which ideas could be aired, brought into opposition, torn apart, and reassembled. The intellectual fervour generated there in the early Hellenistic era can be imagined from the involvement of the Athenian public. When one philosopher, Stilpo, visited Athens men would run from their work to catch a glimpse of him. For Theophrastus' funeral it was said that the entire population turned out. Public honours were heaped upon Zeno the Stoic. Arcesilaus was criticized for being too fond of the mob; and when Epicurus expressly repudiated the idea that philosophers should court the mob, he undoubtedly had the Athenian public in mind.

What factors led to the blossoming of new philosophical schools at the beginning of the Hellenistic period? The empire of Alexander the Great had brought together numerous peoples from Greece to the east Mediterranean and beyond, and cosmo-politanism remained a distinguishing feature of the Hellenistic age. Greek culture found a foothold in nearly every major civilization of the Mediterranean region. Despite the emergence of new centres of learning, notably Alexandria, Athens was well

---

[3] On the nature and status of philosophical schools, see Lynch [23], a useful antidote to the excessively legalistic picture which has long been fashionable.

able to compete as a cultural Mecca. But not on all fronts. Plato's school had fostered not merely philosophical discussion but also mathematical research of the utmost importance; and Aristotle's had become a research centre for a vast range of subjects, literary and scientific as well as philosophical. But by the end of the fourth century the steady growth of the various disciplines had made increasing specialization inevitable. A large part of the brilliant new advances in scientific and literary studies that followed took place in Alexandria, whose rulers, the Ptolemies, offered patronage on a scale which made it difficult to refuse. Philosophy, however, was not so easily uprooted from its ancestral home. For the Hellenistic philosophers, as for Plato, philosophy was a supremely dialectical activity whose life blood was debate and confrontation. Even if another city was broad-minded enough to tolerate the invasion of its public places by these vociferous gurus, it is unlikely that the special atmosphere and the philosophically attuned audiences of Athens could easily have been recreated elsewhere. When Hellenistic philosophers travelled, it was less often to found schools or to spread their message than to serve as court philosophers to the great dynasties that ruled the Mediterranean world. Athens remained unrivalled as the specialist training ground for philosophers.

The empirical and mathematical sciences, including astronomy, were now left to the experts, while philosopher's 'physics' was a largely speculative discipline. Similarly literary studies became a subject for the specialist 'grammarian', while philosophers turned more to linguistic theory. Now that its leading proponents had consciously relaxed, or in some cases renounced, their commitment to the other branches of learning, philosophy itself became a specialist subject, unprecedentedly inward looking. The systems that survived and flourished were those which could offer a single ethical goal towards which all other permitted areas of enquiry might be geared—a goal which sought to encapsulate man's correct stance in relation to the world.

It has always been tempting to see this last development as a deliberate response to a cry for help—an attempt to restore moral purpose to life in an age when dynastic rule had stifled the old type of participatory city-state and was depriving the Greek citizen of a role in the politics of his own city. This claim has not yet been substantiated. Any defence of it would probably require

fuller knowledge than we possess of the social and political back-
grounds from which the various adherents of the Hellenistic
schools emerged; and it must at least be recognized that many of
them came from cities whose roots and recent history lay largely
outside the bounds of Greek civilization. Some, at any rate, of the
new emphasis in philosophy must be attributed to the fact that
it was now for the first time isolated as an entirely autonomous
discipline and one which had to justify itself, often in direct
competition with other branches of learning. As for the blossoming of new schools, one contributory factor must have been supply
and demand, for the spread of Greek culture, by bringing hordes
of new philosophy students to Athens, had created a ready-made
audience for any philosopher bold enough to branch out on
his own.

II

It may be helpful to follow the story for a while through the eyes
of a young Cypriot named Zeno, who typifies the spirit in which
philosophical studies were pursued, and who became in time the
founder of Stoicism, the dominant philosophy of the age. He was
born of at least partly Phoenician stock in 334 B.C. at Citium in
Cyprus, a town of mixed Phoenician and Greek culture. When it
became part of Alexander's empire, as it did within a year of
Zeno's birth, the population's leaning towards Greek culture no
doubt grew, and during Zeno's childhood his father, a merchant,
is said frequently to have brought back books about Socrates
from his voyages to Athens. The passion for philosophy which
these books kindled led Zeno, in 312 B.C. at the age of twenty-
two, to abandon the family business and to take up residence in
Athens in pursuit of a philosophical education.[4] There, thanks to
the private means which he had brought with him, he was able
to sit at the feet of Socrates' various heirs for many years before
finally forming his own school.

The one glaring omission from his curriculum of studies in
this period was attendance at the Peripatos. Aristotle's school,
under the headship of his successor Theophrastus, was clinging

---

[4] The anecdote of his shipwreck at Athens and sudden unplanned encounter with
philosophy (DL VII 2) sounds like a fiction of the Hellenistic conversion-story
industry. For some less fanciful accounts of his arrival see DL VII 4–5.

to its celebrated tradition of polymathy, pursuing in addition to philosophy a whole range of empirical sciences and related disciplines. What kept Zeno away? Perhaps its excessive popularity—for as many as 2,000 students were known to crowd in for the public lectures which Theophrastus gave in the mornings. Perhaps too its polymathy—for a book which Zeno wrote in these early years opened with a denunciation of 'encyclic', or general, education. Zeno's interest was firmly focused on moral and political philosophy, and the kind of mixed bag offered by Theophrastus was not likely to attract him.

Here it should be mentioned parenthetically that the Peripatos, for all its popularity at this time, does not play a leading role in Hellenistic philosophy. Its Aristotelian polymathy was not in the spirit of the age, and, depending as it did on the cohesion of a team of researchers, was too easily dissipated by the departure of individual members to found their own schools or to reap the patronage of Hellenistic monarchs. The school was further weakened by the loss of Aristotle's library on Theophrastus' death, and future members increasingly restricted the range of their studies. However the philosophical writings of Aristotle and Theophrastus were certainly available to any Hellenistic philosopher sufficiently interested to seek them out,[5] and their influence should not be discounted. It is apparent above all in Hellenistic physics and cosmology, and to a lesser extent in ethics, though surprisingly little in logic.

Instead Zeno's first teacher was the Cynic Crates. Cynicism was not a complete philosophical system but a practical approach to life, made fashionable during the middle part of the fourth century by Diogenes of Sinope. Maintaining that the virtue of the wise man is entirely self-sufficient, the Cynics rejected as superfluous all the trappings and conventions of polite society and pursued a bohemian lifestyle. The influence of their self-sufficiency doctrine is pervasive in Hellenistic ethics, and nowhere more so than among the Stoics. The young Zeno's first book proposed radical social reform along strongly Cynic lines. But he never advocated a detached Cynic lifestyle for the individual in existing society.

After a time Zeno parted company with Crates, no doubt in search of a stronger intellectual base for his philosophy. This led

[5] Cf. Lynch [23], 146–9.

him to study with Stilpo, the head of the Megarian school, who lived in Megara but seems to have been a regular visitor to near-by Athens. Stilpo had much of the Cynic in him, but was at the same a teacher of tremendous reputation and something of a sophistical debater. Besides ethics he had an interest in metaphysics. He denied the existence of universals, and, perhaps as a consequence, constructed paradoxical objections to the possibility of predication. Zeno will have had little taste for the paradoxes, but accepted as valid the denial of universals—a step which was to have, as we shall see, profound consequences for Hellenistic epistemology.

Veering yet further in the direction of intellectual respectability, Zeno moved on to the Academy, now headed by Polemo, the third successor of Plato. In the four decades since Plato's death in 347 this institution had lost much of its original momentum. Plato's immediate successors had started out by pursuing some of the metaphysical, ethical, and theological topics in which he had happened to be involved at the end of his life. In their hands the free speculation and research which Plato had fostered gave way to dogma as the attempt to construct a Platonic system gradually fossilized his thought. Polemo himself is known to us almost exclusively as an ethical teacher; and it is above all in ethics that the Academy made its mark on Stoic doctrine.

Under the aegis of so many moralists Zeno may have felt himself inadequately grounded in argumentative technique, for he chose also to study with the leading dialectician of the age, Diodorus Cronus (died c. 284).[6] Diodorus was the most prominent member of the Dialectical school, a circle specializing in logic and in modes of argument. He popularized a range of puzzles which were to become central to Hellenistic dialectic, and at the same time he and his pupils developed propositional logic with such success that it became, in the hands of the Stoics, unrivalled as the logic of the Hellenistic era, quickly eclipsing the term-logic of the Peripatos. One of the leading figures in this process was Philo, a masterly logician who attended Diodorus' lectures in company with Zeno. Philo and Zeno used to practise their debating skills on each other. Zeno himself never valued dialectical debate for its own sake, but he stressed the need to be armed

---

[6] The claims made here about Diodorus are argued more fully in Sedley [24].

against the sophistries of others, and he probably made a significant contribution in his own right to Stoic theory of proof.[7]

There is no need to regard Zeno's metamorphosis from student to teacher as a distinct and datable event. What is clear is that he had the habit of conversing with others in the most celebrated colonnade in Athens, the Painted Stoa, close to the agora. In time a nucleus of like-minded philosophers formed around him. These came to be known as the 'Zenonians', and later as the 'men from the Stoa', or 'Stoics'. Their philosophical work at this date was largely ethical, and had the attraction of preserving the Cynic principle that virtue is self-sufficient and the sole source of happiness, while nevertheless finding an integral role for such 'indifferents' as prosperity, public honour, and health, which were regarded as the raw material of the correct actions (*kathēkonta*) out of which alone a virtuous disposition could be developed. Man's task was to play to the best of his ability the role naturally earmarked for him in a world planned by a provident, immanent deity.

Zeno's successor was Cleanthes, who, formerly a boxer, had attended Zeno's classes in the daytime and earned his living by working at night. If he did not altogether deserve his reputation for being slow witted, he was, at least, of so strongly religious a temperament as to propose that Aristarchus of Samos be charged with impiety for his hypothesis that the sun stays still while the earth goes round it. Even so, he himself did much to further Zeno's work in all its aspects, particularly cosmology, and no history of the Stoa can leave him out of account. It was, however, the third head of the school, Chrysippus, at the end of the third century B.C., who developed Stoicism into a truly major system, overhauling, amplifying, and extending into new areas the work of his predecessors, to so great a degree that his philosophy has become virtually synonymous with 'early Stoicism'. There is no space here to attempt a summary of the full Stoic system, but for readers of this volume it will be of particular relevance that it was Chrysippus who masterminded most of its greatest achievements in logic.

[7] For Zeno's views on logic, see *SVF* I 47–51. For his own possible contribution to theory of proof, cf. his book title *On signs* (DL VII 4), and Brunschwig, Chapter 6 below.

III

It is now time to go back to the beginning of the Hellenistic era, and to chart the progress of an earlier innovator, Epicurus.[8] While Zeno's background lay in the range of philosophies available at Athens, most of them claiming Socratic ancestry, that of Epicurus had been principally in Ionian natural philosophy. He was born in 341 B.C. on the island of Samos, off the coast of modern Turkey. His father was an Athenian settler, and the young Epicurus no doubt felt some affinity for Athenian culture, for when in his early teens he became interested in philosophy it was to the school of a local Platonist, Pamphilus, that he went in search of enlightenment. He was unimpressed by what he heard there, so much so that when at the age of eighteen he had to do his year's military service in Athens he turned down the opportunity of attending lectures at the Academy itself. By now it was the atomist philosophy of Democritus (born *c.* 460) that had won his attention, and once back home he signed up with the Democritean school of Nausiphanes at near-by Teos. (Democriteanism had never established itself at Athens, and remained most closely linked with Democritus' home town Abdera, a colony of Teos.) There too he was contemptuous of the education offered, including as it did such extraneous subjects as rhetoric. But while there he was at least able to extend his knowledge of the Presocratic physical philosophers, who remained thereafter his principal source of inspiration; and he also came under the influence of Pyrrho of Elis, later looked back on as the founder of scepticism. Pyrrho (*c.* 365–*c.* 270) also belonged, if loosely, within the Democritean tradition, but despised learning for its own sake and taught, largely by personal example, a kind of philosophical detachment from worldly affairs. This lifestyle won the admiration of the young Epicurus, and Nausiphanes, who knew Pyrrho personally, found himself constantly bombarded with questions about him. It may well be Pyrrho to whom we should trace back Epicurus' own mitigated doctrine of the philosopher's detachment from the world at large and his disapproval of learning for its own sake. We should also bear in mind that at this formative stage Epicurus must have become familiar with a radical scepticism which,

---

[8] Many of the claims made here are substantiated in Sedley [131].

given his respect for its author, he could not but take seriously. We will return to this point later.

In 311 Epicurus, labelling himself a Democritean, set up his own school in Mytilene; and shortly afterwards he transferred it to Lampsacus, near Troy. Anaxagoras, the great fifth-century natural philosopher, was a local hero at Lampsacus, and the town seems still to have retained an attachment to the staunch materialism associated with his name (Strato, the most materialist of the Peripatetics, who later succeeded Theophrastus, was growing up there around this time). Consistently with this, it was while working there that Epicurus developed the details of his own militantly materialist atomist cosmology.[9] But he also taught at least the rudiments of his rather ascetic brand of hedonism, and formed a close-knit circle of friends among whom its principles could be enacted. This doctrine was evolved in express contradistinction to the hedonism of the Cyrenaics, a minor contemporary school. The Cyrenaics also taught their own sceptical epistemology—a fact which will prove relevant when we come to consider the sources of Epicurus' theory of knowledge.

In 307 B.C. Epicurus and a contingent of his followers migrated to Athens. There, thanks to his right as an Athenian citizen to own property, he bought a house on the west side of town, and a garden just outside the city walls on the road that led to the Academy.[10] 'The Garden' came to be the name of his school. Although it gained a reputation for secrecy and exclusiveness, there can be little doubt that one point of establishing it in Athens was to place it in contact and rivalry with the other leading schools of the day. For instance, the remains of a book which Epicurus wrote ten years later show him rethinking his ideas on language and truth in reaction to the ideas of Diodorus Cronus, and he makes it fairly plain that he has encountered them in debate, not through reading.[11] He also wrote against other figures on the Athenian scene—Theophrastus on physics, Stilpo on the role of friendship.

Epicurus' philosophy is in most ways diametrically opposed to that of Zeno. Man is seen as a chance product of a world which is itself the mechanical product of atoms moving in an infinite void;

[9] See further, Sedley [132], especially 53–4 and n. 73.
[10] See Clarke [22].
[11] Sedley [130], especially 13–17, 48–9, 52–3, 62–4, 71–2.

he nevertheless has free will, and his morality must be contrived by reference to the one goal which we all naturally seek, pleasure. This latter lies chiefly in freedom from anxiety, an end to which all philosophical research must be geared. After his death Epicurus' school survived and spread its teaching for many centuries without much significant modification to its doctrines, earning its best and most enduring publicity in Lucretius' first-century-B.C. Latin poem *De rerum natura*.

IV

We must now go back to the beginning for a third time and see how scepticism made its appearance on the Hellenistic scene. Doubts about man's ability to attain knowledge had an ancestry which was conventionally traced back at least to Xenophanes in the sixth century, and objections to sensory knowledge had been formulated by Parmenides in the first part of the fifth century and soon afterwards by his followers Zeno of Elea and Melissus, and, with reservations, by the atomist Democritus. All of these, and others, came to be seen as forerunners of systematic scepticism, but it was particularly the followers of Democritus who kept scepticism alive in the fourth century. Of these the best known is Metrodorus of Chios, who opened his work *On nature* with the words 'None of us knows anything—not even whether we know anything or not', but then proceeded to offer an elaborate series of cosmological speculations. No doubt by turning his profession of ignorance against itself he was, not unlike later sceptics, conceding that enquiry was still worth while. The same line of thought continues, so far as can be judged from the meagre evidence, through his pupil Diogenes of Smyrna and Diogenes' own pupil Anaxarchus of Abdera. But Anaxarchus' pupil, Pyrrho of Elis, seems to have held purely and simply that nothing can be known, without the subtlety of letting this thesis qualify itself, and, consistently, to have rejected all speculation about the world as a time-wasting source of anxiety.

Curiously, although this blunt approach has less in common with Hellenistic scepticism than the open-ended doubt of Metrodorus, it was Pyrrho, not Metrodorus, who was to become the figurehead of the later sceptical movement. Here it was not the truth about Pyrrho that mattered but the legend, which was permanently established, for better or worse, by his disciple and chief publicist Timon of Phlius. Timon's satirical verses portrayed Pyrrho as the living model of the sceptical life, free from the falsehood and the vanity of lesser, opinionated philosophers; and it may have been largely by his moral example that Pyrrho was felt to have opened a new phase in scepticism.

The official Pyrrhonist school was not established until the first century b.c. But it is significant that Arcesilaus, the key figure in early Hellenistic scepticism, was believed in his own day to have drawn his inspiration from Pyrrho. Born about 315 b.c. at Pitane in Asia Minor, Arcesilaus studied mathematics before taking up his philosophical studies in Athens during the 290s. His first teacher there was Theophrastus, but he soon transferred his loyalties to the Academy, and when in the 270s he was appointed its head he took the astonishing step of instituting scepticism as its official policy. Whether or not Arcesilaus ever met Pyrrho, Timon, who taught in Athens, will have made Pyrrho's scepticism known to him. Indeed, Timon himself was later to satirize Arcesilaus as a hanger-on of Pyrrho and Diodorus, while another contemporary, Ariston of Chios, likened him to a chimaera, 'Plato in front, Pyrrho behind, Diodorus in the middle'. This image neatly encapsulates Arcesilaus' eventual philosophical position. If Pyrrho lay at the back of his philosophy it is because he inspired in Arcesilaus the notion that suspending judgement might actually be more desirable than committing oneself to a dogmatic stance, and not just a bleak expedient in the cause of intellectual honesty as its older advocates had tended to suppose. If Diodorus lay at its heart, it is because Arcesilaus adopted the best dialectical techniques available in his day, those retailed by Diodorus and his associates. For there can be little doubt that these, including above all the Little-by-little Argument, or Sorites, become major weapons in the Academic armoury.[12] If, finally, Plato stood at the front of Arcesilaus' philosophy, it is because Arcesilaus professed to be no innovator but a reviver of the dogma-free dialectic which had characterized the Academy under Plato. This manifesto deserves some sympathy. The post-Platonic Academy had indeed, as we have seen, debilitated itself by paying more attention to Plato's doctrines than to his methods. Arcesilaus could hardly be blamed for seeking the true spirit of

[12] Sedley [24].

Platonism not in this or that metaphysical or ethical dogma but
in the early aporetic dialogues, and, among later dialogues, in
those like the *Theaetetus* and *Parmenides* which could be read as
trying to restore the open-minded dialectic of the early period or
to drag back into the debating chamber theories which were
gaining too facile acceptance in the school. Arcesilaus' whole
object was to keep debate alive. His method was to get one of his
pupils to assert a thesis, then to argue against it while letting the
pupil defend it as best he could—the ideal result no doubt being
an inconclusive one in the manner of early Platonic dialogues.
Thus right from the start his dialectic depended on a regular
supply of dogmatic theses, and it is not at all surprising to hear
that he encouraged his pupils to attend lectures in other schools.
So began the long Academic tradition of confuting the Stoa, by
that date Athens' most fertile and prestigious source of philosophical dogma.

There followed an exciting century and a half of interaction
between the two schools, in which the Academy's role was
parasitic in the sense that it had to work, in sound dialectical
fashion, exclusively with its opponents' terms and premisses, but
also productive in that it kept the Stoics on their toes and stimulated constant revision and defence of their theories. The closeness
of this interaction was intensified by two facts: that Chrysippus
was originally trained by Arcesilaus and his successor Lacydes
before transferring his allegiance to the Stoa; and that Carneades,
a brilliant head of the Academy in the second century B.C., had
himself studied dialectic under Chrysippus' disciple Diogenes of
Babylon before entering his sceptical phase. Carneades' sceptical
method is well elucidated elsewhere in this volume, and can be
passed over here. Although it differed in some respects from that
of Arcesilaus, there is no justification for the tradition of later
antiquity that Carneades inaugurated a new phase—the 'New
Academy', by contrast with Arcesilaus' 'Middle Academy'.

V

Enough of the historical jigsaw has now been assembled to
enable us to stand back and take a look. There is no space in a
brief introduction for any general discussion of the school
doctrines, but the subject of this volume does dictate one over-

riding doctrinal question, how Hellenistic epistemology, with its stress on the problem of justification, came by a character so far removed from that of earlier thought on the subject of knowledge.[13]

Here I would isolate two factors. First, ever since Parmenides the questions asked about knowledge had been dominated by metaphysical concerns. The requirement that the objects of knowledge be in some sense unchanging had been an enduring, if not quite invariable, feature of Plato's and Aristotle's thought, and had helped block the development of any fully empiricist theory of knowledge. Hellenistic philosophers were unhampered by this preoccupation. In Epicurus' simple materialist metaphysics all existence is reduced to atoms, void, and the individual properties belonging to these and to their compounds. Most of the epistemic jobs of Platonic Forms are discharged, without metaphysical complication, by *prolēpsis*, the generic conception of a thing, compounded out of individual sensations of it. This contribution by Epicurus to the empiricist's vocabulary became and remained central to Hellenistic epistemology. For the Stoics only particulars ('somethings') can be significantly named, and nearly all of these are corporeal, for alleged abstract nouns can normally be interpreted as 'this or that body in a certain condition'. Zeno learned from Stilpo arguments which he used to outlaw universals entirely from this scheme as being mere 'quasi-somethings'. The terms used to name them are, for the Stoics, a linguistic convenience and nothing more. As a corollary to this nominalism they tried to derive all kinds of learning, even the acquisition of reason itself, from empirical observation of particulars. The ultimate guarantee, or 'criterion', of truth lies not in any intuited general principles but in individual sensory cognitions. And the same empiricist approach naturally came to be shared by the sceptics—not as their own doctrine, but because the rules of the game obliged them to work with premises accepted by their opponents.

Hence in all the debates of Hellenistic philosophy an empiricist methodology was common ground. It had to be defended, not against a Platonist or an Aristotelian frame of thought, but against

---

[13] On this difference see especially M. F. Burnyeat, 'Aristotle on Understanding Knowledge', in E. Berti, ed., *Aristotle on Science: the 'Posterior Analytics'* (Atti dell' VIII Symposium Aristotelicum (Padua and New York, forthcoming).

scepticism. And it is scepticism that must be seen as the second major factor in determining the Hellenistic approach to the subject.

Here we must once again start by considering Epicurus' position. Democritus had sometimes expressed himself pessimistically about the chances of achieving certainty, and had been inclined to regard the first principles of atomism as the only available objects of knowledge, explicitly denying this status to the sensible properties of things. But he had also proceeded to cast doubt on his own pessimism by imagining the senses' reply: 'Poor mind, you get your evidence from us, then you overthrow us. Our overthrow is your downfall.' His fourth-century followers had, as we have seen, developed the sceptical side of his thought. Epicurus, in consciously reviving the empiricist strand, was reacting to this tendency,[14] plainly eager to establish his own place within the Democritean tradition.

Consequently Epicurus' persistent concern to justify everyday claims of sensory cognition can be attributed to a materialist metaphysics which makes observed particulars the primary objects of knowledge, combined with the obtrusive presence within his own philosophical tradition of arguments denying any route to knowledge of them. These arguments, which appealed largely to optical illusion and to evidence of perceptual subjectivity, were also put to work by the Cyrenaics in establishing their own brand of cognitive pessimism—that knowledge claims should be confined to descriptions of our sense-data, since the relation between sense-data and external objects is beyond our grasp. We have seen that Epicurus' version of hedonism was shaped by his opposition to the Cyrenaics, and there seems no reason to doubt that their gloomy epistemology similarly redoubled his concern to prove the veridicality of sense-data by appeal to the laws of physics.[15] He surmounted the most obvious difficulty of this enterprise, that the laws of physics could themselves only be established if the veridicality of sense-data were already presupposed, by showing scepticism to be an inherently untenable position, both self-refuting and impossible to maintain in practice. Thus the bona fides of Epicurus' enterprise was guaranteed on seemingly *a priori* grounds.

[14] Cf. Lucr. IV 469 ff., and Burnyeat [56].
[15] Cf. Plu. *Col.* for the denunciation by Epicurus' pupil Colotes of the Cyrenaics and of other sceptically inclined philosophers.

Stoicism, initially, was less familiar with the sceptical challenge, and correspondingly less concerned with the justification of claims to sensory cognition. This made its appearance simply as a basic datum of the system. For to Zeno it was obvious that in a providentially designed world the basic tool of learning was supplied for man's advantage, not maliciously to mislead him; and the Stoics always differed from Epicurus in being more preoccupied with the self-supporting structure of their system than with its derivation from first principles. The turning-point came with the attacks of Arcesilaus, which began only towards the end of Zeno's career. Although he constructed arguments against many Stoic tenets, those against the basic criterion of truth, the 'cognitive impression' (*phantasia kataleptike*), were of fundamental importance. Younger Stoics like Persaeus and Sphaerus seem as a result to have shown more circumspection about claims of cognitive certainty, and it was left for Chrysippus to come to the rescue of the 'cognitive impression' with an elaborate set of arguments which put the topic firmly on the map and paved the way for the renewed counterblast of the Academy masterminded by Carneades.

VI

It remains to state, in barest outline, the history of later Hellenistic philosophy. The Stoa continued to flourish. Under Panaetius, who became its head in 129 B.C., and again at the hands of his pupil Posidonius, who set up his own school in Rhodes (these two are the foremost representatives of the period now known as Middle Stoicism), its work underwent certain changes of emphasis which, although of considerable interest, cannot detain us here because of their lack of bearing on epistemology. It should however be mentioned that we possess parts of a work, *On signs,* by the first-century-B.C. Epicurean Philodemus, in which he reports important debates between some distinguished Epicurean forerunners, notably Zeno of Sidon and Demetrius Lacon, and opponents who seem to be Stoics, on the issue of empirical methodology.

Of greater relevance is the history of the Academy in this period. Carneades, who wrote nothing, was succeeded after a brief interval by his pupil Clitomachus, a prolific writer who compiled a detailed record of Carneades' arguments. Clitomachus never pretended that these dialectical gambits represented Carneades' own personal opinion; but meanwhile other Academics, such as Metrodorus of Stratonicea and Philo of Larissa, were beginning to extract positive doctrines from them and to claim Carneades' authority for doing so. Under Philo's subsequent headship the drift back towards dogmatism gathered pace, although the Stoic insistence that certainty can be attained continued to be resisted.

By adopting this weak middle-of-the-road position Philo succeeded in alienating both the dogmatic and the sceptical wings of his school. The result was two separate schisms. In 87 B.C. his disciple Antiochus of Ascalon was outraged to read Philo's defence of his own epistemological position as having been that of all Academic philosophers from Plato onwards, and it was probably at this date that he broke away to form his own school, the Old Academy. His manifesto was to restore what he claimed the sceptical Academy from Arcesilaus to Philo had abandoned, the true philosophy of Plato. But as standard-bearers of 'true' Platonism he invoked not only Plato himself and his early successors, but even Aristotle, Theophrastus, and the Stoics. He in fact read the earlier philosophers through such strongly Stoicizing spectacles that his own system looks much more Stoic than Platonist to the modern eye. Cicero, an important source for this period as well as for earlier Hellenistic philosophy, went along with Antiochus on ethical questions, but remained officially a follower of Philo, to whose semi-sceptical epistemology he consistently adhered. His *Academica* is our primary source for the rift between Philo and Antiochus.

The other schism, a much more poorly documented one, was the work of Aenesidemus. He too seems to have been a member of the Academy under Philo, and to have abandoned it in protest at its excessive dogmatism. He proceeded to found a new, hard-line school of scepticism, the Pyrrhonist school. A continuous line of succession was constructed to demonstrate his direct descent, via a series of teachers and pupils, from Pyrrho. This was probably concocted to establish his intellectual pedigree by implying the priority of his own 'tradition' over that of the sceptical Academy (Pyrrho had predated Arcesilaus). It consequently has little historical value as evidence for an enduring

Pyrrhonist school in the third and second centuries, and it is better to regard Aenesidemus as an innovator. In his work the refutation of Stoicism and of other dogmatic philosophies remained a leading concern,[16] but he also set about bolstering the sceptical position by positive means. To this end he catalogued under ten headings, or 'modes', all the available grounds for suspense of judgement. He also helped develop scepticism's positive moral base, less, it seems, by theorizing in his own name than by setting up Pyrrho's lifestyle as a practical example. Here too the choice of Pyrrho as 'founder' of the school proved to have its advantages.

At this point 'Hellenistic' philosophy should strictly end, but it has become conventional to smuggle in under its coat-tails the remaining history of the Pyrrhonist school down to Sextus Empiricus in the late second century A.D. The justification for this is that Sextus is the only representative of Aenesidemus' school whose work has come down to us in any quantity. Like many of his Pyrrhonist forerunners he was a practising physician, and made some effort to establish consistency between his medical and philosophical methods. There can be no doubt that the work of Aenesidemus bulks large in Sextus' writings However, the exemplary figure of Pyrrho himself has by now largely receded; and Sextus draws on the work of intervening members of the school, especially Agrippa, whose own five 'modes' complemented the ten of Aenesidemus by formally classifying the main forms of anti-dogmatic argument. Sextus' *Adversus mathematicos* is a systematic rebuttal of the leading dogmatic schools, while his other surviving work, the *Outlines of Pyrrhonism*, includes the fullest statement that we possess of the Pyrrhonist's aims and methods.

---

[16] Even his alleged Heracliteanism is to be interpreted as an anti-Stoic dialectical manoeuvre; see Burkhard [45].

Academy	Peripatos	Pyrrhonists	Stoics	Epicureans
		c. 365: Pyrrho born		
347: Plato dies, succeeded by Speusippus			344: Zeno born	341: Epicurus born
339: Speusippus dies, succeeded by Xenocrates				
		c. 334–324: Pyrrho and Anaxarchus in East with Alexander		c. 328: studies under Pamphilus
	322: Aristotle dies, succeeded by Theophrastus	c. 325: Timon born		c. 321: studies under Nausiphanes
314: Xenocrates dies, succeeded by Polemo			312: Zeno arrives in Athens, and in the following years studies under Crates (Cynic), Stilpo, Polemo, Diodorus Cronus	311–310: sets up schools in Mytilene and Lampsacus
				307: founds Garden in Athens
				Colotes fl. c. 310–260
c. 295: Arcesilaus arrives in Athens	Arcesilaus studies under Theophrastus c. 287: Theophrastus dies, succeeded by Strato			
c. 276: Polemo dies, succeeded by Crates			Ariston of Chios, fl. c. 270–250 Persaeus, fl. c. 280–243	271: Epicurus dies, succeeded by Hermarchus
c. 273: Crates dies, succeeded by Arcesilaus who institutes scepticism	c. 269: Strato dies, succeeded by Lycon	c. 270: Pyrrho dies	262: Zeno dies, succeeded by Cleanthes	
242: Arcesilaus dies, succeeded by Lacydes		c. 235: Timon dies	Sphaerus, fl. c. 240–210 c. 232: Cleanthes dies, succeeded by Chrysippus	

c. 219: Carneades born

(?): Carneades becomes head of Academy

155: Carneades on embassy to Rome with Peripatetic Critolaus and Stoic Diogenes
137: Carneades retires through ill health
129: Carneades dies

c. 128: Clitomachus becomes head of Academy
c. 110: Clitomachus dies, succeeded by Philo of Larissa

c. 87: Antiochus breaks away to found Old Academy

c. 79: Philo dies
c. 67: Antiochus dies

45–4: most of Cicero's philosophical works written

c. 90–80 (probably): Aenesidemus breaks away from Academy and revives 'Pyrrhonism'

Agrippa (1st cent. A.D.?) Sextus Empiricus, fl. c. A.D. 200

c. 206: Chrysippus dies, succeeded by Zeno of Tarsus (?): Zeno dies, succeeded by Diogenes of Babylon

c. 152: Diogenes dies, succeeded by Antipater

c. 129: Antipater dies, succeeded by Panaetius

109: Panaetius dies

Posidonius, 135–51

Zeno of Sidon, c. 155–c. 75

Demetrius Lacon, younger contemporary of Zeno
Philodemus, fl. 80–45 B.C.
c. 55 B.C.: Lucretius writes De rerum natura

CAN THE SCEPTIC LIVE HIS SCEPTICISM?

M. F. Burnyeat

HUME'S CHALLENGE

A Stoic or Epicurean displays principles, which may not only be durable, but which have an effect on conduct and behaviour. But a Pyrrhonian cannot expect, that his philosophy will have any constant influence on the mind: or if it had, that its influence would be beneficial to society. On the contrary, he must acknowledge, if he will acknowledge anything, that all human life must perish, were his principles universally and steadily to prevail. All discourse, all action would immediately cease; and men remain in a total lethargy, till the necessities of nature, unsatisfied, put an end to their miserable existence. It is true; so fatal an event is very little to be dreaded. Nature is always too strong for principle. And though a Pyrrhonian may throw himself or others into a momentary amazement and confusion by his profound reasonings; the first and most trivial event in life will put to flight all his doubts and scruples, and leave him the same, in every point of action and speculation, with the philosophers of every other sect, or with those who never concerned themselves in any philosophical researches. When he awakes from his dream, he will be the first to join in the laugh against himself, and to confess, that all his objections are mere amusement, and can have no other tendency than to show the whimsical condition of mankind, who must act and reason and believe; though they are not able, by their most diligent enquiry, to satisfy themselves concerning the foundation of these operations, or to remove the objections, which may be raised against them (David Hume, *An Enquiry Concerning Human Understanding*, § XII, 128).[1]

I begin with Hume, both in deference to the vital influence of Pyrrhonian scepticism on modern thought, following the rediscovery and publication of the works of Sextus Empiricus in

---

[1] Cited from the third edition of Selby-Bigge's edition, with text revised by P. H. Nidditch (Oxford, 1975). One of Nidditch's revisions is restoring the word 'only' to the first sentence of the quoted passage.

the sixteenth century,[2] and because Hume is so clear on the philosophical issues I wish to discuss in connection with Sextus Empiricus. Pyrrhonism is the only serious attempt in Western thought to carry scepticism to its furthest limits and to live by the result, and the question whether this is possible, or even notionally coherent, was keenly disputed in ancient times and had been a major focus of renewed debate for some two hundred years before Hume wrote. My purpose is to return to those old controversies from the perspective of a modern scholarly understanding of Sextus Empiricus.

The background to the passage I have quoted is Hume's well-known contention that our nature constrains us to make inferences and to hold beliefs which cannot be rationally defended against sceptical objections. He has particularly in mind the propensity for belief in external bodies and for causal inference, but not only these. And he has a particular purpose in showing them to be rationally indefensible. Since exposure to the sceptical objections does not stop us indulging in belief and inference, it does not appear that we make the inferences and hold the beliefs on the strength of the reasons whose inadequacy is shown up by the sceptical arguments; for when a belief or a practice is genuinely based on reasons, it is given up if those reasons are invalidated. Since we do not give up the inferences and the beliefs in the face of overwhelming sceptical objections, there must be other factors at work in our nature than reason—notably custom and imagination—and it is to these, rather than to man's much-vaunted rationality, that the beliefs and the inferences are due.[3] In the passage quoted Hume's claim is a double one: first, that what the sceptic invalidates when his arguments are successful, and hence what he would take from us if such arguments could have a 'constant influence on the mind', is nothing less than reason and belief; second, that what makes it impossible to sustain a radical scepticism in the ordinary business of life is that

[2] The exciting story of this influence has been pursued through the ins and outs of religious and philosophical controversy in a series of studies by Richard H. Popkin. See, in particular, *The History of Scepticism, from Erasmus to Descartes* (revised edn., New York, Evanston and London, 1968); 'David Hume: His Pyrrhonism and His Critique of Pyrrhonism', *Philosophical Quarterly* 1 (1951), 385–407; 'David Hume and the Pyrrhonian Controversy', *Review of Metaphysics* 6 (1952/3), 65–81.

[3] On the role and importance of this argument within Hume's general programme for a naturalistic science of man, see Barry Stroud, *Hume* (London, Henley, and Boston, 1977), esp. Ch. 1.

'mankind . . . must act and reason and believe'. A brief comment on each of these claims in turn will give us a philosophical context in which to consider what Sextus Empiricus has to say in defence and advocacy of his Pyrrhonist ideal.

All too often in contemporary discussion the target of the sceptic is taken to be knowledge rather than belief. Sceptical arguments are used to raise questions about the adequacy of the grounds on which we ordinarily claim to know about the external world, about other minds, and so on, but in truth there are few interesting problems got at by this means which are not problems for reasonable belief as well as for knowledge. It is not much of an oversimplification to say that the more serious the inadequacy exposed in the grounds for a knowledge-claim, the less reasonable it becomes to base belief on such grounds. To take a well-worn, traditional example, if the evidence of our senses is really shown to be unreliable and the inferences we ordinarily base on this evidence are unwarranted, the correct moral to draw is not merely that we should not claim to know things on these grounds but that we should not believe them either. Further, in the normal case, that which we think we should not believe we do not believe: it takes rather special circumstances to make intelligible the idea that a man could maintain a belief in the face of a clear realization that it is unfounded. If scepticism is convincing, we ought to be convinced, and that ought to have a radical effect on the structure of our thought.

It is very clear that Hume appreciated this. He presses the Pyrrhonist not on the matter of knowledge-claims, which are easily given up, but on the question whether he can stop holding the beliefs which his arguments show to be unreasonable. Sextus appreciated the point also. The objection that a man cannot live without belief was familiar, indeed much older than the Pyrrhonist movement, since it goes right back to the time when Arcesilaus in the Academy first urged *epochē* about everything.[4] Accordingly,

---

[4] Witness the title of the polemical tract by Arcesilaus' contemporary, the Epicurean Colotes, 'On the fact that the doctrines of the other philosophers make it impossible to live' (Plu. *Col.* 1107 d, 1108 d). The section dealing with Arcesilaus borrowed the Stoic argument that total *epochē* must result in total inaction (ibid. 1122 ab)—essentially, Hume's charge of total lethargy. For the controversy around this issue in the period of Academic scepticism, see the references and discussion in Striker, Chapter 3 below. Subsequently, the Pyrrhonist *epochē* encountered similar criticism: (1) Aristocles *apud* Eus. *PE* XIV 18, 23–4 argues that judgement, hence

Sextus defends exactly the proposition Hume challenged the Pyrrhonist to defend, the proposition that he should, can, and does give up his beliefs in response to the sceptical arguments; and out of this continuing resignation of belief he proposes to make a way of life. Likewise with the Pyrrhonist's abandonment of reason: that too, according to Sextus, is not only desirable but practicable, subject to the complication that the abandonment of reason is itself the result of argument, i.e. of the exercise of reason. Consequently—and here I come to my second point of comment—Hume has no right to assume without argument that it is impossible to live without reason and belief. No doubt it seems an obvious impossibility, but Sextus claims otherwise, and he purports to describe a life which would substantiate his claim. That description ought to be examined in detail before we concede Hume's dogmatic claim that the Pyrrhonist cannot live his scepticism.[5] We ought to try to discover what the life without belief is really meant to be.

BELIEF, TRUTH, AND REAL EXISTENCE

We may begin, as the sceptic himself begins, with the arguments. *Skepsis* means enquiry, examination, and Pyrrhonian scepticism is in the first instance a highly developed practice of argumentative enquiry, formalized according to a number of modes or patterns of argument. The Ten Modes of Aenesidemus (*PH* I 36 ff., DL IX 79 ff.) and the Five of Agrippa (*PH* I 164–77, DL IX 88–9) are the most conspicuous of the patterns, but there are others besides, all of which recur with quite remarkable regularity on page after page of the sceptic literature, and always with the same result: *epochē*, suspension of judgement and belief. These patterns of argument, with this outcome, constitute the essence of scepticism (*skepsis*, enquiry) as that is defined by Sextus Empiricus in the

belief, is inseparably bound up with the use of the senses and other mental faculties; (2) Galen, *De dignosc. puls.* VIII 781, 16–783, 5 K=Deichgräber [10], frag. 74, p. 133, 19–p. 134, 6, asks scoffingly whether the Pyrrhonist expects us to stay in bed when the sun is up for lack of certainty about whether it is day or night, or to sit on board our ship when everyone else is disembarking, wondering whether what appears to be land really is land; (3) Sextus has the lethargy criticism in view at *M* XI 162–3.

[5] I call it dogmatic because Hume offers no argument to support his claim against the alternative, Pyrrhonist account of life and action, available in Sextus or in modern writers like Montaigne.

Outlines of Pyrrhonism; it is, he states, 'a capacity for bringing into opposition, in any way whatever, things that appear and things that are thought, so that, owing to the equal strength of the opposed items and rival claims, we come first to suspend judgement and after that to *ataraxia* (tranquillity, freedom from disturbance)' (*PH* I 8; cp. 31–4). The definition delineates a journey which the sceptic makes over and over again from an opposition or conflict of opinions to *epochē* and *ataraxia*.

The journey begins when he is investigating some question or field of enquiry and finds that opinions conflict as to where the truth lies. The hope of the investigation, at least in the early stages of his quest for enlightenment, is that he will attain *ataraxia* if only he can discover the rights and wrongs of the matter and give his assent to the truth (*PH* I 12, 26–9, *M* I 6). His difficulty is that, as sceptics through the ages have always found, in any matter things appear differently to different people according to one or another of a variety of circumstances, all catalogued in great detail by the Ten Modes of Aenesidemus. We are to understand, and sometimes it is explicitly stated (e.g. *M* VII 392, VIII 18, IX 192, XI 74), that conflicting appearances cannot be equally true, equally real. Hence he needs a criterion of truth, to determine which he should accept. But the sceptic then argues, often at some length, that there is no intellectually satisfactory criterion we can trust and use—this is the real backbone of the discussion, corresponding to a modern sceptic's attempt to show we have no adequate way of telling when things really are as they appear to be, and hence no adequate insurance against mistaken judgements. Assuming the point proved, the sceptic is left with the conflicting appearances and the conflicting opinions based upon them, unable to find any reason for preferring one to another and therefore bound to treat all as of equal strength and equally worthy (or unworthy) of acceptance. But he cannot accept them all, because they conflict. Hence, if he can neither accept them all (because they conflict) nor make a choice between them (for lack of a criterion), he cannot accept any. That is the standard outcome of the sceptic discovery of the equal strength (*isostheneia*) of opposed assertions. So far as truth is concerned, we must suspend judgement. And when the sceptic does suspend judgement, *ataraxia* follows—the tranquillity he sought comes to him, as if by chance, once he stops actively trying to get it; just as the painter Apelles only achieved the effect of a horse's foam when he gave up and flung his sponge at the painting (*PH* I 26–9). All this is compressed into Sextus' definition of scepticism. The sequence is: conflict—undecidability—equal strength—*epochē*, and finally *ataraxia*. The arguments bring about *epochē*, suspension of judgement and belief, and this, it seems, effects a fundamental change in the character of a man's thinking and thereby in his practical life. Henceforth he lives *adoxastōs*, without belief, enjoying, in consequence, that tranquillity of mind (*ataraxia*, freedom from disturbance) which is the sceptic spelling of happiness (*eudaimonia*).[6] But note: the conflict of opinions is inconsistency, the impossiblity of being true together (cf. *M* VII 392); the undecidability of the conflict is the impossibility of deciding which opinion is true; the equal strength of conflicting opinions means they are all equally worthy (or unworthy) of acceptance as true; *epochē* is a state in which one refrains from affirming or denying that any one of them is true; even *ataraxia* is among other things a matter of not worrying about truth and falsity any more. All these notions depend on the concept of truth; no stage of the sequence would make sense without it. And it is a fact of central importance that truth, in the sceptic's vocabulary, is closely tied to real existence as contrasted with appearance.[7]

When the sceptic doubts that anything is true (*PH* II 88 ff., *M* VIII 17 ff.), he has exclusively in view claims as to real existence. Statements which merely record how things appear are not in question—they are not called true or false—only statements which say that things are thus and so in reality. In the controversy between the sceptic and the dogmatists over whether any truth exists at all, the issue is whether any proposition or class of propositions can be accepted as true of a real objective world as distinct from mere appearance. For 'true' in these discussions means 'true of a real objective world'; the true, if there is such a thing, is what conforms with the real, an association traditional to the word *alēthēs* since the earliest period of Greek philosophy (cf. *M* XI 221).[8]

---

[6] The claim that sceptic *ataraxia* alone is *eudaimonia* is argued at length in *M* XI 110–167.

[7] Cf. Stough [29], 142 ff.

[8] If the modern reader finds this an arbitrary terminological narrowing, on the grounds that if I say how things appear to me my statement ought to count as true if, and only if, things really do appear as I say they do (cf. Stough [29], loc. cit.), the

Now clearly, if truth is restricted to matters pertaining to real existence, as contrasted with appearance, the same will apply right back along the sequence we traced out a moment ago. The notions involved, consistency and conflict, undecidability, *isostheneia, epochē, ataraxia,* since they are defined in terms of truth, will all relate, via truth, to real existence rather than appearance. In particular, if *epochē* is suspending belief about real existence as contrasted with appearance, that will amount to suspending all belief, since belief is the accepting of something as true. There can be no question of belief about appearance, as opposed to real existence, if statements recording how things appear cannot be described as true or false, only statements making claims as to how they really are.

This result is obviously of the first importance for understanding the sceptic's enterprise and his ideal of a life without belief. Sextus defines 'dogma'—and, of course, the Greek word *dogma* originally means simply 'belief' (cf. Pl. *Rep.* 538 c, *Tht.* 158 d)— as assent to something non-evident, that is, to something not given in appearance (*PH* I 16).[9] Similarly, to dogmatize, as Sextus explains the term, is what someone does who posits the real existence of something (*hōs huparchon tithetai, PH* I 14, 15, from a context where it has been acknowledged that not everyone would use the word in this restricted sense).[10] Assent is the genus;

---

answer is that his objection, though natural, is anachronistic. The idea that truth can be attained without going outside subjective experience was not always the philosophical commonplace it has come to be. It was Descartes who made it so, who (in the second *Meditation*) laid the basis for our broader use of the predicates 'true' and 'false' whereby they can apply to statements of appearance without reference to real existence. See Burnyeat [59].

[9] The notion of that which is evident (δῆλον, πρόδηλον, ἐναργές) is a dogmatist's notion in the first instance. Things evident are things which come to our knowledge of themselves (*PH* II 97, *M* VIII 144), which are grasped from themselves (*PH* II 99), which immediately present themselves to sense and intellect (*M* VIII 141), which require no other thing to announce them (*M* VIII 149), i.e. which are such that we have immediate non-inferential knowledge of them, directly from the impression (*M* VIII 316). Examples: it is day, I am conversing (*M* VIII 144), this is a man (*M* VIII 316). Sextus declares that this whole class of things is put in doubt by the sceptic critique of the criterion of truth (*PH* II 95, *M* VIII 141–2). Consequently, any statement about such things will be dogma in the sense the sceptic eschews.

[10] The reader should be warned that some interpretations take *PH* I 13–15 as evidence that 'dogma' and 'dogmatize' are still more restricted than I allow, with the consequence that the sceptic does not eschew all belief. It will be best to postpone

opinion, or belief, is that species of it which concerns matters of real existence as contrasted with appearance. The dogmatists, the endless variety of whose opinions concerning real existence provides the sceptic with both his weapons and his targets, are simply the believers; to the extent that it is justified to read in the modern connotation of 'dogmatist', viz. person with an obstinate and unreasonable attachment to his opinions, this belongs not to the core meaning of the Greek term but to the sceptic's argued claim, to which we shall come, that *all* belief is unreasonable. All belief is unreasonable precisely because, as we are now seeing, all belief concerns real existence as opposed to appearance.

HISTORICAL INTERLUDE

We can trace this polemic against belief at least as far back as Aenesidemus, the man who was chiefly responsible for founding, or at any rate reviving, Pyrrhonism in the first century B.C.— some two hundred years or more before Sextus compiled his *Outlines of Pyrrhonism*. Aenesidemus' own *Outline Introduction to Pyrrhonism* was presumably the first work to bear such a title, and we know something of it from a report in Diogenes Laertius (IX 78 ff.; cf. also Aristocles *apud* Eus. *PE* XIV 18, 11). Aenesidemus set out to classify the various modes or ways in which things give rise to belief or persuasion[11] and then tried to destroy, systematically, the beliefs so acquired by showing that each of these modes produces conflicting beliefs of equal persuasiveness and is therefore not to be relied upon to put us in touch with the truth.[12] Most obviously, where our senses deliver consistent reports we tend to be persuaded that things really are as they appear to be,[13] but if we take full account of the different impressions which objects produce on different animals and different people and people in different conditions or circumstances, and all the other considerations adduced under the Ten Modes, we will see that in any such case as much evidence of the

---

controversy until the rest of my interpretation has been set out, but meanwhile the examples in the previous note will serve as well as any to illustrate the sorts of thing about which, in my view, the sceptic suspends judgement.

11 DL IX 78: καθ' οὓς τρόπους πείθει τὰ πράγματα.

12 DL IX 79: ἐδείκνυσαν οὖν ἀπὸ τῶν ἐναντίων τοῖς πείθουσιν ἴσας τὰς πιθανότητας.

13 DL IX 78: πείθειν γὰρ τά τε κατ' αἴσθησιν συμφώνως ἔχοντα.

same kind, or as good, can be adduced for a contrary opinion;
each type of evidence can be matched by evidence of the same
sort but going the other way, each source of belief is a source of
conflicting beliefs.[14] The moral, naturally, is *epochē* about what is
true (DL IX 84); but this is also expressed by saying we must
accept our ignorance concerning the real nature of things (DL
IX 85, 86), which confirms once again the intimate connection
of truth and reality. Then there is the additional consideration
that some of the modes in which beliefs are acquired have little
or no bearing on truth and falsity, as when we believe something
because it is familiar to us or because we have been persuaded of
it by an artful speaker. In sum

> We must not assume that what persuades us (*to peithon*) is actually true.
> For the same thing does not persuade every one, nor even the same
> people always. Persuasiveness (*pithanotēs*) sometimes depends on
> external circumstances, on the reputation of the speaker, on his ability
> as a thinker or his artfulness, on the familiarity or the pleasantness of
> the topic. (DL IX 94, tr. Hicks)[15]

Now this talk of persuasion and persuasiveness has an identifiable historical resonance. In a context (*M* VIII 51) closely
parallel to the passage just quoted, and not long after a mention
of Aenesidemus (*M* VIII 40), Sextus equates what persuades us
(*to peithon hēmas*) with the Academic notion of *to pithanon*.
'*Pithanon*' is often mistranslated 'probable', but what the word
normally means in Greek is 'persuasive' or 'convincing', and

---

[14] Note the partial overlapping between the τρόπους in DL IX 78 and the
δέκα τρόπους, καθ' οὓς τὰ ὑποκείμενα παραλλάττοντα ἐφαίνετο in 79 ff.: cp τά τε κατ'
αἴσθησιν συμφώνως ἔχοντα with Modes I–IV, VII, τὰ νόμοις διεσταλμένα with Mode
V, τὰ μηδέποτε ἢ σπανίως γοῦν μεταπίπτοντα and τὰ θαυμαζόμενα with Mode IX.

[15] I should explain why, without explicit textual warrant, I attribute the content
of this last paragraph also to Aenesidemus. The paragraph is one of two (IX 91–4)
which intrude into a sequence of arguments announced earlier at IX 90. Not only
is it likely, therefore, to derive from a different source, but the sequence of arguments
follows immediately on the account of the Five Modes of Agrippa (IX 88–9), and its
argumentation is largely Agrippean in construction, while the intruding paragraphs
have a certain affinity of content and expression with the section 78–9 which is
definitely associated with the name of Aenesidemus. For example, both passages are
dismissive of belief due to something being familiar (σύνηθες) or pleasing (79:
τέρποντα, 94: κεχαρισμένον). Perhaps the most telling affinity is in the use of the verb
πείθειν to denote the dogmatic belief which the author opposes: the verb does not
occur in (what I suppose to be) the Agrippean sequence IX 88–91, 94–101, nor is it
usual for Sextus to employ it as part of his own technical vocabulary for the key
concept of dogmatic belief. Where he does use it is in discussing Academic
fallibilism, as we are about to see. Cp. also *PH* I 226, 229–30.

Carneades defined a *pithanē* impression as one which appears true (*M* VII 169, 174).[16] The important point for our purposes is that in the sceptic historiography, as in most history books since, Carneades was supposed to have made *to pithanon* the Academic criterion for the conduct of life (*M* VII 166 ff.): a fallible criterion, since he allowed that in some instances we would be persuaded of something which was actually false (*M* VII 175). He also said that our belief is greater—and the Pyrrhonists read him as meaning that it should be greater—when our senses deliver consistent reports (*M* VII 177); this idea, which we saw to be one of Aenesidemus' targets, is the basis for the second and stricter criterion in Carneades' three-level criterial scheme, the impression which is not only *pithanē* but also not 'reversed' by any of the associated impressions. If, then, *to peithon* is the Academic *pithanon*, and if I am right to detect Aenesidemus behind the passages in Diogenes and Sextus where *to peithon* is under fire, then his campaign against persuasion and belief was at the same time a polemic against the Academy from which he had defected.[17] The general purpose of the Ten Modes is to unpersuade us of anything which persuades us that it represents truth and reality. Aenesidemus' more particular target is the idea, which he attributes to the Academy (whether rightly or polemically),[18] that one has a satisfactory enough criterion of action in taking *to be true* that which is persuasive in the sense that it appears true. In Aenesidemus' view, one should not take anything to be true, and he had arguments to show that, in fact, nothing is true (*M* VIII 40 ff.).

I conclude, then, not only that the life without belief was a fundamental feature of Pyrrhonism from Aenesidemus onwards, but that it was put forward by Aenesidemus in conscious opposition to (what he represented as) the teaching of the New

[16] For the correct translation of πιθανός, see Couissin [60], 262, Striker (Chapter 3 below), § III. Getting the translation right is a first step towards undoing the myth of Carneades as a proponent of 'probabilism': see Burnyeat [58].

[17] The evidence for Aenesidemus having begun his philosophical career in the Academy is that he dedicated his *Pyrrhonian Discourses* to L. Tubero, described as a fellow associate of the Academy (Phot. *Bibl.* 169 b 33). Zeller [18], Abt. 2, p. 23 n. 2, is perhaps right in suggesting that because Photius' report of this work (which is mentioned also at DL IX 106 and 116) says nothing of the Ten Modes, it is to be distinguished from the *Outline Introduction to Pyrrhonism* which Aristocles and Diogenes indicate as the place where the Modes were developed.

[18] Both rightly and polemically if his target is Philo of Larissa: see below.

Academy. If the Ten Modes have their intended effect, we will be weaned from the Academic criterion for the conduct of life to Aenesidemus' new Pyrrhonist ideal of a life without belief. It is quite possible, however, that this was not so much a new proposal as the revival of one much older.

The idea that one should live without belief (the word used is *adoxastous*, as in Sextus) is prominent in the most extended doxographical account we possess of the philosophy of Pyrrho himself: the quotation in Eusebius (*PE* XIV 18, 2–4) from Aristocles, a Peripatetic writer of the second century A.D., which gives what purports to be a summary of the views attributed to Pyrrho by his follower Timon.[19] We should not put any trust in our perceptions or beliefs, says the summary, since they are neither true nor false, and when we are thus neutrally disposed, without belief, tranquillity results. It is possible that Aristocles received this report through Aenesidemus himself,[20] but that need not mean it gives a distorted interpretation of Timon's account of Pyrrho. Quite a few of the fragments of Timon which have come down to us are at least suggestive of later Pyrrhonism.[21] Moreover, various stories relating how Pyrrho's friends had to follow him about to keep him from being run over by carts or walking over precipices (DL IX 62—the precipice fantasy may derive from Aristotle, *Metaph.* Γ4, 1008ᵇ 15–16) are exactly of the type one would expect to grow up around a man known for teaching a life without belief. And these stories are old. They are cited from the biography of Pyrrho written by Antigonus of Carystus in the late third century B.C., well before Aenesidemus; in fact Aenesidemus felt it necessary to combat the idea that a philosophy based on suspending belief would make Pyrrho behave without foresight (DL IX 62). This seems rather clear evidence that for Aenesidemus himself the life without belief was the revival of a much older ideal.

It is not difficult, moreover, to guess something of the philo-sophical reasons why Aenesidemus should have resorted to Pyrrho for his model. On the one hand, the Academy at the time of Philo of Larissa appeared less sharply sceptical than it had

---

[19] Timon, frag. 2 in Diels [9]; translation and discussion in Stough [29], Ch. 2.

[20] The ground for this suspicion is a somewhat odd, textually disputed, reference to Aenesidemus tacked on at the end of the summary. See Dumont [46], 140–7.

[21] For discussion, see Burnyeat [57]. The question of the historical accuracy of Timon's account of Pyrrho is a further matter which need not concern us here.

been; in particular, on Philo's controversial interpretation of Carneades (cf. *Acad.* II 78, *ind. Acad. Herc.* XXVI, 4), *to pithanon* could be and was offered as a positive criterion of life.[22] On the other hand, the great difficulty for Academic scepticism had always been the objection—Hume's objection—that total *epochē* makes it impossible to live.[23] The tradition concerning Pyrrho offered a solution to both problems at once. The way to live without belief, without softening the sceptical *epochē*, is by keeping to appearances. This was the plan or criterion for living that Aenesidemus adopted (DL IX 106), again not without some support in the fragments of Timon,[24] and we shall find it elaborated in Sextus Empiricus. It is a pleasing thought that not only does Sextus anticipate Hume's objection, but also, if I am right about the philosophical context which prompted Aenesidemus to his revival of Pyrrhonism, it was in part precisely to meet that objection more effectively than had been done hitherto that Aenesidemus left the Academy and aligned himself to Pyrrho.

LIVING BY APPEARANCES

A sceptical restructuring of thought, a life without belief, tranquillity—these are not ideas that we would nowadays associate with philosophical scepticism, which has become a largely

[22] For the controversy about Carneades, see Striker, Chapter 3 below. That Aenesidemus' target was the Academy of Philo is indicated above all by Photius' report (*Bibl.* 170 a 21–2) that he characterized his Academic opponents as determining many things with assurance and claiming to contest only the cataleptic impression. This corresponds not to Carneades' sceptical outlook but to the distinctive innovation of Philo, according to whom it is not that in their own nature things cannot be grasped but that they cannot be grasped by the Stoics' cataleptic impression (*PH* I 235). The alternative target would be Antiochus, but he does not fit Aenesidemus' scornful description of contemporary Academics as Stoics *fighting* Stoics (Phot. *Bibl.* 170 a 14–17). It would appear that Aenesidemus was also provoked by Philo's claim (*Acad.* I 13) that there were not two Academies, but a single unified tradition reaching right back to Plato. This amounted to the assertion that Plato stood for scepticism as Philo understood it, and Aenesidemus was at pains to deny that Plato could rightly be regarded as a sceptic (*PH* I 222, reading κατὰ τούς with Natorp and noting the disjunctive form of the argument: Plato is not sceptical if either he assents to certain things as true *or* he accepts them as merely persuasive For a decisive defence of Natorp's reading against the alternative κατὰ τῶν, which would mean that Aenesidemus thought Plato was sceptical, see Burkhard [45], 21–7).

[23] Above, p. 22 n. 4.

[24] Esp. frags. 69: 'But the phenomenon prevails on every side, wherever it may go'; and 74: 'I do not assert that honey (really) is sweet, but that it appears (sweet) I grant' (tr. Stough).

dialectical exercise in problem-setting, focused, as I noted earlier, on knowledge rather than belief. Even Peter Unger, who has recently propounded a programme for a sceptical restructuring of thought,[25] does not really try to dislodge belief. Having assiduously rediscovered that scepticism involves a denial of reason, and the connection between scepticism and the emotions, as well as much else that was familiar to Sextus Empiricus, he agrees that all belief is unreasonable, and he even has an argument that in fact no one does believe anything—belief itself is impossible. But he does not really believe this last refinement, since his programme envisages that concepts like *knowledge* and *reason* be replaced by less demanding assessments of our cognitive relation to reality, rather in the spirit of Academic fallibilism; thus it seems clear that, while a great number of our present beliefs would go (for a start, all those beliefs having to do with what is known and what is reasonable), believing as such would remain firmly entrenched at the centre of our mental life. The ancient Greek Pyrrhonist would not let it rest there. He is sceptical about knowledge, to be sure: that is the burden of all the arguments against the Stoics' cataleptic impression—the impression which, being clear and distinct (DL VII 46), affords a grasp of its object and serves as a foundation for secure knowledge. But his chief enemy, as we have seen, is belief. So the question arises, What then remains for a man who is converted by the sceptic arguments to a life without belief, where this means, as always, without belief as to real existence? This is the question we have to ask if we want to probe the secret of sceptic tranquillity.

The sceptic's answer, in brief, is that he follows appearances (*PH* I 21). The criterion by which he lives his life is appearance. In more detail, he has a fourfold scheme of life (*PH* I 23-4), allowing him to be active under four main heads, as follows. First, there is the guidance of nature: the sceptic is guided by the natural human capacity for percipience and thought, he uses his senses and exercises his mental faculties—to what result we shall see in due course. Second comes the constraint of bodily drives (*pathōn anankē*): hunger leads him to food, thirs tto drink, and Sextus agrees with Hume that you cannot dispel by argument attitudes the casual origin of which has nothing to do with reason and belief (*M* XI 148). In this respect, indeed, perfect *ataraxia* is unattainable for a human being, physical creature that he is, and the sceptic settles for *metriopatheia* (*PH* I 30, III 235–6): the disturbance will be greatly moderated if he is free of the additional element of belief (*to prosdoxazein*) that it *matters* whether he secures food and drink. Third, there is the tradition of laws and customs: the sceptic keeps the rules and observes in the conduct of life the pieties of his society.[26] Finally, the fourth element is instruction in the arts: he practises an art or profession, in Sextus' own case medicine, so that he has something to do. All of this falls under the criterion of appearance, but Sextus does not really aim to develop the scheme in practical detail. Once he has pointed us in these four directions, his main concern, and therefore ours here, is with the general criterion of appearance.

In the section of the *Outlines of Pyrrhonism* where it is formally stated that the criterion by which the sceptic lives his life is appearance (*PH* I 21–4), not only does appearance contrast with reality but living by appearances contrasts with the life of belief. Evidently, the mental resources left to the sceptic when he eschews belief will be commensurate with whatever falls on the side of appearance when the line is drawn between appearance and real existence. So it becomes important to ask, as I have not so far asked, just what the sceptic is contrasting when he sets appearance against real existence. By the same token, if appearance is identified with some one type of appearance—and the most likely candidate for this is sense-appearance—that will have restrictive implications for the mental content of the life without belief.

Let us go back briefly to the passage where Sextus gave his definition of scepticism as a capacity for bringing into opposition things that appear and things that are thought etc. When Sextus

---

[26] I have done a little interpretation here, taking τὸ μὲν εὐσεβεῖν παραλαμβάνομεν βιωτικῶς ὡς ἀγαθὸν τὸ δὲ ἀσεβεῖν ὡς φαῦλον in the light of such passages as *PH* I 226, II 246, III 12, *M* IX 49. Note the verb forms τὸ εὐσεβεῖν, ἀσεβεῖν: not attitudes but practices (which were in any case the main content of Greek piety and impiety) are what the sceptic accepts. To say that it is βιωτικῶς, not as a matter of belief, that he accepts the one as good and the other as bad comes to little more than that he pursues the one and avoids the other; in short, he tries to observe the pieties of his society. If custom demands it, he will even declare that gods exist, but he will not believe it (*PH* III 2) or mean it *in propria persona* as do both the dogmatists and the ordinary man (*M* IX 49–50): on the existence of the gods, as on any question of real existence, the sceptic suspends judgement (*PH* III 6, 9, 11; *M* IX 59, 191).

comes to elucidate the terms of his definition, he says that by 'things that appear' (*phainomena*) we *now* mean sensibles (*aisthēta*) in contrast to things thought (*nooumena* or *noēta*) (*PH* I 8–9). This surely implies that he does not always or even usually mean sensibles alone when he speaks of what appears (cp. *M* VIII 216). Some scholars, most recently Charlotte Stough, have taken the sceptic criterion to be sense-appearance, in the narrow meaning, because when Sextus says the criterion is what appears (*to phainomenon*), he adds that the sceptics mean by this the impression (*phantasia*) of the thing that appears (*PH* I 22).[27] But the point here is simply to explain that what the sceptic goes by in his daily life is not, strictly, the thing itself that appears, but the impression it makes on him, and in Sextus' vocabulary (as in Stoic usage—cf. DL VII 51) there are impressions (*phantasiai*) which are not and could not possibly be thought to be sense-impressions. I need only cite the impression, shared by all opponents of Protagoras, that not every impression is true (*M* VII 390). As for *to phainomenon*, what appears may, so far as I can see, be anything whatever. Sextus is prepared to include under things appearing both objects of sense and objects of thought (*M* VIII 362), and sometimes he goes so far as to speak of things appearing to reason (*logos*) or thought (*dianoia*) (ambiguously so *PH* II 10, *M* VIII 70, unambiguously *M* VII 25, VIII 141). Finally, there is a most important set of appearances annexed to the sceptic's own philosophical utterances; as Michael Frede has emphasized,[28] these are hardly to be classed as appearances of sense.

Time and again Sextus warns that sceptic formulae such as 'I determine nothing' and 'No more this than that' (*PH* I 15), or the conclusions of sceptic arguments like 'Everything is relative' (*PH* I 135), or indeed the entire contents of his treatise (*PH* I 4), are to be taken as mere records of appearance. Like a chronicle (*PH* I 4), they record how each thing appears to the sceptic,

---

[27] Stough [29], 119 ff. Stough's initial mistake (as I think it) is to treat the statement as a contribution to a theory of experience. She then elicits the consequence that one perceives only one's own impressions, not the external object, since that which appears *is* (according to Stough's reading of the present passage) our impression. This goes flatly against the innumerable passages where that which appears is the very thing whose real properties cannot be determined, e.g. the honey at *PH* I 20. A further undesirable and unwarranted feature of Stough's interpretation is the divergence it leads her to postulate between Aenesidemus and Sextus (p. 124–5).

[28] Frede [62].

announcing or narrating how it affects him (his *pathos*) without committing him to the belief or assertion that anything really and truly is as it appears to him to be (cp. also *PH* I 197). Clearly it would be impossible to regard all these appearances as impressions of sense.[29] But the practice of argumentative enquiry is so considerable a portion of the sceptic's way of life that they must certainly be included under the sceptic criterion. They are one outcome, surely, and a most important outcome, of his natural capacity for percipience *and thought*. Sense-appearance cannot be all that is involved when the sceptic says he follows appearances.

It may be granted that the conclusion of a sceptic argument is typically that the real nature of something cannot be determined and that we must content ourselves with saying how it appears, where this frequently does mean: how it appears to the senses. But essentially the same formulae are used when the subject of enquiry is, say, the existence of species and genera (*PH* I 138–40), the rightness or wrongness of certain customs and practices (*PH* I 148 ff.), or, quite generally, objects of thought (*noēta*) as contrasted with sensible things (*PH* I 177). Further, the conclusion of a sceptic argument may be also that a certain concept cannot be formed: for example, the concept of man (*PH* II 27). In this connection Sextus contrasts asserting dogmatically that man really is e.g. a featherless two-footed animal with broad nails and a capacity for political science and putting forward this same definition as something merely persuasive (*pithanon*); the former is the illegitimate thing which is the target of his argument, the latter what he thinks Plato would do (*PH* II 28). I think it would be wholly in keeping with the spirit, if not the letter, of this text to add the properly Pyrrhonist alternative of saying what man appears to one to be. For Sextus insists[30] that the sceptic is not prohibited from *noēsis*, the forming of conceptions. He can form his own conceptions just so long as the basis for this is that things he experiences appear clearly to reason itself and he is not led into any commitment to the reality of the things conceived (*PH* II 10).

I suggest, therefore, that the sceptic contrast between appearance and real existence is a purely formal one, entirely independent

[29] *Contra* Stough [29], 146 n. 83.
[30] *Contra* Naess [50], 51.

of subject matter. The sceptic does not divide the world into appearances and realities so that one could ask of this or that whether it belongs to the category of appearance or to the category of reality. He divides questions into questions about how something appears and questions about how it really and truly is, and both types of question may be asked about anything whatever.

In his chapter on the sceptic criterion Sextus says: 'No one, I suppose, disputes about the underlying subject's appearing thus or thus; what he enquires about is whether it is such as it appears' (*PH* I 22). The point is one familiar in modern philosophy, that how a thing appears or seems is authoritatively answered by each individual. When Sextus says that a man's impression is *azētētos*, not subject to enquiry (*PH* I 22), the claim is that his report that this is how it appears to him cannot be challenged and he cannot properly be required to give reason, evidence or proof for it. It is only when he ventures a claim about how something really is that he can be asked for the appropriate justification. It follows that the sceptic who adheres strictly to appearance is withdrawing to the safety of a position not open to challenge or enquiry. He may talk about anything under the sun—but only to note how it appears to him, not to say how it really is. He withdraws to this detached stance as the result of repeatedly satisfying himself that enquiry as to the real nature of a thing leads to unresolvable disagreement. We can understand, now, why the only use the sceptic has for reason is polemical. Quite simply, nothing he wants to say in his own person is such as to require a reasoned justification.[31] Reason is one more important notion which is tied to truth and real existence.

It turns out, then, that the life without belief is not the mental blank one might at first imagine it to be. It is not even limited as to the subject matter over which the sceptic's thoughts may range. Its secret is rather an attitude of mind manifest in his thoughts. He notes the impression things make on him and the contrary impressions they make on other people, and his own impressions seem to him no stronger, no more plausible, than

---

[31] In keeping with this Sextus does not claim knowledge or (*pace* Hossenfelder, [6], 60-1) certainty about how things appear to him. If pressed, the radical Pyrrhonist will actually deny that he knows such things (Galen, *De diff. puls.* VIII 711, 1-3 K= Deichgräber [10], frag. 75, p. 135, 28-30). See further Burnyeat [59].

anyone else's.[32] To the extent that he has achieved *ataraxia*, he is no longer concerned to enquire which is right. When a thing appears in a certain light to him, that no more inclines him to believe it is as it appears than would the fact of its so appearing to someone else. It is merely one more impression or appearance to be noted. Thus the withdrawal from truth and real existence becomes, in a certain sense, a detachment from oneself.

ASSENT AND CONSTRAINT

With this conclusion we reach, I think, the real point of scepticism as a philosophy of life. So thoroughgoing a detachment from oneself is not easy to understand—indeed, it is here that I would locate the ultimate incoherence of the sceptic philosophy—but the attempt must be made if we are to appreciate the kind of restructuring which the sceptic arguments aim to produce in a man's thought, and thereby in his practical life. To this end I must now broach the difficult topic of assent and the will.

I have already explained that assent is a wider notion than belief. The sceptic's non-belief, his *epochē*, is his withholding assent to anything not given in appearance (*PH* I 13). But there are things he assents to: *ta phainomena*, anything that appears. This doctrine is stated in full generality at *PH* I 19–20, with no restriction to any specific class of appearances; although the example to hand is a sensible appearance, the taste of honey, I hold, as before, that Sextus means any kind of appearance and hence that the important further characterization he gives in this connection is to be applied to all appearances without exception.

The further characterization is as follows: things that appear lead us to assent (sc. to them) *aboulētōs*, without our willing it, in accordance with the impression they affect us with (*kata phantasian pathētikēn*). Much the same is said on numerous occasions elsewhere. When the sceptic assents, it is because he experiences two

---

[32] It is of the essence of scepticism, as defined *PH* I 8 and as practised throughout the sceptic literature, to set one person's impressions against those of another. Questions could be raised about the sceptic's entitlement to talk of other people's impressions, and suitable answers could be devised. But on the whole such questions are not raised, any more than the sceptic inquires into the basis for his extensive historical surveys of the views of other philosophers. The radically first-person stance of the scepticisms we are familiar with is a distinctively modern development (cp. p. 25 n. 8 above).

kinds of constraint. First, what he assents to are *kata phantasian katēnankasmena pathē*, states with which we are forcibly affected in accordance with an impression (*PH* I 13). He can assent to an impression, or, as Sextus also puts it (*PH* II 10), he can assent to what is presented in accordance with an impression he is affected with in so far as it appears, because the impression itself, the way the thing appears, is a passive affection not willed by the person who experiences it and as such is not open to enquiry or dispute (*en peisei kai aboulētōi pathei keimenē azētētos estin*) (*PH* I 22); in other words, it is merely what is happening to him now. But second, besides having the impression forced upon us, we are also constrained in these cases to assent. The sceptic yields to things which move us affectively (*tois kinousin hēmas pathētikōs*) and lead us by compulsion to assent (*kai anankastikōs agousin eis sunkatathesin*) (*PH* I 193).

What, then, is the content of the sceptic's assent? Assent is described as assent to something in so far as it appears, or to the state/impression which is its appearing to us, but the expression of this assent is propositional: e.g. 'Honey appears sweet' (*PH* I 20). In another place (*PH* I 13) Sextus puts the point in a negative way: when the sceptic is warmed or chilled, he would not say 'I think I am not warmed/chilled.'[33] Arne Naess takes the negative formulation to be an attempt to articulate the idea that the sceptic does not accept or reject 'It now seems cold to me' as a proposition.[34] I do not find in Sextus any evidence of a contrast between assenting to a state or to the impression of a thing and assenting to a proposition about how something appears to one. We concede, says Sextus (*PH* I 20), that honey appears sweet because we are sweetened perceptually (*glukazometha aisthētikōs*), which I take to mean: we have a perceptual experience featuring the character of sweetness. The sceptic's assent is simply the acknowledging of what is happening to him, and the compulsion to assent, to acknowledge what is happening to him, is equally simple. It is not that there is resistance to overcome, but that there can be no dispute about what the impression is; it is

---

[33] On the translation of θερμαίνεσθαι and ψύχεσθαι, see below.

[34] Naess [50], 8. Naess, however, has a rather special theory about what it is to accept or reject something as a proposition, a theory which is claimed to rescue Pyrrhonism from Hume's critique: see Alistair Hannay, 'Giving the Sceptic a Good Name', *Inquiry* 18 (1975), 409–36.

azētētos, not open to enquiry. The impression is just the way something appears to one, and assent to it is just acknowledging that this is indeed how the thing appears to one at the moment. So far, I have illustrated these points, as Sextus does, by reference to impressions of sense. As it happens, however, at least one of the statements cited occurs in a context describing the attitude of mind which the sceptic brings to the practice of argumentative enquiry. This is the statement (*PH* II 10) that the sceptic assents to things presented to him in accordance with an impression which they affect him with (*kata phantasian pathētikēn*), in so far as they appear to him. Given the context, it is natural to refer the remark to the appearances annexed to the sceptic's various philosophical pronouncements. That the *phantasia*, the impression, is characterized as *pathētikē*, something one is affected with, is no hindrance to this; we have already seen that an impression need not be an impression of sense, and to call it *pathētikē* simply means it is a passivity (*peisis*) or *pathos*, as at *PH* I 22. Sextus is perfectly prepared to speak of a *pathos*, affection, annexed to the sceptic formula 'I determine nothing' (*PH* I 197; cp. I 203). As he explains, when the sceptic says 'I determine nothing', what he is saying is, 'I am now affected (*egō houtō pepontha nun*) in such a way as not to affirm or deny dogmatically any of the matters under enquiry.' At *PH* I 193 this is generalized to all expressions of sceptical non-assertion (*aphasia*) and linked with the topic of compulsory assent to states of appearance. Clearly, 'I determine nothing', as an expression of the sceptic's non-assertion, does not indicate a sense-impression. But it does indicate a *pathos*, a passive affection. It would seem, therefore, that this *pathos*, and assent to it, is forced upon the sceptic as the outcome of his arguments just as much as a sense-impression is forced upon him by an encounter with some sensible object and then forcibly engages his assent.

I think this is right. Look through a sample of sceptic arguments and you will find that a great number of them end by saying that one is forced to suspend judgement, the word most commonly used being *anankazō*, the same word as describes our passive relationship to an impression of sense and the assent it engages. The sceptic assents only when his assent is constrained, and equally when he withholds assent, suspends judgement, this is because he finds himself constrained to do so. A marked passivity in the face of both his sensations and his own thought-processes is an important aspect of the sceptic's detachment from himself. But, once again, there is neither mystery nor effort involved in the constraint.

We are all familiar with the way in which an argument or overwhelming evidence may compel assent. In just this way, the sceptic's arguments are designed to check assent (*epechein* has a transitive use = 'to check', as well as the standard intransitive meaning 'to suspend judgement'). Imagine a man so placed that he really can see no reason at all to believe *p* rather than not-*p*; the considerations for and against seem absolutely equal no matter how hard he tries to resolve the question. Then, as Sextus puts it, he will be checked (*epischethēsetai*—*PH* I 186; cp. I 180, *M* VII 337). If it was a matter of acting where he could see no reason to choose this rather than that, he could toss a coin or simply do whatever one has been brought up to do in the circumstances. In effect, that is what the sceptic does do when he adheres to the conventions of whatever society he lives in without himself believing in them or having any personal attachment to their values. But believing is not like that. Of course, it is a good philosophical question whether it is not possible in some circumstances to decide or will to believe something, but these will have to be circumstances more auspicious than those I have described, where one can literally see nothing to choose between *p* and not-*p*. To quote Epictetus (*Diss.* I 28.3), just try to believe, or positively disbelieve, that the number of the stars is even.[35]

I repeat: try it. Make yourself vividly aware of your helpless inability to mind either way. *That* is how the sceptic wants you to feel about everything, including whether what I am saying is true or false (you are not to be convinced by the reputation or the artfulness of the speaker). That is *ataraxia*. If a tyrant sends a message that you and your family are to perish at dawn unless you commit some unspeakable deed, the true sceptic will be undisturbed both about whether the message is true or false and

---

[35] The example is traditional, i.e. much older than Epictetus. It is a standard Stoic example of something altogether non-evident, which can be discerned neither from itself nor through a sign (*PH* II 97, *M* VII 393, VIII 147, 317; cp. VII 243, XI 59). It occurs also in Cicero's reference (*Acad.* II 32) to certain *quasi desperatos* who say that everything is as uncertain as whether the number of the stars is odd or even, a reference which is sometimes taken to point to Aenesidemus: so Brochard [25], 245, Striker (Chapter 3 below), p. 64.

about whether it would be a good thing or a bad thing to comply with the command. You will be undisturbed not because your will has subjugated the tendency to believe and to be emotionally disturbed, but because you have been rendered unable to find any reason to think anything is true rather than false or good rather than bad. This is not to say that you will do nothing—Hume's charge of total lethargy. Sextus meets this old complaint, first by acknowledging the role of bodily drives like hunger and thirst and by the rest of the fourfold scheme of activity, and in the case of the tyrant (*M* XI 162–6) by saying that of course the sceptic will have his preconceptions, the result of being brought up in certain forms of life (cf. *PH* II 246), and these will prompt him to act one way or the other. But the point is that he does not identify with the values involved. He notes that they have left him with inclinations to pursue some things and avoid others, but he does not believe there is any reason to prefer the things he pursues over those that he avoids.[36]

The assumptions at work here are reminiscent of Socrates, as is much else in Hellenistic moral psychology. The emotions depend on belief, especially beliefs about what is good and bad. Remove belief and the emotions will disappear; as fear, for example, fades when one is dissuaded of one's belief that the thing one was afraid of is dangerous. At least, to the extent that emotions derive from reason and thought, they must disappear when judgement is suspended on every question of fact and value. This will not eliminate bodily disturbances such as hunger and thirst, nor the tendencies to action which result from the endowments of nature and from an upbringing in human society (cf. *PH* I 230–1). For they do not depend on reason and thought. But they will be less disturbing without the added element of belief about good and bad, truth and falsity (above, p. 33). One may feel that this added element of belief is the very thing that gives meaning and sense to a life, even if it is also the source of trouble and disturbance. Without it, the sceptic's life will be a hollow shell of the existence he enjoyed, and was troubled by, prior to his sceptical enlightenment. Such is the price of peace and tranquillity, however, and the sceptic is willing to pay it to

---

[36] Compare, perhaps, Feyerabend's reply to the question why his 'epistemological anarchist' does not jump out of the window: Paul Feyerabend, *Against Method* (London, 1975), 221–2. He notes his fear, and its effect on his behaviour, but he does not endorse any reasons for the fear. See further p. 42 n. 37 below.

the full. Or rather, he is constrained by argument to suspend judgement and belief, and then finds that this just happens to bring tranquillity (*PH* I 28–30; above, pp. 24–5). He exercises no deliberated choice in the matter, any more than when hunger leads him to get food.[37] So far from relying on the will to control assent, the sceptic panacea, beginning with the Ten Modes of Aenesidemus, is to use reason to check all the sources of belief and destroy all trust in reason itself, thereby eliminating the very inclination to believe. The life without belief is not an achievement of the will but a paralysis of reason by itself.[38]

[37] According to Timon, frag. 72, quoted *M* XI 164, the follower of Pyrrho is ἀφυγὴς καὶ ἀναίρετος. According to Sextus (*PH* I 28) he does not pursue or avoid anything eagerly (συντόνως), i.e. he does not mind how it turns out. This detachment in action is interestingly discussed by Hossenfelder [6], esp. 66–74. On Socratic assumptions, it is the logical outcome of the sceptical conclusion that nothing is by nature good or bad, i.e. nothing is really *worth* pursuit or avoidance (Timon, frag. 70 = *M* XI 140, discussed in Burnyeat [57]; *PH* I 27, III 235–8, *M* XI 69 ff.).

[38] The passivity of the sceptic's *epochē* has not, I think, been appreciated in the modern scholarly literature, Hossenfelder [6] excepted. One reason for this is the tendency to read appearance as sense-appearance wherever possible, with the consequence that Sextus' remarks about compulsion are taken to extend no further than bodily and perceptual sensation. That I have already taken issue with. The other reason is that it has been widely held to be common ground to philosophers of different persuasions in the period we are concerned with that 'assent is free' (so e.g. Brochard [25], 138, 391). If that is so, it is easy to assume that, except when the sceptic is compelled to assent, he is free to give his assent or withhold it, and always he chooses—chooses of his own volition—to withhold it.

The idea that assent is free is Stoic doctrine in the first place, and there are indeed plenty of Stoic texts which say that assent is voluntary or in our power. But there are also texts which say that at least some impressions compel assent. The cataleptic impression lays hold of us almost by the hairs, they say, and drags us to assent (*M* VII 257; cp. 405); in another image, the mind yields to what is clear as a scale yields to the weights (*Acad.* II 38; cf. Epict. *Diss.* II 26.7). Assent in such cases is still voluntary because, it would seem, all that is meant by saying it is voluntary is that it depends on my judgement, hence on me, whether I assent or not. At any rate, that is all there is to Sextus' account of the Stoic view in a passage (*M* VIII 397) which explicitly contrasts voluntary assent with involuntary impression. The impression is involuntary (ἀκούσιος), not willed (ἀβούλητος), because whether or not I am affected by an impression does not depend on me but on something else, namely, the thing which appears to me; the impression once received, however, it does depend on me whether I assent to it, for it depends on my judgement. This leaves it quite open what factors influence my judgement, and how, and therefore leaves it open whether the influence could be regarded as in any sense a type of compulsion. In fact, recent studies on the Stoic side have pursued with illuminating results a line of interpretation according to which assent is determined internally, by a man's character and the education of his mind, and is voluntary just because and in the sense that it is internally determined in this way: see Long [106], Voelké [79], and cp. Epict. *Diss.* I 28. 1–5. If that is the content of the doctrine that assent is free, it fits perfectly well with the emphasis I have placed on the passivity of the sceptic's *epochē*. He does not and could not choose *epochē* for the sake of *ataraxia*.

CONTROVERSIAL INTERLUDE

It is time to take stock. A life has been described, and we want to know whether it is a possible life for man. But there is a prior question of some moment to face first: is the life described a life without belief, as Sextus so often claims (*adoxastōs bioumen* etc., *PH* I 23, 226, 231, II 246, 254, 258, III 235)?[39] The sceptic is supposed to content himself with appearances in lieu of beliefs, but it may be objected that, whatever Sextus may say, at least some of these appearances are beliefs in disguise. 'Honey tastes sweet' may pass muster as the record of a perceptual or bodily experience, but when it comes to 'All things appear relative' (*PH* I 135) or 'Let it be granted that the premisses of the proof appear' (*M* VIII 368) or 'Some things appear good, others evil' (*M* XI 19), we can hardly take 'appear' (*phainesthai*) other than in its epistemic sense. That is, when the sceptic offers a report of the form 'It appears to me now that *p*', at least sometimes he is chronicling the fact that he believes or finds himself inclined to believe that something is the case.

This epistemic reading of the sceptic's talk of appearances may be presented in either of two forms: as an objection to Sextus or as an objection to my interpretation of Sextus. In the second version, which I take up first, the claim will be that the sceptic's assent to appearance, as Sextus describes it, is not the assertion of the existence of a certain impression or experience but the expression of a non-dogmatic belief about what is the case in the world. It will then follow that what the sceptic eschews, when he suspends judgement about everything, is not any and every kind of belief about things, but belief of a more ambitious type, which we may call (pending further elucidation) dogmatic belief.[40]

I do not doubt that a good number of the appearance-statements in Sextus Empiricus *can* be read epistemically. But if this fact is to yield an objection not to Sextus but to my interpretation of him, it needs to be shown that the epistemic reading has the approval of Sextus himself. The passage which comes closest to showing

[39] Cp. the talk of stating or assenting to something ἀδοξάστως at *PH* I 24, 240, II 13, 102, III 2, 151.

[40] For the challenge to try to meet this objection I am indebted to the conference and to discussions with Michael Frede. In the space available I cannot hope to do justice to the subtlety with which Frede [63] expounds a very different interpretation of Sextus from that advocated here.

it is *PH* I 13. There Sextus says that some people define a broad
sense of *'dogma'* meaning to accept something or not contradict
it,[41] and with this he contrasts a narrower sense explained by
some (? the same) people as assent to one of the non-evident
things investigated by the sciences. The point of this distinction
is to clarify the sense in which the sceptic does not dogmatize:
he will have nothing to do with *dogma* in the second and narrower
sense, 'for the Pyrrhonist does not assent to anything that is
non-evident'. But he does assent to states with which he is
forcibly affected in accordance with an impression, and such
assent (we are given to understand) is or involves *dogma* in the
broader sense to which the Pyrrhonist has no objection. For
example (an example we have met before), 'He would not say,
when he is warmed or chilled, "I think I am not warmed or
chilled." ' Two questions now arise. First, does Sextus' tolerance
of the broad sense signify approval of an epistemic reading for
appearance-statements generally? Second, does his account of
the narrower sense restrict his disapproval to what we have
provisionally called dogmatic belief?

(1) What the sceptic accepts or does not contradict is 'I am
warmed/chilled'. This is a *dogma* (in the broad sense) inasmuch
as the sceptic thinks, or it seems to him, that he is warmed/
chilled.[42] But it does not follow that it is an epistemic seeming,
in the sense relevant to our discussion, unless its content 'I am
warmed/chilled' is a proposition about what is the case in the
world rather than a proposition about the sceptic's experience.

We must be careful here. The Greek verbs *thermainesthai* and
psuchesthai do not normally *mean* 'I feel hot/cold', although
translators (Bury, Hossenfelder) have a tendency to render them
in such terms here, just because Sextus is illustrating an affection
(*pathos*). They normally mean 'be warmed/chilled'.[43] On the
other hand, neither does 'I am warmed/chilled' necessarily refer
to an objective process of acquiring or losing heat. And my own
view is that to insist that Sextus' illustrative *pathos* must be either
a subjective feeling or an objective happening is to impose a
Cartesian choice which is foreign to his way of thinking.

---

[41] εὐδοκεῖν, on which see Frede [63].
[42] Sextus evidently intends to bring out the semantic connection between δόγμα
and δοκεῖν.
[43] See Frede [63].

Sextus' terminology here is probably Cyrenaic. *Thermainesthai* and *psuchesthai* appear (by a well-motivated editorial insertion) on a list of Cyrenaic terms for *pathē* of perception in Plutarch, *Col.* 1120 e, along with *glukainesthai*, 'to be sweetened', which Sextus uses at *M* VIII 211 (cp. *glukazesthai PH* I 20, 211, II 51, 72, *M* VIII 54, IX 139); *leukainesthai*, 'to be whitened', and the like, applied by Sextus to the activity of the senses, look to be of similar provenance (*M* VII 293 with 190–8). As Plutarch describes the Cyrenaic doctrine which was the original home of this peculiar terminology,[44] it is that I can say *thermainomai*, 'I am warmed', but not *thermos ho akratos*, where this does not mean 'Neat wine is warm' but 'Neat wine is warming' (*thermos* = *thermantikos, Col.* 1109 f.). The case is exactly comparable to one we find in Aristocles (*apud* Eus. *PE* XIV 19, 2–3): according to the Cyrenaics, when I am being cut or burned I know I am undergoing something (*paschein ti*), but whether it is fire that is burning or iron that is cutting me, I cannot say. Do they mean, when they talk of undergoing something, the physical event or the way it feels? To that question *there is no clear answer*, and the terminology makes it impossible to decide. It is the same with Sextus. The reference of these funny verbs is plainly to a perceptual process rather than to the transmission of heat (cf. the case of the neat wine: conversely, the warming of a man so chilled that he could not feel a thing when you rubbed his hands would not illustrate Sextus' point at all), but we should keep the translation 'be warmed/chilled'. The man is being affected perceptually (cf. 'We are sweetened perceptually', *glukazometha aisthētikōs*, at *PH* I 20 and the uses of *thermainein* at *PH* I 110, II 56, *M* I 147, VII 368, IX 69), but we cannot 'split' the affection (*pathos*) into separate mental (subjective) and physical (objective) components. The moral to draw is not that the Pyrrhonist allows himself some beliefs about what is the case, but that scepticism is not yet associated with a Cartesian conception of the self.[45]

If this is correct, *PH* I 13 offers no justification for an epistemic reading of the sceptic's appearance-statements. The broader sense of '*dogma*' is simply the accepting of a perceptual experience as the

---

[44] Plutarch's report shows that the Cyrenaic terminology was caricatured as peculiar.

[45] This is a topic that has come up before: see p. 25 n. 8 above and Burnyeat [59].

experience it is, in the manner we have found amply attested already (above, pp. 38–9).[46] Sextus is not going out of his way to leave room for a non-dogmatic type of belief about matters of real existence. On the contrary, he says that when as a sceptic he makes statements with the verb 'to be', he is to be understood as meaning 'to appear' (*PH* I 135, 198, 200), and he glosses this use of 'to be' at *M* XI 18 in terms which are unmistakably non-epistemic:

The word 'is' has two meanings: (a) 'is actually (*huparchei*)', as we say at the present moment 'It is day' in place of 'It is actually day', (b) 'appears', as some of the mathematicians are accustomed to say often that the distance between two stars 'is' a cubit's length, meaning this as equivalent to 'It appears so and doubtless is not actually so'; for perhaps it is actually one hundred stades, but appears a cubit because of the height and distance from the eye.

He then applies this elucidation to one of the statements that troubled us earlier, 'Some things appear good, others evil' (*M* XI 19).

(2) Moving on to the narrower sense of '*dogma*', the point to observe is that *any* thing which is non-evident is something for the sciences to investigate, the non-evident being by definition that which can only be known by the mediation of inference.[47] The scope for investigation or enquiry will be determined by the extent of things non-evident, 'for', as Sextus says, 'the Pyrrhonist does not assent to anything that is non-evident.' But the Pyrrhonist attack on the criterion of truth abolishes the evidence of everything that the dogmatists consider evident (*PH* II 95, *M* VIII 141–2). Take one of the dogmatists' favourite examples of things too patently obvious to be doubted, 'It is day', which turns up both in connection with the criterion (*M* VIII 144) and in the passage just quoted: the sceptic denies it is evident and, as we have seen, he accepts it only as a non-epistemic statement of appearance, 'It appears to be day [sc. but may not actually be so]'. *Anything* which goes beyond (non-epistemic) appearances is subject to enquiry (*PH* I 19; above, p. 36; cp. *M* VIII 344–5).

In sum, I do not think that one solitary reference to the sciences (for it is not repeated elsewhere in Sextus) in a definition borrowed

---

[46] δοκῶ θερμαίνεσθαι is thus parallel to φαίνεται ἡμῖν γλυκάζειν τὸ μέλι at *PH* I 20.
[47] See p. 26 n. 9 above.

from someone else[48] is sufficient basis to credit Sextus with a distinction between dogmatic and non-dogmatic belief. It is not sufficient even when we add to the scales that Sextus frequently restricts what he suspends judgement about to the question how things are 'in nature' (*pros tēn phusin* etc., *PH* I 59, 78, 87, *et al.*) or how things are 'so far as concerns what the dogmatists say about them' (*PH* II 26, 104, III 13, 29, 135, *M* VIII 3) or, ambiguously, how things are 'so far as this is a matter for *logos* (statement, definition, reason)' (*PH* I 20, 215).[49] Just how restrictive these qualifications are depends on what they are contrasted with, and in every case the contrast is with how things appear, where this, as we have seen, is to be taken non-epistemically. All we are left with, then, is a passive impression (*phantasia*) or experience (*pathos*), expressed in a statement which makes no truth-claim about what is the case. As Sextus sums up the sceptic's avoidance of dogmatism, at the end of the passage which has detained us so long, it is simply this: 'He states what appears to himself and announces his own experience without belief, making no assertion about external things' (*PH* I 15).

To which we may add that if the sceptic did allow himself some belief, opponents of Pyrrhonism would be guilty of serious *ignoratio elenchi* when they bring up the simple instinctive beliefs which, they claim, are inseparable from the use of the senses and from everyday actions (see the arguments from Aristocles and Galen cited p. 22 n. 4 above). Aristocles repeatedly takes his target to be a philosophy which pretends to eschew all judgement and belief whatever, so that he can say that it is inconsistent for

[48] That the two definitions of '*dogma*' are borrowed from some previous sceptic writer is evidenced not only by Sextus' saying so, but by the structurally parallel *PH* I 16–17. Here too we have a contrasting pair of 'someone's' definitions, this time of the term αἵρεσις ('philosophical system'), to one of which the sceptic objects and one he does not, and the first definition, couched (it would appear) in terms of the narrower sense of '*dogma*', can be found almost verbatim in an unfortunately truncated passage of Clement (*SVF* II, p. 37, 8–10), where it is again attributed to 'some people'.

[49] ὅσον ἐπὶ τῷ λόγῳ: it is a nice question for interpretation how to take λόγος here. Bury translates 'in its essence' at *PH* I 20, while *PH* III 65, *M* X 49, XI 165 ὅσον ἐπὶ τῷ φιλοσόφῳ λόγῳ may seem to favour 'reason', but Sextus' own elucidation at *PH* I 20 (what honey is ὅσον ἐπὶ τῷ λόγῳ is what is said about the thing that appears) has decided several scholars for 'statement': Janáček [49], Ch. 2, Hossenfelder [6], 64 n. 124. Perhaps 'theory' would do justice to the resonances of ambiguity (cp. e.g. *PH* III 167, *M* VII 283, VIII 3), provided we remember that what counts as theory and what as evidence is itself part of the dispute between Sextus and his opponents.

the Pyrrhonist to advance any assertion or argument (*apud* Eus.
PE XIV 18, 8–9; 15; 16–17; 24). Sextus, as we have seen, connects dogmatism with claims that something is (simply) true,
and he needs to do so if he is to undercut the ordinary man's
hopes and fears. For clearly, hope and fear can come from any
type of belief about what is or will be the case; it need not be
dogmatic belief in some more stringent sense. What is at issue
here is the ordinary man's ordinary belief that it is good and
desirable to have money, say, or fame or pleasure, and bad to be
without them (*M* XI 120–4, 144–6; cp. *PH* I 27–8). Belief, in the
sense Sextus is attacking, is responsible for *all* the things men
pursue and avoid by their own judgement (*M* XI 142, using *doxa*).
The internal logic of Pyrrhonism requires that *dogma* and *doxa*—
Sextus does not differentiate between these two terms—really do
mean: belief.[50]

Behind this issue of interpretation lies a philosophical question

[50] The same is implied by the original sense of several key words in the sceptical
vocabulary. προσδοξάζειν is the Epicurean term for the judgement or belief which
is added to perception, where perception is ἄλογος, involving no judgemental
element at all (see Taylor, Chapter 5 below). ἀδόξαστός credits the Stoic sage with the
capacity to avoid *all* belief falling short of certainty (DL VII 162). δογματίζειν may
again be Epicurean, as at DL X 120 (the earliest occurrence I can find), where it
appears to mean nothing more stringent than not being in a state of puzzlement
(ἀπορεῖν). The first instance I can find of δογματικός is attributed to Aenesidemus,
who calls the *Academics* δογματικοί because they affirm some things without hesitation
and deny others unambiguously, whereas the the Pyrrhonists are aporeutic (N.B.)
and free of all belief (παντὸς ἀπολελυμένοι δόγματος) and do not say that things are
such rather than such (Phot. *Bibl.* 169 b 36–170 a 2; on the general accuracy of the
relevant sections of Photius' report, see Janáček [66]). Equally, it is Aenesidemus'
contention, as it is Sextus', that one dogmatizes if one gives credence to what is
pithanon (*Bibl.* 170 a 18–20, *PH* I 222, 230).

δόγμα itself may look harder since, although it originally means just 'belief'
(above, p. 26), some contrast with δόξα is indicated by Cicero's translating the terms
decretum and *opinio* respectively. But the reason for this contrast would seem to be
that the Stoics contrast δόξα (mere opinion, defined as assent to something uncertain
or to something false—*Acad.* II 59, 68, 77, *M* VII 151) with κατάληψις and ἐπιστήμη.
They therefore need another word than δόξα for the wise man's belief. The wise man
avoids δόξα (opinion as opposed to knowledge) but he has δόγματα, every one of
them unwavering and true (*Acad.* II 27, 29; cp. *SVF* II, p. 37, 10–11). Notice that
in Cicero's account it is not part of the meaning of δόγμα that it should be firmly
held, but rather the consequence of its being the wise man who holds it: for the
Academics say that all their *decreta* are 'probabilia non percepta' (*Acad.* II 109–10).
Readers of Plato are often perplexed by the way δόξα sometimes means 'opinion' in
contrast to knowledge and sometimes 'belief' or 'judgement' in the broad sense in
which it is a component of knowledge: my suggestion is that δόγμα in Hellenistic
usage conveniently takes over the latter role. It is a broader and more nearly neutral
term than δόξα, not a term for a more stringently defined type of belief.

of considerable interest, the question whether and in what terms a distinction between non-dogmatic and dogmatic belief can be made out. One promising line to start might be to distinguish a belief that honey is sweet and a belief that honey is *really* sweet in the sense that sweetness exists in the honey, as part of its objective nature. Such talk has a familiar philosophical ring where the sensible qualities are concerned, but it would need to be explained what it amounted to when applied to such examples as 'It is day', 'I am conversing' (*M* VIII 144), or 'This is a man' (*M* VIII 316). Again, one may suggest that non-dogmatic belief ir belief not grounded in or responsive to reasons and reasoning— but that will bring with it a breaking of the connection between belief and truth. What Sextus objects to is the accepting of anything as true. Any such acceptance he will count as dogmatizing (*PH* I 14–15; above, pp. 25–6). I do not myself think there is a notion of belief which lacks this connection with truth and, in a more complicated way, with reason.[51] Nor, at bottom, did Hume: else he would not have found it paradoxical that the sceptical arguments fail to dislodge belief. But all I have contended here is that Sextus has no other notion of belief than the accepting of something as true.

DETACHMENT AND PHILOSOPHICAL BELIEF

It remains to consider whether it is an objection to Sextus that many of his appearance-statements seem to demand the epistemic reading which he refuses. One instance out of many would be the following: 'To every dogmatic claim I have examined there appears to me to be opposed a rival dogmatic claim which is equally worthy and equally unworthy of belief' (freely rendered from *PH* I 203). Sextus insists that this utterance is not dogmatic, i.e. not expressive of belief. It is an announcement of a human state or affection (*anthrōpeiou pathous apangelia*), which is something that appears or is apparent to the person who undergoes it (*ho esti phainomenon tōi paschonti*). And this would be all right if 'It appears to me to be so' meant here 'I have some inclination to believe it is so'. Perhaps there could be an experience it was appropriate to record in those terms. But an inclination to believe is the last thing the sceptic wants to enter in his chronicle. The verb 'appears' in the above statement, and dozens like it, is to be

[51] For a contrary view, see Striker, Chapter 3 below, pp. 80–1.

taken non-epistemically, as we have seen. At times, no doubt, the non-epistemic reading is sheer bluff on Sextus' part, but the objector's opposition will itself be no better than bare counter-assertion unless he can muster more to say. I think there is more to say about the appearances annexed to the sceptic's philosophical pronouncements. They form a class of appearances which lie at the centre of the sceptic's conception of himself and his life.

Remember that we know perfectly well *why* it appears to the sceptic that any dogmatic claim has a contrary equally worthy or unworthy of acceptance. It is the result of a set of arguments designed to show, compellingly, that this is in fact the case. Such arguments can compel him to suspend judgement because they compel him to accept their conclusion—to accept, that is, that in each and every case dogmatic claims are indeed equally balanced and hence that one ought to suspend judgement. (Which is often enough, of course, the way Sextus does conclude his arguments.) But accepting the conclusion that *p* on the basis of a certain argument is hardly to be distinguished from coming to *believe* that *p* is *true* with that argument as one's *reason*. In being shown that there is as much, or as little, reason to believe the first-level proposition that honey is bitter as that it is sweet, the sceptic has been given reason to believe the second-level proposition that the reasons for and against are equally balanced. In being shown, both on general grounds and by the accumulation of instances, that no claim about real existence is to be preferred to its denial, he has, again, been given reason to believe that generalization true. Certainly it appears to him that dogmatic claims are equally balanced, but this appearance, so called, being the effect of argument, is only to be made sense of in terms of reason, belief and truth—the very notions the sceptic is most anxious to avoid.[52] He wants to say something of the form 'It appears to me that *p* but I do not believe that *p*', with a non-epistemic use of 'appears', but it looks to be intelligible only if 'appears' is in fact epistemic, yielding a contradiction: 'I (am inclined to) believe that *p* but I do not believe that *p*.' How is this result to be avoided?

[52] Notice that it is for these higher-level generalizations that Sextus invokes the defence of cheerful self-refutation (*PH* I 14–15 and other passages discussed in Burnyeat [55]). Self-refutation presupposes that the propositions do make a truth-claim. Sextus would not need (and could not use) the defence if the generalizations were really the expressions of appearance which he simultaneously claims them to be.

The difficulty is not to be overcome by suggesting that the sceptic emerges from his arguments in a state of bafflement rather than belief. Bafflement could be the effect of arguments for and against; you are pulled now this way, now that, until you just do not know what to say (cf. *M* VII 243). The problem is to see why this should produce tranquillity rather than acute anxiety.[53] Nor should we allow Sextus to deny that the sceptic's philosophical appearances are the effect of argument. He does on occasion claim that the sceptical arguments do not give demonstrative disproof of the dogmatists' views but mere reminders or suggestions of what can be said against them, and through this of the apparently equal strength of opposed positions (*PH* II 103, 130, 177, *M* VIII 289). In the technical terms of the period the arguments are not indicative but commemorative signs. I need not enlarge on the technicalities because (to be blunt) Sextus offers no elucidation whatever of the crucial notion of something's being said *against* a doctrine or belief but not by way of reasons or evidence against it. If the sceptic works through reasoned argument to the point where the reasons on either side balance and reason stultifies itself, if his arguments are (in the now famous phrase) a ladder to be thrown over when you have climbed up (*M* VIII 481), then we must insist that they make their impact through the normal operations of our reason. *Epochē* is not a blind, mechanical effect but, supposedly, the natural and intelligible outcome of following with our human capacity for thought along the paths marked out by the sceptical arguments.

Another suggestion might be that what the sceptic records as the outcome of his arguments is an interrogative rather than an assertive frame of mind: 'Is it the case, then, that contrary claims are equally balanced?' This would fit the sceptic's characterization of himself as *zētētikos*, one who goes on seeking (*PH* I 2–3, 7, II 11), and Sextus does at one point say that some sceptics prefer to take the formula 'No more this than that' as a question, 'Why this rather than that?' (*PH* I 189; cp. *M* I 315). But again we must be careful about *ataraxia*. The sceptic goes on seeking not in the sense that he has an active programme of research but in the sense

---

[53] Cp. Hume's marvellous description of the despair of sceptical doubt, *A Treatise of Human Nature*, Bk I, Pt IV, § VII, p. 268–9 in Selby-Bigge's edition (Oxford, 1888).

that he continues to regard it as an open question whether p or not-p is the case, at least for any first-level proposition concerning real existence. But this should not mean he is left in a state of actually *wondering* whether p or not-p is the case, for that might induce anxiety. Still less should he be wondering whether, in general, contrary claims are equally balanced. For if it is a real possibility for him that they are not, that means it is a real possibility that there are answers to be found; and it will be an immense worry to him, as it was at the very beginning of his sceptical education, that he does not know what these answers are.

In other words, if tranquillity is to be achieved, at some stage the sceptic's questing thoughts must come to a state of rest or equilibrium.[54] There need be no finality to this achievement, the sceptic may hold himself ready to be persuaded that there are after all answers to be had. He is not a negative dogmatist furnished with *a priori* objections that rule out the possiblity of answers as a matter of general principle once and for all (cf. *PH* I 1–3). But *ataraxia* is hardly to be attained if he is not in some sense satisfied—so far—that no answers are forthcoming, that contrary claims are indeed equal. And my question is: How can Sextus then deny that this is something he believes?

I do not think he can. Both the causes (reasoned arguments) of the state which Sextus calls appearance and its effects (tranquillity and the cessation of emotional disturbance) are such as to justify us in calling it a state of belief. And this objection to Sextus' claim to have described a life without belief leads on to an answer to our original question about the possibility, in human terms, of the life Sextus describes.

The source of the objection we have been urging is that the sceptic wants to treat 'It appears to me that p but I do not believe that p', where p is some philosophical proposition such as 'Contrary claims have equal strength', on a par with perceptual instances of that form such as 'It appears (looks) to me that the stick in the water is bent but I do not believe it is'. The latter is acceptable because its first conjunct describes a genuine experience —in Greek terms, a *pathos*, a *phantasia*, which awaits my assent. And it is important here that assent and impression are logically

<hr>

[54] στάσις διανοίας· *PH* I 10; ἀρρεψία, *PH* I 190, *M* VIII 159, 332 a, DL IX 74. Hossenfelder [6], 54 ff., is excellent on this, but I do not think we need go along with him in detecting an ambiguity in the term *epochē*.

independent. For they are not independent in the philosophical case. In the philosophical case, the impression, when all is said and done, simply *is* my assent to the conclusion of an argument, assent to it as true. That is the danger of allowing talk about appearances or impressions of thought: it comes to seem legitimate to treat states which are in fact states of belief, presupposing assent, as if they were independent of assent in the way that sense-impressions can be. For if, beneath its disguise as a mere passive affection, the philosophical impression includes assent, it ought to make no sense for the sceptic to insist that he does not assent to it as true. That would be to contemplate a further act of assent to the assent already given. If the sceptic does insist, if he refuses to identify with his assent, he is as it were detaching himself from the person (namely, himself) who was convinced by the argument, and he is treating his own thought as if it were the thought of someone else, someone thinking thoughts within him. He is saying, in effect, 'It is thought within me that *p*, but *I* do not believe it.' In the right circumstances, that could be said. But not all the time, for every appearance/thought one has.[55] Yet that is what it will come to if absolutely every appearance, higher-level as well as lower-level, is construed non-epistemically.

One of the more memorable sayings attributed to Pyrrho is a remark regretting that it is difficult to divest oneself entirely of one's humanity.[56] (As the story goes, this was his reply to a charge of failing to practise what he preached when once he was frightened of a dog.) Sextus makes out that the sceptic ideal preserves all that is worth preserving in human nature. But it seems to me that Hume and the ancient critics were right. When one has seen how radically the sceptic must detach himself from himself, one will agree that the supposed life without belief is not, after all, a possible life for man.[57]

[55] It is instructive in this connection to read through § II x of Wittgenstein's *Philosophical Investigations*, which discusses among other things Moore's paradox '*p* but I do not believe that *p*'.

[56] DL IX 66, Aristocles *apud* Eus. *PE* XIV 18, 26: ὡς χαλεπὸν εἴη ὁλοσχερῶς ἐκδῦναι τὸν ἄνθρωπον. The source is Antigonus of Carystus, which means, as Long [68] has shown, that the remark probably derives from something in Timon.

[57] This paper has benefited greatly, especially in its last two sections, from helpful criticism at the Conference and at various universities where earlier drafts were read (Amsterdam, Berkeley, Essex, Oxford, Pittsburgh, Rutgers, SMU Dallas, and UBC Vancouver). Among the many individuals to whom thanks is due, I should like to mention Jonathan Barnes, David Sedley, Gisela Striker, and, above all, Michael Frede.

SCEPTICAL STRATEGIES

Gisela Striker

Before I begin an examination of sceptical arguments, I should perhaps say a few words about the term 'scepticism' itself.[1] 'Scepticism', as I propose to use the word, may be characterized by two features: a thesis, viz. that nothing can be known, and a recommendation, viz. that one should suspend judgement on all matters.[2] These two are logically independent of each other, since the thesis is not sufficient to justify the recommendation. Both are susceptible of different interpretations, so that they do not determine the details of a sceptical philosophy. I think it

---

[1] The word 'sceptic' (σκεπτικός), which is traditionally used in histories of Greek philosophy to designate both the Academy from Arcesilaus to Carneades and the Pyrrhonists, seems to have been introduced as a terminological label relatively late in the development of Hellenistic philosophy. Philo Judaeus still uses it in the sense of 'enquirer', as a synonym of 'philosopher' (*De ebr.* 202 W). If, as is often supposed, Philo's source was Aenesidemus, this would seem to indicate that the label did not originate with him (it does not occur in Photius' summary of his book). The earliest extant occurrence of the word in the terminological sense seems to be in Aulus Gellius (IX 5). By the time of Sextus, σκέψις or σκεπτικὴ φιλοσοφία seems to have been the standard designation of the Pyrrhonist philosophy, though not of the Academic: Sextus contrasts the two in *PH* I 4 (cf. Numenius *apud* Eus. *PE* XIV 6, 4, where the use of σκεπτικός probably does not go back to Timon himself, and the title of *PE* XIV 18). Perhaps this was partly due to the influence of Theodosius, who objected to the name of 'Pyrrhonist', and called his own book Σκεπτικὰ κεφάλαια (DL IX 70). But Gellius already claims that both Academics and Pyrrhonists were indifferently called σκεπτικοί (among other things), and this usage has certainly prevailed in the later tradition, presumably as a convenient way of referring to both schools at once. I can see no harm in following tradition in this case.

[2] Cf. DL IX 61; Stough [29], 4. The third feature Stough mentions—'practical orientation'—seems to characterize the sceptics themselves rather than their philosophy (if indeed it applies to the Academics at all, which I find doubtful). I think that her treatment of Greek scepticism is somewhat biased through the overriding importance she attributes to the denial of knowledge as against suspense of judgement. Cf. Frede's review [62].

One should perhaps emphasize that the characterization just given describes scepticism as it were from the outside. Compared to other philosophical doctrines, scepticism would appear as a theory among others, but the sceptics themselves would of course deny that there could be such a thing as a doctrine of scepticism. Hence when I speak of the sceptics' 'position', I should be understood to mean the position they used to argue for, rather than a position they held for themselves. In fact, the question whether or not they did hold a position will be one of the topics of this paper.

would be fair to say that in modern times the thesis has been the more prominent feature, while the ancients seem to have considered the recommendation as equally important. In this paper I will be mainly concerned with the recommendation, i.e. with *epochē*, though the thesis will also come up in the discussion of the sceptics' defence of their position. However, its credentials will not concern us here. I shall start with a problem of interpretation that arises out of the tradition about Carneades. Next, I will discuss the respective replies of Arcesilaus and Carneades to two (Stoic) arguments against scepticism, as examples of two different ways of defending the sceptic position. Finally, I will return to the first problem to see whether the investigation of Carneades' way of arguing can shed some light on it.

I

In a famous passage of Cicero's *Academica*, Clitomachus is said to have affirmed that he had never been able to find out what Carneades' own views were.[3] Now Clitomachus was Carneades' most assiduous student and his successor as head of the Academy. It is no surprise, then, that Carneades' 'own views', if indeed he ever stated them, have been a matter of dispute ever since. It would, I think, be futile to try to settle this question now. What I want to discuss here is one particular point in the dispute, which has in recent times been raised again by Hirzel [48], 162–80. Hirzel pointed out that in Cicero's *Academica* we find two conflicting traditions concerning Carneades' epistemological position. According to the one, attributed by Cicero to Carneades' student Metrodorus and to his own teacher Philo (*Acad.* II 78), Carneades held that the wise man may 'know nothing and yet have opinions' —or, to put it less picturesquely, that though we cannot attain knowledge, we may sometimes be justified in holding beliefs.[4] According to Clitomachus, however, with whom Cicero himself

---

[3] *Acad.* II 139.

[4] *Acad.* II 78: 'licebat enim nihil percipere et tamen opinari, quod a Carneade dicitur probatum: equidem Clitomacho plus quam Philoni aut Metrodoro credens hoc magis ab eo disputatum quam probatum puto.' Cf. also 59, 112, 148. My paraphrase takes account of the point that it is the wise man who is said to know nothing and yet have opinions. This means that it is not only possible to do so— which is trivial—but that it would also be right.

agrees, Carneades maintained this only for the sake of argument. This controversy raises two questions that are not always equally attended to by the commentators. First, we may consider the dispute to be about Carneades' scepticism as an epistemological doctrine. Then the question will be whether he advocated a mitigated form of suspension of judgement, such that a sceptic may have opinions provided that he realizes that he may be wrong; or whether he held the more radical view that the sceptic will assent to nothing at all, i.e. not even have any opinions. Second, given that ancient scepticism seems to consist in an attitude rather than a theory, Clitomachus' remark reminds us of the difficulty involved in treating it as an epistemological doctrine: if scepticism consists in holding no positive views whatever, how are we to take the arguments of the sceptic himself? That is, whether Carneades advocated a weak or a strong version of *epochē*, we cannot simply take it that he was arguing for a doctrine of scepticism—he might just have been refuting some dogmatic thesis.

These two questions are not unrelated. If we follow the tradition of Metrodorus, we might try to apply the theory to itself, saying that Carneades was putting forth his own views with the proviso that they might be false. On the other hand, if we decide to agree with Clitomachus, either we must give an account of how one can be a radical sceptic and yet propose a theory, or we may take it that what appears as a theory is in fact only an argument designed to show that one need not be a dogmatist. It is not quite clear what Clitomachus had in mind when he said that Carneades defended opinions only for argument's sake. On the one hand, he seems to have ascribed to Carneades a radical version of *epochē*, so that we might take him to mean that Carneades advocated strict suspension of judgement. On the other hand, if we remember the remark quoted at the beginning of this section, he might just have meant to say that we should not take even Carneades' epistemological arguments to represent his own views.

Hirzel, apparently addressing himself to the first of our two questions, i.e. whether Carneades advocated strict suspense of judgement or rather admitted some form of justified belief, after a careful study of Cicero's and other evidence, decided to opt for Metrodorus, and in this he has been followed by most modern commentators.[5] The most notable exception is Pierre Couissin who, in an article of 1929 [60], stressed mainly the second problem. He pointed out that the arguments by which Carneades is said to have arrived at his supposedly less radical position can invariably be shown to be directed against the Stoics, and that they always involve premisses taken over from the Stoics themselves.[6] But if these arguments were all demonstrably ad hominem, i.e. consisted in using Stoic premisses to refute the Stoics, then, as Couissin argued, we have no good reason to attribute them to Carneades as his own doctrines. In fact, this type of ad hominem argument is precisely what one should expect from a philosopher who claims not to hold any theory of his own. Besides, if we look at the testimonia which seem to show that Carneades had given up the more radical standpoint of Arcesilaus, we find that their authors usually have some motive for making him look like a dogmatist in disguise—either they were themselves opposed to scepticism and wanted to cite Carneades as an example of the untenability of strict suspension of judgement, like Numenius,[7] or, like Sextus, they tried to draw a clear line between his and their own version of scepticism.[8] Hence Couissin concluded that 'il est à présumer que Carnéade . . . n'a professé aucune doctrine positive' ([60], 268).

Keeping these caveats in mind, we might still try to find an answer to our first question in the sense that, whether he endorsed it or not, Carneades might have consistently advocated either the stronger or the weaker form of epochē. Now while Hirzel tried to decide this primarily on historical grounds, the main reason why his view has found so many adherents seems to be rather the systematic one that what is sometimes described as Carneades' 'softening up' of the sceptic position amounts to a perfectly good brand of scepticism itself. After all, Carneades never claimed that we can have certainty about anything, and one does not cease to be a sceptic—at least in the modern sense—by admitting the possibility of plausible or reasonable belief. So perhaps the charge

[5] Brochard [25], 134 f.; Robin [28], 99; implicitly Goedeckemeyer [26], 64; Stough [29], 58, to quote only a few prominent names. Hartmann [47], 44, thinks that the positions of Clitomachus and Metrodorus come to much the same. Similarly dal Pra [27], 298.
[6] This was actually noted already by Sextus, cf. M VII 150, IX 1.
[7] Apud Eus. PE XIV 8, 4; cf. XIV 7, 15.
[8] Cf. PH I 226–31.

of weakness that seems to be brought against Carneades in some of our sources really misses the point by identifying Academic scepticism with the more radical Pyrrhonist position, which does indeed exclude the possibility of justified belief. Thus in the latest history of Greek scepticism, Charlotte Stough barely mentions our problem in a footnote ([29], 58). She simply starts from the assertion that 'Academic Skepticism is not a development of Pyrrhonism, but a second, and rather different, Skeptical philosophy' ([29], 34), and then tacitly follows the tradition which ascribes to Carneades an epistemological doctrine of justified belief. Now it is probably true that Academic and Pyrrhonian scepticism are distinct and initially independent developments; and their respective arguments for the sceptical attitude are indeed different. Yet I do not think that this fact really solves the puzzle with which we are concerned. But let me try first to show why one might think so by considering the arguments each school brought forward for their official epistemological attitude of *epochē*.

The question of the reasons for suspension of judgement is fairly easy to answer in the case of Pyrrhonism (though this need not necessarily apply to the historical founder or ancestor of the school himself): Sextus makes it quite clear that the argument behind the sceptic's attitude is *isostheneia*, or the 'equal force' of contradictory propositions in the fields of both sense perception and theory.[9] This argument is based on the famous 'tropes' as well as on the lengthy discussions of conflicting theories in Sextus' own books *Adversus mathematicos*, which typically end with a statement to the effect that, there being no way to decide which one of the parties to the dispute is right, the sceptic will suspend judgement.[10] Now this argument leads directly to *epochē*: if we have no reason whatever to prefer any proposition to its contradictory, clearly the most reasonable thing is to avoid a decision and keep clear of any positive belief.

In contrast with this, the case seems to be more complicated

---

[9] The evidence for this abounds in *PH* I. Some very explicit passages are *PH* I 8, 196. Others are listed s.v. ἰσοσθένεια in Janáček's Index [8]. That this argument eventually acquired the paradoxical status of a dogma of Pyrrhonian scepticism, which could be invoked against a theory even in the absence of strong counter-arguments, appears from *PH* I 33–4.

[10] e.g. *PH* I 61, 88, 117, *M* VII 443, VIII 159. Sextus describes the procedure in *PH* II 79.

for the Academics. We usually find two reasons given for Academic *epochē*: first, the 'opposition of propositions' (*enantiotēs tōn logōn*, DL IV 28) or the conflict between equally well-supported contradictories, and second, *akatalēpsia*, or the thesis that 'nothing can be known'.[11] The first of these is of course a version of *isostheneia*. The Academics tried to induce suspension of judgement in their hearers by arguing on both sides of a thesis, and it is usually assumed that the arguments for and against were of equal weight. But they do not seem to have extended this type of argument beyond the field of theoretical dispute.[12] With regard to sense perception they seem to have relied on their famous argument against the Stoic *kataleptikē phantasia* which Carneades later generalized to apply to every conceivable 'criterion of truth'.

Now this argument by itself provides no sufficient ground for suspension of judgement. Numenius does indeed try to assimilate it to *isostheneia*,[13] but this is a mistake: the argument does not show that we always have good reasons to believe the contrary of what appears to us to be the case, but only that for each sense-impression, however clear and distinct, we can describe conditions such that a qualitatively undistinguishable impression would be false. Even if doubts about the truth of *p* may in a sense be called reasons for believing not-*p*, it certainly does not follow that these reasons are as good as the initial reasons for holding *p*. All that can be derived from this argument is that we can never be certain that a given impression is true. And in order to get from this to *epochē*, one needs some additional premiss—as e.g.

---

[11] For the first, cf. DL IV 28 (Arcesilaus), Eus. *PE* XIV 4, 15, *Acad.* I 45, Galen, *Opt. doctr.* 1, p. 40 K (p. 82, 1–5 M). For the second, Eus. loc. cit., *Acad.* loc. cit., cf. II 59, Galen, *Opt. doctr.* 2 p. 43 K (p. 85, 4–8 M). For the term ἀκαταληψία, DL IX 61, *PH* I 1 (further references in Janáček's Index [8] s.v.), Galen, *Opt. doctr.* 1 p. 42 K (p. 83, 16 M).

[12] Cf. de Lacy [67], and following note.

[13] *Apud* Eus. *PE* XIV 8, 7: παραλαβὼν γὰρ ἀληθεῖ μὲν ὅμοιον ψεῦδος, καταληπτικῇ δὲ φαντασίᾳ καταληπτὸν [sic] ὅμοιον καὶ ἀγαγὼν εἰς τὰς ἴσας, οὐκ εἴασεν οὔτε τὸ ἀληθὲς εἶναι οὔτε τὸ ψεῦδος, ἢ οὐ μᾶλλον τὸ ἕτερον τοῦ ἑτέρου, ἢ μᾶλλον ἀπὸ τοῦ πιθανοῦ. As de Lacy notes, the last words indicate that Numenius found the Carneadean 'theory of probability' inconsistent with the principle of οὐ μᾶλλον. So it is, but then the Academic argument against the Stoics is not a form of οὐ μᾶλλον. According to de Lacy, the only other source which ascribes οὐ μᾶλλον to the Academy with regard to perception is Hippolytus (*Haer.* 1.23.3), who does not distinguish between Academic and Pyrrhonian scepticism (cf. de Lacy [67], 68, nn. 1, 2).

that one should not hold a belief unless one is absolutely certain
of its truth.

So while the argument from conflicting theories provides
sufficient ground for suspension of judgement with regard to
philosophical doctrines—especially if, as some of our sources
suggest, the refusal to take sides is considered as a didactic rule,
by which the Academics sought to avoid the influence of mere
authority on their students[14]—the argument from *akatalēpsia*
seems rather weak. Moreover, it is clear that the Academics saw
that they needed an extra premiss to argue from this to *epochē*:
they insisted, against the Stoics, that their argument against
katalēptikē phantasia does not imply the conclusion that 'everything
will be as uncertain as whether the stars are even or odd in
number'.[15] And Carneades' own 'theory of criteria' shows how
the gap can be filled if certain knowledge is not available. So why
should the Academics have accepted the thesis that one should
not hold 'mere' opinions?

In a famous argument by which Arcesilaus proved that the
Stoic Sage will have to suspend judgement on all matters, this
premiss is taken over explicitly from the Stoics.[16] The Stoics'
reason for holding it was, of course, that the wise man will have
something better, namely knowledge, to go by, so that he
doesn't need opinions. But this can hardly have been why the
sceptics accepted the thesis. Cicero suggests that their reason
was that they wanted to avoid error;[17] and since they had shown
that no opinion is exempt from doubt and hence immune against
error, they preferred to abstain from belief altogether. But again
this insistence on avoiding error could easily have been taken
over from the Stoics—Cicero emphasizes that Zeno and Arcesilaus
agreed on this point (*Acad.* II 66). If one does not hold, like the
Stoics, that errors are sins, there seems to be no good reason left
why one should not hold an opinion with the express proviso
that it might be wrong. And this is just what Carneades is said to
have maintained (*Acad.* II 148).

[14] Cf. Cic. *Acad.* II 60, *ND* I 5. 10, *Div.* II 150, Galen, *Opt. doctr.* 1 p. 41 K (p. 83,
2–5 M).

[15] *Acad.* II 32, 54, 110, *PH* I 227, Numen. *apud* Eus. *PE* XIV 7, 15. For the example
cf. *M* VIII 147, *PH* II 97.

[16] *Acad.* II 77, cf. 66, 68, *M* VII 155–7, Augustine, *Contr. Acad.* II v 11, cf. ibid.
II vi 14, III xiv 31.

[17] *Acad.* I 45, cf. II 66, 68, 115.

As far as the Academic argument goes, then, Carneades seems to have had very good reasons to adopt a mitigated scepticism, and no very strong reasons to advocate strict suspension of judgement. Thus one might be inclined to discount Clitomachus' testimony as coming from a sceptic over-anxious to avoid all appearance of dogmatism.[18] Commentators who have followed roughly this line of thought could then also conclude that we may take Carneades' theory of criteria to express his own point of view, so that we may treat this as his official doctrine, for which, of course, he would not want to claim dogmatic certainty.[19]

However, as I indicated before, this does not really solve the puzzle about Carneades' alleged advocacy of belief. For in the passage where Cicero reports, with explicit reference to Clitomachus, what is sometimes described as Carneades' theory of 'qualified assent'[20], he insists that the sceptic will adopt a positive or negative attitude without assent (*Acad.* II 104). The positive attitude is typically described as 'following' or 'using' a presentation, or as 'approving' of it.[21] Now opinion, at least according to the Stoic terminology in which the debate usually took place, implies assent, and so, according to Clitomachus' testimony, Carneades seems to have considered something less than or distinct from opinion. And in spite of the plausibility Carneades' own theory seems to give to a doctrine of justified opinion, there might have been reasons to insist on strict suspension of

[18] Cf. dal Pra [27], 297 f.

[19] Cf. e.g. von Arnim [54], 1968, Long [20], 95.

[20] Reid [7], note to *Acad.* II 104, Hicks [19], 344, Stough [29], 65. This expression is no doubt inspired by Cicero's words in *Acad.* II 104, where he translates Clitomachus as saying that there are two modes of suspending assent, only one of which the sceptic accepts. This could be understood to mean that the sceptic's 'approval' is a qualified form of assent. But, as Hirzel already pointed out ([48], 168 n. 1), the Greek original probably had only the word ἐποχή or ἐπέχειν. Even if, as Couissin has argued ([61] 390 ff.), ἐπέχειν originally meant suspending assent, it could be given a wider sense, so that it is no contradiction if Clitomachus goes on to say, in the same passage, that the wise man may react positively or negatively provided he does not assent ('dum sine adsensu') (cf. Couissin, ibid. 392).

[21] 'Sequi': *Acad.* II 8, 33, 35, 36, 59, 99, 108 (cf. *M* VII 185 κατακολουθεῖν, 185 ἑπόμενος,187 ἕπονται); 'uti': *Acad.* II 99, 110, cf. *M* VII 175 χρῆσθαι, 185 παραλαμβάνειν; 'probare': *Acad.* II 99, 104, 107, 111, *PH* I 229–31 (πείθεσθαι). It is true that Cicero does not always observe the terminological distinction between 'adsentiri' and 'adprobare', but he emphasizes it in crucial passages. Although Sextus does indeed use συγκατατίθεσθαι twice in *M* VII 188, his distinction between the Academic and the Pyrrhonist sense of πείθεσθαι in *PH* I 229–30 suggests that πείθεσθαι was the official Academic term.

judgement. The Academics used to justify their method of arguing pro and contra everything by saying that all alternatives must be investigated in order to find the truth.[22] One might say that for someone who has not yet found the truth it would be more advisable to refrain from assenting altogether, since accepting a proposition, even with due reserve, might prevent one from continuing the search.

Furthermore, Carneades' own 'doctrine of criteria', whether it was accepted as true or only as plausible, clearly amounts to an epistemological theory. Now the evidence for Academic suspension of judgement with regard to philosophical theories is much stronger than that for universal *epochē*—in fact, it seems to be implicit in their very method of arguing on both sides of a thesis without arriving at a decision; and hence we should be hesitant to ascribe to Carneades any doctrine, even of qualified status.

Our doubts will be confirmed by remembering, what Couissin has persuasively argued, that the alleged doctrines of both Arcesilaus and Carneades involve Stoic premisses or at least concepts. However, I do not think with Couissin that this entirely establishes their *ad hominem* character. For although these theories were undoubtedly prompted by Stoic arguments, we should perhaps distinguish between anti-Stoic arguments which attack positive Stoic doctrines and arguments by which the sceptics defended their own position against Stoic objections. The so-called positive doctrines of the sceptics were developed as defences of scepticism, as I will try to show; and here we seem to have two possibilities: either the Academics merely pointed out that the objections were untenable, e.g. by showing that the arguments were inconclusive even on Stoic premisses, or by appealing to some other philosophical theory which did not share the premisses used in the Stoic objections. This seems to have been the strategy of Arcesilaus, and it seems obvious that we have no reason to ascribe to him the doctrines he used in this way. On the other hand, the sceptics could also have tried to defend a sceptical epistemology as an alternative to the Stoic theory of knowledge, in which case it would at least be possible that they were expressing their own views. The second alternative seems to

[22] Cic. *Acad.* II 60, *ND* I 11.

have been Carneades' procedure: he outlined a theory to show that it was not necessary to be an epistemological dogmatist. Whether this represents his own view, we will have to consider later on.

In the following section I will try to analyse the debate in which the sceptics' arguments were developed in order to show how these theories originated as replies to specific Stoic objections. It will, I think, be instructive to consider the reactions of both Arcesilaus and Carneades in turn. Incidentally, our analysis should also serve to answer Hirzel's question as to whether Carneades defended a weaker or a stronger form of *epochē*. Finally, I will return to the second of our initial questions to see whether a closer scrutiny of Carneades' arguments can help us to decide the question of their status.

II

The debate we are to consider turns around an argument that has been, besides the notorious self-refutation argument,[23] the cornerstone of anti-sceptic criticism ever since: I mean the argument that scepticism 'makes life impossible'[24] by leading to total inactivity. For brevity's sake I will refer to this as the *apraxia* argument.[25]

There are two versions of this argument, which are kept distinct by Cicero though not by our other sources: the first attacks the sceptic thesis that nothing can be known, the second is directed against the possibility of total suspension of judgement. The first objection claims that the sceptic will never be able to decide what to do, the second, that he will not even be able to act at all. These two points are obviously connected—if the sceptic is to act in a reasonable way, he will need a method of deciding what to do—but for purposes of exposition it will be

---

[23] For this argument cf. Burnyeat [55].

[24] τὸ ζῆν ἀναιροῦσιν, Plu. *Col.* 1108 d, cf. 1119 cd, DL IX 104, *Acad.* II 31, 99.

[25] For this term cf. Plu. *Col.* 1122 a. Sextus' term is ἀνενεργησία, cf. *M* XI 162 and ἀνενέργητος in *PH* I 23, 24, 226, *M* VII 30. The argument was used by the older Stoics, as Plutarch's reference to it shows; it is actually still older, since Aristotle already uses it as an argument against οὐ μᾶλλον, *Metaph.* Γ4, 1008ᵇ 10–19. Augustine calls it 'fumosum quidem iam et scabrum, sed . . . validissimum telum' (*Contr. Acad.* III xv 33). It seems to have pretty well survived beyond antiquity.

clearer if we follow Cicero in treating the two objections
separately.[26]

The first argument, then, is as follows: if nothing can be known,
then we will have no standard by which to decide either what is
the case or what we should do; hence we will be reduced to
inactivity or at least be entirely disoriented in practical matters.
The alleged consequences of *akatalēpsia* are often graphically
illustrated by examples designed to bring out its absurdity, e.g.
Plu. *Col.* 1122 e: 'But how comes it that the man who suspends
judgement does not go dashing off to a mountain instead of to
the bath . . . ?'[27] This shows that in order to act we must be able
to find out, presumably by means of sense perception, what is
the case. But we must also have some idea of what it will be best
to do, or, as the Stoics claimed, in order to act virtuously, we
must know what will be the right thing to do (*Acad.* II 24–5);
that is, we need both factual and normative knowledge.[28] But
since the latter kind of knowledge is—at least according to the
Stoics—based upon the former, the discussion of this objection
is often restricted to the factual case.

Now since this argument does not purport to show that
scepticism is self-contradictory, but only that it has paradoxical
consequences for the conduct of life, one possible reply would
consist in simply accepting the conclusion, and merely pointing
out that it is not the sceptic's fault if everything is as uncertain as
whether the stars are even or odd in number. This reply is actually
mentioned by Cicero (*Acad.* II 32), who treats it however as the
view of some 'desperados' to whom he will pay no further
attention. We do not know who these people were, but it seems
not impossible, as Brochard has suggested ([25], 245), that Cicero
had in mind some Academic radicals like Aenesidemus. However
this may be, neither Arcesilaus nor Carneades took this move.
Instead, they showed that the argument is invalid, since in the
absence of knowledge we are not left entirely without a standard.

[26] Cicero introduces the first version in *Acad.* II 32, the second in 37; he replies
to the first in 99 and 103, to the second in 104 and 108–9. In 78 he correctly observes
that the argument about ἐποχή has nothing to do with the debate about the possibility of knowledge (see below, p. 75). The distinction is also implied in Plu. *Col.*
1122 a–e, where a–d deals with the second version, e–f with the first.

[27] Cf. the stories about Pyrrho, DL IX 62.

[28] Sextus stresses the normative side in *M* XI 163, the factual side comes out e.g.
in *PH* I 21–4 (on the criterion of the sceptic philosophy).

Arcesilaus' reply[29] is recorded by Sextus (*M* VII 158): he said that 'The man who suspends judgement will guide his choices and rejections, and his actions in general, by the standard of the reasonable (*to eulogon*). It has long been noticed that the term *eulogon* comes from the Stoics.[30] A 'reasonable' or 'probable' proposition is defined by them as one which 'has more tendencies to be true than to be false, like "I shall live tomorrow" ' (DL VII 76). As far as factual propositions are concerned, then, *to eulogon* would seem to be what is probable. The term *eulogon* also occurs in definitions of 'appropriate act' (*to kathēkon*): an appropriate act is one which when done has a reasonable justification (*eulogos apologia*). The justification would be in terms of what is in accordance with human nature, so that in these cases *eulogon* seems to mean 'reasonable' rather than 'probable'.[31] It seems clear, in any case, that both in factual and in practical matters *to eulogon* could be invoked where knowledge was not to be had.[32]

[29] A different answer is suggested by Plutarch, *Col.* 1122 ef: ὅτι φαίνεται δήπουθεν αὐτῷ βαλανεῖον οὐ τὸ ὄρος ἀλλὰ τὸ βαλανεῖον, καὶ θύρα οὐχ ὁ τοῖχος ἀλλ' ἡ θύρα, καὶ τῶν ἄλλων ὁμοίως ἕκαστον. ὁ γὰρ τῆς ἐποχῆς λόγος οὐ παρατρέπει τὴν αἴσθησιν, οὐδὲ τοῖς ἀλόγοις πάθεσιν αὐτῆς καὶ κινήμασιν ἀλλοίωσιν ἐμποιεῖ διαταράττουσαν τὸ φανταστικόν, ἀλλὰ τὰς δόξας μόνον ἀναιρεῖ, χρῆται δὲ τοῖς ἄλλοις ὡς πέφυκεν. This is not explicitly attributed to Arcesilaus, and Plutarch might of course have been influenced by later—Pyrrhonist—sources, as he seems to be in the parallel passage 1118 ab, where the key term is φαινόμενον. However, there is some indication that he might here be using an older source. For in the preceding chapter (1122 a–d) he has reported an argument which must be older than Carneades, since it was already attacked by Chrysippus (Plu. *Stoic. rep.* 1057 a). There the word φυσικῶς seems to have a crucial role (cf. below, p. 69) and the same word is taken up a few lines later in a quotation from Plato (*Rep.* 458 d) φυσικαῖς οὐ γεωμετρικαῖς ἑλκόμενος ἀνάγκαις. Again in the passage just quoted the sceptic is said to use his senses ὡς πέφυκεν. The word φυσικῶς also occurs in DL's biography of Arcesilaus, DL 36: φυσικῶς δέ πως ἐν τῷ διαλέγεσθαι ἐχρῆτο τῷ φημ' ἐγώ . . . in a way which suggests that it goes back to something Arcesilaus himself would say—he probably used it to point out that he attached no theoretical weight to his assertions. It appears, then, that Arcesilaus sometimes referred to nature rather than to τὸ εὔλογον to account for the actions or statements of the sceptic. If this is correct, it would of course explain the notable absence of εὔλογον from our passage in Plutarch and also from *PH* I 220–35, where Sextus could have easily used it to mark the difference between Academic and Pyrrhonian scepticism (cf. Couissin [60], 255 f.). Incidentally, this could also show that Arcesilaus was indeed closer to the Pyrrhonists than Carneades.

[30] Cf. von Arnim [53], 1167 f., Couissin [60], 249, Robin [28], 61 ff.

[31] For this point cf. Tsekourakis [78], 26–8; a good example for this sense of εὔλογος seems to occur in a quotation from Chrysippus, Galen, *Plac. Hipp. Plat.* IV 4.141, p. 356 M (*SVF* III, p. 126, 29 ff.).

[32] I suppose the following quotation from Chrysippus might serve to illustrate the kind of reasoning involved (Epict. *Diss.* II 6.9): Διὰ τοῦτο καλῶς ὁ Χρύσιππος λέγει ὅτι 'Μέχρις ἂν ἄδηλά μοι ᾖ τὰ ἑξῆς, ἀεὶ τῶν εὐφυεστέρων ἔχομαι πρὸς τὸ τυγχάνειν

So Arcesilaus, in suggesting 'the reasonable' as a criterion, was simply pointing out to the Stoics that their own theory already provided a second-best guide to action which, given the impossibility of knowledge, would have to serve as the only one. Hence, in obvious parody of Stoic doctrine, he went on to argue that *to eulogon* will also be sufficient for virtuous action (*katorthōma*) —he simply substituted the definition of *kathēkon* for that of *katorthōma* (*M* VII 158). The *ad hominem* character of Arcesilaus' reply seems to me evident, and I can see no reason to take this as his own view, let alone a 'rationalist' alternative to Carneades' empiricism, as Hirzel suggested[33]—Sextus' report is the only testimony we have for this argument of Arcesilaus', and there is no suggestion that he would have explained the 'reasonable' in any way different from the Stoic.

It seems equally obvious that this reply could hardly satisfy the Stoics, whose distinction between virtuous and merely 'appropriate' acts was based upon the difference between the perfect knowledge of the sage and the weak and fallible 'opinion' of the fool. Although we have no explicit record of Stoic counterarguments to Arcesilaus on this point, I think this comes out rather clearly in the arguments with which Carneades was later confronted.[34] Moreover, the Stoics could have objected that a reasonable justification would itself have to be based on knowledge, e.g. of human nature—after all, only the sage does the correct thing for the right reason[35]—and Arcesilaus seems to have made no effort to explain how the sceptic will arrive at the view that this or that proposition is probable or reasonable. So Arcesilaus' 'theory' seems to amount to not much more than a ready rejoinder, with no attempt to deal with the problems raised by the Stoic objection.

Before we consider Carneades' reaction to the same argument, let us look at Arcesilaus' position with regard to the second

---

τῶν κατὰ φύσιν: αὐτὸς γὰρ μ' ὁ θεὸς τούτων ἐκλεκτικὸν ἐποίησεν. Εἰ δέ γε ᾔδειν ὅτι νοσεῖν μοι καθείμαρται νῦν, καὶ ὡρμην ἂν ἐπ' αὐτό. Cf. also the anecdote about Sphaerus, Athen. VIII 354 e and DL VII 177—though I have some doubts about that, since it seems obvious that Sphaerus should have simply said that he was not a sage. It illustrates, however, the use of εὔλογον for factual statements.

[33] Cf. Hirzel [48], 182n.
[34] Cf. the argument that the wise man must have certainty in order to be virtuous, *Acad.* II 23–5, 27, Stob. *Ecl.* II 111, 18 ff. W (*SVF* III, p. 147, 1 ff.).
[35] Cf. the testimonia in *SVF* III, p. 138 f.

version of *apraxia*. This is directed against the sceptic thesis that it is possible to withhold assent on all matters, and now the point is not just that the sceptic will not know what to do, but that he will be literally reduced to total inactivity because (voluntary) action logically implies assent. Here the Stoics were relying on their theory of voluntary action.

They held that voluntary action involves three things: presentation (*phantasia*), assent (*sunkatathesis*), and impulse or appetite (*hormē*), which is sometimes said to be itself a kind of assent.[36] The presentation, in the case of action, should be the thought, whether prompted by an external object or arising from the agent's thinking, that the agent should do a certain action.[37] The agent's assent to this presentation results in or 'is' an impulse which leads to action. Now the fact that assent is in our power, i.e. can be freely given or withheld, accounts for the point that the agent acts voluntarily and is thus responsible for his action. If assent were not in our power—so the Stoics argued—moral praise or blame could not be justified. But since action implies assent, we can indeed be held responsible for what we do.[38] This Stoic conception of the role of assent is obviously similar to Aristotle's theory of choice (*prohairesis*), and the Stoics may indeed have brought out the implications of Aristotle's way of speaking at times as if every voluntary action were preceded by a *prohairesis*.[39]

Given this theory, the objection to *epochē* amounts to the claim that, since it is logically impossible to act voluntarily without assent, the sceptic will with every single action he performs

---

[36] Cic. *Fat.* 40 ff., *Acad.* II 25, 108, Plu. *Stoic. rep.* 1055 f–1057 c, Alex. Aphr. *De an.* 72, 13 ff., *Fat.* 183, 5 ff., Sen. *Ep.* CXIII 18. ὁρμή a kind of συγκατάθεσις: Stob. *Ecl.* II 88, 1 W (*SVF* III, p. 40, 27), cf. Alex. Aphr. *De an.* 72,26.

[37] Cf. Sen. *Ep.* CXIII 18, and Plu. *Stoic. rep.* 1037 f.

[38] For the Stoic doctrine of 'free will' cf. the testimonia in *SVF* II, p. 282–98, and Long [106].

[39] The analogy has been noted by Long [103], 337–9; for Aristotle cf. J. M. Cooper, *Reason and Human Good in Aristotle* (Cambridge, Mass., 1975), 6–10. Lest this theory seem exceedingly implausible, it should perhaps be noted that it need not be taken to imply that every single voluntary action is preceded by a conscious mental act of assent. The Stoics were well aware that we often act without reflection (cf. e.g. Plu. *Stoic. rep.* 1057 ab). But in order to ascribe responsibility to an agent, we must at least assume that he was aware of what he was doing, i.e. that he knew some appropriate description of his action, and that the doing or not doing the action depended on him (not necessarily that he could have acted otherwise—as the Stoics pointed out, cf. Alex. Aphr. *Fat.* 182.4–20, 196.24–197.3). The Stoics represented these conditions as a decision to act upon a given proposition, without thereby implying that we are always conscious of the decision.

abandon his theoretical attitude of suspension of judgement, and demonstrate its practical impossibility. Arcesilaus' reply to this has been preserved by Plutarch, *Col.* 1122 b ff.:

The soul has three movements: sensation, impulse, and assent. Now the movement of sensation cannot be eliminated, even if we would; instead, upon encountering an object, we necessarily receive an imprint and are affected. Impulse, aroused by sensation, moves us in the shape of the action directed towards a suitable goal: a kind of casting weight has been put in the scale of our governing part, and a directed movement is set afoot. So those who suspend judgement about everything do not eliminate this second movement either, but follow their impulse, which leads them instinctively to the good presented by sense.

Then what is the only thing that they avoid? That only in which falsity and error can arise, namely forming an opinion and thus interposing rashly with our assent, although such assent is a yielding to appearance that is due to weakness and is of no use whatever. For two things are requisite for action: sense must present a good, and impulse must set out for the good so presented; and neither of these conflicts with suspension of judgement. (tr. Einarson/de Lacy)

As the terminology indicates, Arcesilaus is again using Stoic premisses as far as possible: thus the presentation that activates impulse is said to be of something as *oikeion* (in accordance with the agent's nature); *phantasia* and *hormē* are used in the Stoic sense, only *sunkatathesis* is tendentiously called *doxa* (opinion), presumably on the well-known ground that, according to the Academics, any case of assent will be a case of opinion.[40] Though Plutarch cannot have taken his report from Arcesilaus himself, who wrote nothing, we can infer from the fact that Chrysippus argued against the view defended in this passage (Plu. *Stoic. rep.* 1057 a) that it goes back to Arcesilaus, and the wording suggests that Plutarch was using a reliable source.

Arcesilaus begins with a Stoic thesis about the faculties of the soul involved in action, and then goes on to argue that one of these, assent, is superfluous, since *phantasia* and *hormē* alone are sufficient. He may well be relying on Peripatetic teaching here, since Aristotle maintains in several places that some voluntary

[40] *M* VII 156, *Acad.* II 67.

actions are done without *prohairesis*.[41] But Arcesilaus would of course have to hold that assent was never necessary, so that all action can be explained in terms of *phantasia* and *hormē* alone. And here his reply would again obviously appear unsatisfactory to the Stoics. The only word in Plutarch's text which refers to the way in which *hormē* leads to action is *phusikōs*. Einarson and de Lacy translate 'instinctively'. This may be too strong, since it would seem to imply the implausible view that we always act by instinct. Arcesilaus might have left open the possibility that we can 'naturally' decide to act without assent. But then the Stoics would be entitled to an explanation of how this is possible. If on the other hand we take *phusikōs* in the strong sense, then it would seem that moral responsibility was ruled out. If Arcesilaus was right about the possibility of acting without *doxa* or *sunkatathesis*, he may have shown that assent was not implied by the concept of voluntary action. But clearly this would not amount to a satisfactory explanation of voluntary action, which is what the Stoics were trying to give with their theory of *sunkatathesis*. It is no surprise, then, that Chrysippus and Antipater are said to have violently attacked the Academics for this 'theory of action'.

Here again, I can see no good reason to consider Arcesilaus' rejoinder to the Stoic argument as a positive doctrine of his own. All he does is to maintain, possibly relying on Peripatetic doctrine, that assent is not necessary for action. He does not in the least try to deal with the central point of the Stoic theory. He seems merely to insist that an alternative is possible, perhaps that we could explain all action merely in terms of *phantasia* and *hormē*, but he offers no account of the difference between voluntary and, e.g., instinctive action. Nor would it be fair to think that he meant to commit himself to the view that there is no such thing as moral responsibility. In fact, his answer to the first objection seemed to outline, though not seriously, an account of morally right action, which would of course presuppose a framework for the distinction between voluntary and involuntary action.

As far as Arcesilaus is concerned, then, we may conclude that there is no evidence for ascribing any positive epistemological doctrine to him—and indeed in respect of *epochē* he is unanimously described as having been more strict than Carneades.

---

[41] *EN* 1111^b 6–10, cf. 1112^a 14–17, *MA* 701^a 28–36.

III

As I have indicated above, Arcesilaus' replies could hardly satisfy the Stoics; and so it is not surprising that Carneades was confronted with more elaborate versions of the same objections. It is very likely that these were worked out by Chrysippus, who is said to have saved the Stoa from the onslaught of the Academy, and even to have forestalled the later attacks of Carneades (Plu. *Comm. not.* 1059 a–c).

Carneades' reaction to both objections is in several respects very different from that of Arcesilaus. To the first argument— that the sceptic makes 'everything uncertain'—he replied with his well-known theory of criteria. According to this theory, which is most fully expounded by Sextus (*M* VII 166 ff.), although we can never be certain that any particular presentation of ours is true, we may with reasonable hope of being right use those that (a) are plausible (*pithanos*); (b) do not conflict with any other presentation given in the same situation; and (c)—if time permits this—have been tested with regard to the circumstances in which they have arisen—e.g. whether the perceiver is awake, in good health etc., whether the object is large enough, not too distant, etc.

Now this looks first and foremost like a theory of evidence for factual propositions rather than a theory of criteria for action.[42] Sextus' examples are all of the factual kind ('This is Socrates'; 'There's an ambush over there'; 'There's a snake in the corner'), though the connection with action is made in the ambush—and

---

[42] 'Theory of evidence' is presumably too strong; cf. Burnyeat [58], who argues that the 'theory of criteria' develops the suggestion that the wise man will hold opinions—the second horn of the dilemma posed by Carneades to the Stoics; cf. p. 76 below—rather than trying to refute the objection that everything will be uncertain within a context of strict suspension of judgement. Now the 'plausible presentation' is cited by Cicero as answering the 'omnia incerta' objection (*Acad.* II 32) or a version of ἀπραξία (*Acad.* II 99, cf. also Numen. *apud* Eus. *PE* XIV 8, 4), and Clitomachus combines it with the thesis that the wise man will withhold assent in *Acad.* II 99–101 and 104. Sextus himself recognizes that a criterion for the conduct of life is needed to avoid total inactivity (*PH* I 23; *M* VII 30), and I take it that the objector in *M* VII 166 is making the same point. The occurrence of the term συγκατατίθεσθαι in Sextus' report (*M* VII 188) might simply be due to carelessness on the part of Sextus, who tends to treat the πιθανόν theory as official Academic doctrine (which it actually became with Philo). In *PH* I 229–31, on the other hand, he seems to avoid συγκατατίθεσθαι, suggesting rather that the term used by both Academics and Pyrrhonists was πείθεσθαι. Cf. p. 61 n. 21 above for the terminology.

snake—examples, where the person will have to act without
delay, since it might cost his life to stay and check whether he is
right. But if Sextus' report is correct, Carneades seems to have
been primarily concerned to refute the suggestion that *akatalēpsia*
implies total uncertainty in factual matters. Besides, as Sextus
reports it, the theory seems to apply only to perceptual judgements. But obviously the conditions given for consistent or
'tested' presentations could easily be extended beyond that field.
So Cicero adduces the case of a man trying to decide whether to
go on a sea journey: if there is no indication that the ship might
sink—the weather is good, winds are favourable, the ship is well
equipped and has a reliable captain etc.—he will conclude that
he may confidently start on his journey, although of course he
cannot exclude the possibility of an unexpected disaster (*Acad.* II
100). In this case, of course, the Stoics would have admitted that
knowledge could not be had, so that 'the probable' would have
to be followed. So it is presumably no accident that in the
exposition of his criteria Carneades insisted on cases in which,
according to the Stoics, *katalēpsis* might have been possible, in
order to show that even these leave room for doubt.

Now Cicero says in a number of places that the plausible is
also to serve as a practical criterion.[43] It is not so obvious how
it could be used as a guide to moral judgements, and indeed it
might not have been intended to. But there might be a reason
why Carneades was content to discuss perceptual judgements:
when the Stoics insisted that we need a 'criterion of truth', they
would always start by defending their conception of *katalēptikē
phantasia*. One often finds it asserted that the Stoics recognized
katalēptikē phantasia also outside the field of sense perception. I
have argued elsewhere[44] that this may be a mistake—at least we
have no sufficient evidence for this assumption. That does not
mean that knowledge in other fields does not depend upon
katalēptikē phantasia, but that the way in which it does is more
complicated than is often realized. Thus, e.g. the man who
assents to 'I should take a walk now' (Seneca's example) clearly
does not assent to a sense impression. But neither does he assent
on the same grounds as he would to a sense impression—say,
perspicuity or some other 'mark of truth'. Rather, he assents to

---

[43] *Acad.* II 32, 104, 110, cf. *M* VII 175.
[44] [21], Appendix, 107–10.

this as to something appropriate or in accordance with his nature (*oikeion*).[45] It is true that the Stoics recognized certain things as being immediately felt as *oikeia*, so that in those cases (where the object of the desire is perceived by the agent) one might perhaps speak of *kataleptikē phantasia*.[46] But this was only an initial stage, and it seems quite obvious that in the majority of cases assent to a proposal for action would have to depend on the agent's generalized notion of what is in accordance with (his own or universal) nature.[47]

Hence against Arcesilaus' suggestion that the sceptic could use 'the reasonable' as a guide to action the Stoics might have objected that we have no way of even establishing that something is reasonable unless we can rely on our notions of what is in accordance with nature, and these in turn must be based on *kataleptikē phantasia*.[48] This is why they maintained that the sceptic who denies the possibility of knowledge based on perception also eliminates the possibility of deciding what to do. Carneades, in concentrating on the case of sense perception, was therefore meeting the Stoics on their own ground. However, his own theory does not go far enough to show how the transition to moral questions would have to be made. If I am right in suggesting that the Stoics used the 'common notions' to account for this, Carneades might perhaps have tried to explain how even non-cognitive sense impressions can be the basis of general concepts. But although we know that the common notions did play a part in the debate between the Stoa and the Academy (Plu. *Comm. not.* 1059 bc), the relevant arguments on this point do not seem to have been preserved.

In his refutation of the first objection, then, Carneades developed an alternative theory which might serve some of the

---

[45] *Acad.* II 25.

[46] Cf. *Acad.* II 30, 38. The last passage suggests a parallel rather than an indentification of the perception of facts and perception of things as οἰκεῖα. Similarly, Plu. *Stoic. rep.* 1038 c.

[47] Cf. the accounts of οἰκείωσις, DL VII 86, Cic. *Fin.* III 20 f., 33, and the definition of the *summum bonum*, ibid. 31: 'vivere scientiam adhibentem earum rerum, quae natura eveniant, seligentem quae secundum naturam et quae contra naturam sint reicientem.' I suppose that if moral judgements or practical decisions were always made with reference to οἰκεῖα or ἀλλότρια, then a 'fool' would have a mistaken idea of what is in accordance with nature, rather than thinking that accordance with nature is irrelevant. For a detailed account of οἰκείωσις and the Stoic epistemology of moral judgement cf. Pembroke [114] and Long [105].

[48] Cic. *Acad.* II 30-1, *Fin.* III 21.

purposes of the Stoic theory based on *katalēptikē phantasia*. And although Carneades, like his predecessor, used a Stoic framework —thus the distinction between plausible and true presentations, i.e. ones that appear correct to the perceiver, and ones that do in fact correspond to reality, was taken from the Stoics (*M* VII 242 ff.) —the theory itself seems to be his own.[49] It does not, indeed, provide for the Stoic distinction between the wise man, whose every action is supposed to be based on knowledge, and the fool, who will have to rely on opinions. There is no explicit reply in *Academica* II, as far as I can see, to the argument that virtue requires knowledge, advanced in 23–5. But Cicero indicates in several places that the temerity which lies in rash assent may itself be the greatest mistake to be avoided:[50] it might be better to be a modest sceptic than to be an arrogant dogmatist. Moreover, Sextus in one place (*M* VII 184) says that the greatest caution should, 'according to the followers of Carneades', be used with regard to questions pertaining to happiness—so Carneades' theory does provide a way of distinguishing between rash and prudent decisions. But with the examples of the ambush and the snake he points out at the same time that this distinction may not be generalized to separate the wise man from the fool— in some situations, there simply is no room for a careful examination of evidence.

[49] It seems to me that Couissin and, following him, dal Pra underestimate Carneades' originality by stressing only the fact that he took his basic concepts from Chrysippus. If he took over the materials, he did not also take over the arguments; and in fact it seems that he was indeed original e.g. in pointing out that impressions should not be considered in isolation, and in the attention he paid to the methods we in fact use to ascertain the truth of a given factual statement. (For an account which stresses Carneades' innovations—even a little too much, perhaps—cf. Stough [29], 50–64). It will not do to treat Carneades' theories, even if they were polemically formulated, as reductions *ad absurdum* of the Stoic doctrines, as dal Pra does ([27], 275): one does not demonstrate inconsistencies in other people's theories by adding inconsistent premises. Carneades did not show that the Stoics were contradicting themselves—and they very likely did not contradict themselves, in spite of Plutarch's collection of superficially incompatible theses—but that some of their premises were wrong. One should not let oneself be taken in by the Academic trick of making it appear that Academic conclusions follow from Stoic premises alone. And apart from his criticism of Stoic doctrines, Carneades also tried to show that nothing absurd follows if we drop the disputed premises—in fact, as Cicero puts it (*Acad.* II 146), the sceptic only throws out what is never the case, but leaves everything that is needed. Hence Carneades' philosophy was not entirely negative— though it does not follow that he ever constructed a system for himself. Cf. Robin's more balanced evaluation, [28], 128–9.

[50] *Acad.* II 68, 87, 108, 115, 128, 133, 138, 141.

If the Academics sometimes followed the Stoics in discussing epistemology or ethics in terms of the sage,[51] they probably did this only because this terminology provides a convenient way of talking about what one should do, as opposed to what one normally does do, or what can in principle be done as opposed to what everybody can do. If the wise man is he who always does as he should do, certainly no one would claim to be a sage (cf. *Acad.* II 66); but it does not follow that the sage is super-human. So the 'Academic sage', whom Cicero in some places contrasts with the Stoic (*Acad.* II 105; 109–10; 128), will perhaps be more cautious and prudent than the rest of us, but he like all ordinary humans will have to be content with what is plausible.

Considering the contrast between Arcesilaus and Carneades in their reaction to the 'omnia incerta' argument, we might indeed be inclined to think that Carneades was developing his own views. After all, he is offering a new solution to the Stoic problem of how to choose between presentations, and, moreover, this solution is consistent with his scepticism at least to the extent that it incorporates the thesis that nothing can be known.

There remains, however, the difficulty that in advocating an epistemological theory Carneades would have abandoned the Academic practice of arguing for and against without coming to a conclusion. If he did present the theory as his own view, he must be considered, at least in Sextus' sense, as a dogmatist, even if one of qualified status. We will come back to this point after we have considered Carneades' reply to the second version of the *apraxia* argument.

Both Chrysippus and Antipater are said to have argued at great length against those who 'maintained that upon the advent of an appropriate (*oikeia*) presentation [we] immediately have an impulse to act without giving in or assenting' (Plu. *Stoic. rep.* 1057 a). I have mentioned already what seems to have been the main point of their criticism: namely that voluntary action implies assent, which is in our power; and that those who deny

<hr />

[51] Cicero has couched his entire discussion in *Academica* II in these terms, cf. 57, 66, 115. For references from other works cf. Reid's note on *Acad.* II 66 ([7], 254). Sextus and Plutarch write in terms of 'the man who withholds judgement' or 'the Academics' and similar expressions (*M* VII 158, 173, 174, 179, 184, *PH* I 229, 230, Plu. *Col.* 1122 c–e; cf. also Clitomachus in *Acad.* II 104). It is not implausible that the Academics adopted this terminology precisely when they were arguing against the Stoics.

this are implicitly denying the possibility of morally responsible action. This argument appears in its most explicit form in *Acad.* II 37–9. Lucullus had already argued that action implies assent (25); now he insists that virtuous action in particular depends on assent as that which is in our power: 'and most important of all, granting there is something in our power, it will not be present in one who assents to nothing. Where, then, is virtue, if nothing rests with ourselves?' The passage concludes with a restatement of the Stoic doctrine that action implies assent, from which it would follow that he who rejects assent thereby takes away all action from life.

Carneades' counter-argument is again much more elaborate than Arcesilaus'. First, he seems to have pointed out to the Stoics that their argument would be of no help towards establishing the possibility of knowledge: if knowledge is impossible, and action implies assent, all that follows is that the wise man, in order not to remain inactive, will have to assent to a presentation that does not yield knowledge—he will have to hold opinions. That this was the point of Carneades' alleged acceptance of opinion seems to me to come out clearly in the two passages in which Cicero refers to it in his speech for scepticism. To start with the second, *Acad.* II 78: Here Cicero claims that the only point of controversy that remains between Stoics and sceptics is the question whether there can be a *kataleptikē phantasia*—the question of *epochē* is not relevant here since, as Carneades said, 'The wise man could have no knowledge and yet hold opinions.' The question about withholding assent is presumably the *apraxia* argument, which was the main Stoic argument against *epochē*.[52] Cicero is pointing out that this does not belong to the controversy about the possibility of knowledge because, as Carneades had shown, it could at best serve to show that the wise man must assent to something, which means, if the sceptics are right, that he must hold opinions—it cannot be used to argue that knowledge must be possible.

[52] Sometimes indeed supplemented by the argument that we cannot help assenting to what is evident, so that the sceptic would in fact be mistaken about his own attitude, cf. *Acad.* II 38 and 107. Sextus (*M* VII 257) ascribes this argument to the 'younger Stoics' (ibid. 253) which might indicate that it was not part of the original doctrine, but added as an argument against the sceptics. It is not, of course, inconsistent with their doctrine of the voluntariness of assent—that does not amount to the claim that we can choose what to believe, which would be absurd, but that we are responsible for giving in to false presentations, cf. Brochard [72], 9 ff.

In a similar way, the earlier passage *Acad.* II 67–8 shows how Carneades turned the *apraxia* argument against the Stoics. There Cicero reports two arguments, the one going back to Arcesilaus, by which he proved to the Stoics that their sage would have to suspend judgement on all matters: 'If the wise man ever assents to anything, he will at some time hold an opinion; but the wise man will never hold an opinion; therefore, he will not assent to anything' (cf. *M* VII 156–7). The second argument is expressly ascribed to Carneades: he is said to have sometimes conceded as a second premiss that the wise man will sometimes assent—from which it followed that he will also hold opinions. It is quite clear, as Couissin saw ([60], 261), that these two arguments were designed to build up a dilemma for the Stoics: given the first (sceptic) premiss, either they will keep the thesis that the wise man has no opinions, which will then lead to *epochē*, or they will—following the *apraxia* argument—insist that the wise man must sometimes assent, in which case he will be reduced to having opinions. It is significant that the premiss that the wise man will sometimes assent is called a concession ('dabat') on the part of Carneades—obviously the apparent concession was made in order to deduce a conclusion that was inacceptable to the Stoics. Hence I think Cicero is perfectly right when he follows Clitomachus in thinking that Carneades advocated opinion only for the sake of argument.

It is an entirely different question, of course, whether Carneades may have said, like Cicero (*Acad.* II 66), that he himself, or people in general, would sometimes have opinions. This could simply be ascribed to human weakness—after all, as Cicero rightly insists (*Acad.* II 108), consistent suspension of judgement is no easy task. But it does not amount to the claim that we are sometimes justified in holding opinions—the thesis expressed in the Stoic way by saying that the wise man will hold opinions. As far as Carneades' alleged advocacy of opinions goes, then, it seems that the question may be settled in favour of Clitomachus.

It remains to be seen how Carneades dealt with the argument that action implies assent. If he had really conceded this point to the Stoics, we might be inclined to think his position was that the necessity to be active in some sense justifies our having opinions, whether these themselves are well grounded or not. But it is perfectly clear, from Cicero's quotations of Clitomachus' books, that he did not make this concession. Instead, he pointed out that the Stoic argument confuses two things under the term *sunkatathesis*. If the two factors involved are distinguished, it turns out that it is indeed possible to act freely without assent. The two crucial passages are *Acad.* II 99–101 and especially 104.

The first passage refers to the already familiar distinction between 'cataleptic' and plausible presentations, saying that the wise man will 'approve of' the plausible ones and 'use' them as a guide to action. Apart from the implicit distinction between 'approving' or 'using' and assenting, it is not yet made clear how the wise man is to avoid assent in his actions. In the second passage, Clitomachus introduces an explicit distinction between two modes of suspension, and a corresponding distinction between two ways of reacting to presentations: in one sense, *epochē* is taken to mean that the wise man will not assent to anything, in another, that he will refrain from reacting either positively or negatively. Now, while the Academics hold that he should never give his assent, they allow him to say 'Yes' or 'No', following plausibility, so that he will have a method to direct both his actions and his theoretical thinking. Cicero insists that the sceptic's positive reaction is not assent.

The point of Carneades' distinction can perhaps best be brought out by reconsidering briefly the role of assent in the Stoic theory. The Stoics used the concept of assent in both their epistemology and their theory of action. In the theory of knowledge, the distinction between having a presentation and assenting to it, which Cicero explicitly attributes to Zeno (*Acad.* I 40–1), seems to be based on the fact that we may, and indeed often do, have presentations without believing them to be true. Hence we can distinguish the act of accepting a presentation as true from the mere 'having' an impression, which is caused by factors outside our control.[53] This distinction has become part of the European tradition, its latest prominent descendant being perhaps Frege's distinction between the mere grasping of a thought and the judgement that the state of affairs expressed by a proposition is a fact.[54]

Now, in the theory of action, *sunkatathesis* is said to have the

---

[53] Cf. *Acad.* II 145, M VIII 397.
[54] The Stoics are duly praised for their discovery in Brochard [72], 46 ff. As so often, the basic insight seems to come from Aristotle, cf. *de an.* III 3 428a 24–b 9.

additional feature of leading to action—that is, besides denoting the acceptance of a proposition as true (e.g. 'I should do X'), it also denotes the decision to do the action prescribed by the proposition. This is why the Stoics sometimes said that impulse (*hormē*) is a kind of assent. Hence the role of assent in action seems comparable rather to Aristotle's *prohairesis* than to Frege's 'Urteil'.

The Stoics did apparently distinguish the theoretical and the practical side of such acts of assent, saying that the assent is given to the proposition (*axiōma*) while the impulse is directed towards the (action-) predicate (*katēgorēma*) contained therein;[55] but they obviously held that in practical matters, the judgement 'I should do X' is identical with the decision to do X, and necessarily followed by the action of doing X.

What I take Carneades to be pointing out to them is that judging that one should do a thing and deciding to do it are not the same: an agent may decide to do a thing without accepting it as true that he should do it, and this means that he can act voluntarily without assenting in the theoretical sense. Thus, e.g. the man who runs away from a suspected ambush need not believe that there really is an ambush, nor, consequently, that it was the right thing for him to run away—his action is prompted

---

[55] This is how I understand the somewhat unclear passage from Stob. *Ecl.* II 88.1 W (*SVF* III, p. 40.27–31): πάσας δὲ τὰς ὁρμὰς συγκαταθέσεις εἶναι, τὰς δὲ πρακτικὰς καὶ τὸ κινητικὸν περιέχειν. ἤδη δὲ ἄλλων μὲν εἶναι συγκαταθέσεις, ἐπ' ἄλλο δὲ ὁρμάς· καὶ συγκαταθέσεις μὲν ἀξιώμασί τισιν, ὁρμὰς δὲ ἐπὶ κατηγορήματα, τὰ περιεχόμενα πως ἐν τοῖς ἀξιώμασιν, οἷς συγκαταθέσεις; *pace* Tsekourakis [78], 77 f., who takes it that all assent is or is followed by ὁρμή. Apart from the obvious implausibility of this view (for which cf. Alex. Aphr. *De an.* 72.20 ff.), there seems to be no good evidence to support it. Tsekourakis quotes Porphyry *apud* Stob. *Ecl.* I 349.23 W (*SVF* II, p. 27, 6) τῆς συγκαταθέσεως καθ' ὁρμὴν οὔσης as saying that assent is a kind of ὁρμή, but in fact Porphyry seems to say only that assent is voluntary. (For this use of καθ' ὁρμήν cf. Nemesius, *Nat. hom.* XXVII 250 Matthaei: περὶ τῆς καθ' ὁρμὴν ἢ κατὰ προαίρεσιν κινήσεως, ἥτις ἐστὶ τοῦ ὀρεκτικοῦ; cf. also Alex. Aphr. *Fat.* 182.4–20, where καθ' ὁρμὴν κίνησις seems to mean intentional or spontaneous movement.) Porphyry is simply setting out the Stoic theory of αἴσθησις, and the clause quoted by Tsekourakis is apparently taken up a few lines further down by εἰ μὴ συγκατάθεσις εἴη τῶν ἐφ' ἡμῖν. From the Stobaeus passage Tsekourakis infers that there must have been other than practical ὁρμαί, and he suggests that these might be acts of assent to theoretical propositions. Now I am not sure whether πρακτικὰς really qualifies ὁρμάς—it could just be explicative; and it seems obvious from the definitions of ὁρμή given by Stobaeus himself, *Ecl.* II 86.17 (*SVF* III, p. 40, 4 ff.), and others that ὁρμή is always directed towards action. If πρακτικαί ὁρμαί were only a subclass of ὁρμαί, one might suggest that they were so called in counter-distinction to the affections (πάθη), which were also a kind of ὁρμαί (*SVF* III, p. 93, 4 ff., 9 ff., p. 94, 3 ff.). The attribute πρακτική might have served to distinguish between decisions immediately preceding action and dispositional states also due to assent.

by the suspicion that there might be an ambush, and he acts without regard to his possible doubts as to whether he really has to run or not. So even if the Stoics would not have accepted, on theoretical grounds, the most glaring counter-examples to their identification, viz. cases of *akrasia*, where the agent judges that he should not do a thing and yet does it, there would be ways of making it clear that a decision to act is not identical with a moral judgement about the act.

Now while this shows that we can act without assent, Carneades' distinction still permits us to draw the line between voluntary and involuntary actions where the Stoics wanted to draw it, since a decision to act, though it is not assent, may be just as much in the agent's power.

The distinction between deciding to act upon a proposition and accepting it as true can be carried over by analogy to the theoretical field. I may decide to use a proposition, say, as a hypothesis, without thereby committing myself to its truth: thus a scientist who puts a hypothesis of his to the test should not be supposed to assume it to be true, though he will of course choose the hypothesis he finds most likely to be true. Hence, if Carneades' distinction is kept in mind, it turns out that the sceptic is free both to act and to speculate about matters of fact without accepting any proposition as true.[56]

In this case, Carneades may be considered as proposing a modification of the Stoic theory. While keeping the initial distinction between having a presentation and reacting to it, he replaces the unitary Stoic conception of assent by the two parallel notions of deciding to act—for practical matters—and using (as a hypothesis)—for theoretical questions. Since these two are sufficient as a basis for action or for theorizing, the sceptic can without paradox refrain from assent in the full sense of accepting as true. So Carneades' reply to the second version of the *apraxia* argument shows that he successfully vindicated the possibility of strict *epochē*.

[56] The Carneadean distinction between accepting as true and adopting as a basis for action provides the background for the later Pyrrhonist distinction between criteria of truth and criteria for action or for the conduct of life (*PH* I 21; *M* VII 30). For this is not a distinction between theoretical and practical questions, as one might think at first glance: clearly the Pyrrhonist withholds judgement on both fields. The point is that he acts in accordance with what appears to him to be the case without committing himself to the truth of his impressions.

One might be inclined to object at this point, with Hartmann [47], 44, and dal Pra [27], 298, that the difference between the positions of Metrodorus and Clitomachus—provisional assent on the one hand, positive attitude on the other—is insubstantial. The important similarity seems to lie in the fact that on both accounts propositions can be assented to or adopted on the basis of evidence—and this is the main point of distinction between the rational attitude of Academic scepticism and the irrationalism of the Pyrrhonists (cf. *PH* I 23–4; 229–38; *M* XI 165–6). But apart from the, to my mind, important clarification of the two aspects of Stoic *sunkatathesis* in the theory of action, the distinction does not seem negligible in the theoretical field either: for, leaving aside for the moment Stoic terminology, Carneades might be considered to suggest an alternative theory of belief such that assenting or accepting as true is not a necessary ingredient.[57]

To say that belief need not imply assent does not mean, to be sure, that the concept of assent has no application—it probably does, e.g. in cases where, after an argument or a proof, we come to see the truth of a proposition and hence accept it as true.[58] But we should not generalize this model to apply to all cases of belief.[59] Apart from the implausible suggestion that beliefs are always acquired in this way, which might be circumvented by saying that the theory at bottom claims no more than that we take what we believe to be true (and, in the case of the Stoics, that we are responsible for what we believe), it is not clear whether belief really implies taking to be true. For an acceptance theory of belief does not seem to take sufficient account of the fact that our beliefs may vary in degree. Accepting a proposition *p* as true would seem to exclude accepting not-*p* also, at least consciously, and yet it would seem that a person may quite consistently believe that *p* but also, less confidently, that not-*p*, as e.g. when someone says 'I believe I saw him yesterday, but it may have been

---

[57] I owe this point to Rolf George.

[58] I think it would be correct to say that we assent to a proposition because we (already) believe it, so that assent is not part of any belief (cf. B. Mayo, 'Belief and Constraint', *Proceedings of the Aristotelian Society* 64 (1963/4), 139–56; cited from A. P. Griffiths (ed.), *Knowledge and Belief* (Oxford, 1967), 147–9); but let us set this aside for the moment, using 'assent' in the sense of 'accepting as true'.

[59] For the difficulties involved in this cf. H. H. Price, 'Some Considerations about Belief', *Proceedings of the Aristotelian Society* 35 (1934/5), 229–52; repr. in Griffiths, op. cit., 41–59, whose theory is in many respects strikingly similar to the Stoic—or rather a revised 'Carneadean' version of it.

the day before.' A man who sincerely believes that his house will not burn down may still take out fire insurance because 'You can never be sure.' It will not do in such cases to replace partial belief that *p* by full belief that probably-*p*, since degree of probability and degree of belief do not always go together.[60] Hence partial belief should be identified neither with taking to be probable nor with—even provisionally—taking to be true. Now of course this goes beyond the controversy between the Stoics and the sceptics. We have no evidence to suggest that Carneades criticized or rejected the Stoic analysis of *doxa*. But in expounding Carneades' theory of criteria Sextus repeatedly points out that credibility and hence also conviction may vary in degree.[61] It is not so clear whether Carneades distinguished between degrees of confirmation and degrees of conviction. But there is a point to his distinction between assent and the positive attitude of the sceptic which is lost if we interpret him, on the lines of Metrodorus, as advocating provisional assent. Accepting as true might be considered as the limiting case of the positive attitude, justifiable only by certainty, and a certain amount of confidence is not the same as even provisionally assumed certainty.

If we introduce for a moment a terminological distinction between opinion—as defined by the Stoics—and belief, we might say that the sceptic, according to Carneades, will have no opinions, though he may have more or less firm beliefs. To be sure, this is not the complete indifference of the Pyrrhonian sceptic, but it is strict *epochē* in the sense of total abstaining from assent.

We can now come back to the question whether Carneades put his theory of 'using plausible presentations' forward as his own epistemological view. In a way, it is tempting to say that he did, since, given his distinction between accepting as true and adopting as a hypothesis, we might say that this was presumably the hypothesis which he himself adopted. Also, the theory is at least his own view in the sense that it is not anyone else's view. But

[60] For the theory of partial belief cf. F. P. Ramsay, 'Truth and Probability', in his *The Foundations of Mathematics and Other Logical Essays* (London, 1931), 156–98, and D. M. Armstrong, *Belief, Truth and Knowledge* (Cambridge, 1973), 108–10.

[61] *M* VII 173, 178, 181, 184: it depends on the importance of the question at hand whether the sceptic will be content with a merely plausible presentation or whether he will look for confirmation to make it more reliable.

then we have to consider also the framework within which Carneades developed his theory. Before he expounds Carneades' theory of criteria, Sextus reports an argument by which Carneades purported to show that there could be no absolute criterion of truth whatsoever (*M* VII 160–5). The first part of this argument takes its premisses obviously from the Stoics, and consists in showing that the only possible criterion would have to be the Stoic *katalēptikē phantasia*. Later on, in developing his own criteria, Carneades is again relying on Stoic theory.[62] So if we were to attribute this theory to him as an exposition of his own view, we would have to take it—as e.g. Stough [29], 41, explicitly does—that he accepted a great deal of the Stoic doctrine without any argument. And this, I think, is rather unlikely.

To understand what he was trying to do we should remind ourselves of the Academic methodology. A good example of this is provided by the way Carneades argued on ethical questions. Cicero tells us that he sometimes defended a certain view with such vigour that he was taken to hold the theory himself (*Acad.* II 139). On most occasions however, he seems to have argued for a different thesis—but, as Cicero emphasizes, only in order to attack the Stoics (*Acad.* II 131; *Tusc.* V 84). On the occasion of the famous embassy to Rome he argued with equal force and ingenuity for and against justice on two consecutive days (Cic. *Rep.* III 9: Lact. *Inst.* 5.14.3–5). This is the procedure which Cicero describes as 'comparing claims and bringing out what can be said with regard to each opinion' ('conferre causas et quid in quamque sententiam dici possit expromere', *Div.* II 150), and for which the Academics found it necessary to argue both for and against all other philosophers (*ND* I 11; *Acad.* II 60).

Now while Carneades' ethical theses seem to have been adopted for purely critical purposes—he appears to have argued that the Stoics ought to have adopted 'his' definition of the highest good, as Arcesilaus had argued earlier that the Stoic sage ought to suspend judgement on all matters[63]—one might say that in his epistemology he went beyond this in making a case for the possibility of consistent scepticism. In contrast with Arcesilaus, he was apparently not content with criticizing the Stoics and refuting their objections; he worked out alternative solutions to

---

[62] This has now been shown in detail by Burnyeat [58].
[63] Cf. Long [102].

the problems that the Stoics had set themselves. But this is of course also a way of showing that the opposite of the Stoic theses can be maintained with equal plausibility. If we are inclined to ascribe some of those alternatives to Carneades as his own theories, this may be due to the fact that, instead of producing a situation where both alternatives have the same weight, he seems quite often to have outweighed his opponents. But this brings in our own judgement—as far as Carneades himself was concerned, it seems most likely that he remained uncommitted both with respect to the framework in which the problems of his day arose, and with respect to the solutions he himself or others happened to offer.*

* I have benefited greatly from the criticism and advice of Rolf George, whose visit to Göttingen luckily coincided with the writing of this paper, and from comments by Myles Burnyeat, Wolfgang Carl, and Günther Patzig.

TRUTH AND KNOWLEDGE

Julia Annas

In the debate on the question, 'What is the criterion of truth?'[1] the answer provided by the Stoics was, in the main,[2] *katalēpsis* or *kataleptikē phantasia*. I shall translate these as 'apprehension' and 'apprehensible presentation'.[3] These are problematic concepts, as difficult as the much-debated question of 'the criterion of truth' itself. This discussion tries to bring out some ways in which the debates were clouded by the Stoic failure to distinguish clearly between questions about what we can know and questions about what is the case, and to realize that truth is a metaphysical notion, not an epistemological one.

Apprehension is assent to an apprehensible presentation,[4] and we are told many times what the latter is: an apprehensible presentation is a presentation from an existing object and impressed and stamped according to the object, such as could not come from a non-existent object.[5] A presentation is in turn an impression on the soul; Zeno called it an imprint on the soul, but Chrysippus, thinking this too literal and liable to mislead,

---

[1] Graeser [75], 68 (cf. Hartmann [47], 4) holds that the question of a criterion of truth was not one the Stoics faced until forced to do so by the challenge of their opponents in the sceptical Academy. But this cannot be right; Zeno was forced by Arcesilaus' criticisms to modify his definition of the apprehensible presentation (e.g. *Acad.* II 77, Numen. *apud* Eus. *PE* XIV 5–6, esp. 732 a and 733 a–c), so he already defended a theory of apprehensible presentations as the criterion. (Possibly he was attacking the Epicurean view that all presentations (not just all perceptions) were true; see *SVF* II 78, and Striker [133].)

[2] DL VII 54 offers what look like various alternative criteria, but these are not rivals to the apprehensible presentation (see Rist [33], 133–4, Long [69]). The word 'criterion' itself did not imply that what was put forward was a guarantee of truth, rather than just a means or way of judging (see Striker [21]); but the Stoics did think of a criterion as a guarantee (see above n. 1).

[3] I do not want here to go into the vexed question of whether the word καταληπτική had a suggestion of activity (as in 'apprehen*sive*') or of passivity (as in 'apprehen*sible*'). On this see Sandbach [121], 14–15, Graeser [75], 45–50.

[4] M VIII 397: ἔστι μὲν οὖν ἡ κατάληψις ... καταληπτικῆς φαντασίας συγκατάθεσις. See Graeser [75], 41 n. 9.

[5] M VII 248: ἀπὸ ὑπάρχοντος καὶ κατ' αὐτὸ τὸ ὑπάρχον ἐναπομεμαγμένη καὶ ἐναπεσφραγισμένη, ὁποία οὐκ ἂν γένοιτο ἀπὸ μὴ ὑπάρχοντος. See *Acad.* II 18, 77, and *SVF* IV (index), s.v. φαντασία καταληπτική.

called it an alteration of the soul (*M* VII 227-31, 236). An apprehensible presentation, then, is one which not only comes from an existent thing but reflects this so faithfully that it could not be mistaken for a mere hallucination or the like. A presentation fails to be an apprehensible one not only if it is a presentation of a non-existent object, but if it presents an existent object in such a way that it could be confused with any other existent or non-existent object, however similar. An apprehensible presentation has, in Sextus' words, a unique particular quality which enables the person who has it to discriminate with the proper skill, and not confuse its object with any other object whatsoever (*M* VII 252). This last condition amounts to a considerable constraint, for it shows that the Stoics accepted some form of what is now called the identity of indiscernibles.[6] Their opponents made much of the fact that even the Stoic wise man might be unable to discriminate between presentations of twins, or of two eggs; but the Stoics had a good reply to this, namely, that if the two items *were* different then they were discernible in principle, but not necessarily to the Stoic however wise, who would therefore suspend judgement (*Acad.* II 53-8, *M* VII 408-11, 416).

Apprehensible presentations are the criterion of truth because they can be guaranteed to put us in touch with the way the world really is. They do not reveal everything about it, but what they do reveal can be utterly trusted. They enable us to judge correctly about some experiential facts, and for the empiricist Stoics all truth is built up from what is delivered through the senses. The ancient sources are very sketchy on the way in which the input of sense was actually to provide the constituents of truth extending beyond empirical matters, and the problem is complicated by the fact that later writers sometimes proceed as though there could be apprehensible presentations that do not come through the senses. I follow Striker in holding that the latter view is not to be ascribed to the old Stoa, and shall in this paper consider

---

[6] Cf. Rist [33], 137, Graeser [75], 54 and n. 41. The Leibnizian term is quite appropriate in spite of the different role played by the principle in his system. For the Stoics, more than spatiotemporal co-ordinates are required to differentiate two individuals, since each individual has its own unique and particular ἰδίως ποιόν; but it by no means follows that even the wisest of us will be in a position to recognize this. Not all presentations are apprehensible, and the Stoics' opponents need to find a counter-example within the class of presentations claimed to be such by the Stoics.

only apprehensible presentations which do come through the senses.[7]

Difficulties at once suggest themselves over the relation of apprehension to the apprehensible presentation. Pohlenz ([116], 174–86, [32], 59–63) made an attempt to solve these by making a historical claim. Zeno, he conjectured, began by making the agent's apprehension the criterion of truth. This is suggested by the famous simile in which he presented the stages of cognition (*Acad.* II 145): presentation was compared to the open hand with outstretched fingers, apprehension to the clenching of the fist, and knowledge to the secure grasp of the clenched fist by the other hand. This certainly seems to place what is criterial on the side of the agent, rather than of what is presented to him. Chrysippus, according to Pohlenz, disagreed and made the apprehensible presentation, rather than the agent's apprehension, the criterion of truth. Pohlenz's thesis has been severely criticized,[8] and it is clear that it cannot stand as a historical claim. None the less it points up a genuine problem in the Stoic theory, and critics who rightly claim that we have no reason to ascribe radically different views to Zeno and Chrysippus are unconvincing when they go on to claim that there are no real philosophical difficulties in the thesis which they both share.

The ancient evidence on this subject allows of widely differing interpretations. In what follows I shall try to sharpen our perception of the difficulties by bringing out the two lines into which the interpretations fall. (In doing this I shall have to make a considerable amount of reference to the work of other scholars, and to the text through them, but this seems the clearest way to organize the material so as to bring out what is persistently problematic about it.)

I shall call the first line 'the coherence interpretation'. It stresses apprehension rather than the apprehensible presentation, and finds the criterion of truth in the way the particular apprehension fits into the body of rationally accepted beliefs. As with modern coherence theories of truth, the coherence interpretation stresses considerations of knowledge rather than of truth, failing to separate the two sharply. It succeeds in fitting the theory of

---

[7] Striker [21], Appendix, 107–10. The opposing view is defended by Bonhöffer [71], 228–32. Cf. Sandbach [121], 12.

[8] Sandbach [121], 15–18, Rist [33], 138 ff.

apprehensible presentations into Stoic doctrines taken as a whole (especially the moral doctrines), rather than doing justice to particular pieces of evidence. It gives the Stoics a theory which is defensible against sceptical attacks, and appeals to those who would like them to have a plausible defence against those attacks. Against this I set 'the correspondence interpretation'. This looks less like a modern 'correspondence theory of truth' than the coherence interpretation looks like modern coherence theories; this is because modern theories do sharply separate questions of truth from questions of epistemological justification. A modern 'correspondence theory of truth' consists in an explication of the claim that truth is a relation of correspondence between selected linguistic and non-linguistic items (propositions and facts, for example). This leaves the ontology and epistemological status of these items quite open, and even Tarksi's theory can count as a correspondence theory of truth.[9] But the Stoics did not make this sharp distinction. The correspondence interpretation, however, makes less appeal to considerations of knowledge than the coherence interpretation does, and lays more weight on the apprehensible presentation and the way this is defined for us in the ancient sources than on the notion of the agent's apprehension. In consequence, it does more justice to particular pieces of evidence we have about apprehensive presentations, though at the cost of producing a theory which it is difficult to fit into Stoicism as a whole (especially the moral doctrines). And it gives the Stoics a theory which is philosophically naïve, and exposed to the most obvious sceptical attacks.

I shall begin with the coherence interpretation, which takes off naturally from Zeno's simile, which stresses the agent's response. Of course, all similes have their limits, and we should not read it as giving any support to the idea that justification depends in any way on subjective feelings of certainty. Nobody attains to apprehension merely by feeling confident about the veridicality of his experience; apprehension is different from misplaced certainty because it is *right*. However, how is this to be ensured? The obvious move is to go beyond the agent's immediate feelings

---

[9] D. Davidson, in 'Reality without Reference', *Dialectica* 31 (1977), 247–58, even takes the extreme view that a Tarski-style theory of truth can be used to *construct* a theory of reference, rather than using reference to construct a theory of truth.

to his employment of reason or *logos*. There have to be rational
procedures for checking and certifying that the presentation concerned does fulfil the conditions necessary for assent to be
bestowed, and these are stringent, since the presentation must
reflect the object with exactness in its utter particularity.[10]
Apprehension must go beyond the immediate experience and
give it some kind of context.

This is an attractive idea. It is all very well for Austin to claim
that there just are obvious differences between being presented
to the Pope and imagining or dreaming being presented to the
Pope (*Sense and Sensibilia*, 48–9). The sceptic can always reply that
no experience can guarantee its own veridicality. Whatever the
difference or differences claimed to be criterial for judging between
veridical and non-veridical experience, there could be an experience that had all the favoured marks but was not veridical. This
was the response immediately made by the sceptical Academy, and
one would like to think that it did not catch the Stoics completely
unawares. How could anyone think that presentations just are
apprehensible or not, as if this were like the obvious empirical
difference between being and not being red?

Apprehension is assent to the right sort of presentation in the
right sort of way. Now assent or holding true requires a proposition, or at least some proposition-like entity. This is a point made
early on by Arcesilaus (*M* VII 154) and one which it was natural
for the Stoics to accept, given their stress in the logical writings
on assertion, truth, and proposition. For them 'true' and 'false'
have their primary application to propositions, so even though
presentations are true or false, this is so by virtue of some
proposition's being true or false in each case. This is clear from
the account offered by Sextus as *M* VII 244. So a presentation
must be the kind of thing which has a content which can be
expressed in propositional form. As Striker puts it ([133], 134):
'The Stoics seem to have thought that sense impressions are
transformed into propositions by a kind of automatic translation

---

[10] Cicero (*Acad.* I 42) says that apprehension is so called 'non quod omnia quae
essent in re comprehenderet, sed quia nihil quod cadere in eam posset relinqueret'
(cf. Sandbach [121], 14), which supports the idea that the presentation need not
reflect the object in *all* its particularity. But in view of *M* VII 252, the point must be
that the presentation does reflect its object in a uniquely particular way, but that not
all facts about the object are relevant to doing this.

(cf. DL VII 49). One has only to read the British Empiricists to realize that the transition from mental images to meanings of words may seem to be an easy one.'

So a presentation, while in itself an imprint or alteration, not the kind of thing which can be true or false, is to be thought of as something with a content which can be expressed in a proposition, and this is true or false. 'The Stoics say that some sensibles and some intelligibles are true, but the sensibles not directly but by reference to their corresponding intelligibles' (*M* VIII 10). This need, on this interpretation, to bring in something other than the mere imprint, may explain why other criteria of a predominantly intellectualist nature are attributed to the Stoics, like 'right reason' and in particular 'perception and (pre)conception' (*aisthēsis* and *prolēpsis*) attributed to Chrysippus. These are not, however, to be regarded as alternative criteria to the apprehensible presentation, but rather as necessary conditions for there to be an occurrence of a criterial apprehensible presentation. If we do take them as having criterial force, we get bizarre results, as in Gould's account ([74], 48–66). Gould claims that, at any rate for Chrysippus, the question of whether we accept a sense-presentation as coming from a real object, or as being a mere hallucination or phantasm, is settled by whether or not it coheres with the concepts or common notions that we have built up. Orestes in his madness thought that his presentations of the Furies came from real objects; in his right mind he would have known that this was not so. 'Why? Because they were not sufficiently like the family of presentations of young girls which he has stored away in his memory. No one of *them* has dragon-like features. It is this family of presentations or this common notion which exercises the decisive control, and this, I believe, is the reason why Chrysippus calls common notions the *chief criteria* of truth.' However, the platitude that we tend to dismiss 'wild' sensory experiences that we cannot bring under familiar concepts, as being hallucinatory, has no tendency to show that these concepts are our criterion for truth. On Gould's interpretation, when Captain Cook first saw a dodo, since he could not bring this experience under any concept that he already possessed, this showed that dodos did not really exist; but this is absurd.

More is required, then, than merely bringing the sense-experience under the concepts possessed by the agent. What is required is indicated by the presence of 'right reason' (*orthos logos*) as one of the Stoic criteria; the sense-experience must fit into the rational system of perceptions and beliefs that the percipient has. It must be tested by rational procedures to see if it fulfils the conditions laid down for being an apprehensible presentation: does it come from an existing object, and does it mirror this in all its particularity so accurately that it could not be illusory? The presentation must be tested and checked by the perceiver's reason, i.e. presumably, by whatever rational procedures he has mastery of.[11]

So far, apprehension guarantees the apprehensibility of a presentation by fitting it into the system of concepts the perceiver has, where the determining factor is not their possibly varying and fortuitous content, but the rational structure of the system and the rationality of the testing procedures recognized as authoritative. This looks very like a coherence theory of truth, and this is indeed what we find in the expositions of Watson and of Rist. Watson makes the claim about coherence most explicitly ([80], 37, 51, 53): '. . . the new piece of information must fit into the so far established world picture, and *katalēpsis* cannot be separated from *logos*, the particular act from the general disposition. For truth, then, there must be coherence.' Coherence seems to be a sufficient condition for truth: 'The private articulation of reality . . . can be relied upon because its coherence is guaranteed by the very nature of Logos'; 'If coherence is the guarantee of truth, incoherence will be responsible for *error*'.

This interpretation gives due prominence to the way that the Stoic theory of truth fits their doctrines about Logos and the articulated rational system it forms. It also does justice to the way in which presentations have an articulable content which can be assented to. If assenting to a presentation involves assenting to a proposition or *lekton*, then a coherence theory of truth seems more obvious: the truth of the presentation is guaranteed by the place it finds within the whole coherent system of Logos embodied in *lekta*. The Kantian tone of this may cause us discomfort; I shall come back to this discomfort and try to make it more precise, but

---

[11] The notion of testing by rational procedures seems to be a point on which Stoics and sceptics may have influenced each other fruitfully, though of course they differed fundamentally over the degree of certainty such procedures could yield. (Compare *M* VII 242 ff. with Carneades' suggested procedure at VII 166–90.)

first I shall consider Rist's view in more detail, since it adds an important factor.

Rist stresses the role of apprehension and makes it, in so far as it expresses Logos, criterial for a presentation's being apprehensible, because he wants to stress the role of the wise man in Stoic epistemology. This is no accident since he clearly wishes to bring the wise man's epistemological role more into line with his moral role. In doing so, Rist is led to bring out some extreme consequences of the coherence view, which are not so obvious in what Watson says (though they are, I think, implicit in it).

Like Watson, Rist links the percipient's apprehension with the whole rational system of Logos which individuals may grasp and exemplify only to a very imperfect degree. This brings out clearly an implication of the coherence interpretation which has hitherto been missed, namely that since individuals partake of Logos to varying degrees, it will be the wise man, and not just anybody, who will have properly used the correct rational procedures to test the credentials of a proffered presentation, and who will therefore be the one to certify it as being in fact an apprehensible one. Someone with less grasp of these rational procedures—inclined, perhaps, to haste and carelessness and the other defects to be removed by a training in Stoic dialectic—may not achieve this, and his hurried and ill-informed judgement may not be correct as to the truth of presentations. (DL VII 46 catalogues the relevant virtues; among them is *amataiotēs* or 'non-empty-headedness', the disposition to refer presentations to 'correct reason', *orthos logos*.) It is, then, the wise man, intelligent and informed, who gives a presentation its certificate as being apprehensible. According to Rist, 'In Zeno's picture of the process of grasping facts, only the wise man will assent to every particular recognizable presentation in so far as it is recognizable.' (Quotations are from Rist [33], 133–51.) If assent to a presentation is a free act which the wise can bring off correctly while the ignorant and ill informed cannot, there can be nothing about the presentation *itself* which compels assent. If there were, then wise and foolish alike would be compelled to assent, and there would be no room for the wisdom of the wise man to make any difference to his judgement; in which case it would not be the Logos embodied in him which certified the presentation as valid. Here the intrinsic nature of the presentation does drop out as irrelevant to the criterion, and we get a pure coherence theory, with the implication that what Rist calls 'recognizable presentations' need not always be recognized. '. . . Although they ought to be believed, they are not always believed. Only the wise man will have the sense to believe them in all cases. It would, then, be incorrect to call these presentations "irresistible" . . .' 'Although they ought to be believed, there is no reason for saying that they must be believed, let alone that they will be believed.'

Rist gets support from the passage at *M* VII 253–7 where it is said that 'younger Stoics' added to the criterion the condition that there must be 'no obstacle' if there is to be assent. For we have cases like that of Admetus seeing Alcestis returning from the dead, where there is an apprehensible presentation but the percipient does *not* recognize it as such, and does so only when given further information enabling him to understand the overall situation. Rist stresses the fact that even where there is no obstacle in these cases, the apprehensible presentation only 'practically' (*monon oukhi*, 257) drags us by the hair to assent. Even in these cases, he claims, they cannot have held that we *have* to assent; if this was their doctrine then it must have been unorthodox. But this is one of the comparatively few cases where we do find a *change* in doctrine recorded, presumably to meet objections, and we cannot decide on the basis of it what 'orthodoxy' must have been.

A strong objection to Rist is that he assimilates apprehension too much to knowledge in making it the preserve of the wise. In Zeno's illustration, knowledge was a further stage, involving support by other truths. Knowledge for the Stoics was always *systematic*. But nothing more is needed to get us there if we need coherence with the body of accepted beliefs before we have apprehension. However, knowledge should not differ from apprehension in too minimal a way. One of the few things we do know about Zeno is that he distinguished apprehension from knowledge on the grounds that it was *not* the preserve of the wise. 'Between knowledge and ignorance he placed that apprehension of which I have spoken, and he did not count it a peculiarity of either the good or the bad' (*Acad.* I 42). This is echoed by Sextus (*M* VII 152 ff.) who tells us that Arcesilaus objected to precisely this doctrine.

Even if we avoid this mistake, however, there are other objections to a coherence interpretation. Firstly, there is the problem inevitable for any coherence theory, namely that if coherence is sufficient for truth (as it must be if the presentation has no intrinsic feature compelling our assent) then the world seems to drop out. Truth is assured by the way an individual bit of information fits, or fails to, into the coherent overall world-picture; but this idea has plausibility only for some types of statement, and is least plausible for the type that the Stoics were most interested in. Coherence has plausibility as a test only for highly abstract or theoretical statements, hardly for perceptual reports, which are the paradigm of statements whose truth-values can be established one by one, in a non-holistic way. This difficulty is sharpened by the fact that the Stoics give such ontological and logical prominence to particulars and to statements about them. On a coherence interpretation, since beliefs stand or fall as a body, this emphasis is odd, or just a mistake. Further, the sceptics attacked the doctrine of apprehensible presentations on the assumption that these could be tested individually, without going beyond the bounds of the particular experience. They have been criticized for doing this (by Watson, for example, [80], 68–9), but what they were doing was surely the natural, not the unnatural thing to do.

A second objection is the absurdity of the result that the wise man is the authority and the norm on accepting presentations; for while he might well be the filter for moral views, how can he be the norm for the deliverances of *sensation*? We cannot avoid this difficulty, because the empiricist cast of Stoicism demands that apprehensible presentations come through the senses. But if the wise man is the perceptual norm, then not only is he the only wise, beautiful, sane man, and so on, he is the only man with 20–20 vision, good hearing etc. What could 20–20 vision be, other than the state of the wise man's visual apparatus? But this is ridiculous. Being wise and good may improve your judgement about many things, but it can't do anything for your eyesight.

Thirdly, this view can do nothing with important features of the apprehensible presentation as it is defined for us several times in the sources. We are told that it is something that comes from an existing object, and that it is 'stamped and sealed' in accordance with the nature of the object. One is tempted by this language to think of it as a kind of mental picture or image, reflecting the

features of the object producing it. But whether or not it should
be thought of as a picture, it is certainly a *representational* item.
However, since on the coherence interpretation what are accepted
or rejected are judgements which express the content of the
presentation, there is no obvious way in which its representational
features can be what make it an apprehensible one. But it is these
features that are stressed in Zeno's definition and any variants on
it; these do not even mention the proposition expressing the
articulable content, but tell us that a presentation is apprehensible
when it creates an impression which presents its object in such a
way that it could not be confused with any other object whatsoever. It is the representational features which are to compel
our assent; so on a view according to which our assent is not
compelled, they are redundant. They are even somewhat misleading, since they suggest that anybody has to assent to a
representation if it is apprehensible; which on this interpretation
is not true.

We do, then, seem to be forced back on to some form of the
correspondence interpretation: there is something in the nature
of the presentation itself which makes it apprehensible. We do
not create the perceptible world, as the coherence view is in
danger of falling into holding; we face it, and it barrages us with
presentations, some of which are veridical and some not.

An important point here is that from the philosophical point of
view the representational nature of the Stoic presentation may be
misleading. We grasp the presentation and through it grasp the
object: the presentations thus do form a screen between us and
the real things they come from. Modern representational theories
of this type tend to regard themselves as being vulnerable to the
sceptical challenge that perhaps all we can really know are the
presentations; we can never penetrate through to the real things
that cause them. Attempts to meet the sceptic tend to take the
form of trying to show that there can be a convincing argument
to bridge this gap; and since this endeavour has never prospered,
it tends to be assumed that a representational theory is a mere
half-way house, an unsatisfactory position that is already in pawn
to the sceptic and already doomed. The Stoic theory, however,
is philosophically much nearer to that familiar Aunt Sally, pre-
sceptical naïve realism. For if a presentation is of such a sort that

it cannot be false, it can be grasped as securely as the object itself can for a naïve realist. What does it matter if a presentation intervenes between me and the table, if the presentation is such that it cannot but be veridical? The claim that my experiences can be relied upon to be veridical, in standard cases, has the same status for both theories. The correspondence interpretation commits one to thinking of the Stoics as naïve realists of a type;[12] there just are some presentations which are self-intimatingly veridical.

The first major objection to this interpretation is that it gives the Stoics a theory which is *too* naïve, disagreeably so. It is simply dogmatism to insist that some presentations just are apprehensible, announcing their own veridicality. Moreover, the objections are overwhelmingly obvious. Arcesilaus at once objected that there could be, for any true presentation, a false one which was indistinguishable from it (*M* VII 401 ff.). Moreover, Sextus' 'younger Stoics' may have recognized this point and tried to meet it when they admitted that there were apprehensible presentations which did not in fact receive assent because there was an 'obstacle', as in the case of Admetus and that of Menelaus meeting the real Helen in Egypt. If this is the case, then apprehensible presentations cannot in every case be self-announcing and compel our assent, and we have to face the objection put succinctly by Sandbach ([121], 18–19): 'How are such presentations to be recognized? How is a man to know that he is right to give them his assent?' It is prima facie undesirable to give the Stoics a theory so naïve as to be helpless in the face of this reasonable challenge.

There is an obvious response to this. This is to claim that the sceptical question cannot be answered, but that this does not matter because properly speaking it should not even arise; we have to take some things for granted, and in matters of perception the reasonable place to stop and refuse sceptical challenges is at the level of statements that everyone would agree on. This seems to have been the defence offered by Antiochus (*Acad.* II 17 ff.), and it is promising; it has interesting affinities with modern holistic arguments which deny the need for foundations in epistemological enterprises. Since the Stoics prided themselves on the holistic character of their system, we would expect this

[12] Cf. Schofield, Chapter 11, pp. 284–6 below.

form of argument to appeal; but this does not seem to have been the case. The only defences of their position that we can find, apart from attempts to undermine their opponents' arguments, are distressingly unsophisticated. There is, for example, the claim at *M* VII 260, that it is mad to admit that there are objects and deny that we can have a grasp of them; which begs the question at issue completely. Further, the argument retailed at *M* VII 155–7, to the effect that if there are no apprehensible presentations then nothing will be securely grasped and the wise man will have to suspend judgement, shows that the Stoics were committed to a foundationalist approach.

Interestingly, we are told that Chrysippus wrote in defence of 'common sense and the senses' (Plu. *Stoic. rep.* 1036 cd)—though we are also told that he undermined the ostensible aim by providing better arguments against their trustworthiness than for it—so it is not impossible that he may have held that the only philosophical defence possible, or needed, for the idea that apprehensible presentations are self-announcing, was a common-sense one. Sandbach presents such a defence:

There must be some presentations that are immediately acceptable, that are self-evidently true. That is what constitutes a cognitive presentation. It is the attitude of common-sense that most presentations are of this sort. In ordinary life every man has no doubt that what 'appears to him' is really there, that the sun *is* shining, that those objects are pomegranates, that a waggon and horses are bearing down on him. ([121], 19)

However, will this do? We might well expect the sceptic to respond, 'So what?' In ordinary life every man has no doubt that health is better than disease, and that incest is always wrong, but the Stoic wise man is supposed to correct him on these. Why should his views on pomegranates be incorrigible? Indeed the pomegranates example reminds us embarrassingly that there are occasions when the ordinary man, and even someone more careful, can be put right, as Sphaerus was.

The commonsense view can be backed up by the consideration that we must found our beliefs somewhere so that we can get on with the more important business of living in a good manner. Pohlenz says of Zeno that for him it was a 'praktisches Postulat' that we can have some reliable knowledge. But this seems misguided. Is a commonsense epistemology the *right* 'praktisches Postulat' for a moral theory as revisionary as Zeno's? Why is it all right to found all knowledge on the plain man's beliefs about the world, when this very knowledge will overturn some of his most cherished beliefs in the spheres of morals, physics, and logic? While the coherence interpretation falls into absurdity by making the wise man the perceptual norm, this view falls into the opposite error of being too determinedly commonsensical. Even if the Stoics *were* concerned only to get on to the ethics and metaphysics, and to cobble up any old theory of knowledge to get going, the naïve correspondence theory would be the *least* obviously suitable theory. The coherence theory fits in much better with the moral theories and the role in them of the wise man.

Thirdly, just as the coherence interpretation could do little with the features of the apprehensible presentation that made it a representation of an object, so the correspondence interpretation can do little with the feature that plays a vital part in the coherence interpretation, namely the fact that the presentation receives assent and so must have an articulable content the expression of which is a proposition. Since on this view it is the representational features of the presentation itself that guarantee that the perception is veridical, the assent we make to the articulation of its content is not what makes it apprehensible. Indeed, on this view it is hard to see why we need to bring in the idea of assenting to a presentation, rather than to a proposition associated with a presentation. The presentation announces itself; we grasp it; any assent to an articulable content registers this grasp, but is redundant from the epistemological point of view. Sandbach is instructively embarrassed by the relation of assent and presentation. He says ([121], 13) that the presentation gives information about the external object, and that 'it is this information to which we can assent or refuse to assent.' But then it is strictly speaking not the case that what we assent to is the *presentation*, and what the Stoics actually say has to be called misleading. 'The proposition "There is an apple" is not identical with the presentation, but is in some sense included in it, and put before the mind by it. Hence, although it may be inaccurate, it is psychologically intelligible to say that one assents to a presentation' ([34], 88). However psychologically intelligible, it is misleading if it suggests that assent is what is epistemologically basic, for on this view that cannot be so.

If we bear this in mind, we may be more sympathetic to Arcesilaus' objection (*M* VII 154) to the Stoics, that strictly speaking one assents not to a presentation but to a proposition (*logos*). This is usually dismissed as a carping and pedantic point, since after all the Stoics did have an explicit and fairly clear account of how presentations are true and false in a way derivative from the truth and falsity of propositions. But Arcesilaus was raising this point as an objection to the specific claim that *apprehension* was assent to an *apprehensible* presentation, not the claim that we assent to presentations in general; and in this context he is surely making a good point. If an apprehensible presentation is what Zeno defined it to be, then apprehension should be a matter of our being struck by the representational features which were the subject of Arcesilaus' dispute with Zeno; and in that case, while we might be caused as a result to assent to some proposition, it is misleading to say that we assent to the presentation itself. This suggests that it is up to us to decide whether or not the presentation reflects its object with utter faithfulness; but it is precisely this that the definitions were concerned to deny; according to them, in some cases a presentation is so utterly faithful to its original that we just cannot reject it, and, if so, assent to its propositional content must be secondary.

In fact there is a certain unavoidable tension in the apprehensible presentation and the way it has both representational features and an articulable content. Of course there is no conflict between these features as such, and on any account of truth it must be the case that what is assented to is a propositional item, so that the presentation must have both kinds of features. The problem arises when we press the question, what makes the apprehensible presentation the criterion of truth; for it is hard to see how both sets of features can be essential to a presentation's being an apprehensible one. If it is our assent, backed up by Logos, which certifies the presentation as being apprehensible, then the accuracy with which it reflects or pictures its object seems to be dispensable —indeed, it can be overruled. And if what makes it apprehensible is just the utterly unmistakable and particular way it reflects its object, and we cannot resist this, then the fact of our assent registers this, but cannot be what makes the presentation apprehensible, and so appears redundant from the standpoint of its being the criterion of truth.

The conflict of the coherence and correspondence interpretations on this point suggest that the Stoics were, in fact, unclear about the relation of perception and thought.[13] The coherence interpretation gives them a philosophically more interesting theory, while the correspondence interpretation does more justice to the texts. The notion that what is epistemologically basic is the encounter between perceiver and representational item, and that assent is derivative, fits what we are told about the way propositional thinking derives from the input of sense. ' . . .Presentation comes first; then thought, which is capable of expressing itself, puts into the form of a proposition that which the subject receives from a presentation' (DL VII 49). On the coherence view, since assent is primary, general concepts are already required for there to be an apprehensible presentation; and this seems to get the Stoic picture of concept-acquisition the wrong way round. It may be claimed that this objection conflates the genetic question of how thought is produced as a result of sensory experience, with the different question of whether experience is epistemologically more basic than propositional thought. But the Stoics show no signs at all of recognizing such a distinction, any more than Locke does, and it is not helpful to import it into an interpretation of them.

We have seen that both interpretations have a good deal of footing in the evidence and the general probabilities about Stoic doctrine. Both explain some puzzling facts about the doctrine of apprehensible presentations, while keeping, or even creating, other difficulties. I have tried to indicate, in the way I have characterized the lines of thought, why this might be so. Proponents of the coherence view concentrate on the question of how we can know that some of our experiences are veridical. They find the correspondence interpretation unsatisfactory because it has no way of coping with this demand, and appears crude. Proponents of the correspondence interpretation are impressed by evidence

---

[13] This comes out in the waverings of interpreters on this point. Stough [29], 36–7 and n. 7, can do even less with the connection between representational features and propositional content than Sandbach. Kneale [43], 150–1, doubts, given the evidence, that the Stoics had a clear theory here.

suggesting that the Stoics clung to the belief that there really are some experiences which cannot but be veridical. The fact that neither interpretation can be ruled out and that both have much plausibility suggests that the Stoics never sorted out the two distinct questions, 'Are there any experiences whose veridicality can be guaranteed?' and, 'Can we know that there are any experiences whose veridicality can be guaranteed?'

Such evidence as we have suggests that Zeno began with a naïve theory that never envisioned that the two questions might be different. He laid it down that there were some experiences which were guaranteed as veridical and were self-intimatingly so. The sceptical attack, begun by Arcesilaus in Zeno's lifetime, concentrated on the second claim: there could be a presentation, they countered, that was in all respects like an apprehensible one, but false, and indistinguishable *as far as we know*. The 'younger Stoics', moving to meet this kind of objection by insisting that there must be 'no obstacle' for an apprehensible presentation to serve as the criterion, were both bringing in considerations of coherence, and thinking about conditions for knowledge rather than conditions for truth. So on the whole the correspondence interpretation fits Zeno's original definitions best, whilst the coherence interpretation best fits the theory of the 'younger Stoics' who had made some defensive moves against the sceptical attack. However, we cannot find a radical change of doctrine, as Pohlenz did. Nor can we find a recognition of the difference between a theory of knowledge and a theory of truth. If there had been either, the debate with the sceptics would surely not have dragged on for so long so inconclusively, and with its tendency to produce the frustrated feeling that each side was talking past the other.

It is no accident, then, that there is something deeply unsatisfactory about the Stoic candidates for answering the question, 'What is the criterion of truth?' The claim that there are apprehensible presentations is sometimes seen as an answer to the problem of what makes our statements about the world true, and sometimes seen as an answer to the problem of how we can be assured of knowing anything. And the Stoics are never quite sure whether they are producing a 'naturalized epistemology' or refuting Cartesian doubts.

This is all the more frustrating since in another context they made a distinction about truth which is very relevant to the matter in hand.

A distinction which we are informed about in some detail through Sextus is the Stoic distinction between truth (*hē alētheia*) and the true (*to alēthes*).[14] The formulation, which does not at once suggest anything very obviously comprehensible to us, is explained as follows (*PH* II 81–3):

> The true is said to differ from truth in three ways—in essence, composition, potency. In essence (*ousia*) since the true is incorporeal (for it is judgement and 'expression' [*lekton*]) while the truth is a body (for it is knowledge declaratory of all true things, and knowledge is a particular state of the regent part, just as the fist is a particular state of the hand, and the regent part is a body) . . . In composition (*sustasis*), because the true is a simple thing, as for example 'I converse', whereas truth is a compound and many true cognitions. In potency (*dunamis*) since truth depends on knowledge but the true does not altogether so depend.

Thus, truth is a system of true items which is regarded as being known by an agent and therefore as being material, since all mental states and dispositions are identical with physical states. The true, however, is exemplified by a single true proposition, which for the Stoics is an immaterial *lekton*. What is ascribed to the person who has truth is not omniscience (as is pointed out by Long [69], but infallibility: everything claimed to be true by someone who possesses the disposition of knowledge which is the truth, is as he says it is, but it is not implied that he knows everything which is in fact true. The distinction of essence or being comes with the distinction between the true as a proposition and the truth as a state or disposition, since it is part of Stoic metaphysics that the former is incorporeal whilst the latter is identified with a physical state. It is therefore important that the true is a proposition whilst the state which is the truth is not propositional: ' . . . truth does not in Stoicism consist of propositions, but of a coherent and comprehensive structure of valid general concepts . . .' (Long [108]). The third difference, that of *dunamis* or function ('potency' is a bad translation) is harder to explain. Sextus' discussion, however, makes it clear that the distinction resides in the relation of truth and the true to the

---

[14] See Long [107], 98–102, and [108] (where nn. 4 and 5 refer to other discussions).

person concerned, particularly the wise man. Truth is identified with knowledge, and this is not achieved by merely coming out with particular statements which happen to be true. For knowledge more than this is required, principally the building up into a systematic structure which is so often stressed in Stoic epistemology. The wise man's disposition is knowledge: without it we have the true but not truth, and with it we have the truth even if on a particular occasion we do not have an utterance of the true. Someone with knowledge may utter propositions which are not examples of the true, without losing the truth which he possesses—as when, for example, the wise man deceives people about some occurrence; what he utters is not the true, but he is not lying, because his intent is good and springs from knowledge.

Since truth and the true are so different, we would expect there to be repercussions for any theory of truth, and in particular for the question of the criterion of truth. A criterion of truth guarantees that what is said is as it is said to be. But much will hang on whether we have an example of the truth or an example of the true. For a particular proposition might report things correctly and yet, although being an example of the true, not be an example of the truth, because not asserted by someone with knowledge. The true does not imply truth.

Nowhere in the sources are there any indications that this distinction between truth and the true was thought relevant to the question of the criterion of truth. Sextus reports the distinction at length, yet never attaches it to considerations about the criterion. And yet the distinction does seem to be highly relevant. Of course the Stoics might well use the expression 'criterion of truth' in common with other philosophical schools, without meaning to confine it to truth in their sense (as opposed to the true),[15] but this does not totally explain the absence of connection we find.

Prima facie there ought to be a difference of criterion between truth and the true. For truth is a coherent system, is identified with knowledge, and is the possession of the good and wise man. Whereas the true is not yet a system, does not yet amount to knowledge, and can concern particulars which all are competent to judge about.

[15] That they did talk of a 'criterion of truth' is strongly suggested by DL VII 54; cf. also VII 49, and VII 46.

Now obviously these differences reflect rather strikingly the different views of the criterion of truth which I have labelled the coherence and correspondence interpretations. For if the coherence interpretation is right, it is, ultimately, Logos which certifies a presentation as being apprehensible; and in this case Logos forms a coherent system and the presentation is accepted because it fits in; we find surprisingly little distinction between apprehension and knowledge; and the wise man is the guarantor of truth. On the other hand, if the presentations report on their faces that they are apprehensible, then they can be reported in particular statements that are examples of the true; apprehension of them does not yet amount to knowledge; and the wise man has no obvious advantage over the plain man when it comes to getting them right. To put it crudely, it looks as though the Stoics need a coherence theory of the truth and a correspondence theory of the true. Since the Stoics never applied this distinction between the truth and the true to the question of the criterion of truth, it is not surprising that both the coherence and the correspondence interpretations have a great deal of plausibility in coping with the evidence.

It is ironical that the Stoics drew this careful distinction between truth and the true, and also probably distinguished different senses of 'criterion'[16] and yet never thought to link the two in any way. If they had done so, perhaps they might have thought that their search for a criterion of truth might be in fact a search for two different things: truth and knowledge. If we go on to ask why this was so, we shall no doubt come up with answers which are too vague and speculative to be really helpful. One very general answer is that they were not working in a philosophical climate conducive to drawing this distinction; their part of philosophy called 'Logic' covered what he would call epistemological questions, and we can see quite well nowadays how a preoccupation with 'philosophical logic' can push epistemological questions into the background.[17] But one point worth mentioning in this connection, of less generality, is the role of the wise man in Stoicism. The wise man is the one with knowledge; he is also the norm. We can discern a tendency (not peculiar to the Stoics,

[16] Striker [21], 102–7, Long [69], 4.

[17] Though the Epicureans may have succeeded in separating the two to some extent; see the essay by C. C. W. Taylor, Chapter 5 below.

of course) to think that reality is what the wise man tells us is so. The considerations that might make this convincing come from the moral sphere, but would tend to prepare the way for accepting the wise man's beliefs, the system of knowledge, as being *constitutive* of reality in any sphere, including that of reporting on everyday experience. Hence we can see the temptation both of the coherence interpretation, which uncomplicatedly makes the wise man the norm in every sphere, and of the correspondence interpretation, which rejects this as absurd at the level of standard perception where we feel intuitively that anybody's honest report is as good as anyone else's. What I have tried to bring out is that there is an unavoidable unclarity in the Stoic views on these topics; but also the fact that this is not a fortuitous problem, but arises from deep sources of disunity within Stoicism itself.[18]

---

[18] I have benefited greatly from discussion at the symposium and the comments of those present. I am especially grateful to Myles Burnyeat, Troels Engberg-Pederson, Anthony Long, Malcolm Schofield, and David Sedley.

Since writing this paper I have read Kerferd [96], where he defends the view that *phantasiai* are true or false, and objects of assent, directly and not in a sense derivative from that applying to propositions. I think, however, that this is compatible with my claim that there is a tension between *phantasia* as representational item, and *phantasia* as truth-bearer (either directly or indirectly).

'ALL PERCEPTIONS ARE TRUE'[1]

C. C. W. Taylor

Epicurus is reported by Diogenes Laertius (X 31) as having said that perceptions (or perhaps 'the senses' or 'sense-impressions', which are also possible meanings of Epicurus's own term *aisthēseis*) are among the criteria of truth; this report is confirmed by two passages of Epicurus himself, at DL X 50–2 and 147. By itself this need imply nothing more than the merest common sense; of course perception and the senses must have some role in determining what is the case and what is not, and hence which statements are true and which are false. But the matter is not so straightforward. For, firstly, *aisthēsis* and related words are used in a wider range of contexts than 'perceptions' and its cognates: e.g. cases of hallucination are sometimes said to involve *aisthēsis* (see below). Secondly, Epicurus is also said to have maintained the much more obviously controversial thesis that every *aisthēsis* is true. In this paper I shall try to establish what he meant by those statements, to clarify the relation between them, and to consider their wider implications for his epistemological and physical theory.

I turn first to the doctrine that all *aisthēseis* are true, for which the evidence has been helpfully collected by Gisela Striker [133]. No version of it occurs in the texts of Epicurus himself, but the following doctrines, or versions of the same doctrine, are attributed to him by other writers.

1. Every *aisthēton* is true (*M* VIII 9: *Ep. ta men aisthēta panta elegen alēthē kai onta . . . pantōn de tōn aisthētōn alēthōn ontōn;* 63: *Ep. elege men panta ta aisthēta einai alēthē, kai pasan phantasian apo huparchontos einai . . .*). Cf. ibid. 355, every *aisthēton* is reliable (*bebaion*).

[1] I am indebted to the participants in the Oxford conference for pointing out serious defects in the original version of this paper. I trust that I have profited from their criticisms. I am especially grateful to Gisela Striker, from whose publications on this topic I have learned a great deal, and to Malcolm Schofield and David Sedley for their detailed suggestions for improvements.

2. Every *aisthēsis* and every *phantasia* is true (Usener [13], no. 248: Aetius; Usener [13], p. 349, 5–6: Aristocles *apud* Eus.).

3. Every *phantasia* occurring by means of *aisthēsis* is true (Plu. *Col.* 1109 ab).

4. Every *phantasia* is true (*M* VII 203–4, 210).

5. *Aisthēsis* always tells the truth (*M* VIII 9: *tēn te aisthēsin . . . dia pantos te alētheuein*; 185: *mēdepote pseudomenēs tēs aisthēseōs*). Cf. the passages in Cicero referred to by Striker, to the effect that the senses are always truthful.

It appears likely that most of these formulations differ from one another only verbally. Thus Sextus is the only writer cited above to use the term *aisthēton* ('sense-content'[2]), and his use of the term strongly suggests that it is interchangeable with *phantasia* ('appearance'). This appears particularly from *M* VII 203–4, where the thesis that *phantasia* is always true is supported by a number of examples from the various senses, e.g. 'The visible (*horaton*) not only appears (*phainetai*) visible, but in addition is of the same kind as it appears to be', which are summed up in the words 'So all *phantasiai* are true.' Here, then, what is true of *aisthēta* is taken to be true of *phantasiai* as a whole; further evidence that Sextus regards the terms as coextensive is given by *M* VIII 63–4, where he represents Epicurus as counting Orestes' hallucination of the Furies as a case of *aisthēsis*, and therefore as true. Again, in the passage from Aristocles cited above, quoted by Eusebius, *aisthēsis* is treated as interchangeable with *phantasia*, since the thesis introduced by means of both terms (i.e. 2 above), is expressed in the course of the passage firstly as the thesis that every *aisthēsis* is true and then as the thesis that every *phantasia* is true. If these writers treat *aisthēton* and *phantasia* as strictly coextensive terms, they misrepresent Epicurus, who distinguishes *phantasiai* of the mind (e.g. appearances in dreams) from *phantasiai*

---

[2] I use the term 'sense-content' as roughly equivalent to the Greek *aisthēton*, to indicate the informational content of a perceptual or quasi-perceptual act, without commitment to the objective reality of that content. For example, if some honey tastes sweet to me, I have an *aisthēton* of the sweet, whether or not the honey really is sweet. I interpret Epicurus as holding that in every instance of *aisthēsis* we have some sense-contents, as regarding hallucinations as instances of *aisthēsis*, and as saying of cases of perceptual illusion such as that of the oar's looking bent that the sense-content is true, though some belief which we may form as a result of having that sense-content may be false.

of the senses (DL X 50–1). In strict Epicurean doctrine, then, *aisthēta* are a species of *phantasiai*. But the misrepresentation is not crucial, since Epicurus clearly holds that both sensory and non-sensory *phantasiai* are always true (ibid.: for the Epicurean view of the 'truth' of dreams, see below). In the passages from Sextus cited under 5 above, where *aisthēsis* is said always to tell the truth and never to lie, it is possible to render the word as 'sense' (equivalent to 'the senses'), 'perception', 'sensation' (i.e. the faculties thereof), 'the (particular act of) perception', or 'the (particular) sensation (occurring in the perceptual context)'. But however we render it, the thesis that *aisthēsis* always tells the truth is presented either as following immediately from the central thesis that all *aisthēta* are true, or as entailing it, or as restating it. The precise logical relation of the two theses (if indeed they are two) is impossible to determine from these passages; by the same token, their intimate logical interconnection is displayed by both. Our evidence, then, indicates that ancient writers regularly attribute to Epicurus or the Epicureans the doctrines that every *phantasia* is true and that every *aisthēton* is true. Though strictly *aisthēta* are a species of *phantasiai*, differentiated by their causation via the sense-organs, some later sources appear to make no distinction between the terms. In some reports the doctrine that every *aisthēton* is true appears to be expressed as 'Every *aisthēsis* is true'; in others, where *aisthēsis* may mean 'sense' or 'faculty', the thesis that *aisthēsis* always tells the truth is inextricably interwoven with the thesis that all *aisthēta* are true.

We find, then, in the texts of Epicurus the doctrine that sense-contents are among our criteria for discriminating what is true from what is false, and we find ascribed to Epicurus by later writers the doctrine that all sense-contents are true. This ascription is confirmed by Epicurus' remarks at DL X 50–2, though the doctrine is not explicitly stated there. Some of these writers clearly regard Epicurus as holding that the former doctrine implies the latter, and as maintaining the latter because he was committed to it by the former. Thus Aristocles (loc. cit.) says that people who hold that every *aisthēsis* and every *phantasia* is true do so from the fear that, if they said that any *aisthēseis* were false, they would have no criterion nor any sure or reliable standard (sc. of truth). Similarly Plutarch interprets the Epicurean thesis that all *phantasiai* arising by means of *aisthēsis* are true as leading to

the consequence that all perceptible objects are a mixture of all
the qualities which they seem to have in any conditions of perception; the Epicureans accept *that*, he says, because if they didn't
they admit that their standards would go to pot and their criterion
altogether disappear (*Col.* 1109 a–e). Did Epicurus in fact hold
that if *aisthēseis* are among our criteria of truth, then *aisthēseis* must
themselves be true? And if he did, can we see why?

This second question may appear surprising. To some people
it may just seem obvious that any criterion of truth must itself
be true, and anyone who thinks so will naturally assume that it
must have been obvious to Epicurus also. But so far from being
obvious, it is not even true. By 'criterion' we understand 'something used in discriminating, judging, or determining'.[3] In
general, it is plainly false that, whenever we distinguish F from
G (where 'F' and 'G' stand in for names of properties), that by
means of which we distinguish is either F or G. This may be so
in some cases, e.g. we may discriminate straight from crooked
lines by applying a straight ruler (*kanōn*). But, while it is true that
Epicurus used the term *kanōn* as equivalent to *kritērion* (*apud* DL
X 129: his work dealing with criteria of truth was entitled *Kanōn*,
DL X 31), it would be gratuitous to suppose that he reached his
doctrine by generalizing from this single instance in the face of
the multitude of counter-instances where the terms *kanōn* and
kritērion are equally at home. Thus, in the required sense of
'criterion' taste is the criterion of sweet and sour, but taste (i.e.
the sense of taste) is itself neither sweet nor sour; sight is the
criterion of black and white, but is itself neither black nor white.
The general point holds also for the special case of distinguishing
truth from falsity. Thus sometimes we find out the truth about
some matter by looking, but it does not make sense to say that
looking is true (or that it is false). Thus to attribute to Epicurus
either the general assumption that any criterion of F-ness must
itself be F, or the special assumption that any criterion of truth
must itself be true, is to attribute to him a fairly obvious falsehood.
There is, however, no need to attribute either assumption to him.
Rather, the evidence indicates that he held that all *aisthēseis* must
be true because of the particular sort of criterion that *aisthēseis* are,
and that his reasons for holding that a criterion of *that* sort must

[3] See Striker [21].

itself be true were better than the untenable assumptions which we have just dismissed. The sort of criterion in question is *evidence*. *Aisthēseis* are used in discriminating truth from falsehood in that they provide evidence on the basis of which we judge (*krinomen*) what is true and what false, just as the evidence of witnesses in a court is used by the judge to determine the truth of the matter in dispute. And just as the evidence of the witnesses must itself be true in order that a sound verdict be arrived at, so the evidence of *aisthēseis* must be true if we are to attain to knowledge of the world. The choice of forensic terminology is not, of course, accidental, but rather reflects Epicurus' own descriptions of the role of *aisthēseis*. They are treated as witnesses in a legal action, whose word may be challenged or accepted, and whose evidence may be used to establish the claims of other parties as true, or convict them as false. So at DL X 146: 'If you fight against all *aisthēseis*, you will not have anything by reference to which you can pass judgement on those which you say have spoken falsely.' Here *aisthēseis* say things, and the sceptic is inclined to condemn them as lying witnesses. (*Anagōgē*, 'referral', can also have a legal sense, that of referring a dispute to an arbitrator, as in a third-century treaty from Delphi.[4]) The forensic analogy is reflected in the Epicurean terminology for the process by which beliefs are confirmed or refuted by the evidence of *aisthēseis*; a belief is true if it is 'witnessed for' (*epimartureitai*) or 'not witnessed against' (*ouk antimartureitai*), false if it is witnessed against or not witnessed for (DL X 50-1; cf. *M* VII 210-16). *Aisthēseis*, then, are reliable witnesses; nothing can convict them of falsehood (*dielengksai*). Since what they say is true, we may use it as evidence (*sēmeia*) from which to arrive by inference at conclusions about what we are not directly aware of (ibid. *hothen kai peri tōn adēlōn apo tōn phainomenōn chrē sēmeiousthai*; cf. DL X 38, 87, 97, 104).

It is, then, the forensic analogy of the evidential role of *aisthēsis* which commits Epicurus to the doctrine that *aisthēseis* are true, rather than the implausible assumptions which I dismissed earlier. That analogy itself does not support the thesis that *all aisthēseis* must be true: judicial procedures depend on testimony, though witnesses frequently lie, misremember etc. The stronger thesis

---

[4] E. Schwyzer, *Dialectorum Graecarum Exempla Epigraphica Potiora* (Leipzig, 1923), 328a, II A 17.

rather depends on the *basic* character of the evidence of *aisthēseis*. *Aisthēseis* have to be true if we are to have any knowledge or well-founded beliefs about the world; for all such knowledge and belief is inferential, justified ultimately by appeal to the evidence which *aisthēseis* provide. If we challenge any piece of that evidence itself, we can do so only by appeal to further evidence of the same kind, but we can give no reason why we should prefer one piece of evidence to another. Hence the only alternative to total scepticism is undifferentiated acceptance of *aisthēseis* as true (DL X 146–7). Epicurus might then seem to present an early version of the familiar empiricist doctrine of the foundations of knowledge; sense-contents provide the immediate, i.e. non-inferential data by inference from which we arrive at, or at least justify, beliefs about physical objects, other persons etc. But in fact the empiricist doctrine aligns rather awkwardly with the forensic analogy; for on the empiricist view, as represented by Locke or Berkeley, we have immediate and complete knowledge of our sense-contents themselves, and proceed to more or less risky inferences from that knowledge to knowledge and/or belief about the external world. In terms of the forensic analogy, the fundamental empiricist thesis that we have immediate and incorrigible knowledge of our sense-contents ('ideas' in some versions, 'sense-data' in others) would surely have to be expressed as follows, that our sense-contents are totally reliable witnesses *as to what they themselves say*. So if a sense-content says 'My evidence is as follows: *p*', there can be no doubt that that is what its evidence is, namely that *p*. But what we want from a witness is not just to be sure what his evidence is, but in addition to be sure that his evidence is *true*. We want a guarantee not merely that he says that *p*, but that it is true that *p*, and it is clear that the empiricist thesis that we have incorrigible knowledge of what his evidence is cannot provide such a guarantee. So if Epicurus' thesis that all *aisthēseis* are true is interpreted just as the thesis that we cannot be mistaken about what *aisthēseis* we have, it cannot do justice to the evidential role which he assigns to *aisthēseis*.

This brings me to the central question of this paper, viz. what did Epicurus mean by his thesis that all *aisthēseis* are true? We have seen that a superficially plausible account of that thesis, viz. that we have incorrigible awareness of our sense-contents, is insufficient to account adequately for the fundamental status of the thesis in Epicurus's epistemology. We might, of course, be forced to conclude that Epicurus failed to recognize the inadequacy; but at least it provides us with a motive to look for another interpretation which will represent the thesis as complying more closely with Epicurus' intentions. In this connection we must take notice of two connected points which I have hitherto ignored. Firstly, I have taken it for granted that Epicurus' thesis was that all *aistheseis* are *true*, and have raised the question how that is to be understood. But, as is well known, *alethes* may in context mean 'real' rather than 'true', or may be ambiguous between the two senses. Moreover, there is some evidence to suggest that the Epicurean thesis may have been that all *aistheseis* are in some sense real. Secondly, Epicurus appears to have insisted that every *aisthesis*, in contrast with belief, is *alogos*. Whatever that means precisely, there is a prima-facie inconsistency in the claim that what is lacking in *logos* is none the less true, since truth and falsity surely apply in the first instance to *logos* or *logoi*, to speech or things said. This difficulty might be thought to support the suggestion that *alethes* should in this context be understood as 'real' rather than as 'true'. My next task, therefore, is consideration of that suggestion; in the course of that consideration I hope to explain what Epicurus had in mind in describing *aistheseis* as *alogoi*.

The suggestion is derived from two ancient sources, DL X 32 and *M* VIII 9. Diogenes' statement comes at the end of his summary, paraphrased above, of the role of *aistheseis* as a criterion. After describing how thoughts (*epinoiai*) are formed by the operation of various mental processes on *aistheseis*, he adds 'And the visions (*phantasmata*) of madmen and those which occur in dreams are *alethe*, for they have effects (*kinei*); but that which is not has no effect' (*to de me on ou kinei*). Here the thought seems plainly to be that only something real can have any effect on anything. But dreams and visions manifestly have effects, most obviously on the behaviour of those subject to them. So dreams and visions are real things. Sextus is even more explicit. 'Epicurus' he says, 'said that all *aistheta* are *alethe* and things that there are (*onta*); for he made no distinction between calling something *alethes* and calling it existent' (*huparchon*). It is noteworthy that both contexts also contain a reference to the thesis that *aisthesis* is *alogos*. In Diogenes this occurs in 31 immediately after the list of criteria, including *aisthēseis*. Diogenes's words are 'For every *aisthēsis*, he (i.e. Epicurus) says, is *alogos* and receptive of no memory; for it is not stimulated (*kineitai*) by itself, nor, being stimulated by something else, can it add or take away anything.' Sextus' report is similar: 'And *aisthēsis*, which is receptive of the things presented to it, neither taking away nor adding nor altering anything, since it is *alogos*, always tells the truth and receives what there is just as it is in reality (*kai houtō to on lambanein hōs eiche phuseōs auto ekeino*). But while all the *aisthēta* are *alēthē*, the things we believe (*ta doxasta*) differ, and some are true and some false . . .' It is tempting to offer the following explanation of the thesis that *aisthēsis* is *alēthēs* and of its connection with the doctrine that *aisthēsis* is *alogos*. The thesis is simply the thesis that every instance of *aisthēsis*, including dreams and hallucinations under *aisthēseis* since those states consist in the reception of impressions similar to those of perception proper, is a real event, consisting in the reception by the physical organism of a pattern of physical stimulation (in terms of the atomistic theory of mental functioning, a bombardment of large numbers of *eidōla* in very rapid succession). *Aisthēsis* is *alogos* in that *aisthēsis* is the purely physical event of the reception of stimulation; being purely physical it lacks any mental content, and hence cannot be true or false. It merely reproduces the external stimulation without addition or subtraction, as the wax reproduces the impression of the signet which is pressed into it. Truth and falsity belong to the judgements which we make about the physical process of stimulation, characterizing it as the perception of this or that. This interpretation is tempting in so far as it explains how *aisthēseis* could sensibly be described both as *alētheis* and as *alogoi*, in so far as it does justice to the evidence which suggests that *alētheia* should be taken in this context as 'reality', and in so far as it frees Epicurus' theory from such absurdities as the claim that the madman's hallucinations are true.

But these advantages are bought at too high a price. This account suffers from the basic defect of having altogether abandoned the evidential role of *aisthēseis*. For on this account *aisthēseis* themselves don't say anything; they are purely physical events whose occurrence is reported, correctly or incorrectly, in thought. But a witness who says nothing is no witness; and if anything in this area is clear, it is that Epicurus regards *aisthēseis* as witnesses to the reality of things. Further, this interpretation is inadequate even with respect to those very passages adduced in its support. The identification of its inadequacy will, I hope, lead us to a more correct understanding of the thesis that all *aisthēseis* are *alētheis*.

If we look again at *M* VIII 9, we see that Sextus' first point is that Epicurus made no distinction between 'true' and 'real'; consequently he defined 'true' as 'that which is as it is said to be' and 'false' as 'that which is not as it is said to be'. This amounts to a conflation of the notions of 'true' and 'real', and of 'false' and 'unreal'. 'True' and 'false' apply properly to what is said or thought; consequently an account of truth along these lines ought to take the form of the Aristotelian formula 'Truth is saying of what is that it is, and of what is not that it is not' (*Metaph.* 1011ᵇ 26). 'Real' and 'unreal', on the other hand, characterize entities or states of affairs as in the Epicurean formula, but characterize them independently of what is thought or said. The conflation of the two pairs of notions in the Epicurean formula suggests that Epicurus is not interested in any contrast between a report and what it reports, but in the systematic correlation between a true report and the reality of what it reports. Consequently Sextus' report moves immediately from the claim that all *aisthēta* are *alēthē kai onta* to the assertion that *aisthēsis* always tells the truth, since it represents the reality which impinges on it exactly as it is, without addition or diminution, the whole being finally summed up as 'While all the *aisthēta* are true, some things that we believe are true and some false.' It is clear that the contrast, central to the interpretation we are considering, between purely physical *aisthēsis*, which is reported, and thought, which reports it, is inconsistent with Sextus' evidence in this passage. For *aisthēsis* itself, Sextus tells us, reports the physical stimulation which gives rise to it. The special status of *aisthēseis* as witnesses is due to the fact that the reports which *aisthēsis* gives represent that physical stimulation with perfect accuracy. And the accuracy of those reports is guaranteed by the fact that *aisthēsis* is *alogos*. What this seems to mean is that *aisthēsis* lacks the capacity to form any judgement about the pattern of stimulation presented to it; its function is restricted to representing it as it is. But that representation has a content to which truth and falsity are applicable; the special feature of that representation is that in fact it is always true. We might perhaps be inclined to identify *aisthēta* with the physical stimulation, which is real, as distinct from *aisthēsis,* which reports that stimulation, and which is true. But that would be to impose on the passage a sharper distinction than the text warrants. In view of the conflation of the concepts of truth and reality which occurs in this passage (see above), it is much more plausible that no clear distinction is drawn between the putative bearers of those predicates, *aisthēsis* and *aisthēton.* This is supported by the evidence presented earlier that Sextus uses the term *aisthēton* interchangeably with *phantasia.* The latter term denotes an act of mental representation or the content of such an act, 'something's appearing so and so'. It is, therefore, unlikely that in this passage Sextus uses the term *aisthēton* to denote a purely physical entity, *in contrast with* a kind of mental representation.

This leaves us with the evidence of DL X 32. Now it is undisputed that the point there is that the *phantasmata* of madmen and dreamers are real, since they have effects, and only real things can have effects. But this is ambiguous as it stands. For it is unclear whether what is meant is that the states of having an hallucination or having a dream are real states, since those states have effects, e.g. they produce movements and utterances on the part of the people who have them, or that the objects present to the mind in those states are real objects, since those objects have effects, e.g. they induce beliefs on the part of those to whom they are present. The use of the word *phantasmata*, rather than *phantasiai*, might suggest the latter, but the lack of any systematic distinction between terminology for mental acts and that for objects of such acts makes it unsafe to rely on the terminological point alone. The evidence of two further passages dealing with hallucinations does indeed support the latter interpretation against the former, but indicates at the same time that Diogenes' very compressed report omits a central feature of Epicurus' view of such phenomena.

The passages in question are Plu. *Col.* 1123 bc and *M* VIII 63–4. Plutarch chides Epicureans for holding that none of the 'sights and extraordinary things' which occurs in dreams and visions is 'an optical illusion or false or insubstantial' (*parorama . . . oude pseudos oude asustaton*), but that they are all *phantasiai alētheis* and physical objects (*sōmata*) and shapes which come from the surrounding environment. Here the conflation between act and object is very marked: a class of phenomena is said to be neither false nor insubstantial, but actually to consist of physical objects *and* real/true *phantasiai*. It is clear that the physical reality of the objects of dreams and visions is a central Epicurean dogma. Like the objects of any other mental processes, these objects are a sort of physical objects, viz. films of atoms emitted from the surfaces of three-dimensional aggregates of atoms. But the conflation between act and object apparent in this passage should prompt us to ask whether the Epicurean thesis that such objects are *aletheis* was simply the thesis that they are real (i.e. physical) objects. Is it not likely that Epicurus also held some view about the way these items were represented in the *aisthesis* of the dreamer or the visionary, a view which was also expressed in the thesis that those objects are *aletheis*? The passage from Sextus clearly indicates that this is the case. 'Epicurus,' he says, 'said that all the *aistheta* are *alethe*, and that every *phantasia* arises from something that there is, and is just as the thing which stimulates the *aisthesis*' (*toiauten hopoion esti to kinoun ten aisthesin*). This sentence gives us both aspects of Epicurus' theory of the *aletheia* of *aistheseis*: the things which stimulate *aisthesis* are real, physical things, namely *eidola*, and they are represented in *aisthesis* exactly as they are. We should recall the evidence presented earlier that *aisthesis* is incapable of altering in any way the things which it represents. This general theory of the *aletheia* of *aisthesis* is then applied to what would ordinarily be considered a case of false *aisthesis*, viz. Orestes' hallucination of the Furies. 'So in the case of Orestes . . . his *aisthesis* which was stimulated by *eidola* was *alethes* (for the *eidola* were there), but his mind believed falsely when it thought that the Furies are solid objects.' Given the general theory just stated the explanatory clause 'for the *eidola* were there' (*hupekeito gar ta eidola*) should be understood as 'for the *eidola* which stimulated his *aisthesis* were there just as they were represented in his *aisthesis*.' We see, then, that Diogenes' testimony of the reality of dreams and visions is seriously inadequate. The *phantasmata*, i.e. things appearing to the mind, which occur in those states are *alethe* not merely in that they are real physical objects, but also in that they really are exactly as they are represented in *aisthesis*. As we should expect, the reality of the things represented is inseparable from the truth of the representation. Diogenes' evidence is, therefore, insufficient to support the suggestion that the Epicurean doctrine that *aisthēseis* are *alētheis* merely reduces to the claim that *aisthēseis* are real, physical events. On the contrary, given Epicurus' epistemological requirements it is an indispensable part of that doctrine that *aisthēsis* is not merely a response to physical reality but a faithful representation of that reality.

That this is a general feature of *aisthēsis*, and not merely a feature of the special cases of dreams and hallucinations, is amply attested by the sources. In addition to the evidence of Sextus cited earlier (*M* VIII 9) to the effect that *aisthēsis* is 'receptive of the things presented to it, neither taking away nor adding nor altering anything', we may cite *M* VII 210, 'It is proper to *aisthēsis* merely to receive what is present and stimulates it, e.g. colour, but not to discriminate that the thing here is one thing and the thing here another. Therefore all the appearances which arise in this way are true, but the beliefs are not all true . . .' (adopting Usener's supplementation of the text). The obscure expression 'not to discriminate that the thing here is one thing and the thing here another' refers to the application of this theory to phenomena of perceptual illusion, perspective etc. The large rectangular tower looks small and round when seen from a distance, because when the *eidōla* reach the eye they actually are small and round, the large, rectangular *eidōla* emitted by the tower having been reduced in size and altered in shape by friction with the atoms in the space between the tower and the observer. *Aisthēsis* faithfully reproduces the actual state of the *eidōla* when they reach the eye, but it is no part of the business of *aisthēsis* to distinguish the small round *eidōlon* which you get when you look at the tower from *here* (i.e. from a distance) from the large rectangular one which you get when you look at it from *here* (i.e. from close up). That is the work of opinion, not of *hē alogos aisthēsis*; opinion is distorted when it gives rise to the belief that the same object is visually presented (*phantaston*) under both conditions, and is hence mispresented when one looks from a distance.[5] Two passages from

---

[5] This seems to give the best account of what is meant by 'discriminating that the thing here is one thing, and the thing here another'. Other suggestions, e.g. that Sextus is saying that while *aisthēsis* registers that *this* is, e.g. green and this blue, it is not *aisthēsis* but *logos* which identifies the green thing as grass and the blue thing as the sky, introduce ideas irrelevant to the purpose of the passage, which is to give

Plutarch's *Adversus Colotem*, dealing with different kinds of perceptual phenomena, present essentially the same picture. In 1121 ab he presents the Epicurean theory of illusion in much the same way as Sextus; when the rectangular tower looks round in the distance, and the straight oar in water looks bent, then the sense-organ comes into contact with an *eidōlon* which is round, and one which is bent, and *aisthēsis* receives an accurate imprint of that (*tēn . . . aisthēsin alēthōs tupousthai*). At 1109 a–e the phenomena are those of perceptual relativity, e.g. that the same water feels warm to one person and cold to another. Here the explanation is once again that each person's experience faithfully reproduces the actual character of the *eidōla* which he receives; the water itself contains atoms of both kinds, which are registered by observers whose sense-organs are in the appropriate condition to receive them. Disagreement on whether the water really is warm or cold reflects failure to distinguish the *eidōla* which make contact with the sense-organs from the aggregates of atoms which emit them.

So far, then, the evidence suggests that the Epicurean thesis that all *aisthēseis* are *alētheis* is not to be interpreted as the thesis that we have incorrigible acquaintance with our sense-contents. Nor is it merely the thesis that all *aisthēseis* are real, either in its trivial version, viz. that every occurrence of *aisthēsis* is a real event, or, in the more substantial version, viz. that every instance of *aisthēsis* consists in the stimulation of the sense-organ by a real, physical object. Rather, it is the thesis that every instance of *aisthēsis* consists in the stimulation of the sense-organ by a real object which is represented in *aisthēsis* exactly as it is in reality. If we need further evidence in favour of that interpretation, and against the 'incorrigible acquaintance' interpretation, it is provided by the context of the first passage from Plutarch just mentioned, *Col.* 1120 c ff. Here Plutarch is dealing with Colotes' critique of the scepticism of the Cyrenaic school; he represents him as rejecting, and indeed as making fun of the fundamental sceptical thesis that, while we do indeed have incorrigible acquaintance with our own sense-contents, that amounts merely to knowledge of an internal state, providing no ground for any justifiable

---

the Epicurean explanation of the source of the (erroneous) belief that misperception occurs. This source is the failure to distinguish distinct perceptual objects in distinct conditions of perception, a failure attributable to opinion, not to perception itself.

inference about anything external to the percipient. Plutarch states this position in its own technical terms: the percipient is 'sweetened' when something tastes sweet to him, 'embittered' when something tastes bitter to him, 'illumined' when he seems to see light etc., 'since each of these experiences has its own particular incontestable clarity in itself' (tōn pathōn toutōn hekastou tēn enargeian oikeian en hautōi kai aperispaston echontos).[6] Colotes apparently made fun of this curious terminology, pointing out that the sceptic ought not to say that something was a man or a horse, but rather that he himself was 'manned' or 'horsed', i.e. was in a state of seeming to see a man or a horse. Plutarch attempts to show that Colotes' own position does not differ from the one which he is attacking; he urges that just as the sceptics admit infallible knowledge of sense-contents but do not allow any knowledge of anything beyond them, so the Epicureans must admit that, while they have knowledge of the eidōla which impinge on them, they can have no knowledge of the external objects which, they claim, emit those eidōla. This is undeniably a difficulty for Epicurean epistemology, as for any representational theory of perception, but the point which concerns us here is that Plutarch's attempt to assimilate the Epicurean position to the sceptical one itself throws into relief the basic difference between the two. For the sceptic's starting-point (and his finishing-point too, for that matter) is knowledge of one's own perceptual states, 'perceptual sweetening' etc., whereas the Epicurean starts from direct acquaintance with physical objects impinging on the senses. The sceptic declares insoluble the problem of justifying the inference from descriptions of perceptual states to statements about external objects. For the Epicurean, on the other hand, descriptions of perceptual states are already descriptions of a percipient in contact with the physical world. The inference which he has to justify is not that from experience to the external world, but the inference from descriptions of eidōla to descriptions of their causes. This is put beyond doubt by Plutarch's description of the Epicurean position:

When a round eidōlon comes into contact with us, or again a bent one, they say that our aisthēsis is truly imprinted, but they don't allow us to affirm as well that the tower is round and the oar bent; they guarantee their experiences and appearances (phantasmata) as reliable, but are not

[6] Cf. M VII 190–8, PH I 10.

willing to admit that the external things are that way. And just as they [i.e. the sceptics] ought to say 'horsed' and 'walled', not 'horse' and 'wall', so these people have to say that their sight is 'rounded' and 'bended', not that the oar is bent or the tower round. For the *eidōlon* by which the sight is affected is bent, but the oar from which the *eidōlon* comes is not bent (1121 ab).

The evidence which I have presented seems to me to establish my contention that the Epicurean thesis that all *aisthēseis* are *alētheis* is not the familiar empiricist axiom that we have complete and incorrigible acquaintance with our sense-contents, as expressed e.g. by Hume (*Treatise* I iv 2): 'Since all actions and sensations of the mind are known to us by consciousness, they must necessarily appear in every particular what they are, and be what they appear'. I have not, of course, argued that Epicurus denied that axiom, or maintained anything inconsistent with it; I have merely argued that that is not what he means by 'All *aisthēseis* are *alētheis*.' But our incidental treatment of the thesis that *aisthēsis* is *alogos* has shown that Epicurus accepted another dogma of empiricism, viz. the view that, in contrast with its active role in forming concepts and making judgements, in perception the mind is passive, merely reproducing data which are presented to it. A paradigm expression of this view is provided by Locke (*Essay* II i 25):

These simple ideas, when offered to the mind, the understanding can no more refuse to have, nor alter when they are imprinted, nor blot them out and make new ones itself, than a mirror can refuse, alter, or obliterate the images or ideas which the objects set before it do therein produce. As the bodies that surround us do diversely affect our organs, the mind is forced to receive the impressions; and cannot avoid the perception of those ideas that are annexed to them.

Allowing for the fundamental difference that Locke is talking about the passive reception of mental impressions, whereas the Epicureans were concerned with the passive reception of physical *eidōla*, this passage is strongly reminiscent of the sources for the Epicurean doctrine that *aisthēsis* is *alogos*. All our sources for that doctrine (DL X 31, M VII 210, VIII 9, Aristocles, loc. cit.) associate it closely with the assertion that *aisthēsis* cannot alter the data presented to it in any way, but merely reproduces them as it were photographically. The analogy of the camera is, though

anachronistic, quite an apt expression of the Epicurean view.
Their thought seems to have been that, like the camera, *aisthēsis*
cannot lie, since *aisthēsis* puts no construction on what it 'sees'
nor compares it with what it remembers (DL, loc. cit. *mnēmēs*
oudemias dektikē), but, like the camera, merely records what is
before it. But it is precisely this passivity in the face of stimulation
which gives *aisthēsis* its evidential value; after all, what better
evidence could there be that Brutus stabbed Caesar than a
photograph of him stabbing Caesar? The paradox that *aisthēsis*
is both a witness and *alogos* is thus resolved. *Aisthēsis* is *alogos* in
that it can't think about what it sees, and thus can't misrepresent
it. But it tells us what it sees, in just the way that a camera does,
by presenting it, and thus has maximum evidential value.

The photographic analogy has the further advantage of
emphasizing a fundamental difficulty in the Epicurean doctrine
that *aisthēseis* are a criterion of truth. For we are able to treat
photographs as evidence only because we know how cameras
work; we know what kind of casual process is necessary for the
production of a photograph, and so are able to infer back from
the image to the reality which must have produced it. Similarly,
we are entitled to treat *aisthēseis* as reliable witnesses to reality only
if we already accept the Epicurean account of the physical processes which give rise to them.[7] For if we don't already accept that
perception consists in the physical impact on the sense-organs of
films of atoms emitted by physical objects, and in the passive
mirroring of those films in consciousness, then we have no reason
to accept the fundamental premiss that *aisthēsis*, being in the
required sense *alogos,* must be inerrant. Why should *aisthēsis* not
process the physical stimuli which it receives, so that the same
physical data are perceived differently by observers in different
perceptual conditions? That suggestion does, after all, provide
a perfectly plausible account of many cases of perceptual relativity,
e.g. the same wine's tasting sweet to the healthy man and sour
to the sick man. One might respond that in that situation the
observers have different data, since things do appear differently
to them. But that is to interpret 'data' as 'sense-contents' instead
of as 'physical stimuli'; the Epicurean theory requires the latter

---

[7] This may perhaps be the force of the obscure statement (DL X 32) that the
reality of perceptions guarantees the truth of *aisthēseis* (*to ta epaisthēmata d' huphestanai*
pistoutai tēn tōn aisthēseōn alētheian).

interpretation, since the nerve of that theory is precisely that sense-contents exactly mirror the physical stimuli which excite them. If that claim is abandoned we have to retreat to the claim that we cannot be mistaken about what sense-contents we have. I hope to have shown that that is a retreat from the Epicurean position, not a restatement of it.

It is no accident that the examples which our sources rely on in elucidating that position concentrate on the spatial properties of the *eidōla*, viz. size and shape. For the thesis that *eidōla* are represented in perception exactly as they are in reality is most readily applicable to just those properties. *Eidōla* are physical structures, composed of atoms whose only intrinsic properties are size, shape, weight and 'the necessary accompaniments to shape' (e.g. propensity for certain sorts of motion: DL X 54). Such structures themselves have objective size and shape, which may be reproduced faithfully or inaccurately in perception. But since they are composed of individual atoms which lack such secondary properties as colour, taste, and smell, and since they are individually imperceptible, a succession of *eidōla* being required to stimulate the sense-organ, they cannot themselves be said to possess colour, taste, or smell. So if the same wine tastes sweet to the healthy man and sour to the sick man, what becomes of the Epicurean thesis that the *aisthēsis* of each man is true? It cannot sensibly be maintained that the healthy man's *eidōla* really are sweet, and the sick man's really are sour, for imperceptible things have no taste. Perhaps, then, the thesis is that the *aggregate* of *eidōla* which each receives really is as each tastes it. But here 'really is' seems to come to no more than 'really tastes', and that in turn to no more than 'really tastes to him', in which case the thesis that every *aisthēsis* is true reduces to the triviality that whatever tastes etc. a certain way to someone really tastes etc. that way to him. As far as I can see, the theory can be saved from this trivialization only by means of providing a theoretical identification of e.g. real sweetness as a phenomenal property associated with a specific physical structure S (e.g. a structure of smooth particles, Lucr. IV 622–4). Then the thesis that the perception of sweetness is true would be the substantial thesis that, whenever anything tastes sweet to a percipient, that percipient is being stimulated by *eidōla* of structure S. The Epicurean theory certainly provides the materials for such identifications (see especially Lucretius' account of hearing, smell, and taste, IV 522–721): it is less clear that either Epicurus or his followers grasped the theoretical necessity for them.

The Epicurean thesis that all *aisthēseis* are true provides, then, no independent support for the physical theory. Rather it presupposes that theory, in two ways. As regards the perception of shape and size, the theoretical account of the mirroring of *eidōla* in perception is required to explain the sense in which perception is true. As regards the perception of secondary qualities, the role of the theory is to identify a certain physical structure as what is truly perceived. The theory predicts that whatever is perceived as a phenomenal property, e.g. sweetness, will in fact be an instance of that structure; the truth of the perception consists in its fulfilling that prediction. In advance of the theory as a whole, the claim that all perception is true requires independent support. Epicurus seems to have thought that that support could be provided by epistemological considerations, in that the only alternative to the acceptance of the claim is total scepticism, which he regarded as an absurd or self-defeating doctrine. Thus at DL X 146–7 he asserts that rejecting all *aisthēseis* together or any particular one alike lead to the abandonment of any criterion of what is true and false. It is implied that that is an unacceptable position, though it is not stated why it is unacceptable. Perhaps his thought is that scepticism itself requires the conceptual distinction between truth and falsehood, and that that distinction itself presupposes the ability to tell which things are true and which false, which in turn presupposes a means of telling, i.e. a criterion. That there was an Epicurean argument along these lines is proved by Lucr. IV 473–9:

Yet even if I were to concede that he [i.e. the sceptic] does know this [i.e. that he knows nothing], let me ask him this: since he has previously seen nothing true in things, how does he know what knowing and again not knowing are? What has produced his conception of the true and the false? What has proved that the doubtful differs from the certain? You will find that your conception of the true was produced by the senses first of all, and that the senses cannot be refuted.

Perhaps an expansion of this point, or perhaps a separate one, is the argument that reason cannot give grounds for rejecting the evidence of perception, since reason itself originates from or depends on perception. This is certainly Epicurean, as it is reported both in the same passage of Lucretius, 'Moreover, what must be held to be more trustworthy than the senses? Will reason, arising from false sense, be strong enough to speak against them, reason which arises solely from the senses? Unless they are true, all reason also becomes false' (482-5), and in the corresponding summary in DL X 32: 'Nor again can reason [refute *aisthēseis*], for all reason depends on *aisthēseis*.' This is obviously a descendant of Democritus' famous 'Complaint of the Senses' (frag. 152 Diels–Kranz), 'O wretched mind, you receive your evidence from us, and do you overthrow us? Our overthrow is a fall for you', and can be developed into an argument to show that scepticism is self-refuting.

Epicurus had, then, some good arguments, or at least the materials of such arguments, which he could advance against scepticism without presupposing his physical theory. His method thus displays a subtle interaction of epistemological and metaphysical considerations. The fundamental epistemological requirement is that every *aisthēsis* should be true, i.e. that whatever seems to be the case should in some sense or other actually be the case. It then becomes part of the task of the general theory of nature to specify the sense or senses in which what seems to be actually is. It is an astonishing achievement of atomism, both in its fifth-century and in its Epicurean version, to have provided an even reasonably plausible account of the satisfaction of this requirement as part of a comprehensive account of the world. But problems remain. For the sceptic can reasonably claim that the account of how things always are as they seem is, in the last resort, empty. For example, how is the claim that sweetness is always the taste of a structure of smooth atoms to be tested? Suppose microscopic examination revealed that in some cases the atoms were smooth, but in others spiky. If both the microscopic and the gustatory observations are, in the theoretical sense, 'true', then we have two sets of atoms instead of one. No doubt we could add to the theory a description of how a structure of smooth atoms emits a structure of spiky ones, but the problem of verification arises there again, and so on at every level. The basic difficulty is that a theory of objective reality which is not subject to any constraint by experience must be empty of actual content.[8] Epicurus could have avoided this difficulty only by abandoning his fundamental

---

[8] For discussion of the same problem in fifth-century atomism see Taylor [134].

epistemological requirement and facing up to the sceptical challenge to find a way of discriminating veridical from non-veridical experience. The subsequent history of philosophy to the present indicates the formidable nature of that undertaking; the Epicurean alternative, though ultimately unsuccessful, was well worth exploring.

PROOF DEFINED*

Jacques Brunschwig

In this chapter I shall analyse and compare two parallel passages in Sextus (*PH* II 134–43, and *M* VIII 300–15), which chronicle the efforts made by the Hellenistic philosophers to arrive at a satisfactory definition of proof (*apodeixis*). I shall make occasional use of a third passage in Sextus (*M* VIII 411–23) which contains closely related material. This third text has the advantage of explicitly guaranteeing the Stoic origin of the doctrines it expounds,[1] whereas the other two make no ascription to any particular author or school;[2] its point of view, however, is a little different: it aims simply to classify the various types of argument, *logos* (cf. *M* VIII 411, 424), whereas the other two texts undertake that task in the hope of thereby reaching a definition of a particular species of argument, viz. proof (cf. *M* VIII 300, 315; *PH* II 135, 143). That difference has been neglected by the few commentators who have offered a close analysis of these familiar texts:[3] Urs Egli regards the passages as strictly comparable accounts of two distinct theories about the same subject matter ([41], 61); Benson Mates treats the texts bearing on the theory of proof as though their primary aim was to classify the different types of argument, and he finds them less interesting than those passages which testify to another, and equally Stoic, classification of arguments—

---

* Translated by Jennifer Barnes.

[1] See *M* VIII 425 (τοῖς ἀπὸ τῆς στοᾶς). The Stoic origin of the other two texts is widely accepted. *SVF* II, p. 89.3–10 prints no more than eight lines of extracts from *M* VIII 310 and 314. Other texts have preserved a different Stoic definition of proof from the one I am going to analyse: according to that condensed definition, a proof is 'an argument which concludes to what is less well apprehended by way of things better apprehended' (cf. DL VII 45: λόγον διὰ τῶν μᾶλλον καταλαμβανομένων τὸ ἧττον καταλαμβανόμενον περαίνοντα; *Acad.* II 26: 'itaque argumenti conclusio, quae est graece ἀπόδειξις, ita definitur: ratio quae ex rebus perceptis ad id quod non percipiebatur adducit'.) I shall return later to this definition and to its relation to the definitions which will occupy us (see below, n. 22 and p. 146).

[2] *M* VIII 300–15 uses the first person (καλοῦμεν, 302; φημί, 304); but near the end it uses a third-person expression (ὑπογράφουσιν 314). In *PH* II 134–43 Sextus regularly refers to an unnamed school (τί φασιν, ὥς φασίν, ὃ λέγουσιν, 135; εἰώθασί, 143).

[3] See esp. Mates [44], 58–63, 110–11; Egli [41], 61–4; Frede [42], 118; Gould [92]; Barnes, Chapter 7 below, pp. 161–81

a classification which involves the celebrated notion of an 'indemonstrable' (*anapodeiktos*) argument.[4] That latter classification gives a different sense to the word '*apodeixis*' from the one to be investigated here: it has been the subject of many penetrating studies,[5] and I shall leave it alone.

The two texts which I consider central, *PH* II 134–43 and *M* VIII 300–15, each present a definition of *apodeixis* by way of a carefully elaborated dichotomous analysis of its genus, *logos*;[6] and they do so in terms which are superficially similar. But there are numerous differences between the two texts which oblige us to analyse them separately, following, as far as possible, the inner logic of each of them.[7] For reasons which will emerge later, I shall begin by looking at the *M* version—though I shall not scruple to compare it to the *PH* version when the need arises.

The *M* version can be divided schematically as follows: (1) argument to justify locating proof in the genus *logos* (*M* VIII 301); (2) definitions of *logos* and of the elements of a *logos* (301–2); (3) dichotomous division of the genus *logos* along these lines (303–9):

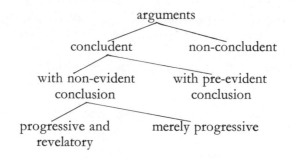

(4) first recapitulation of the series of divisions, in the form of a definition of proof (310); (5) supplementary elucidations of that

---

[4] Basic texts: DL VII 76 f.; *PH* II 156 f.; *M* VIII 223 f.; cf. Mates [44], 63 ('another classification of valid arguments which seems more important than that just discussed').

[5] Cf. Mates [44], 63 f.; Kneale [43], 162 ff.; Frede [42], 127 f.

[6] In several passages Sextus also says that proof is a species of the genus sign (σημεῖον); cf. the references given by Barnes, Chapter 7 below, p. 179 n. 22. Later on we shall see how this double allegiance is to be explained (below, nn. 14, 22).

[7] The differences between my analysis and Egli's derive in the main from the fact that he does not follow this method. Thus ([41], 62–4), he arranges in parallel columns pieces extracted from each of the three texts, thereby suppressing bridge passages and recapitulations as important as *M* VIII 310 and 314.

recapitulation (311–13); (6) second recapitulation, introducing two new definitions of proof (314).

Let us look in turn at each of the parts of that schematic plan.

(1) Sextus offers the *M* version as an explication of the notion of proof (cf. 300), and he begins by locating it within the generic notion of *logos*. He gives the following justification for that inclusion: a proof 'is certainly not a perceptible object, but a sort of movement and assent of thought (*dianoias tis kinēsis kai sunkatathesis*)—and those are logical things (*logika*)' (301). That argument does not amount to much: it seems to presuppose that everything that is not perceptible is 'logical', a presupposition falsified, in Stoic doctrine, by time, the void, and space, which are incorporeal without therefore being 'logical'; further, everything 'logical' is not necessarily a *logos* in the strict sense of the word, i.e. an argument: for example, a proposition (*axiōma*) is certainly something 'logical', but it is not a *logos*. Note also that the *PH* version does not offer this feeble argument—or indeed any argument at all—for the inclusion of the notion of proof in the generic notion of *logos*: it thinks that the point is self-evident (*PH* II 135).

(2) In 301–2, the *M* version defines a *logos* as 'what is composed of premisses (*lēmmata*) and conclusion (*epiphora*)'. This definition, with its typically Stoic terminology, appears again in practically the same form in the *PH* version; the latter, however, is more particular about the formal accuracy of its definition: it uses a noun for the proximate genus of the *definiendum*, stating that a *logos* is 'a *system* composed of premisses and conclusion' (135).

The two versions differ more sharply when it comes to defining what a premiss is. The *M* version has this (302): 'We call *lēmmata* not certain assumptions which we wrest [sc. from our interlocutor], but those which our interlocutor grants (*didōsi*) and concedes (*parachōrei*) because they are obvious (*tōi emphanē einai*).' By insisting on the goodwill and bona fides of the dialectician, and on the ease with which his interlocutor will grant him the 'obvious' premisses which he submits for his approval, this definition runs a clear risk from a logical point of view: it implicitly supposes, or tempts us to suppose, that a premiss is always a *true* proposition—for it is granted by virtue of its being 'obvious'.[8] Now that presupposition strongly discourages the development of logical theory; for it leads us to neglect the interesting case where we reason correctly from false premisses— the case which enables us to distinguish clearly between the genuinely logical question of the validity or invalidity of an argument, and the extralogical question of the truth or falsity of its component propositions. And in point of fact, as we shall see, the *M* version will not introduce an explicit distinction among logically concludent arguments between those that may be described as true (because their premisses and conclusions are true), and the rest.

Here now is the definition of a premiss in the *PH* version: 'We call *lēmmata* the propositions (*axiōmata*) which are assumed by agreement (*sumphōnōs lambanomena*) for the establishment of the conclusion' (136). This is a more restrained and a more abstract definition, in which the psychological and dialectical connotations are far less apparent. Admittedly, it does not expressly state that one can examine 'by agreement' what would follow logically from false premisses, but neither does it exclude that possibility, and its difference from the *M* definition might well be inspired by a desire to leave room for false premisses. At any rate, the *PH* version, unlike the *M* version, draws, as we shall see, a careful distinction between the logical concludency of an argument and the truth of the propositions it contains; and we may properly regard this difference as deriving from the difference between the definitions of a premiss in the two versions.

As far as the definition of the conclusion is concerned, the two versions are again in agreement, except that once more *PH* alone refers to the proximate genus: according to *M* (302) the conclusion is 'that which is established (*to kataskeuazomenon*) from the premisses'; according to *PH* (136), it is 'the proposition (*axiōma*) established from the premisses'. Given that a *logos* is not

---

[8] I assume that ἐμφανής ('obvious') implies ἀληθής ('true'), both because of the context, which contrasts propositions wrested by guile or by force with premisses asked for in good faith, and because of the word itself, which seems to refer to the evidence of the thing itself. The proposed definition leaves no room for false premisses—neither false premisses recognized as such both by the dialectician and by his partner and required by the former for the purposes of his argument, nor false premisses recognized as such by the dialectician but not by his partner. If the premiss is false but not recognized as such by either of the interlocutors, then matters proceed just as if it were true.

always concludent, we must surely give a proleptic sense to '*to
kataskeuazomenon*'—'what is to be established from the premisses',
and not 'what is actually established from the premisses'. The
criterion for picking out the conclusion of a *logos*, whether concludent or non-concludent, is probably its position—it comes last
in the *logos*—and the fact that it is introduced by way of the
particle 'therefore' (*ara*).

M 302, like *PH* II 136, gives as an example of a *logos* the
celebrated argument: 'If it is day, it is light; it is day: therefore,
it is light.' *M* explains carefully, *PH* briefly, which are the
premisses of the argument and which the conclusion.

(3) After those preliminary definitions of a *logos* and its constituent elements, the *M* version launches out on the series of
dichotomies which I summarized in the diagram above. I shall
now comment on each of its successive stages.

(3A) The first dichotomy (303–5) divides *logoi* into concludent
(*sunaktikoi*) and non-concludent arguments. Sextus describes the
criterion for this distinction in the following way: 'Concludent
arguments are those in which, once the premisses are agreed to
hold (*huparchein*), the conclusion also clearly follows from the
agreement to the premisses (*para tēn toutōn sunchōrēsin akolouthein
phainetai kai hē epiphora*).'[9] This definition, which is in some
respects reminiscent of Aristotle's definition of the syllogism[10]
(and, indeed, also of his definition of the 'perfect' syllogism[11]),
seems to me to muddle psychological considerations of clarity
('*phainetai*') and logical considerations of formal validity ('*akolouthein*'). If we take it literally (at least on the interpretation I have

---

[9] Two notes on the translation. (i) καί ('also') connects the conclusion to the
premisses: if the premisses are true, it too is true. Cf. the καί in 304 (καὶ τὸ δεύτερον).
(ii) One might hesitate between 'It clearly follows' and 'It seems to follow' as a
translation of ἀκολουθεῖν φαίνεται. The second version, which may be better favoured
by the ordinary rules of grammar, seems to me to be excluded by the context,
which aims at giving a definition of a *concludent* argument. If the conclusion 'seems
to follow', without actually doing so, will we have an argument which is, purely
and simply, concludent?

[10] See *APr.* I 1 24b 18–20. Note in particular the parallel between τεθέντων
τινῶν and τῷ ταῦτα εἶναι in Aristotle, and συγχωρηθέντων ὑπάρχειν τῶν λημμάτων
and παρὰ τὴν τούτων συγχώρησιν here. On the point of these qualifications, which
are intended to exclude superfluous or 'redundant' premisses, see Barnes, below
pp. 168–9.

[11] See *APr.* I 1 24b 22–4. Compare the 'clarity' (φαίνεται: above n. 9) of the
inference in the Stoic case with the clarity of the logical necessity in Aristotle's
'perfect' syllogisms (πρὸς τὸ φανῆναι τὸ ἀναγκαῖον).

just given), we shall have to classify as non-concludent 'Lewis
Carroll' arguments—arguments which are logically valid but so
complex that the logical connection between premisses and conclusion is no longer evident.

The following portion of the text does not make this much
clearer. Non-concludent arguments are defined only in a negative
way ('those which are not of this type': *hoi mē houtōs echousin*, 305);
and that really tells us nothing more. As an example of a
concludent argument, the same passage (303–4) gives us the
well-worn: 'If it is day, it is light; it is day: therefore, it is light';
but the accompanying commentary merely underlines the
muddled thinking. The argument is concludent, the text reports,
because

If we grant the truth of the conditional (*dothentos men alēthous einai tou
sunēmmenou*) . . . and if we also grant that its antecedent holds (*dothentos
de huparchein kai tou prōtou tōn en autōi*) . . . its consequent will of
necessity be concluded (*kat' anankēn suneisachthēsetai*) because of the
holding of the premisses (*dia tēn toutōn huparxin*).

There is no mention here of the clarity of the link between
premisses and conclusion, and we note the appearance of the idea
of necessity which was absent from the initial definition of
concludency. But these little changes make the whole thing
tautological: the commentary boils down to saying that the
argument is concludent (*sunaktikos*) because it is necessary to
conclude (*suneisachthēsetai*) to its conclusion.

Note finally that a detail of this commentary seems to confirm
that the M version presupposes that only *true* premisses are to be
reckoned with: we are told that once the premisses are allowed
to be true (*dothentos men alēthous einai . . . dothentos de huparchein*), the
conclusion necessarily follows, not because of the agreement we
gave to the premisses which were hypothetically taken as true,
but categorically, because of the actual truth of the premisses (*dia
tēn toutōn huparxin*).[12] This slide from agreement about truth to

---

[12] If he did not presuppose the truth of the premisses, the author ought, I think,
to say 'because of the agreement given to the premisses' and not, as he does,
'because of the truth of the premisses'. For the identity between ὕπαρξις and truth cf.
the parallel descriptions of the premisses: δοθέντος μὲν ἀληθοῦς εἶναι τοῦ συνημμένου,
and δοθέντος δὲ ὑπάρχειν καὶ τοῦ πρώτου (the difference is no doubt due to a desire
to distinguish between the types of truth possessed by the two premisses: the major
is a complex conditional proposition, whose truth is not given by perceptual
evidence; the minor is simple and its truth rests immediately on perception).

actual truth shows that for the author of the M version a premiss worthy of the name is always a true proposition.

When the PH version comes to the problem of the criterion for concludency, it differs importantly from the M version, and suggests a criterion which is famous for a rigour and a precision which have only been fully appreciated since the modern rebirth of logic (cf. Mates [44], 74). For we now read (137) that an argument is concludent 'when the conditional which has as its antecedent the conjunction of the premisses of the argument and for its consequent the conclusion, is sound (*hugies*)';[13] in other words, an argument '*p*, *q*; therefore, *r*' is concludent if and only if the conditional proposition 'If *p* and *q*, then *r*' is true.[14] Doubtless the problem is shelved rather than solved by this definition: the concludency of an inference depends on the truth of its associated conditional, and we have still to discover the criterion for the truth of a conditional—a problem which, as we know, gave rise to interminable disputes in the schools of the period.[15] But at least the problem of concludency was clearly reduced to another well-formed problem, and it was freed from any intrusive psychological elements. The continuation of the text of PH (137) shows how the new criterion for concludency is satisfied by the argument 'If it is day, it is light; etc.' (the text here has now been correctly understood and restored after centuries of distortion[16]); but unfortunately the author does not make clear by reference to

[13] ὑγιής (from which the modern term 'valid' originates) is used by the Stoics both of a logically valid argument and also of a true proposition. Mates [44], 136, says that in the latter sense the word is 'interchangeable with ἀληθής', citing M VIII 125–8, 244 ff. It is worth observing that these examples only concern *complex* propositions (conditionals, conjunctions). See Barnes, below, p. 169, n. 11.

[14] The criterion of concludency given by M VIII 411–23 is first expressed in an elliptical and scholastic manner (an argument is concludent 'because it is formulated in a sound form', διὰ τὸ ἐν ὑγιεῖ ἠρωτῆσθαι σχήματι—I do not know why Egli [41], 64, finds in this 'the exact formulation'); but it is then explained in the same terms as in PH II (cf. 416–17). This connection between the form of an argument and the form of an associated conditional enables us to understand how a proof can be called a species of sign (see above, p. 126 n. 6). For a sign is 'the antecedent in a sound conditional, which reveals the consequent' (M VIII 245). Thus a proof can be considered as a species of sign; 'for it makes clear the conclusion, and the conjunction of its premisses will be a sign of the truth of the conclusion' (M VIII 277).

[15] Sextus himself makes this point in a polemical context (cf. M VIII 426–8).

[16] Read, with Mates and against the manuscripts and various editorial proposals: εἰ ⟨ἡμέρα ἐστί, καὶ εἰ ἡμέρα ἐστί, φῶς ἐστι⟩, φῶς ἐστιν. Cf. Mates [44], 110–11 and [110].

which criterion the associated conditional is held to be
true.[17]

(3B) If we now return to the M version, a new dichotomy
appears (305–6): it consists in distinguishing, among concludent
arguments, between those which conclude to something pre-
evident (*prodēlon*) and those which conclude to something non-
evident (*adēlon*).[18] It is thus a property of the conclusion alone that
makes the difference. We may ask two questions about this
property. The first is whether the non-evidence of the conclusion, in arguments of the second class, belongs specifically to
one or other of the three categories of *adēla* distinguished by the
Stoics. Those categories are: (a) things that are non-evident once
and for all (*kathapax*), like the exact number of grains of sand in
Libya; (b) things that are non-evident by nature (*phusei*), like the
invisible pores of the skin; and (c) things which are non-evident
for the time being (*pros kairon*)—things evident by nature, but
temporarily prevented from being so by external circumstances,
like the city of Athens for someone who is not there.[19] We may
certainly exclude the first category: no argument could conclude
to something non-evident *kathapax*—for such things can never
fall under human understanding (*anthrōpinē katalēpsis*), whereas
demonstrated conclusions are objects of rational understanding
(cf. M VIII, 147; DL VII 52). But there is no reason in the text
of the M or the PH versions to exclude either of the two remaining
categories: the fact that the arguments in the second class of our
dichotomy are described as having a non-evident conclusion,
without any further qualification, leads us to suppose that this

---

[17] The parallel text at M VIII 411–23 is fuller on this point. It reports that a
conditional is true if it is never the case that its antecedent is true and its consequent
false. That seems to be the criterion ascribed to Diodorus (cf. PH II 110; M VIII
115–17).

[18] On the notions of ἄδηλον and πρόδηλον cf. PH II 97–9; M VIII 144–7.

[19] If an argument allows us to conclude to a thing which is by nature non-evident,
that thing does not thereby become evident; its ἄδηλον character is not annulled by
the knowledge which the argument allows us to acquire about it (see, correctly,
Barnes, below, pp. 177–8. But exactly the same goes for a conclusion which is
temporarily non-evident: if you prove at Oxford that the city of Athens exists, its
existence remains for the moment ἄδηλον; only by going there can you put an end
to its non-evidence. In the same way, a microscope will annul the non-evidence of
the pores in the skin; but the Stoics never envisaged that possibility (as is shown by
their use of the word νοητοί, literally 'intelligible', for those invisible pores). That is
so despite the use of the word δηλωτική at M VIII 277, and the imperfect 'percipiebatur' in Cicero (above, p. 125 n. 1).

non-evidence can be either temporary or permanent, either accidental or natural.

The second question about the pre-evidence or non-evidence of the conclusion is whether we are dealing with an *absolute* property of the conclusion, to be determined simply from its own content, or rather with a *relative* property which the conclusion has in relation to the premisses or to one of the premisses. The two examples in the *M* version of arguments with pre-evident conclusions are accompanied by comments somewhat lacking in coherence in this respect. In the analysis of the first ('If it is day, it is light; etc.'), it is stated that the conclusion 'It is light' is evident to the same degree (*ep' isēs phainomenon*) as the premiss 'It is day', that is to say, as the minor premiss alone.[20] (Nothing is said of the relationship between the conclusion and the conditional major premiss, whose self-evidence—whether it is seen as rational or as inductive—cannot be granted quite the same status as the perceptual self-evidence which belongs to the minor premiss and to the conclusion.) On the other hand, the second example ('If Dion walks, Dion moves; the first; therefore the second'[21]), it is said that the conclusion 'is one of those things patent in itself (*tōn autophōratōn hupērchen)*'. The specific property of the conclusion is therefore sometimes presented as relative and sometimes as absolute. The *PH* version is simpler and clearer on this point; it only gives one example of an argument with a pre-evident conclusion (the first of the two examples above), and it is content to state that its conclusion ('It is light') is *prodēlon* (140).

Of the two classes distinguished in the present dichotomy, it is the class of arguments with a non-evident conclusion that is relevant to the theory of proof. The ancient idea of *apodeixis* implies, as is plain enough in Aristotle, that the premisses are 'better known' than the conclusion (cf. *APo.* I 2 71ᵇ 21 f.). But in Aristotle's view the premisses, at least in the paradigm cases, must be better known 'by nature' or 'in themselves' than the conclusion; and that implies that they must be further removed than the latter from the immediate data of perception. For the Stoics, on the other hand, and in the empiricist climate of the

---

[20] Read τῷ ἡμέρα ἐστι, for the MSS reading τῷ εἰ ἡμέρα ἐστιν (305).

[21] For the sake of brevity I here use (as Sextus often does elsewhere) the hybrid formulation which the Stoics called λογότροπος (cf. DL VII 77).

Hellenistic schools in general, an argument will only be probative if it allows us to establish a conclusion which it is impossible (*de facto* and/or *de jure*) to verify by direct observation, and to establish it by means of premisses which themselves, it seems, must be immediate.[22] While Aristotelian knowledge is knowledge of the cause, Stoic proof, we might say in a Cartesian vein, is proof from effects.[23]

However, it would be wrong to reduce the self-evidence required of the premisses to perceptual self-evidence. Let us look at the two examples in the *M* version that illustrate the idea of an argument with a non-evident conclusion. In the first example ('If sweat flows through the skin, there are invisible (*noētoi*) pores in the flesh; the first; therefore the second') we can say that the non-evident conclusion rests on the one hand on the rational self-evidence of the major conditional premiss, and on the other hand on the perceptual self-evidence of the minor premiss. The second example ('That whose separation from the body causes men to die is the soul; it is separation of the blood from the body that makes men die; therefore, the blood is the soul') has a different logical structure; it seems nevertheless that the epistemological standing of the premisses is the same as in the previous example: a rational or semantic type of self-evidence for the major premiss, and an empirical kind of self-evidence for the minor.

I have one last comment to make on this section of the dichotomy in the *M* version—the last comment, but perhaps not the least, even though it is negative in form: whereas the *PH* version, as we shall see, divides concludent arguments into *true* and *non-true* arguments and only then distinguishes, among true arguments, between those that have a pre-evident conclusion and

[22] For the moment I say that it is a necessary condition, since the *M* version identifies proof with a particular species of argument with non-evident conclusion; but note that, according to the abbreviated definition of ἀπόδειξις which I cited above (p. 125, n. 1), it is a sufficient condition (and Egli [41], 62, calls this 'the old Stoic definition of proof'). I shall return to this problem later. Again, I say that the conclusion must be empirically unverifiable *de facto* and/or *de jure* in order to leave open the two possibilities of ἄδηλον πρὸς καιρόν and ἄδηλον φύσει. In any case, this condition on probativeness explains perfectly why a proof is included in the genus sign (see above, nn. 6, 14). As for the premisses, they are in principle πρόδηλα ; but see below, p. 152 and n. 45.

[23] Or, in the more up to date vocabulary of Barnes (below, p. 181), 'an inference to the best explanation'.

those that have a non-evident conclusion, the *M* version ignores this intermediate stage. This is certainly not mere chance, nor a textual aberration—we shall have a proof of that later on when we examine what I have called the first recapitulation. Rather, the 'omission' is a direct consequence (and, conversely, a confirmation) of that presupposition which the *M* version has already made, both in its notion of concludency and in its definition of the premisses: since the author has implicitly admitted, from the very beginning, that a premiss is always a true proposition, he has no reason to make the distinction among concludent arguments which the author of the *PH* version introduces.

(3C) The next dichotomy (307–9) divides the class of arguments which have a non-evident conclusion. It consists of discriminating between those that 'lead us from the premisses to the conclusion in a merely progressive (or: processive) way (*ephodeutikōs monon*)' and those that lead us 'at the same time in a progressive way and in a revelatory way (*ephodeutikōs hama kai ekkaluptikōs*)'. In order to understand this distinction, reasonably described by Mates ([44], 61), as 'by no means clear', we must take a close look at the definitions and the examples which accompany it.

We read that the first category contains 'the arguments which clearly depend on faith and memory (*hoi ek pisteōs kai mnēmēs ērtēsthai dokountes*)'. These are illustrated by the following example: 'If some god has told you that this man will be rich, he will be rich; this god (I point to Zeus, say) has told you that this man will be rich; therefore this man will be rich.' In this kind of case, we are told, we accept the conclusion 'not because it is established by the force of the argument put forward, but because we have faith in the god's assertion (*ouk ek tēs tou protathentos logou dunameōs kataskeuasthen, alla tōi pisteuein tēi tou theou apophansei*)'. To illustrate the second category, that of arguments 'at the same time progressive and revelatory', the text returns to the example that proves the existence of pores in the skin,[24] and explains that the premisses of such a proof teach us, by their very nature (*ek tēs autōn phuseōs*) to draw the conclusion 'in accordance with a

---

[24] According to Egli [41], 64, this example is 'an alien replacement for the original example, which we still find at *M* VIII 422 [*sic*; read: 423]'. The example of a probative argument in that passage is this: 'If this woman has milk in her breasts, she has conceived; the first; therefore, the second.' Egli does not say, and I cannot see, why we should suppose that this example is more 'original' than the other.

progress of something like this sort (*kata tina toiautēn ephodon*)'
(the phrase betrays some mild embarrassment): 'It is impossible
for a liquid to flow through a solid and non-porous body; but
sweat runs through the body; therefore the body cannot be solid
but must be porous.' Our author's embarrassment is readily
explained; for his 'justification' of the original argument amounts
in effect to replacing it by another argument, in which the original
major premiss, of the form 'If p, then q', gives way to its contra-
positive, qualified by a modal operator, 'If not-q, then necessarily
not-p.' It is hard to see how this new argument could be an
adequate foundation for the original argument of which it is
merely a transformation.[25]

I will now return to the dichotomy as a whole. Leaving on one
side the special problems raised by the possibility of our pointing
to Zeus,[26] and hearing his words, it seems to me that the real
difficulty of this passage lies in the fact that the reasons the author
gives for distinguishing between the two types of argument are
not those that actually distinguish them. According to our author,
we do not accept the conclusion of an argument such as the one
about the oracle because it is established 'by the force of the
argument' or 'by the force of the premisses'.[27] (Incidentally, that
should impel him to deny that such an argument is concludent,
if he bears in mind his own earlier definition of a *logos sunaktikos*.)
Rather, we accept it because 'we have faith in the god's assertion',
and probably also because we recall times when we have been able
to establish the veracity of the gods in general and/or of Zeus in
particular. (However, memory, though linked with faith in the
abstract description of this type of argument, receives no further
mention in the commentary on the example.) In the argument of
the oracle, we might say, pure reason is subordinate to or
dependent upon (*ērtēsthai*) something else; but scientific proof, as
illustrated by the argument of the pores, is put forward as a

[25] To be quite fair, I should point out that the major premiss of the first argument
talks of sweat and flesh, whereas that of the second talks in general of liquids and
solids; thus the author hopes to justify the first argument by showing it to be a
particular case of a general law. But it is left for the author of *PH* to bring out
clearly how the proof is rooted in the conceptual content of the notions of solidity
and liquidity (see below, p. 153).

[26] On this see Frede [42], 55; Lloyd [101], 286. On the general problem of δεῖξις
see also P. Pachet·[113].

[27] Barnes (below p. 178), cites, with references, various parallel expressions.

strictly autonomous process in which the conclusion, fully deserving the name '*epiphora*' (which reminds us of garnering and the harvest home), grows like a ripe fruit on the intertwining branches of the premisses.

It is therefore in the relation between the premisses and the conclusion that our author finds the distinction between the two types of argument: he writes (cf. 308) as if this relation were intrinsic and rational in the one case, extrinsic and fideistic in the other; and as if faith in the god's announcement played exactly the same role in the latter case as the logical force of the argument does in the former. In this, it seems clear to me, he is at best confused. In order to accept the conclusion of the oracle argument (if we do accept it) we must both recognize the logical force of the argument, which rests on the formal structure of the relation between its premisses and its conclusion, and also grant the truth of the premisses, and in particular of the conditional major premiss, which demands an act of faith in the veracity of the gods: we must be both good logicians and good pagans. At the logical level, the relation between premisses and conclusion is exactly the same in the oracle argument and in the pore argument: it is that of the 'first indemonstrable' of Stoic theory (cf. *PH* II 157; *M* VIII 224; DL VII 80), later christened *modus ponens*: if p, then q; p; therefore, q. It goes without saying that the logical force of *modus ponens* remains the same, whatever we may substitute for the variables 'p' and 'q'; as soon as the conditional, together with its antecedent, are presented as true, the truth of the consequent follows necessarily, by virtue of the meaning of the connective 'If . . . then . . .'; it really does not matter what kind of criteria we choose—rational, inductive, mystical, or Heaven knows what—to test or verify the conditional premiss.

So what is different in the two cases distinguished by the present dichotomy is not the logical relation between the premisses and the conclusion of the argument; it is rather the epistemological relation between the antecedent and the consequent of the conditional major premiss; in particular, it is, at least implicitly, the nature of the criterion that we use when judging that premiss to be true. The celebrated squabble about the truth-conditions of the conditional thus crops up again in the theory of inference (as long, of course, as we limit ourselves to arguments in *modus ponens* form; and in practice that is what our author does here,

although he knows, as we saw above,[28] that there are other kinds
of arguments with non-evident conclusions): just as we distinguish
different truth-conditions for the conditional, graded from the
weakest to the strongest, so we can distinguish classes of
inferences with conditional major premisses, according to how
many or how few of those criteria are satisfied by that premiss.

That is surely the reason why the division that interests us now
is not, as before, a simple dichotomy of the genus by way of the
presence or absence of a specific feature (like, for instance, the
distinction between concludent and non-concludent arguments);
rather it is a complex dichotomy, using two characteristics of
which one (progressiveness) belongs to both the classes distinguished while the other (revelatoriness) belongs to one only.
Since the division is tacitly put forward as being exhaustive, we
must deduce that there are no arguments which are revelatory
without being progressive; in other words, that revelatoriness
implies progressiveness—but not vice versa.

Although our text only distinguishes two classes of arguments
with conditional major premisses, it is tempting to compare it
with the celebrated list, given elsewhere in Sextus, of the four
distinct criteria of truth for the conditional, each stronger than
its predecessor and weaker than its successor,[29] and to ask by
reference to which of those criteria the major premisses of the
oracle argument and of the pore argument are judged to be true.
The former ('If some god has told you that this man will be rich,
he will be rich') must be put fairly low on the scale: it is acceptable
to a Philonian, for (if you have 'faith') you will agree that it is
not the case that its antecedent is true and its consequent false;
but it must be held false by a Diodoran, for there will be a time
(beginning from the death of the Croesus in question) when its
antecedent will be true and its consequent false.

---

[28] Cf. the argument of 306 about blood and the soul (cited above, p. 134). There is
nothing to indicate how we should locate an argument of this sort in the present
dichotomy. Thus our author has not divided the genus he says he has.

[29] Cf. PH II 110 f.; M VIII 112 f.: the criterion of Philo (a conditional is true if
it is not the case that its antecedent is true and its consequent false); the criterion of
Diodorus (if it has not been and is not possible that its antecedent is true and its
consequent false); the criterion, usually ascribed to Chrysippus, of 'connectedness'
or συνάρτησις (if the contradictory of the consequent conflicts, μάχεται, with the
antecedent); the criterion of 'implication' or ἔμφασις (if the consequent is contained
potentially, περιέχεται δυνάμει, in the antecedent).

As for the conditional major, 'If sweat flows through the skin, there are invisible pores', that is no doubt thought of as satisfying a criterion similar to that of 'connectedness' (*sunartēsis*): our author supports it by saying that 'through a solid and non-porous body [negation of the consequent], it is impossible (*adunaton*) for a liquid to flow [generalization of the antecedent]'; and according to the criterion of *sunartēsis*, a conditional is true when the negation of its consequent is incompatible (*machetai*) with its antecedent (*PH* II 111). Although he does not explicitly say so, the author of the *M* version tends, I think, to distinguish between *a priori* and empirical impossibility: I assume that he would classify an argument as 'revelatory' when the antecedent, '*p*', of its conditional major, and the consequent, '*q*', are such that the conjunction '*p* and not-*q*' is *a priori* impossible, in the sense that its impossibility can be seen merely by inspecting its terms. (Thus a non-porous body through which sweat flowed would qualify, independently of any experience, as both compact and non-compact.[30]) On the other hand, he would classify as non-revelatory an argument where the conjunction '*p* and not-*q*' could not be ruled out merely by inspection of its terms, but could be excluded empirically, by appeal to 'memory' of cases in which *q* has been experienced in association with *p*, and by an act of 'faith' in the unfailing repetition of that association.

I have two further notes to make on the present dichotomy.

(1) It is certainly closely connected with the Stoic theory of 'signs' (*sēmeia*), and with the distinction which the Stoics, beginning perhaps with Zeno, made between a 'commemorative' (*hupomnēstikon*) and an 'indicative' (*endeiktikon*) sign.[31] A commemorative sign is one which signals the existence of something temporarily non-evident (*pros kairon adēlon*); it owes its value as a sign, and its name of 'commemorative' sign, to our *memory* of the occasions on which it has been present in *observable* association

---

[30] In 309 the word ἀδύνατον must, I think, be interpreted in the sense of *a priori* impossibility. In the same way, the possibility that Zeus is lying, or had made a mistake, is a purely *a priori* possiblity, and not one guaranteed by actual experience.

[31] On signs see *PH* II 99–102; *M* VIII 151–5; and the account by Verbeke [122]. Zeno wrote Περὶ σημείων (DL VII 4); cf. Rist [119], esp. pp. 389–90 (Rist translates σημεῖα by 'signals' in order to avoid possible confusion with σημαίνοντα, 'signs' or 'signifiers').

with that of which it is a sign. Thus smoke can be considered a
sign, or a signal, of a fire which, though bright enough in its own
nature, is temporarily invisible. An indicative sign, on the other
hand, is one which signals something naturally non-evident
(*phusei adēlon*); thus it cannot owe its signalling capacity to our
observation of a constant conjunction between it and what it
signals, for the latter is in principle unobservable; it must rather
be 'by its own nature and constitution' (*ek tēs idias phuseōs kai
kataskeuēs*) (*M* VIII 154) that it makes us 'conclude rationally'
(*logizometha*) (155) to the existence of what it signifies; for
example, bodily movements are indicative signs of the existence
of the soul, which is itself always and in principle invisible.

Those characteristics fit perfectly with the dichotomy we are at
present examining. For, on the one hand, the future wealth of our
protégé of Zeus is quite certainly a temporary *adēlon*, since we shall
have to wait at most a few decades before it is manifest to every
eye; and faith in the words of the god is, as we have seen,
implicitly founded on our memory (*mnēmē*) of the many occasions
on which we have been able to see for ourselves the efficacy of his
prophecies. On the other hand, the existence of invisible pores in
the skin is naturally *adēlon*, as we know, and the flow of the sweat
is a revelatory sign of them by the very nature of the premisses
(*ek tēs autōn phuseōs*) which serve to prove it. Thus we may suggest
that the author of the dichotomy before us divided the genus he
had reached (the genus of concludent arguments with a non-
evident conclusion) by applying the distinction between *adēlon
phusei* and *adēlon pros kairon*, and by adapting to the theory of
proof the distinction between the corresponding species of sign.

(2) We might try to delineate more nearly the class of 'merely
progressive' arguments, and at the same time to determine more
precisely the nature of 'revelation', by asking the following
question: in the conditional, 'If some god has said to you that
this man will be rich, he will be rich', which are the elements
without whose presence we should be obliged to place the
argument in a different category? A series of imaginative modifications to the example will enable us to separate the essential
from the accidental here.

(a) The asymmetry between a major premiss with an indefinite
subject ('some god') and a minor premiss with a definite subject
('this god') is an interesting feature of many examples of Stoic

arguments;[32] but our argument would remain in the same class, I think, if we were to replace the indefinite expression 'some god' by a definite expression ('this god'), or even by what the Stoics called an 'intermediate' expression ('Zeus').[33]

(b) It would surely still belong to the same class if the god had declared himself on some subject other than the economic prospects of a given individual: every argument beginning 'If some god says to you that p . . .' will be 'merely progressive', provided only that p is *adēlon* (the argument 'If some god has said to you that it is day . . .' would have a pre-evident conclusion). But note that p need not be a temporary *adēlon*: if a god decided to tell us that there were 10^{853946} grains of sand in Libya, we should have to take his word for it, even though we had no hope, in this case, of testing it; and if he decided to tell us that there are invisible pores in the skin, that would not make his words into an 'indicative' sign of the existence of those pores. A mistaken utterance is not an *a priori* impossibility—not even from divine lips; and whatever a Stoic god may say, his word is never a 'revealed truth', and his message is no apocalypse. Thus the fact that the proposition p in the oracle example refers to the future is not essential: the *prophetic* aspect of the example is accidental.

(c) We can place in the class of 'merely progressive' arguments every argument beginning 'If x has said to you that p', provided that the range of x is restricted to speakers who are known empirically to be always reliable[34]—the divinity of a speaker is simply the limiting case of this, a case peculiarly favourable to the 'faith' which we can have in his words.[35] The *religious* aspect of our example is no more essential to it than its prophetic aspect.

(d) We might perhaps think that we can go no further, and

---

[32] On this see Imbert [95], esp. 240–1. This functional difference between major and minor premiss is sometimes reflected in Stoic terminology: λῆμμα is reserved for the major and πρόσληψις is used to name the minor premiss (see e.g. DL VII 76).

[33] Cf. *M* VIII 96–7, and the analogous classification, using a different vocabulary, at DL VII 70 (discussed by Goulet [93]).

[34] It is true that the Sage, who possesses knowledge of all truths, sometimes utters falsehoods (cf. *PH* II 80–3; *M* VII 38–45; and the discussion by Long [108]); but if it is true of the Sage, it must be true, *a fortiori*, of God—and if we admit such a possibility, the major premiss of the argument will be (empirically) unacceptable.

[35] Oddly enough, the manuscripts omit the word 'θεῶν' in the *PH* version of the oracle argument (141); the editors restore it, adducing the parallel in the *M* version. The opposite solution, proposed by Mutschmann, is to rely on *PH* and expel the word from *M*; but that is not very convincing.

that the *verbal* aspect of the example cannot be suppressed without removing it from the category of 'merely progressive' arguments. If that is so, we shall have to say that 'revelatory' arguments are those whose conclusions rest on the sort of evidence proper to signs of the type later called 'natural' (the flowing of sweat would be a 'natural' sign of the porousness of the skin), and that 'merely progressive' arguments are those whose conclusion rests on the trust we place in certain producers of verbal signs. The distinction will thus approximate to the later distinction between arguments from authority and arguments from reason. But if my remark (1) is correct, that cannot be right. The distinction between indicative and commemorative signs is not at all the same as that between natural and verbal signs: thus smoke, a typical example of a natural sign, is taken by the Stoics to be a *commemorative* sign of the temporarily invisible fire which causes it, because the association between smoke and fire is supported, in their view, by no more than an empirical regularity (*PH* II 100; *M* VIII 152). Hence, we must classify as 'merely progressive' and not as 'revelatory' every argument in which the major premiss is a conditional whose antecedent is a commemorative sign of its consequent, even if that sign has nothing to do with the making of any verbal statement (e.g. 'If there is smoke, there is fire; the first; therefore the second').

Thus we see that the author of the *M* version perhaps took as essential to his example certain features which are not in fact so—I mean the aspects of prophecy, of religion, and of language. He underlines the part played by man's faith in the word of god; but, as I have already noted, he pays little attention to the role of memory: he mentions it alongside faith in his definition of non-revelatory arguments (*ek pisteōs kai mnēmēs*: 308), but he does not comment on it, and indeed he never mentions it again in his discussion (*pistis* reappears alone at the end of 308: *alla tōi pisteuein tēi tou theou apophansei*). Now memory and faith seem to be indissolubly linked in the functioning of commemorative signs: memory of past experiences would do us no good unless it bred a faith that the future would see them repeated in similar fashion; and faith in signs would be blind if it did not rest on the memory of those observations which support it.[36] We know,

---

[36] This functional complementarity of memory and faith prevents me from following a suggestion made by Jonathan Barnes, who wondered if μνήμη refers to

moreover, that memory gave the commemorative sign its name, and that the role of memory is regularly emphasized in descriptions of the functioning of this sort of sign (*PH* II 100; *M* VIII 152–3); we know also that when Sextus concentrates his sceptical polemic on the indicative sign, and spares the commemorative sign, that is because the former is the tool *par excellence* of the dogmatic philosophers, who claim with its help to transcend the level of the phenomena, whereas the latter is something we must all of us make use of and have confidence in it if we are to live our daily lives (*to gar hupomnēstikon pepisteuetai hupo tou biou*: *PH* II 102; *touto gar para pasi koinōs tois ek tou biou pepisteuetai chrēsimeuein*: *M* VIII 156).[37] In these circumstances, it is perhaps not too rash to suppose that in trying to apply the distinction between the two types of sign to his classification of arguments, the author of the *M* version mistook the meaning of the word '*pistis*'—he took it in a religious sense, although in his sources it referred only to the 'trust' which we spontaneously place in the regularity of natural phenomena.

Let me end this long commentary on the dichotomies of the *M* version by setting out the definition of proof which they implicitly contain. Admittedly, it is never stated in the paragraphs we have analysed (301–9) that a proof is an argument 'at the same time progressive and revelatory'; but that must surely be the case, given that the goal of the whole series of dichotomies is the definition of proof, and that the series culminates with arguments that are 'at the same time progressive and revelatory'. Thus we may conclude that the dichotomies of *M* imply the following definition of proof: *a concludent argument, with a non-evident conclusion, which is at the same time progressive and revelatory*. I propose to call this *Definition R*, to mark the particular role which revelation plays in it; that characteristic, as we shall see, will be what differentiates it from the other definitions that we shall encounter.

(4) In 310 Sextus himself proceeds to give a recapitulation of

---

'reliance on one's own experience' and πίστις to 'reliance on that of others'. If that were so, I think we should have to say that non-revelatory arguments depend on faith *or* on memory; but our author says that they depend on faith *and* on memory.

[37] One might object that it is a matter of trust in commemorative signs and not, properly speaking, of trust in natural phenomena. But if we place trust in a commemorative sign, surely that is only because we have a basic trust in the regularity of nature and because we assent to what will later be called the 'principle of Induction'.

the sort which I have just presented on my own account. That he
is speaking here *in propria persona*, drawing the moral from the
texts he has just reproduced or paraphrased, is shown clearly
enough by his mode of expression ('That being so, proof *must be
. . .*': *opheilei einai*). But we notice at once that there is an important
difference between the definition he claims to draw from the
series of dichotomies and the one I drew from the text a moment
ago. This is what he says: 'This being so, a proof must first of all
be an *argument*, secondly *concludent*, thirdly *true* (*triton kai alēthēs*),
fourthly *having a non-evident conclusion*, fifthly *revealing this by the
force of the premisses*.' This new definition includes the notion of
revelatoriness which R contains; but it also includes the notion
of truth which is absent from R. I shall call it *Definition C*, since
it contains the conjunction of these two notions.[38]

It is tempting to explain the difference between Sextus' recapitulation and the text he professedly recapitulates by supposing
either that the dichotomies in 303–9 mentioned truth in a
paragraph which has been accidentally lost, or that the notion was
later added to the recapitulation in 310 by some *lector eruditus*. But
the next part of the text in my view excludes each of those
hypotheses.

(5) For in 311–13 Sextus tries to justify the addition of the
notion of truth by giving an example of an argument which is
'concludent but not true', i.e. which is valid from the point of
view of formal logic but which has a false premiss and leads to a
false conclusion. This discussion is connected to the previous
paragraph by the particle '*goun*' ('However that may be, this much

---

[38] Definition C has been subject to very different assessments. Barnes refers to it,
in a general way, as 'the Stoic analysis of proof' (below, p. 165 n. 6); Egli ([41], 62),
on the other hand, thinks it is 'not Stoic in origin'. His general thesis about the three
texts on the definition of proof is that they incorporate two distinct definitions:
(i) an 'old Stoic' definition containing three features (an argument that is concludent, true, and demonstrative): the main text for this is *M* VIII 411–23, and it is
the same as the abbreviated definition preserved by Diogenes Laertius and Cicero
(cf. above, p. 125 n. 1); that will appear later as my Definition T. (ii) There is a
definition which is 'not Stoic in origin', consisting of five points (an argument which
is concludent, true, with non-evident conclusion, revealing its conclusion by the
logical force of the premisses—but it is illogical to count the feature 'argument' as
one of the five points in this definition): this is attested by *M* VIII 310 and *PH* II 143, and it is my Definition C. According to Egli,
Sextus mixed up these two theories of proof in the two expositions which are not
explicitly called Stoic (i.e. *PH* II 134–43 and *M* VIII 300–15); and his source was a
treatise of Clitomachus which attacked the Stoic theory of proof.

is clear . . .'); and that, I think, proves both that the present case was not adverted to in the earlier dichotomies, and also that Sextus took it upon himself to introduce the notion of truth into the recapitulation—as he must if he is to take the new case into consideration.[39]

Sextus' example (311) is this: '(When it is day), "If it is night, it is dark; it is night; therefore, it is dark" '. No doubt Sextus borrowed the example from some other source—we find it performing the same function at *PH* II 139 and also at *M* VIII 413. Nevertheless, it is notable that when Sextus explains why such an argument must be called concludent, he here refers to the criterion of concludency of the *M* version (*dothentōn gar autou tōn lēmmatōn huparchein, sunagetai kai hē epiphora*—compare that with the expressions of 303-4). In the *PH* version his explanation invokes the rigorous criterion of concludency which, as we have seen, is characteristic of that version:[40] Sextus is a conscientious and an intelligent worker; and he does not ignore the differences between the various sources he uses.

And here is a further indication of that professional conscientiousness: having inserted an additional chapter into the story, Sextus tidies things up by listing once again all the chapters which follow the one he has added. Thus he next gives an example of an argument which, though concludent and true, is not probative, since its conclusion is pre-evident (312: the example, again, is the celebrated 'If it is day, it is light . . .'—stated, presumably, in the daytime; the example has already been adduced, to the same end, in 305). Next, he gives (313) an example of an argument which, though it is concludent and true, and has a non-evident conclusion, is not probative, since it does not reveal the conclusion (the example of the oracle).

(6) After this reworking of the material, with its complementary elucidations, we feel the need for a new recapitulation which will finally set our thoughts in order. A second recapitulation does indeed appear in 314; but it appears in a most unexpected

---

[39] Egli [41], 64, considers 311-14 to be an addition by Sextus himself; he notes that if you pass directly from 310 to the second half of 314 (ἔνθεν καὶ οὕτως . . .), you get a sequence of thought entirely comparable to that in *PH* II 143. But he has not seen that the addition was made necessary by Sextus' decision to introduce τρίτον καὶ ἀληθής into the definition of proof (310).

[40] Cf. *PH* II 139 (where we should read, with Mates [44], 111 n. 30: εἰ νύξ ἐστι, καὶ εἰ νύξ ἐστι σκότος ἐστί, σκότος ἐστίν); *M* VIII 415-17.

form. For Sextus begins by laying down a new definition of proof, which tallies exactly neither with R nor with C. Here it is: 'When all these characteristics are found together, and the argument is *concludent and true and establishing* (*parastatikon*) *a non-evident conclusion*, there is a proof.' Like C and unlike R, this definition includes the notion of truth; but unlike both C and R, it does not explicitly contain the notion of revelation: to mark those peculiarities, I shall call it *Definition T*.

Definition T is, according to Egli (above, p. 144, n. 38), the old Stoic definition; even so, I must defend its independent reality against possible objections by Barnes (below, p. 178, n. 21) and his readers. I entirely agree with Barnes that the notion of revelation is 'a crucial feature of the Stoic notion of proof' (see the many references he cites); moreover, the abbreviated Stoic definition (cited above, p. 125, n. 1) basically comes down to just that. But in my view this notion has neither the same sense nor the same function in all the relevant texts. We may indeed say that all the Stoic authors who applied themselves to the subject of proof agreed that the conclusion of an *apodeixis* is 'revealed' by its premisses; but that did not mean the same thing for all of them: some took the word 'revelation' in a narrow sense, others in a broad sense, perhaps without being quite aware of the difference.

(i) The narrow sense goes along with the idea that there are several ways of establishing a non-evident conclusion, and that only one of those ways can properly be called 'revelatory': every 'revealed' conclusion is non-evident, but a non-evident conclusion can be reached without being 'revealed'. In this narrow sense of the word, it will be stated that the conclusion of a proof is revealed 'by the force of the premisses' (and not simply 'by the premisses'). From this point of view, the notion of revelation must be introduced into the definition of proof as a specific difference, independent of the others, allowing us to subdivide the class of arguments with non-evident conclusion. That is what happens in Definitions C and R.

(ii) The broad sense of the word 'revelation' goes along with the idea that a non-evident conclusion is revealed merely by the fact that, though non-evident, it is nevertheless reached: the conclusion of a true concludent argument is revealed if and only if it is non-evident. The existence of this broad sense is, I think, clearly attested: it is plainly to be seen at *M* VIII 422–3, where it is said that in a probative argument 'the conclusion, being non-evident, is revealed by the premisses (*tēn epiphoran adēlon ousan ekkaluptesthai hupo tōn lēmmatōn*), and that the argument about lactation (see above, p. 135, n. 24) 'having as a conclusion the non-evident proposition "This woman has conceived", reveals it through its premisses (*adēlon gar echōn to sumperasma, to keknēken ara hēde, touto dia tōn lēmmatōn ekkaluptei*).' (On the same note, observe that the idea of revelation figures in the definition of sign in general (cf. *M* VIII 245; *PH* II 104); for, although it appears in the definition of the indicative sign, it does not, despite its position, do so as a specific difference of that sort of sign (*PH* II 101). If it is thus true that proof is a species of sign (cf. above, nn. 6, 14, 22), and that a proof is 'revelatory of its conclusion' (*PH* II 131), it would be wrong to infer that the type of sign in question is only the indicative sign.) In the broad sense of the word, revelation need not appear in the definition of proof as an independent condition: it is implied by the condition that the conclusion be non-evident. And that is just what happens in Definition *T*.

In Definition *T*, as it is formulated at the beginning of 314, '*parastatikos*' is indeed, as Barnes says (p. 165, n. 7), a synonym for '*ekkaluptikos*'—but only in the broad sense of the latter term. The use of '*parastatikos*' here may well be specifically intended to avoid any confusion with the narrow sense of '*ekkaluptikos*'. Thus it is not surprising that Sextus can immediately present another definition, which contains the word '*ekkaluptōn*', as though it were an alternative formulation of Definition *T*

For at this point Sextus clearly wants to work his way towards yet another new definition of proof—a definition which he professedly borrows from a written source. This is how he presents it (314): 'That is why they also describe it (*hupographousin*) as follows: A proof is *an argument which, from agreed premisses, reveals in a concludent fashion a non-evident conclusion* (*apodeixis esti logos di' homologoumenōn lēmmatōn kata sunagōgēn epiphoran ekkaluptōn adēlon*).' This definition contains, in an arbitrary order but in more or less literal form, most of the constituents of the definitions we have already met: the generic notion of argument (*logos*); concludency (*kata sunagōgēn*); perhaps truth (*di' homologoumenōn lēmmatōn*—assuming that a premiss is only agreed to if it is true); non-evidence of the conclusion (*epiphoran adēlon*); revelation (*ekkaluptōn*). The most remarkable thing about this definition, in my view, is that it has evidently not been obtained by way of dichotomous divisions.[41] Grammatically speaking, it does not possess the conjunctive structure which comes from a succession of divisions (and which Definition *C* for example, characteristically does possess); it has what might be called an organic structure: its several components are centred about the participle '*ekkaluptōn*' which is completed by an object ('*epiphoran adēlon*') and by various qualifications introduced by different prepositions (*di' homologoumenōn lēmmatōn*; *kata sunagōgēn*). To mark that structure, let us call this formula *Definition S*. Its author is plainly concerned neither to set its constituents in a branching logical order, nor to give any precise idea of those classes of arguments which lack one or other of the characteristic marks of probative argument.

Thus the reader of version *M* has come across no less than four definitions of proof: *R, C, T,* and *S.* But there is still a surprise in store for him; for if he was at least able to recognize in all four definitions a common Stoic inspiration, he now (314) finds the last of them illustrated by an example which is none other than the famous Epicurean demonstration of the existence of the void from the existence of motion.[42] On that final note of astonishment, let us end our analysis of this tortured text, the genesis of which was evidently complicated in the extreme.

I turn now to *PH* II 134–43. That version is simpler and more straightforward than *M*, and I have already anticipated some of its essential features: thus I shall be able to proceed—as you may well hope—with a little more dispatch.

Sextus himself indeed evinces the same desire for brevity. At the beginning of the chapter he promises to expound shortly (*suntomōs*) the theory of proof, 'trying first to explain in a few words (*dia bracheōn*) what they say (*ti phasin*) proof is'. As if to give an immediate example of his wish to be brief, he does not bother to say that *apodeixis* belongs to the genus *logos*, nor—*a fortiori*—to explain why it does.

His account can be put schematically as follows: (1) opening

---

[41] I do not think that it can have been 'put together' from the five points listed at *M* VIII 310, as Egli [41], 62, suggests.

[42] Cf. Epicurus *apud* DL X 40; *M* VIII 329 (=Usener [13], no. 272).

statement of a definition of proof (135)—this is in fact Definition
S, and all that follows is offered as a series of elucidations designed
to make the sense of that definition more intelligible; (2) definition
of *logos* and of its elements (135–6); (3) dichotomous division of
the genus *logos* (137–42) along the following lines:

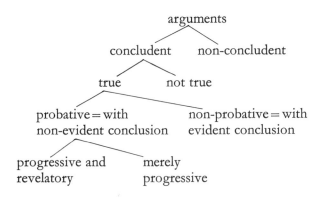

arguments
    concludent   non-concludent

    true   not true

  probative = with   non-probative = with
  non-evident conclusion   evident conclusion

  progressive and   merely
  revelatory   progressive

(4) Recapitulation, and *reprise* of Definition *S* which the whole
discussion was designed to justify (143).

As in the case of the *M* version, I shall now consider in a little
more detail each of the successive parts of this text.

(1) Definition *S* is brought onto the stage as a classic definition
(*hōs phasin*). What follows is designed to clarify the content of the
definition: 'What they say will be more clear from what follows.'
But these elucidations are probably not Sextus' own handiwork;
rather, I think that he takes them from a different source—at
least the final sentence of the chapter (143) suggests such a
conjecture: 'It is in this way, then, that they are accustomed
(*eiōthasi*) to explain the notion of proof' (cf. Egli [41], 64).

(2) While the definition of *logos* is practically the same as that
in *M*, the definition of the premisses is significantly different; but
I have nothing to add to what I have already said on the matter.

(3) The sequence of dichotomies contains several important
points which demand our attention:

(3A) As we have seen, the division of *logoi* into concludent and
non-concludent arguments (137) is grounded on a different
criterion of concludency from the one used in the *M* version—a
criterion which has won the admiration of modern logicians.

(3B) Concludent arguments are next subdivided into 'true' and 'non-true' arguments (138–9). A concludent argument is true when 'not only is the conditional which has the conjunction of its premisses as antecedent and its conclusion as consequent sound (so that, on the new criterion, the argument is concludent), but also both the conclusion and the conjunction of its premisses, which forms the antecedent of that conditional, are true.' For the conjunction to be true, each of the premisses must of course be true; and if it is so, then the conclusion too will be true.[43]

There is no need to comment on the change in sense of the word 'true', which applies to an argument in the *definiendum* and to a proposition in the *definiens*—the point has often been noticed (cf. Mates [44], 132). Rather let us remember that the distinction between concludent arguments which are true and those which are not true—a distinction which is fundamental from a logical point of view—was absent from the dichotomies of *M*. As if to underline its importance and its novelty, *PH* carefully explains (139) how an argument can be concludent without being true; he uses an example ('If it is night, it is dark; etc.', stated in daylight) which we have already met in the elucidations which Sextus added to the first recapitulation in the *M* version (311).[44]

(3C) In 140 true arguments are, in their turn, subdivided into two classes: some are 'probative' (*apodeiktikoi*), viz. those which 'from pre-evident premisses (*dia prodēlōn*) lead to a conclusion which is non-evident (*adelon ti sunagontes*)'; others are 'non-probative', viz. those which 'are not of that sort'. With regard to this dichotomy, I confess that at first it seemed to me evident that there was an absolute identity between probative argument (*logos apodeiktikos*) and proof (*apodeixis*); but since Barnes holds the contrary opinion (below, p. 178, and n. 21), I must find some arguments to justify my intuitive identification of the two things.

First, and from a general point of view, let me say that in a division of the genus *logos* which is designed to produce a definition of the species *apodeixis*, it would be very odd if the

---

[43] Strictly speaking, the truth of the conclusion should not appear in the definition of a true argument, on pain of redundancy. That is why Mates [44], 111 n. 29, proposes to excise the words καὶ τὸ συμπέρασμα in 138. He has not noticed that at the end of 139 Sextus quotes another Stoic definition of a true argument, which proves that the Stoics did not shrink from such a redundancy: 'They also say that a true argument is one which establishes a true conclusion from true premisses.'

[44] Here again the text has only recently been rightly understood and emended; cf. Mates's correction, above, p. 145 n. 40.

differentia *apodeiktikos* were introduced at any level other than that at which the species *apodeixis* is reached: would you tolerate a classification of animals in which the notion of *human animal* was introduced at an earlier level than that of *man*? That would surely be more than 'infelicitous'.

But I can also adduce a textual argument, drawn from *M* VIII 411–28: that long polemical passage is designed to test whether the Stoics (named at 425) can, in their logical theory, fulfil 'the claim of proof' (*hē tēs apodeixeōs huposchesis*) (411). How does Sextus conduct the test? He explains in detail that there are three classes of argument, each included in its predecessor; viz, concludent arguments, true arguments, and probative arguments (*apodeiktikoi*: 411–12, 424); and he shows that, given the relations of inclusion among those classes, if we can prove that concludent arguments are 'undiscoverable' (*aneuretos*), we shall thereby have proved that neither true nor probative arguments can be discovered (425). Thus it appears that in order to rebut 'the claim of proof', it is necessary and sufficient to rebut the claim of probative argument: nowhere is there the least suspicion of a distinction between proof and probative argument.

Hence it is, I believe, legitimate to hold that in the series of dichotomies in the *PH* version, the paragraph which introduces the notion of probative argument (140), at the same time marks the stage at which the notion of proof is reached. Thus proof—and here we have an important innovation compared to the *M* version—is no longer a subdivision of the species *argument with a non-evident conclusion*; rather it is identical with that species itself.

The dichotomy raises a second question. Probative arguments are there defined as 'leading from pre-evident premisses to a non-evident conclusion'. If we take the definition literally, we shall have to countenance three distinct types of non-probative argument: those whose premisses and conclusion are pre-evident; those whose premisses and conclusion are non-evident; and those whose premisses are non-evident and whose conclusion is pre-evident. The text does not, however, make that complicated move. The author of the *PH* version is content to give two examples: one of a non-probative argument (that of the day and its inevitable light), which is explicitly classified as such because its conclusion is pre-evident; and one of a probative argument (that of the pores and their ceaseless sweat), which is explicitly classified as such because its conclusion is non-evident.

Thus it appears that it is not essential to the *PH* definition of proof that the premisses be pre-evident. That might perhaps encourage us to expel from the text the words '*dia prodēlōn*' (the words are not echoed in the later appearances of the definition at 141 and 143, and they have no parallel at the corresponding stage in the dichotomies of *M*, 305–6); and it seems in particular to show that the Stoic concept of proof is not strictly limited to inferences founded directly upon the data of sense-experience: the Stoic theory *can*—even if it rarely *does*—recognize as proofs arguments whose premisses are not pre-evident but have themselves been proved by a sequence of one or more pro-syllogisms in which the only pre-evident propositions are the initial premisses of the probative chain.[45]

(3D) The next dichotomy (141–2) divides arguments with non-evident conclusions into those which are 'merely progressive' and those which are 'at the same time progressive and revelatory'. This section reproduces for the most part the corresponding section of the *M* version, which I have analysed at length. The essential difference is that here (although the text does not explicitly say so[46]) we are dealing with a distinction between two types of proof; for proof has already been identified as argument to a non-evident conclusion. The author of *PH* thinks that the argument about the oracle is no less a proof than the argument about the pores, whatever other differences there may be between them. That apart, the text of *PH* is here very similar to that of *M*: the definitions, the examples, and the comments, are pretty well identical in the two versions—though the author of *PH* is both more concise and more precise.

That general similarity sets in higher relief two differences to

---

[45] According to Barnes, below, p. 181, 'linked series of syllogisms, such as constitute an Aristotelian science, will not be found among the Stoics.' However, they allow that the premisses of an argument can be proved by means of another argument (cf. the 'third rule' of their metalogic, Alexander, *in APr.* 278.6 ff.: 'If from two propositions a third is deduced, and if there are propositions from which one of the premisses can be deduced, then the other premiss together with these propositions will yield the conclusion').

[46] As Barnes rightly remarks (below, p. 178 n. 21), Sextus never says that he is distinguishing two types of ἀπόδειξις, and he offers 143 as a summary of the whole of 134–42 (including the last dichotomy, 141–2). I shall suggest later on a possible explanation for this state of affairs (below, p. 159 n. 53).

which I must draw attention. (i) Commenting on the example of
the oracle, the author of *M* said (308) that we accept its conclusion
'not because it is established by (*ouk ek*) the force of the argument
put forward, but (*alla*) because we have faith in the god's
assertion'. In his note on the same example (141), the author of
PH significantly weakens the contrast and says that 'we give our
assent to the conclusion not so much (*ouch houtōs*) because of the
necessity of the premisses as (*hōs*) by our faith in the statement of
the god.'[47] That modification seems to indicate that the author of
PH discreetly removed the error committed by *M*: acceptance of
the conclusion, in the example of the oracle, certainly depends on
our admitting the premisses, and hence on our 'faith' in divine
veracity; but it also depends, essentially, on the formal validity of
the reasoning.

(ii) The second nuance is no less significant: in attempting to
show why the argument of the pores is 'revelatory', the author of
M, as we have seen, found himself a trifle embarrassed, and he
tried to ground it on another piece of reasoning which had no
very plausible claim to serve as a foundation for the original
argument. Now the author of *PH* expresses himself with the
assured vigour and technical accuracy of a competent logician
(142): 'The flowing of the sweat is revelatory of the existence of
pores because we grasp in advance (*dia to proeilēphthai*) that a
liquid cannot pass through a solid body.' In the word '*proeilēphthai*'
we can hear an echo of the celebrated Stoic notion of *prolēpsis*
(preconception, or prenotion);[48] and we thus see that the author
of *PH*, instead of courting the danger of an infinite regress by
resting one argument on another, justifies the argument of the
pores by grounding it on the criterion of preconception, which
forms the absolute basis for the dogmatists' attempt to transcend
the phenomena.[49] It is because we read directly, from our preconceptions of solidity and liquidity, that a liquid cannot pass
through a solid, that we are able to understand the phenomenon
of the flowing of the sweat as a revelatory sign of the existence of
pores in the skin, even though those pores are irreducibly
invisible.

[47] I am not sure that the strange phrase οὐχ οὕτως . . . ὡς . . . should be translated
like this; but I do not see any plausible alternative.

[48] I owe this point to Gisela Striker.

[49] On the 'canonical' role of πρόληψις see Goldschmidt [128]; Schofield, Chapter
11 below.

(4) Now that the series of dichotomies is at an end, we expect the author of *PH* to set out the definition of proof which they implicitly contain. Given our analysis of the preceding text, that definition should be formulated as follows: a proof is *an argument which is concludent and true, and which has a non-evident conclusion* (i.e. is probative). That definition is simply Definition *T*; and the account of *PH*, up to this point, can be considered a clear and coherent explication of it. But things become a little perplexed in Sextus' last paragraph (140), where he proceeds, as he did in *M*, to offer on his own account a recapitulation of the sort I have just made. I translate the whole of the paragraph:

> Thus a proof must be both an argument (*kai logos*), and concludent (*kai sunaktikos*), and true (*kai alēthēs*), and having a non-evident conclusion (*kai adēlon echōn sumperasma*) and [this word is omitted in one of our sources for the text[50]] revealed by the force of the premisses (*kai ekkaluptomenon*—or simply *ekkaluptomenon*—*hupo tēs dunameōs tōn lēmmatōn*). And that is why it is said that a proof is an argument which, from agreed premisses, reveals in a concludent fashion a conclusion which is non-evident.

The last sentence of that paragraph poses no problems: we recognize Definition *S*, which was announced at the start of the chapter and which the remainder of the chapter was designed to elucidate. But the first part of the paragraph causes difficulty. If we keep the text transmitted by the Greek manuscripts (i.e. including the '*kai*'), we must acknowledge that Sextus has extracted from the dichotomies a definition different from the one which they imply: they imply Definition *T*, as we have just seen; but Sextus seems to extract from them Definition *C*.

But that difficulty can be overcome with the help of the variant reading offered by one of our sources for the text. For we have seen that the conjunction 'and' (*kai*), which the recapitulation regularly places before each component of the definition, is exceptionally missing, in one of the authorities for the text, before '*ekkaluptomenon*'—i.e. before the very term which causes the difficulty. Now a variant of that sort standardly indicates that a gloss has probably been interpolated into the text—the syntactical

---

[50] Viz. the Latin translation of Sextus, preserved in the MS Parisinus Lat. 14700. Mutschmann dates this translation to the thirteenth century; he thinks that it represents an archetype independent of that of the Greek manuscripts, and he ascribes to it an importance equal to that of the manuscripts for the establishment of the text.

hiatus created by the interpolation being left empty by some copists and filled up by others. In the circumstances I do not hesitate to suggest that we athetize the whole expression *'kai ekkaluptomenon hupo tēs dunameōs tōn lēmmatōn'*.[51] Thus emended, the text, I think, no longer presents any difficulty. The recapitulation gives Definition *T*, which is just what can be properly extracted from the dichotomies. Moreover, Sextus is right in thinking that the definition obtained in the recapitulation allows him to explain Definition *S*, which he goes on to quote; for even though the former no longer contains *'ekkaluptomenon'* (after the emendation I propose), whereas the latter contains *'ekkaluptōn'*, nevertheless the property of having a non-evident conclusion, which is included in Definition *T*, implies, as we have seen, that the conclusion is 'revealed' in the broad sense of the term.

Having analysed and compared the two texts of *M* and *PH*, I shall now give a summary in the form of a table containing the different definitions of proof we have encountered, together with their constituent elements:

		logos	*sunaktikos*	*alēthēs*	*adēlon sumperasma*	*ekkaluptikos*
		argument	concludent	true	with non-evident conclusion	revelatory (narrow sense)
R	*M* VIII 301–9 (implicit in the dichotomies)	+	+	−	+	+
C	*M* VIII 310 (first recapitulation)	+	+	+	+	+
T	*M* VIII 314 (second recapitulation) *PH* II 137–40 (implicit in the dichotomies) *PH* II 143 (emended text) *M* VIII 411–24	+	+	+	+	−
S	*M* VIII 314 *PH* II 135 *PH* II 143	+	+ (*kata sunagōgēn*)	? (*di' homologoumenōn lēmmatōn*)	+	? (*ekkaluptōn*)

[51] Kayser and Mutschmann preserve the text as transmitted by the Latin translation, i.e. they keep ἐκκαλυπτόμενον . . . λημμάτων but do not print the καί; that

Now let us ask the following question: what are the most conservative hypotheses by means of which we can give an historical explanation of the complex state of affairs I have tried to describe? We can, I think, make a few plausible conjectures.

(1) Of the four distinct definitions of proof which our texts present, the oldest must be Definition *S*. Unlike all the others, its structure, as I have already noted, does not reflect a dichotomous division. It is hard to imagine that it was formulated on the basis of the dichotomies of *M* or of *PH* (*pace* Egli [41], 62); and it is very easy to imagine that those dichotomies were elaborated after the event, in order to justify and explain Definition *S*. Remember too, that in the *PH* version the chapter on proof opens by citing this definition, and presents a unitary attempt to elucidate it.

Moreover, we should note that the other definitions preserve, with hardly any disagreement, those elements of *S* which contain no ambiguity: that is true for the defining characteristics *argument*, *concludent*,[52] *having a non-evident conclusion*. On the other hand, the characteristics over which Definitions *R*, *C*, and *T* disagree are precisely those which *S* expresses in a relatively obscure manner. One might well have hesitated, for example, over the phrase '*di' homologoumenōn lēmmatōn*': did the author of *S* presuppose that a premiss is 'agreed to' if and only if it is true? According to your answer to that question, you will be led in one of two directions: either you will explicitly specify that the premisses of a proof, unlike those of certain arguments which are concludent but not probative, must be true (that is what *C* and *T* do); or else,

---

is unconvincing, given the distinction I make above: it amounts to preserving the notion of revelation in the narrow sense (cf. ὑπὸ τῆς δυνάμεως τῶν λημμάτων) without giving it the status of an independent condition in the definition. My surgical solution is, despite appearances, less rash. Sextus' text has certainly been interlarded with interpolations of this sort, produced by the action of competent, or semi-competent, readers. Myles Burnyeat kindly drew my attention to two of them, whose author he wittily proposes to baptize 'Lector Sublogicus': *M* VII 243 (where the manuscripts give ἢ ἀπιθάνων, rightly rejected by von Arnim, Mutschmann, and Bury); and *M* VII 158 (where the manuscripts give οὐ περὶ πάντων ἐπέχων, which is generally and rightly corrected to ὁ περὶ πάντων ἐπέχων).

[52] συνακτικός is a correct gloss on κατὰ συναγωγήν, as *PH* II 170 shows (κατὰ συναγωγήν, τουτέστι συνακτικῶς).

presupposing that every 'agreed' premiss is true, you will omit the specification as being superfluous (that is what R does).

Again, you might wonder if the word '*ekkaluptōn*' in Definition S describes a relation which holds between an argument and its conclusion whenever that conclusion is non-evident; in that case you will hold that a non-evident conclusion can only be reached by 'revelation', and you will take that word in a broad sense. Or does the word rather describe a particular form of the relation, which must be considered as specifically characterizing the notion of proof? In that case you will hold that there are several ways of reaching a non-evident conclusion, only one of which can properly be called 'revelatory'; and you will take that word in its narrow sense. In the former case, there is no need explicitly to introduce the notion of revelatoriness into the definition of proof, since it is already implied by the non-evidence of the conclusion (that is what Definition T does); in the latter case you must put 'revelatoriness' into the definition as an independent feature (that is what R and C do). Thus the differences between R, C, and T have their roots in the least clear parts of S.

So we may posit the existence of an original author whose contribution to the mass of material we have studied consisted simply in supplying us with Definition S—he left to others the tasks of justifying that definition, and of elucidating its obscurities. Let us call this author Mr S. We can issue the following identikit picture of him: Mr S is a pioneer; he likes phrases that are well-turned and pregnant with meaning; he enjoys a prestige so great that his assiduously pious heirs will produce volumes of systematic and elucidatory commentary on his words.

(2) The earliest of the attempts to deduce Definition S by way of a series of dichotomies must have been that of M VIII 301-9, which implicitly contains Definition R. For we find there many indications that its author has not reached the same level of logical competence as the author of the PH version, who seems to have conscientiously corrected his mistakes. The author of the M dichotomies defines the notion of a premiss so as to exclude the possibility of arguing validly from false premisses; consequently, he does not feel the need to distinguish between a class of concludent arguments with true premisses and a class of concludent arguments with false premisses. He defines concludency in such a way that psychological clarity appears as a

component of logical validity. Having introduced a fairly complex distinction between 'merely progressive' arguments and arguments which are 'at the same time progressive and revelatory', he seemed to us incapable of giving an exact description of their difference: failing to grasp that the logical structure of the two examples he analyses is the same, he confuses an epistemological difference, which bears on the type of truth possessed by one of the premisses, with a logical difference, which bears on the type of relation between premisses and conclusion. I attempted to show that in making this distinction he tried to adapt to the theory of proof a distinction which had its origin in the theory of signs; and I ventured to suggest that he wrongly interpreted the notion of 'faith' in a religious sense.

For this second character in our story, whom I shall call Mr R, we can construct the following identikit: Mr R. is a zealous commentator on Mr S; a fairly mediocre logician; a man preoccupied with religious matters to the point of giving a religious twist to notions which originally had no such connotation.

(3) The *PH* version of the dichotomies, and Definition *T* which it implies (and which it explicitly states, if my textual suggestion for 143 is accepted), are chapters of our story due to the intervention of a third character, Mr T. Mr T took up again the task undertaken by Mr R; but he possessed resources of an incomparably superior kind to devote to the service of Mr S. Mr T can, I think, be given a later date than Mr R; for some of the differences we see between the work of the two men can only be properly explained if we allow that Mr T knew the work of Mr R, approved of it in principle, and used his own talents as an accomplished logician to improve upon it.

We noted, you will remember, the following modifications: Mr T adopts a new definition of the notion of a premiss, which dissipates Mr R's confusion between an 'agreed' and a true proposition; he distinguishes clearly between concludent arguments with true premisses and concludent arguments with false premisses, and he thereby stresses that the logical validity of an inference is independent of the truth of its constituent propositions; he formulates a criterion of concludency that is admirable in its rigour. He has enough respect for Mr R not to sacrifice the latter's distinction between 'merely progressive' arguments and 'progressive and revelatory' arguments, even though, in his view, the distinction no longer bears upon the definition of proof as such.[53]

For these reasons (if we may continue our little game of identikit portraiture) we shall describe Mr T as follows: he was a logician of genius, no less attached than Mr R to the memory of Mr S; he undertook the same task as Mr R, but with distinctly superior resources; he had sufficient respect for Mr R to try to preserve whatever could be preserved of his work, but he did not shrink from correcting his errors with consummate self-assurance—and sometimes, perhaps, with a touch of irony.

(4) We had four definitions of proof; and thus far only three characters have been introduced into our hypothetical history of their origins. But three characters are enough: now that we have found fathers for definitions *S*, *R*, and *T*, only *C* remains parentless; but we need not look further than Sextus himself to file our fourth paternity suit. For Definition *C* was put forward as a recapitulation, probably composed by Sextus himself, of the series of dichotomies in *M* VIII 301–9, i.e. of the series composed by Mr R; but instead of extracting from that series Definition *R*, which it implies, Sextus proposed a definition which preserved all the characteristics of *R* but added to them the notion of truth, and he thus obtained Definition *C*; that addition then obliged him to produce some complementary commentary. Now the notion of truth is the mark of Definition *T*, which Sextus knew, and which he had in front of him not only when he wrote up the *PH* version but also when he wrote up the *M* version—for he cited it there (to the reader's surprise) in what I have called the second recapitulation (314). Thus it is highly probable that Sextus himself completed *R* by adding to it the notion of truth which he borrowed from *T*. Definition *C*, then, will simply be a hybrid produced by Sextus from his two originals; and it will be the only one of our definitions which is not properly Stoic.

(5) My investigations lead me, finally, to a conclusion which I neither foresaw nor desired: plainly, Mr S is very like Zeno (he is the founder of a school, and he has a taste for pithy expression— cf. DL VII 18, 20, 23, 24); Mr R makes us think of Cleanthes (he lacks intellectual finesse, he is interested in religious affairs, he is devoted to his predecessor's work—cf. DL VII 37, 170, 174;

[53] That will be why this dichotomy is retained in the *PH* version (cf. above, p. 152 n. 46).

and, of course, the *Hymn to Zeus*); and Mr T summons up Chrysippus (he is a brilliant logician; and he adopts towards his immediate predecessor a complex attitude compounded of respect, impatience, and mild irony[54]). Those similarities of character and circumstance, however, are not enough in themselves to warrant the identification of the three masters of the Old Stoa with the three logicians who seem to have turned their minds to the problem of the definition of proof. But a small detail gives substance to our hypothesis. We have seen that Mr T was the first to use the criterion of preconception to underpin the argument of the pores—the example of a revelatory probative argument. Now we know from Diogenes Laertius (VII 54) that Chrysippus added preconception to the criteria of truth. And if Chrysippus is Mr T, who are Mr S and Mr R if not Zeno and Cleanthes, his two predecessors at the head of the school? But enough of such speculation: for further information, please apply to your local clairvoyant.[55]

---

[54] Cf. DL VII 179: Chrysippus often said to Cleanthes that Cleanthes need only teach him the doctrines and he would find the *proofs* for himself; clearly, then, he thought himself better equipped than his master from that point of view.

[55] This is a revised version of the paper delivered at the Conference at Oriel College; I have been greatly benefited by remarks made by several participants, in particular by Gisela Striker, Myles Burnyeat, Michael Frede, Geoffrey Lloyd, and especially (both during and after the Conference) by Jonathan Barnes. I thank them all; and I also thank Jennifer Barnes for kindly undertaking the English translation.

PROOF DESTROYED

Jonathan Barnes

I

Sceptical philosophers customarily attack both perception and ratiocination; they question the salubrity of the sources from which we hope to draw our knowledge, and they cast doubt upon the reasonings whereby we expect to purify, canalize, and extend our understanding of the world. Scepticism of the reason is less discussed than scepticism of the senses, but it is no less menacing.

Rustic sceptics, who pretend to doubt everything, may, as Aristotle thought, deserve punishment rather than counter-argument; but urbane sceptics, whose doubt is both systematic and circumscribed, pose a sensible threat to our intellectual aspirations. And when the urbane sceptic turns his attention to matters of reason, one of his prime targets is the science of formal logic. John Locke, that prince of sceptical urbanity, is nowhere more vigorous than in his attack on syllogistic (which for him constituted the sum total of formal logic): the syllogism, he alleges, is not 'the great Instrument of Reason' (*Essay* IV xvii 4, p. 670, 34 Nidditch); formal logic fuddles our native wits and obfuscates the clear lines of natural deduction; 'to an ingenuous Searcher after Truth, who has no other aim, but to find it, there is no need of any such Form' (ibid. 675, 6); prudent scientists will ignore the artifices of the Schoolmen, and construct instead 'a Chain of *Ideas* . . . visibly link'd together in train' (ibid. 673, 19). The Lockean view, which in truth was largely cribbed from Descartes,[1] has never lacked support.

Lockean sceptics who doubt the utility of formal logic will train their guns on the theory of formal proof or demonstration. For the citadel of proof stands at the confluence of the two great streams of logic and epistemology; and it is therefore a natural object for sceptical siege. So, at least, it was for the ancient

---

[1] See J. A. Passmore, 'Descartes, the British Empiricists, and Formal Logic', *Philosophical Review* 62 (1953), 545–53; on Locke's attitude to logic see esp. W. S. Howell, *Eighteenth Century British Logic and Rhetoric* (Princeton, 1971), 264–98.

sceptics. And the major part of this chapter will narrate one clever manoeuvre in their campaign. Having scrutinized the attacking force, I shall turn briefly to the defenders and ask what damage and what losses they suffered from the sceptical investment. But first let me set down a few facts about the campaign as a whole.

Aristotle, whose *Posterior Analytics* is the first essay on the theory of proof, took part in a dispute over the nature, and the very possibility, of formal demonstration. Galen, the most passionate advocate among the ancients of the demonstrative art, tells us that his contemporaries were still engaged in the same debate.[2] And we know from the evidence of Sextus Empiricus that the centuries between Aristotle and Galen witnessed similar disputations.

The sceptical philosophers of the Hellenistic age gave the theory of proof a sound drubbing: there is no such thing as a demonstrative argument, they said; and if there were, it would be of no utility. Sextus patches together a lengthy account of their reasoning at *PH* II 134–92, and again at *M* VIII 300–481 (see also *PH* I 60, 122–3; II 113–14; *M* II 106–12). His immediate sources will doubtless have included Agrippa, the Pyrrhonian, whose arguments against proof are summarized by Diogenes Laertius (IX 88–91), and Clitomachus, the star pupil of Carneades, whom we know to have written *Refutations of Proof* and who was well versed in Peripatetic and Stoic philosophy.[3]

According to tradition, the sceptics were not the only sect who scorned proof: Epicurus despised logic and the paradigmatically demonstrative science of geometry, and he managed to corrupt the mathematician Polyaenus into sharing his view; and a later Epicurean, Zeno of Sidon, conducted an assault on Euclid. But Epicurus was himself no logical ignoramus; and Zeno may have argued, not that Euclidean proof is a mug's game, but rather that Euclid himself did not show sufficient logical rigour. In any

---

[2] For Aristotle see *APo.* A 3 (cf. J. Barnes, 'Aristotle, Menaechmus and Circular Proof', *Classical Quarterly* 26 (1976), 278–92); for Galen see *Ord. lib. prop.* XIX 52 K= *Scripta Minora* II 82, 3–10 (there is a list of Galen's writings on proof in *Lib. prop.* XIX 39–45 K=*Scr. Min.* II 115, 19–121, 4; the Galenian material on proof is collected and discussed by Müller [137]; see also Egli [41], 90–1).

[3] Several scholars have speculated on Sextus' immediate sources (see esp. Natorp [51], 258–64; dal Pra [27], 185–7, 385–7; Egli [41], 48–50, 61–73); none is wholly convincing, and the matter awaits a detailed examination of the whole Sextan context.

event, Epicureanism had its logicians: Sextus reports an anonymous Epicurean defence of demonstration (*M* VIII 337–336a); and he rehearses an argument in favour of the possibility of proof which he ascribes to Demetrius of Laconia (*M* VIII 348–66). Demetrius is known from other sources to have taken a logical interest in the theory of signs, and to have written at some length on the subject of geometry.[4] But it was the Stoics in whom the theory of proof found its Hellenistic champions. Like Aristotle, the Stoics were gifted logicians; unlike Aristotle, they were profoundly concerned with epistemological issues: it is only to be expected that they should have devoted some thought to the nature of formal proof. In their view, we are told, 'the matter of logic is argument; but its aim is knowledge of demonstrative procedures—for everything else culminates in this, viz. the giving of scientific demonstrations' (Ammonius, *in APr.* 9.26–9). And 'they say that they embarked on the art of logic not simply in order to know what follows from what, but in particular in order to know how to distinguish truths and falsehoods by means of demonstrative arguments' (*PH* II 247).

Sextus reports that 'the Stoics seem to have given particular precision to the forms of demonstration' (*M* VIII 396); he purveys the complex Stoic analyses of the concept of proof; and he indicates that the Stoics made some attempt to repel the sceptical attack on demonstrative argument (*PH* II 185–6; *M* VIII 463–9). 'All things', according to the Stoics, 'are seen by consideration through arguments' (DL VII 83); and demonstration 'contributes greatly to the correcting of our beliefs' (DL VII 45). Those general remarks are given particular content in several accounts of Stoic doctrine—Cicero's Stoic texts, for example, are marked by a special attention to demonstrative rigour.

If we turn to individual Stoics, the documentation is less rich. At least four of Chrysippus' numerous books were, to judge from

---

[4] Epicurus 'totam dialecticam et contemnit et irridet' (*Acad.* II 97); and the Epicureans τὴν διαλεκτικὴν ὡς παρέλκουσαν ἀποδόκιμαζουσι (DL X 31—note the verb παρέλκειν; cf. Cic. *Fin.* I 22); Polyaenus 'qui magnus mathematicus fuisse dicitur . . . Epicuro adsentiens totam geometriam falsam esse credidit' (Cic. *Acad.* II 106; cf. *Fin.* I 20); on Zeno see Proclus, *in Euc.* 214–18; for Demetrius on signs see Philodemus, *Sign.* XXVIII 13–XXIX 15, on geometry see the papyri in V. de Falco, *L'epicureo Demetrio Lacone* (Naples, 1923). For Epicurus, see Long [20], 29–30; for Zeno see Vlastos [125]. Further details, references, and bibliography in Sedley [132], 23–6.

their titles, collections of demonstrations (DL VII 197, 201, 202); and Diogenes of Babylon 'says that music is useful with regard to knowledge; for there are very many definitions and divisions and demonstrations in the science of harmony' (Philodemus, *Mus.* 89, 24–7 = *SVF* III Diog. 87). For the other older Stoics there is no explicit evidence.

Matters are different in the case of Posidonius. He, according to Galen, 'was brought up on geometry and was more accustomed than the other Stoics to follow out proofs' (*Plac.Hipp.Plat.* V 390 K = 362.5 M = T 83 Edelstein–Kidd); and Strabo calls him 'demonstrative'—in the logical sense (II 3.5 = T 46 E–K). Posidonius undertook to defend Euclid against Zeno of Sidon (Proclus, *in Euc.* 199, 3–200, 6 = F 46 E–K): his researches led him to develop a branch of the logic of relations, and to reflect upon the proper canons of demonstrative rigour (Galen, *inst.log.* XVIII = F 191 E–K). Moreover, he was a polymath, who attempted to supply proofs in the various sciences he studied (e.g. Simplicius, *in Phys.* 291. 21–292. 31 = F 18 E–K); and his concern to give explanations of things fits well with that probative purpose (Strabo, II 3.8 = T 85 E–K). Admittedly, Posidonius was something of an eclectic—Strabo calls him an 'Aristotelizer' (ibid.)—but there is little reason to doubt that his interest in proof was a part of his Stoic no less than of his Aristotelian heritage.[5]

The theory of proof was a talking-point and a matter of controversy in the Hellenistic schools. To what extent the history of that controversy can be reconstructed I do not know; and I shall imitate Sextus' usual practice by speaking impersonally of 'the sceptics' and 'the Stoics': my interest is in the substance rather than in the historical course of the Hellenistic disputes.

II

A: LOGICAL REDUNDANCY

Sextus offers Stoic accounts of proof in three separate passages (*PH* II 135–43; *M* VIII 301–15, 411–23), from which it emerges that a demonstration is an argument (*logos*) which is concludent

---

[5] On the matter of this paragraph see esp. Kidd [97].

(*sunaktikos*) and true (*alēthēs*), which has a non-evident (*adēlon*) conclusion, and which reveals (*ekkaluptein*) that conclusion. The analysis calls for a few brief comments.[6]

An argument or *logos* is 'a system composed of premisses and a conclusion' (*PH* II 135); and we may represent a Stoic *logos* as an ordered pair, $<\pi, \sigma>$, where π is a set of propositions, $\{a_1, a_2, \ldots, a_n\}$ (the putative premisses), and σ is a single proposition (the putative conclusion). An argument is *sunaktikos* if 'the conclusion follows the conjunction of the premisses' (*M* VIII 415); i.e. $<\pi, \sigma>$ is concludent if σ follows from the conjunction of the members of π. (I shall return to concludency shortly.) And a concludent argument is true if 'both the conclusion and the conjunction of its premisses are true' (*PH* II 138).

A true argument is only a demonstration if its conclusion, σ, is something 'non-evident' or *adēlon* (e.g. *M* VIII 305), and if it is 'revelatory' or *ekkaluptikos* of that conclusion.[7] A demonstration is thus an *illuminating* argument: its conclusion is a dim truth which its torch lights up for the eye of knowledge to see. But to say that is only to exchange one metaphor for another; and I shall have to return later to the matter of revelation or illumination.

So much for the Stoic analysis: let us now turn to the sceptical attack. At *M* VIII 429–447 Sextus adverts to 'the formal theory of conclusive and non-conconclusive arguments': 'conclusive (*perainōn*)' is synonymous with '*sunaktikos*', and Sextus is about to sketch a theory which classifies non-concludent arguments or fallacies. The theory is explicitly ascribed to the Stoics (435) who 'say that non-conclusive arguments come about in four ways: either in virtue of disconnectedness, or in virtue of redundancy,

---

[6] The Sextan passages have been analysed in detail by Brunschwig in the preceding Chapter. He discovers *four* distinct definitions of proof in them; but all four contain all and only the elements of what, in the text, I loosely call 'the' Stoic analysis. (Brunschwig's Definitions R and S do not *explicitly* contain the notion of truth; but they both implicitly assume that a demonstration has true premisses—and that is enough for my purposes. Brunschwig's T contains the notion of revelation, but only in a weak form: I shall return to that point later.) For the major part of my paper, what I say, generally, about 'the' Stoic concept of proof is compatible with everything in Brunschwig's subtle analysis. I may be allowed to add that my understanding of all these issues has been greatly influenced and improved by many discussions with Jacques Brunschwig.

[7] Revelation is a crucial feature of the Stoic notion of proof: see *PH* II 131, 134, 135, 143, 177, 178; *M* VIII 140, 277, 299, 310, 314, 422, 423. In the first of the two definitions at *M* VIII 314, the word 'ἐκκαλυπτικός' does not appear; but the definition contains the synonymous 'παραστατικός' (see *PH* II 178∼*M* VIII 392).

or in virtue of being propounded in an incorrect form, or in virtue of a deficiency' (429).

Sextus proceeds to explain the four types of fallacy (430–4), and he then employs each in turn to attack the theory of proof. The second type of fallacy appears on the stage at 438–43: the sceptics argue that the first of the five Stoic 'indemonstrables' is guilty of redundancy; that it is therefore non-concludent; and that no demonstration can properly be couched in its form.

At *PH* II 146–67 the same material is more generously reproduced: 146–51 recount the fourfold typology of fallacy, which is now ascribed to 'the Dialecticians'; and 156–67 consider redundancy. Here Sextus argues that redundancy infects more than the first indemonstrable—it infects all five of the indemonstrables, and also the 'perfect' syllogisms of the Peripatetics. Since 'the Dialecticians lay these down as the foundation of all inferences' (166), it will follow that all formal arguments are guilty of redundancy, that none are concludent—and hence that none can be used to formulate proofs.

The Argument from Redundancy is thus very simple: all formal inferences are redundant; no redundant arguments are concludent; hence no formal inferences are concludent, and no proofs can be expressed by way of formal logic.

Sextus' word for redundancy is '*parolkē*', and the verb '*parelkein*' means 'be redundant'. The term is not restricted to logical contexts but has a perfectly general sense: Apollonius Dyscolus, for example, frequently uses it in a semantic context (observing, say, that the prefix '*en-*' in '*enantios*' and '*enanchios*' *parelkei*; for those adjectives are respectively synonymous with '*antios*' and '*anchios*', and in each case the prefix is semantically idle (*Adv.* 183.25–184.2)).[8]

Logically speaking, an argument is said to be non-concludent 'by virtue of redundancy' if one or more of its premisses are redundant; that is to say, if a premiss is logically idle, or makes

---

[8] For other occurrences of '*παρέλκειν*' see e.g. A. D. *Pron.* 3.6; 27.19; 38.3; Alex. Aphr. *in Top.* 428.20; 430.21; 431.1; *PH* II 77, 255; III 265; cf. Stephanus, *Thesaurus Linguae Graecae*, s.v.—'*παρέλκειν*' contrasts with '*συμβάλλειν*' (*PH* II 175), '*συντείνειν*' (A.D. *Synt.* I.4), '*εὐχρηστεῖν*' (*M* I 209); '*παρέλκων*' with '*ἀναγκαῖος*' (A.D. *Synt.* I.3), '*χρηστός*' (Alex. Aphr. *in APr.* 278.29). One of the literal senses of '*παρέλκειν*' is 'draw out'; hence 'spin out' or 'be prolix'; from which it is a short step to 'be redundant'. In another sense, a prudent rider who takes a spare mount with him may be said *παρέλκειν* it (see Hdt. II 102; Suid. s.v. *ἄμιπποι*); but it is, I fear, a little fanciful to see an equestrian metaphor in our use of the word.

no contribution to the inference. Sextus gives the following example:

> (A) (1) If it is day, it is light
>   (2) It is day
>   (3) Virtue is beneficial
> Therefore: (4) It is light

'For that virtue is beneficial is superfluously assumed along with the other premisses; since it is possible to exclude it and to draw the conclusion, "It is light", from the two remaining premisses, "If it is day, it is light", and "It is day" ' (M VIII 431; cf. 439). In short, proposition (3) is redundant in (A) because the *logos* $<\{(1), (2)\}, (4)>$ is concludent; and (A) is a redundant argument because premiss (3) is redundant in it.

The general idea of logical redundancy is not difficult to grasp; and those with a penchant for precision may be encouraged by Sextus' illustration to offer the following formal definition: *an argument,* $<\pi, \sigma>$, *is redundant* iff there is some α_i in π which is redundant in $<\pi, \sigma>$; and *a member of* π, α_i, *is redundant in an argument* $<\pi, \sigma>$ iff there is a proper subset, ρ, of π, not containing α_i, such that $<\rho, \sigma>$ is concludent.

Now our Sceptical Argument from Redundancy assumes that no redundant argument is concludent; indeed, it claims to borrow that assumption from the Stoics themselves. To most modern logicians the assumption will seem outrageous: redundancy is inelegant and aesthetically displeasing, but it does not amount to a *logical* fault. On the contrary, all redundant arguments are, logically speaking, impeccable; for all such arguments are in fact concludent. If ρ is a proper subset of π, and $<\rho, \sigma>$ is concludent, then $<\pi, \sigma>$ is concludent; if σ follows from ρ, then it follows from π—for π is simply ρ with an addition or two, and the addition of premisses to a concludent argument cannot produce a non-concludent argument.

Thus the sceptical assumption that redundant arguments are inconcludent is totally false; and its falsity is so obvious and so elementary that we should hesitate to ascribe it to the subtle logicians of the Porch.[9]

---

[9] 'By all the usual tests these [redundant arguments] would be perfectly valid arguments, though inelegant. Perhaps Sextus made a mistake here, or perhaps he was following an inferior handbook' (Mates [44], 83); Egli [41], 48–52, develops that view in detail; there is a more sympathetic account in C. L. Hamblin, *Fallacies* (London, 1970), 92–3.

That depressing conclusion has been reached too hastily; and the sceptics deserve a better hearing. Let us begin by looking briefly at Aristotle; for Sextus, in *PH* at least, implicitly ascribes the assumption that redundancy breeds inconcludency to the Peripatetics as well as to the Stoics.

The term '*sullogismos*' is the Aristotelian counterpart to the Stoics' '*logos sunaktikos*'. According to Aristotle, a *sullogismos* is a *logos* in which 'certain things being posited, something other than the things posited follows of necessity by their being the case' (*APr.* A 1 24^b 18–20; cf. *Rh.* A 2 1356^b 16–17). The phrase 'by their being the case (*tōi tauta einai*)' is glossed as 'because of them': if $<\pi, \sigma>$ is a *sullogismos* then if the members of π are true, σ follows *by virtue of their truth*. Now if σ holds because of ρ, and if ρ is a proper subset of π, it is plausible to infer that σ does *not* hold because of π; if σ holds in virtue of ρ alone, then it does not hold in virtue of π. Of course, if π's members are all true, then σ is true; but σ will not follow *by virtue of* the truth of π's members, but rather by virtue of the truth of a proper subset of π's members.

It follows that if $<\rho, \sigma>$ is a *sullogismos*, then $<\pi, \sigma>$ is not a *sullogismos*; that is to say, it follows that a redundant argument cannot be an Aristotelian *sullogismos*.

That interpretation of Aristotle may seem pedantic to the point of madness; and it is not suggested by the *Prior Analytics*' gloss on the phrase 'because of them'.[10] But it was the interpretation of no less a commentator than Alexander of Aphrodisias, who remarks that 'by this additional phrase [sc. 'by their being the case'] arguments which contain a redundant premiss are ruled out' (*in APr.* 22.30–23.2; cf. *in Top.* 13.25–14.2; 432.2–3; 568.18–23).

Moreover, the interpretation has Aristotle's own authority behind it. In *Topics* Θ 11 he asserts that 'there are five ways of criticizing an argument in itself . . . Again, <you may criticize an argument> on the grounds that a *sullogismos* would come about even if some of the premisses were removed—for sometimes people assume more than the necessary premisses, so that

---

[10] 'To follow "because of them" is for there to be no need of any external term in order for the necessity to come about' (*APr.* A 1 24b 21–2).

the *sullogismos* does not come about by their being the case (*tōi tauta einai*)' (161ᵇ 28–30). A little later there is an illustration of this deductive fault, after which Aristotle comments: 'What is the trouble? Is it that it makes obscure the cause on which the argument depends?' (162ᵃ 32–4).

Suppose that <ρ, σ> is a *sullogismos*, in which ρ contains 'the necessary premisses'; and imagine that a man assumes more than those premisses and tries to infer σ by way of the argument <π, σ>. Aristotle says that we should criticize <π, σ> on the grounds that 'the *sullogismos* does not come about by their being the case', or that 'it makes obscure the cause on which the argument depends'. The context of the criticism is dialectical, but its content comes from the official definition of a *sullogismos*: Aristotle is plainly saying that a redundant argument, <π, σ>, offends against the *tōi tauta einai* condition; and he must be taken to imply that no redundant arguments are *sullogismoi*.

Aristotle thus held that redundancy was a logical flaw, in that it debars an argument from the title of *sullogismos*; and the later Peripatetics did not dispute their master's view. The sceptics were therefore right to ascribe to the Peripatetics the assumption that a *sullogismos* cannot be redundant. Were they also right in ascribing the corresponding assumption to the Stoics? To answer that question we must look more nearly at the Stoic notion of concludency.

According to Sextus, a Stoic argument is concludent iff 'the conditional having as antecedent the conjunction of the premisses and as consequent the conclusion is sound (*hugiēs*)' (*PH* II 137). Let '*p*' express the conjunction of the members of π, and let '*q*' express σ; then <π, σ> is concludent iff 'if *p*, then *q*' is sound. The word 'sound' may here be replaced by 'true';[11] so that <π, σ> is concludent iff 'if *p*, then *q*' is true.

But when is a Stoic conditional true? Sextus records four ancient analyses of the conditional (*PH* II 110–11; cf. *M* VIII 112–18). The third account is stated thus: 'Those who introduce connectedness (*sunartēsis*) say that a conditional is sound whenever

---

[11] In logical contexts 'ὑγιής (sound)' is contrasted with 'σαθρός' (*PH* II 42), 'μοχθηρός' (ibid. 105), 'φαῦλος' (ibid. 150), 'ψευδής' (ibid. 200). It is often coupled with 'ἀληθής' *PH* II 42), and Sextus uses 'ὑγιής' and 'ἀληθής' interchangeably when talking of conditionals (*PH* II 110; *M* VIII 417, 426). Of course, 'ὑγιής' does not mean 'true' (Sextus explains it by way of reliability: a conditional is ὑγιής if it 'preserves the consequence': *M* VIII 112; cf. VII 78); but 'If *p*, then *q*' is ὑγιής iff it is true.

the contradictory of the consequent conflicts (*machētai*) with its antecedent' (*PH* II 111). Diogenes Laertius expressly ascribes that analysis to the Stoics (VII 73); and there is good reason, of an inferential kind, to attribute it to Chrysippus in particular (see Cic. *Fat.* VI 12). It may well be that some Stoics flirted with rival analyses of the conditional; but it is beyond serious doubt that Sextus' third account was official Stoic doctrine.[12]

Alas, that account is not pellucid: in particular, the two notions of 'connectedness' and 'conflict' cry out for elucidation. As for conflict, various sources tell us that two propositions conflict if they are incompatible (e.g. Apollonius, *Conj.* 218, 22–3); but that is hardly helpful. A compressed text in Alexander promises better: 'A thing is consequential (*akolouthon*) if it is necessary for it to be the case by something else's being the case (*tōi heteron einai*); a thing is conflicting (*machomenon*) if it is necessary for it not to be so' (*in Top.* 93, 10). Alexander's '*tōi heteron einai*' is to be taken in the same way as Aristotle's '*tōi tauta einai*'; and his comment may be paraphrased as follows: 'One proposition, σ, is consequential <upon another, σ',> iff <if σ' holds then> necessarily σ holds because σ' holds; and one proposition, σ, is conflicting <with another, σ',> iff <if σ' holds then> necessarily σ fails to hold <because σ' holds>'. Thus σ and σ' conflict iff, assuming that σ' holds, σ fails to hold because σ' holds. Alexander does not attribute that account of conflict to the Stoics; but '*machesthai*' is not a term of Peripatetic logic, and it is not implausible to suppose that Alexander is transcribing a Stoic view.

Thus 'If *p*, then *q*' is true iff π and the negation of σ conflict, i.e. iff if *p*, then not-not-*q* because it is the case that *p*, i.e. iff if *p*, then *q* because *p*. That harmonizes reasonably well with Sextus' account of Stoic concludency in *M* VIII 302 and 304, if we overlook the psychologism which insinuates itself into those texts.

For information on connectedness or *sunartēsis* we might turn to a passage in Philodemus' tract *On Signs*. The question there at issue is how we can establish that 'this is connected (*sunērtēsthai*) to that by necessity' (XXXV 5); and it emerges that mortality

---

[12] Full references, discussion, and bibliography in Frede [42], 80–93. DL reports that, according to the Stoics, arguments are inconclusive 'if the contradictory of the conclusion does not conflict with the conjunction of the premisses' (VII 77): that fits exactly with Sextus' account of Stoic concludency provided that we assume the συνάρτησις analysis of the conditional.

say, is 'connected' to man only if 'man, according as (*katho*) and in so far as (*hēi*) he is man, is mortal' (ibid. 15).[13] Connectedness here is a relation between properties: F-ness is connected to G-ness iff anything G is F in so far as it is G. But Philodemus' account is easily adapted to the case of propositions: σ is connected to π iff if the members of π are true, then σ holds in virtue of their truth, i.e. iff if p, then q because p.

And now Stoic concludency has taken on a Peripatetic aspect: $<\pi, \sigma>$ is an Aristotelian *sullogismos* only if σ holds in virtue of the truth of π; and $<\pi, \sigma>$ is a concludent argument for the Stoics only if 'If p, then q' is true, and hence only if σ holds in virtue of the truth of π. Redundant arguments cannot be Peripatetic *sullogismoi*; no more can they be Stoic *logoi sunaktikoi*. Thus the Stoics did indeed hold, as the sceptics allege, that no redundant arguments are concludent.[14]

But why should any self-respecting logician suppose that if $<\pi, \sigma>$ is a concludent argument, then σ must hold in virtue of the truth of π? And what, in any case, is the force of 'in virtue of' in such a supposition?

A further passage in Sextus may help. The first of his four types of fallacy happens 'by virtue of disconnectedness (*diartēsis*)'; and Sextus says, by way of explanation, that disconnectedness occurs

when the premisses have no communality (*koinōnia*) or connectedness (*sunartēsis*) with one another and with the conclusion; e.g. in the argument 'If it is light, it is day; but corn is being sold in the market: therefore it is light.' For we see that in this argument 'If it is day it is light' has no agreement (*sumpnoia*) or connection (*sumplokē*) with 'Corn is being sold in the market', nor does either of them with 'It is light'; but each is disconnected from the others. (*M* VIII 430)

That text contains some puzzling features;[15] but it shows that

---

[13] Philodemus later adds '*παρό*' to '*καθό*' and '*ῇ*' (XXXII 33); and he offers four different interpretations of those three terms (XXXII 33–XXXIV 24). But he explicitly says that the Stoics failed to discern the finer distinctions he himself makes.

[14] Sextus' ultimate source was perhaps Chrysippus' treatise *On Redundant Arguments* (DL VII 195).

[15] But surely '*εἰ ἡμέρα ἔστι, φῶς ἔστιν*' has some *κοινωνία* with '*φῶς ἔστιν*'? The parallel text in *PH* gives a different illustration: *εἰ ἡμέρα ἔστι, φῶς ἔστιν · ἀλλὰ μὴν πυροὶ ἐν ἀγορᾷ πωλοῦνται · Δίων ἄρα περιπατεῖ* (II 146). There each proposition plainly lacks *κοινωνία* with *each* of the other two (*PH* simply says that they lack *ἀκολουθία*, and fastidiously avoids the rich vocabulary of *M*). It is tempting to

*dis*connectedness is a matter of lack of communality, or irrelevance; and it thus suggests that connectedness is a matter of communality or relevance. In that case, it will be a necessary condition for the truth of an implication that its antecedent has something in common with, or is relevant to, its consequent; and we can give at least some account of 'in virtue of': σ will hold in virtue of π only if π (i.e. only if each a_i in π) is relevant to σ.

That view is not obviously silly. Consider again argument (A). If I produce that argument, claiming to infer (4) from (1)–(3), you may well demur: I can infer (4) from (1) and (2); but proposition (3) has nothing whatever to do with the inference—it is otiose, inert, logically idle. If (1)–(3) are all true, then so too is (4); but it does not follow that I can infer (4) from (1), (2), *and* (*3*): the inferential relation holds only between (4) and (1)–(2).

Some modern logicians have attempted to systematize the thoughts vaguely expressed in the last paragraph: they hold that σ' entails σ only if σ' and σ are tied together by a bond of relevance, and that an inference is valid only if its premisses are relevant to its conclusion. I suggest that Aristotle and the Stoics anticipated that theory: their logic is at bottom a 'logic of relevance'; and their objection to redundant arguments is based upon the notion, however imperfectly grasped, of 'relevant implication'.[16]

In the major part of this section I argued laboriously that the

---

introduce the appropriate *PH* example into *M* by emending the text; and *M* certainly is corrupt here (for we must read: οὔτε τὸ εἰ ἡμέρα ⟨ἔστι, φῶς⟩ ἔστιν ἔχει . . .). But *M*'s bad example is repeated at 435. Perhaps Sextus used a poor source for *M*; or perhaps his copy of his source was already textually corrupt.

[16] But consider this argument:
    (1) Chrysippus was a Hellenistic philosopher
    (2) Epicurus was a Hellenistic philosopher
    Therefore: (3) There was at least one Hellenistic philosopher
On the one hand, the argument seems to be redundant; for $\langle\{(1)\}, (3)\rangle$ is surely concludent. On the other hand, neither (1) nor (2) is irrelevant to (3)—(3) holds *both* in virtue of (1) *and* in virtue of (2).

To escape from that difficulty, we need to modify our earlier definition of redundancy: a redundant premiss is not one which merely *happens* to be superfluous to the argument, but one which *cannot* pull any logical weight or lend its force to the inference. Christopher Kirwan has suggested the following definition:
    a_i is redundant in $\langle\pi, \sigma\rangle$ iff a_i is a member of π and a_i
    is a member of no minimal adequate subset in $\langle\pi, \sigma\rangle$
(ρ is a minimal adequate subset in $\langle\pi, \sigma\rangle$ iff ρ is a subset of π, and ρ strictly implies σ, and no proper subset of ρ strictly implies σ).—For a comprehensive account of modern studies in the 'logic of relevance' see A. R. Anderson and N. D. Belnap, *Entailment* (Princeton, 1975); they briefly examine Stoic συνάρτησις at pp. 435–52.

Stoics (and the Peripatetics) did indeed regard redundant arguments as non-concludent; and that their view of redundancy rests on a central feature of their notion of concludency. I have just suggested that there are connections between the ancient notion of concludency and certain modern views about 'relevant implication'. I do not claim that the Stoics were right (and in any case, my interpretation of their view is sketchy); but I do claim that their attitude to redundancy is worth taking seriously, both for philosophical and for historical reasons. For we cannot hope to understand the fundamental ideas of logic if we merely ignore such things as relevant implication; and we shall not comprehend any ancient system of logic unless we reconstruct it upon the implicational foundations laid down by its original builders.[17]

C: REDUNDANCY AND FORMAL LOGIC

So much for one premiss of the Argument from Redundancy. I now move to the other premiss, which states that all formal arguments are redundant. I shall restrict myself to the first of the Stoic 'indemonstrables', as Sextus does in *M* VIII: like Sextus, I assume that the first indemonstrable is of the form $<\{^\ulcorner$ if σ', then $\sigma^\urcorner$, $\sigma'\}$, $\sigma>$, and I use the hackneyed example:

(B)   (1) If it is day, it is light
      (2) It is day
Therefore: (3) It is light

According to the sceptics, argument (B) is redundant; and it is redundant because the informal argument:

(C)   (1) It is day
Therefore: (2) It is light

is concludent. For (C) stands to (B) as $<\rho$, $\sigma>$ to $<\pi$, $\sigma>$. Here are Sextus' words:

These, then, are the celebrated indemonstrables; and they all seem to me to be nonconcludent by virtue of redundancy. For instance—to begin with the first—either it is agreed that 'It is light' follows 'It is day', which is its antecedent in the conditional 'If it is day, it is light', or it is unclear. But if it is unclear, we shall not grant the conditional as agreed; but if it is pre-evident that, given 'It is day', of necessity 'It

---

[17] For some discussion of ancient concludency see Frede [88], 6–10.

is light' is the case, then if we say that it is day, it is inferred that it is light—so that an argument of the sort 'It is day; therefore it is light' suffices, and the conditional 'If it is day, it is light' is redundant (*PH* II 159).

For they will say either that its being light follows its being day, or that it does not follow. And if it follows, once it is agreed that 'It is day' is true, 'It is light' is immediately inferred—and that was the conclusion. But if it does not follow, it will not follow in the case of the conditional either, and for that reason the conditional will be false, since its consequent does not follow its antecedent (*M* VIII 441-2).

The passages offer parallel but distinct arguments. Each considers whether, in argument (B), (3) follows (2); and each presents the Stoic with a dilemma. The dilemma of *PH* is this: either it is evident that (3) follows (2), or it is unclear; the dilemma of *M* is simpler: either (3) follows (2), or it does not.

The first horn of *M*'s dilemma is dangerous. For if (3) follows (2), then argument (C) is concludent—so that argument (B) is redundant. In general, if σ follows σ', then $<\{\sigma'\}, \sigma>$ is concludent; and hence $<\{^{\ulcorner}$ if σ', then $\sigma^{\urcorner}, \sigma'\}, \sigma>$ is redundant. And the first horn of *PH*'s dilemma points in the same direction; for if it is evident that (3) follows (2), then (3) follows (2).

But the second horn of each dilemma is a blunt prong. Suppose, as in *M*, that (3) does not follow (2): premiss (1) of (B) will then be false, as *M* asserts; but it certainly does not follow that (B) is redundant—an argument with a false premiss is not for that reason a redundant argument. Equally, if, as in *PH*, it is unclear whether (3) follows (2), we may well hesitate to grant (1); but that does not show that (1) is redundant.

In short, each dilemma fails because its second horn is powerless to impale us. And in *M* at least Sextus recognizes the failure; for although he introduces the dilemma, as in *PH*, by saying that 'the argument propounded in the first mode [i.e. the first indemonstrable] is inconclusive', he ends it as follows: 'Thus as far as the logical theory mentioned above goes, one of two things results: either arguments propounded in the first mode are found to be inconclusive, since their hypotheticals are redundant; or they are wholly false, since their hypotheticals are false' (VIII 442). The conclusion of *M*, in other words, is not that all first indemonstrables are redundant, but that all first indemonstrables are either redundant or false.

Now that disjunctive conclusion does in fact follow from the argument in M, and it is equivalent to the proposition that all true first indemonstrables are redundant. Since Stoic proofs are, by definition, *true* arguments, that conclusion is no less damaging than the simpler one that all first indemonstrables are redundant. The dilemma of *PH* yields the disjunctive conclusion that all first indemonstrables either are redundant or have a non-evident premiss; or, equivalently, that all first indemonstrables with pre-evident premisses are redundant. According to *PH* II 140, an argument is only a proof if 'it concludes to something non-evident by way of things that are pre-evident.' If that is so, then the dilemma of *PH* is as lethal as the dilemma of M.

The sceptical dilemmas do not show what they pretend to show; but their failure is trivial—for they actually show something equally fatal to the art of formal demonstration.

The sceptics' opponents squirmed a little. Some probably urged that argument (C), and in general arguments of the form $<\{\sigma'\}, \sigma>$, are not concludent, on the grounds that no single-premissed arguments or *logoi monolēmmatoi* are concludent. Aristotle and the Peripatetics rejected *logoi monolēmmatoi*, and so did Chrysippus; but their view is not worth tracing out here.[18] Others maintained that argument (C) is enthymematic—an elliptical version of (B) (see Alexander, in *APr.* 17.18–24; *in Top.* 9.8–17); but in order to do so they were obliged to produce a new analysis of concludency.

The plain fact is that the sceptics were right: given the Stoic analysis of concludency, the first indemonstrable is demonstratively useless. That is the central core of the Argument from Redundancy. Of course, the Argument does not establish the vacuity of formal logic or justify Locke's predilection for native intuition over artificial syllogizing; for it bears, as I have expounded it, upon only one principle of formal inference. Still less will the Argument show that 'there is no demonstration'. But for all that it has a certain significance: it points to an incoherence at the heart of Stoic theorizing about logic and knowledge.

For Aristotle see e.g. *APr.* A 15 34a 17; A 25; for the Peripatetics, see esp. Alex. Aphr. *in APr.* 17.10–18.7; *in Top.* 8.16–9.19; cf. Ammon. *in APr.* 27.14–33; 32.10–2; Philop. *in APr.* 33.10–24; for Chrysippus see *PH* II 167; *M* VIII 443. The Stoic Antipater rejected this orthodoxy (*PH* II 167; *M* VIII 443; Apuleius, *De int.* VII 184.20–3; Alex. Aphr. *in Top.* 8.16–18); but we hear no details of his argument. See further Mueller [112].

III

How distressed should the Stoics have been by the sceptical attack on their formal logic? Was their theory of proof entirely overthrown by the Argument from Redundancy? Or could they have settled in a Lockean posture, admiring demonstration but rejecting as otiose the claims of formal proof? To answer that question we must look at the purpose of Stoic proof.

According to Locke, reason has four degrees: 'The first, and highest, is the discovering, and finding out of Proofs; the second, the regular and methodical Disposition of them, and laying them in a clear and fit Order, to make their Connexion and Force be plainly and easily perceived; the third is the perceiving their Connexion; and the fourth, the making a right conclusion' (IV xvii 4, 669.27–32). And Locke holds that formal logic cannot serve the first of those rational ends: it is not an instrument of reason, nor a device to be employed in the discovery of scientific truths.

Locke was attacking his own contemporaries; and they could appeal to a tradition running back to antiquity. Among the ancients, the most vigorous advocate of their view was undoubtedly Galen. Galen was an amateur of logic; and he made a special study of *apodeixis*. He recommended that no scientist should start work until he had mastered the technique of formal demonstration; and he held explicitly that that technique provided a method, and the only true method, of discovery. He maintained that ·every science must proceed by first assembling a set of axioms, and then deducing, by way of formal inferences, its body of theorems. Geometry provided Galen with his model; but he believed that all sciences, including his own science of medicine, should apply the geometrical method.[19]

Now Aristotle, as I have argued elsewhere,[20] did not hold the Galenian view of *apodeixis*. Rather, he ascribes an expository and didactic function to demonstration: the theory of proof provides an intellectual showcase in which our pieces of knowledge can be

---

[19] See Müller [137] 417–19, and e.g. Galen, *Meth.med.* X 30, 10–39, 4 K; *Simp. med.* XI 462, 5–12 K; *Ord.lib.prop.* XIX 52–3 K–*Scr.Min.* II 82, 21–83, 6. Note that Galen himself thought that neither Aristotelian nor Stoic logic provided an adequate grounding for a theory of proof, which he sought rather in geometry (*Lib.prop.* XIX 39 K=*Scr.Min.* II 116, 19–117, 16; *Plac.Hipp.Plat.* V 226 K=184, 11–185, 8 M).

[20] See Barnes [136].

displayed to their best advantage, and it gives a pedagogical procedure whereby science may be transmitted from teacher to pupil. Aristotle, like Descartes, had observed that, 'as for logic, its syllogisms . . . serve rather in explaining to others the things one knows . . . than in learning them' (*Discours*, pt. II).

Of course, the connection between proof and knowledge is not merely extrinsic. To know that q is, in many cases, precisely to possess a proof $<\pi, \sigma>$; and if it is demonstrable that q, then a man knows that q iff he has a demonstration that q (*APo*. A 2 71^b 28-9). But that does not show that proof is a heuristic device: it is one thing to hold that acquiring knowledge that q is coming to grasp a proof of σ, another to recommend researchers to sit at their desks and syllogize.

Should we ascribe to the Stoics an Aristotelian or a Galenian conception of proof? Galen had a great admiration for Posidonius; and there is little doubt that he attributed his own view of the purpose and importance of proof to his Stoic forebear. Is that attribution correct? And did the Stoics in general believe that proof was a valuable, or even an indispensable, heuristic tool?

If $<\pi, \sigma>$ is an Aristotelian demonstration, then the members of π are more familiar than, and explanatory of, σ (*APo*. A 2 71^b 21); and it is those features which give a proof its epistemological character. The corresponding feature of a Stoic demonstration is that the members of π must be 'revelatory' of the non-evident (*adēlon*) conclusion, σ. At first sight, that appears to show that a Stoic proof is an instrument of discovery; for it is natural to suppose that a 'revelation' is a making plain, and that a 'revelatory' inference makes clear what was previously unclear—that it promotes the conclusion from a post of obscurity to a position of light.

But a closer examination of Stoic theory shows that to be mistaken. The Stoics distinguished three kinds of non-evidence: some things, they held, are 'once and for all (*kathapax*) non-evident, if they are not of a nature to fall under our apprehension'; others are 'temporarily (*pros kairon*) non-evident, if they have a clear nature but are made temporarily non-evident for us by some external circumstances'; others are 'naturally (*phusei*) non-evident, if they are not of such a nature as to fall under our clear perception' (*PH* II 97-8; cf. *M* VIII 144-7). Plainly, non-evidence is not a characteristic that can be alleviated or cured by a proof:

no argument can make evident what is non-evident; and hence 'revelatory' inference cannot be a matter of raising a proposition from a state of obscurity to a state of lucidity.

What, then, is revelation? Our sources give no very satisfactory answer to the question. Sextus implies that if σ′ reveals σ, then 'by attending to the former, we get an apprehension of the latter' (*M* VIII 253); and we must grasp σ′ *before* we grasp σ 'in order that, by being known beforehand, it may lead us to a conception of the object that becomes known by way of it' (*PH* II 119). Elsewhere he adds that the revelation is achieved by the 'power (*dunamis*)' of the premisses (*PH* II 143; *M* VIII 310) or of the argument (*M* VIII 308); or, more informatively, that the premisses 'by their own nature teach us to establish' the conclusion (*M* VIII 309).

In a proof there must be a 'natural' connection between premisses and conclusion, such that knowledge of the former permits us to grasp the latter. If we consider the standard examples of Stoic demonstrations, we may conjecture what that natural connection was meant to consist in.

Take the following inference (*PH* II 142; *M* VIII 309):

(D)   (1) If sweat flows through the skin, there
            are imperceptible pores in the flesh
       (2) Sweat flows through the skin
Therefore: (3) There are imperceptible pores in the flesh

It is clear that in argument (D) the conclusion *explains* the premisses; or rather, that the non-evident state of affairs described by the conclusion accounts for the evident fact set down in premiss (2). Other illustrative proofs exhibit the same feature: a punctured lung explains bronchial discharge (*M* VIII 252); pregnancy accounts for lactation (ibid. 423); motion is possible because there is void (ibid. 314); bodily movements depend on the soul (*PH* II 101; *M* VIII 155). In any concludent argument, the conclusion holds in virtue of the premisses; in a demonstrative argument, the conclusion will also express the state of affairs underlying and explaining the overt facts recorded in the premisses.[21]

[21] Brunschwig (above, p. 146) agrees with me (above, p. 165 n. 7) that revelation is an essential feature of Stoic proof; but he distinguishes between two senses of 'reveal' ('ἐκκαλύπτειν'). His *narrow* sense corresponds to the sense I sketch in the

Sextus' account of the different types of *adēla* prefaces his discussion of the Stoic theory of signs (*sēmeia*). Now he says more than once that proof is a species of sign,[22] and he asserts that that is so because a proof 'is revelatory of the conclusion' (*PH* II 131; cf. *M* VIII 140, 277). The Stoics distinguished two sorts of sign: 'commemorative' signs signify what is temporarily non-evident; 'indicative' signs signify what is naturally non-evident; and an indicative sign is defined as 'an antecedent proposition in a sound conditional, revelatory of the consequent' (*PH* II 101; cf. *M* VIII

---

text; his *broad* sense is simply this: ⟨π, σ⟩ reveals σ iff ⟨π, σ⟩ is a true argument and σ is non-evident. Since Brunschwig holds that only *broad* revelation is invoked in Definition *T* (the last of the three Stoic definitions, the one tentatively associated with Chrysippus—and, presumably, the official Stoic line), he in effect maintains that revelation in *my* sense forms no part of the most polished Stoic account of proof.

No ancient author, to my knowledge, explicitly distinguishes between two senses of 'ἐκκαλύπτειν' in that fashion; and certainly Sextus' long discussions of proof, to which the distinction should be of the last importance, betray no knowledge of it. Nor can I find the distinction implicit in the text which Brunschwig cites, *M* VIII 422–3. (On revelation and signs, see below, p. 180 n. 24.) Thus I am not convinced of the reality of Brunschwig's distinction; and in consequence, I incline to doubt the existence of his Definition *T*.

But, as Brunschwig clearly shows, there is a grave difficulty with my own view. *PH* II 134–43 proposes to explain what ἀπόδειξις is; by 140 Sextus has set out all the ingredients of Definition *T*, and he says that they together constitute a λόγος ἀποδεικτικός. We naturally suppose that 'λόγος ἀποδεικτικός' is a synonym for 'ἀπόδειξις': thus Brunschwig argues that the *definition* of ἀπόδειξις is completed by 140, with Definition *T*, and that 141–2 introduce a distinction between two *types* of ἀποδείξεις, one of which is characterized by being ἐκκαλυπτικός in the narrow sense.

I am obliged to reject that interpretation, and to suppose that, here at least, Sextus does not use 'λόγος ἀποδεικτικός' as a synonym for 'ἀπόδειξις'; rather, 'λόγος ἀποδεικτικός' designates—most infelicitously—a genus of which ἀπόδειξις is one species. Now that, I readily admit, is not very palatable; but I believe that Sextus at least was able to swallow it. For his text, as Brunschwig allows (p. 152, n. 46), gives no hint that 141–2 introduces a distinction between types of ἀποδείξεις; and since he explicitly offers the definitions of 143 as a summary or recapitulation of 134–42, he must have considered 141–2 as an integral part of the *analysis* of ἀπόδειξις. (In 143 I retain the phrase which Brunschwig excises.) And if Sextus can tolerate the infelicity, cannot we do so too?

The issue requires further discussion. Those readers who share Brunschwig's view may take my text to be talking about only *some* of the Stoic analyses of proof.

[22] e.g. *PH* II 96, 122, 131, 134; *M* VIII 140, 277, 299. Of course, the sign is not, strictly speaking, the genus of demonstration: a demonstration is a species of *logos*. At *M* VIII 277 Sextus explains: 'Demonstration is agreed to be by genus a sign; for it is clarificatory of its conclusion, and the conjunction of the premisses will be a sign of the holding of the conclusion.' That is, if ⟨π σ⟩, is a demonstration then π reveals σ, so that π is an indicative sign of σ. On the theory of signs see Verbeke [122].

245).[23] Thus if proofs are signs, they are indicative signs; and the conclusion of a proof will be something *naturally* non-evident. Just as, in a proof, the premisses 'by their own nature teach us to establish' the conclusion (*M* VIII 309), so an indicative sign 'of its own nature and constitution is said to all but cry aloud and signify that of which it is indicative' (*M* VIII 154).[24]

That connection between proof and the indicative sign has an important corollary. What a sign signifies must be non-evident; but the sign itself must be pre-evident (*M* VIII 172–3). It follows that the premisses of a proof must be pre-evident; and that is just what Sextus says: a proof 'concludes to something non-evident by way of things that are pre-evident (*dia prodēlōn*)' (*PH* II 140). But if that is right, then the Stoics cannot allow *sequences* of proofs, in which the conclusion of one argument is used as a premiss for the next; for any proved proposition will be non-evident, and therefore ineligible to appear as a premiss. Stoic proofs, unlike Aristotelian proofs, are strongly individualistic: they do not club together to form systematically concatenated demonstrative sciences.[25]

All that is, I fear, somewhat speculative and rather vague: a full account of the function and importance of Stoic proof will demand greater philosophical precision and more scholarly textual analysis. But if what I have said is roughly correct, it has several consequences for our understanding of the history of proof; and I end by indicating three of them.

First, Stoic and Aristotelian proofs differ sharply in their

[23] Brunschwig (above, p. 147) argues that the notion of revelation is not specific to the *indicative* sign, since it appears in the definition of sign *in general* at *PH* II 104 and *M* VIII 245. But those two texts refer exclusively to *indicative* signs: each occurs in the sceptical critique of the indicative sign, after Sextus has explicitly said that his discussion will be concerned *solely* with that species of sign (*PH* II 102; *M* VIII 156).

[24] Sextus' language here, and in the texts cited on p. 178, calls to mind the fourth of his accounts of the conditional: 'Those who judge by ἔμφασις say that a conditional is true if its consequent is included δυνάμει in its antecedent' (*PH* II 112). There is some evidence, admittedly slight, for connecting ἔμφασις with the Stoics (see Frede [42], 92): perhaps the Stoics suggested that if σ′ is an indicative sign of σ, then ⌈if σ′, then σ⌉ satisfies the condition of ἔμφασις.

[25] That is a surprising—even an outrageous—conclusion. Brunschwig (above, p. 152) hopes to evade it by suggesting that the phrase 'διὰ προδήλων' at *PH* II 140 is an interpolation. But even if his suggestion is right, we are left with the association between signs and proof. If we are to restore sequences of proofs to the Stoics, we must suppose that Sextus' account of their views is badly garbled.

attitude to explanation. Each type of proof is, in a loose sense, explanatory; but whereas in an Aristotelian demonstration the premisses supply material which explains the conclusion, in Stoic demonstrations the order of explanation is reversed—an ideal Stoic demonstration is, in a modern jargon, an inference to the best explanation.

Secondly, Stoic proofs serve to advance our knowledge: a demonstration provides a route (presumably the sole route) to knowledge of the non-evident explanations of the phenomena. It does not follow that such proofs are, in the Galenian sense, instruments of research; and it may be that a Stoic proof is no more than a formal medium for the presentation of indicative signs.

Finally, inferences to the best explanation are unlikely to require complex deductive techniques: linked series of syllogisms, such as constitute an Aristotelian science, will not be found among the Stoics. In that case, the Stoic formal logic will be largely irrelevant to Stoic theory of proof;[26] and the Stoics need not have been dismayed by the sceptical contention that their five indemonstrables were demonstratively useless.

---

[26] Mueller [112], 185, suggests that the Stoics actually recognized this: 'The Peripatetics . . . insisted on the claim, believed for many centuries after them, that their logic was the instrument of science. We do not know the Stoic response to this claim, but it is reasonable to suppose that they retreated to the view that the theory of deductive inference was a technical discipline, studied for some ethical end, perhaps, but not as the method of scientific discovery.' But see the texts cited above, p. 163; and cf. Frede [88], 23–4.

STOIC LOGIC AND
ALEXANDRIAN POETICS*

Claude Imbert

In Chapter XV of the treatise *On the Sublime*, pseudo-Longinus takes two sources of sublimity which the previous chapters have identified (*eidos* and *pathos*), and summarizes them under the single concept of *phantasia* or presentation.[1] He thus unites a Platonic notion which sees the sublime as the effect of a transcendent vision of the Forms (*Symposium*), with a theory deriving from the Sophists (or even from Homer), according to which a divine inspiration possesses the poet's body and determines his words (*Ion*). Longinus relies on a general thesis about the nature of language: 'the term *phantasia*', he explains, 'is used generally for anything which in any way suggests a thought productive of speech (*gennētikon logou*)' (XV 1). Without pausing over a definition which he takes to be thoroughly familiar, he adds that in rhetoric and aesthetic theory the term has a more specialized sense: it designates that state of emotion or enthusiasm by virtue of which a speaker can *see*, and make his audience *see*, whatever he is talking about.

A *phantasia* is thus a vision which can be communicated in its entirety by language: language makes *phantasiai* explicit, and *phantasiai* bring language into existence. Donald Russell has remarked on the Stoic origin of the doctrine;[2] and his observation is confirmed by the immediate context. For Longinus cites the madness of Orestes (Eur. *Orest.* 255 ff.) to illustrate the visionary origin of lyrical sublimity; and Orestes' ravings were a favourite example in the Stoic handbooks. Thus Sextus refers to Orestes in a doxographical passage (*M* VII 245) which tries to explain how a presentation may give rise to a proposition (*axiōma*) which is

---

* Translated by Jonathan Barnes.

[1] I adopt the standard translation, trying (as far as possible) to disembarrass it of any Cartesian or Lockean connotations. This chapter may, in a sense, be read as an attempt to define the Stoic notion of *phantasia*.

[2] See his edition and translation of *On the Sublime* (Oxford, 1964), 120; D. A. Russell and M. Winterbottom, *Ancient Literary Criticism* (Oxford, 1972), 477 n. 1.

neither true nor false: when Orestes sees Electra as a Fury, his presentation is partly correct (for it derives from an actual object present to him), and partly incorrect (for it refers to a non-existent Fury). Similarly, Aëtius, reporting a Stoic distinction, invokes Orestes' madness in order to contrast an inadequate presentation, which he calls a *phantasma*, with an apprehensive presentation (*SVF* II 54). Finally, Quintilian alludes to a picture of Orestes pursued by the Furies as an example of the genius of the painter Theon of Samos: 'He is renowned for his depiction of imaginary visions, known as *phantasiai*'.[3]

In general, throughout the period of Middle and Roman Stoicism, treatises on rhetoric (Varro, Cicero, Quintilian[4]) draw on the history and theory of the plastic arts in order to explain how an artist can experience and communicate a vision which, while constituted by elements taken from reality, does not derive from any particular empirical model. Such a vision aspires to penetrate the secrets of nature which perception of its own accord cannot attain; and it reveals them to others by the various modes of expression or 'translation' (*hermēneia*). Quintilian speaks in such terms of Phidias, the beauty of whose Zeus 'seems actually to have added something to his established sanctity, so near did the majesty of the work come to that of the god' (*Inst.* XII x 9). Similarly, Philostratus praises Phidias for having con-ceived a Zeus who is not merely the expression of an imitative or anthropomorphic theology: his statue manifests a wisdom and an imaginative power which have both heuristic and didactic force in that they can prefigure and express in a single sign the cosmic nature of the god. 'If you entertain a thought of Zeus, you must see him along with the sky, the seasons, and the stars, as Phidias once tried to do' (*VA* VI 19).

Panofsky long ago observed how un-Platonic that aesthetic theory is; for it ascribes the conceiving of visible signs to the artist's intellectual faculty.[5] Those signs enlarge our untutored

---

[3] *Inst.* XII x 6: 'concipiendis visionibus, quae phantasias vocant, praestantissimus est' (for the identification of the Orestes theme, see R. G. Austin's edition (Oxford, 1948), note ad. loc.); cf. VI ii 29.

[4] On Varro as a historian of painting and sculpture, and as a source for Quintilian, see J. J. Pollitt, *The Ancient View of Greek Art* (New Haven, 1974), 79–81; idem, *The Art of Rome* (Englewood Cliffs, 1966), XVI and XX.

[5] See E. Panofsky, *Idea—ein Beitrag zur Begriffsgeschichte der älteren Kunsttheorie* (3rd ed., Berlin, 1975), esp. 6–13; the lecture was given in 1923, in the series Vorträge der Bibliothek Warburg.

perceptions, educate them, and lead them on to the truth; and they dare to rival theology. Independently of Panofsky, Pollitt recognized the important role played in the theory by *phantasia*:[6] under the influence of art, it guides our inexperienced perceptions towards that synoptic view of nature and god to which they aspire. Like Russell, these two historians of art noted the Stoic inspiration behind the theory.

Other evidence could readily be gathered in support of the testimony of Longinus and the others I have cited (Lucian and Pliny come to mind): together, such passages show how a notion proper to Stoicism came to acquire the status of a commonplace. In Alexandrian eyes, the theory had enough vigour and novelty to serve as an axiom for the critics and historians of art, and for the masters of the craft of rhetoric. It offered an alternative, well adapted to the art of Alexandria, to the theory of imitation which Aristotle develops in the fourth chapter of the *Poetics*. '*Phantasia* . . . is a wiser craftsman than imitation; for imitation can only create what it has seen, whereas presentation can equally well create what it has not seen; for it will hypothesize it by reference to what exists' (Philostratus, loc. cit.). The theory confirms the essential unity of the arts and sciences: epistemologically speaking, sculpture, painting, anatomical drawings, astronomical models, and the boldest of theological treatises, all lie on a single continuum. According to the *Canons* of artists and orators established at Pergamum and Alexandria, the graphic arts were developed before the literary or discursive arts; and thanks to that historical dissociation, engineered by nature, they can shed a powerful light on that synoptic understanding which characterizes the goal of science but which cannot be directly approached. *Phantasia* thus has greater heuristic value than abstraction—and here too we have something thoroughly Stoic: the arts and sciences are, as it were, new organs of perception which perfect and complete the sensory equipment given us by nature. The theory depends, moreover, on an indirect and purely philosophical argument; for the existence of apprehensive presentations and of 'prenotions' is, in the last analysis, deduced from the existence of the arts and sciences.[7]

---

[6] See *The Ancient View* . . ., 63–5, and the texts assembled in the glossary, s.v. *phantasia*, 201–5.

[7] On the unity of the arts and sciences, treated as new forms of perception, see *Acad.* II 31; Plu. *Demetr.* 1. On the conceptual function of 'prenotions', see Goldschmidt [128].

In the light of that wide diffusion of the Stoic notion of presentation, and in the light of its 'productive' claim, we must revise the modern view which limits the interest of Stoic logic to dialectic and, in particular, to the theory of deduction: the ancients, as we have seen, judged matters differently. If we wish to restrict ourselves to the theory of the syllogism, we must at least relate it to what were its actual starting-points. Now 'the Stoics place first in order the theory of presentation and perception, because the criterion by which truth is known is, generically speaking, presentation, and because the theory of assent, and of apprehension and thought, which precedes the others, cannot be constructed without presentation' (DL VII 49). However obscure it may seem to modern logicians, it is undeniable that the Stoics derived their methods of inference from certain presentational structures. Moreover, that fact should explain the peculiarities of Stoic syllogistic and, in particular, it should solve two problems which have stumped modern commentators—whether, like Łukasiewicz and Mates, they have tried to assimilate Stoic logic to the post-Fregean propositional calculus, or whether, with more scholarship and less prejudice, they have simply compared the one system to the other.[8] Those questions are: (1) why do Chrysippus' five inferential schemata fail to mesh with any formalizations of the propositional calculus? (2) what is the epistemological significance of those schemata?

Our answers must depend on the interpretation we give to the Stoic notion of a *lekton*.

Without going into details, let me say that the argument for rejecting Łukasiewicz's interpretation of Stoic logic relies as much on the way Chrysippus selects and formulates his five 'indemonstrables', as on the semantic or metalogical concepts of adequacy, truth, completeness, and extensionality. It will be said that if the Stoics did not formulate a logical calculus, at least they came near to doing so. But in what sense? The notion of a 'precursor' is as irrelevant to the history of logic as it is to the history of science in general.[9] In any case, it is neither the concept of a *calculus* nor the rudimentary formalism of the Stoic fragments

---

[8] See Frede [42], a study based on a detailed analysis of the Alexandrian commentators.

that prevents us from comparing Stoic and modern logic: after all, we have explicit definitions of the truth-functional connectives, and explicit formulations of Gentzen's rules, and we may set them alongside the techniques of inference, more complex but no less precise, which the Stoics proposed. Rather, the difficulty is rooted in the debatable and debated notion of a *proposition*.

As we know, difficulties with the notion of truth led Frege to distinguish between logical truth and the adequate representation of facts, and to abandon his projected *lingua caracteristica* in favour of the construction of a logical calculus. (See his *Logische Untersuchungen.*) The logical and the epistemological aspects of natural language being thus separated, it proved possible to define the truth-functional connectives quite independently of any application they may have. There is no need to tie Boolean algebra to truth-values, nor truth-values to certain segments of natural language: a Boolean calculus does not imply any particular logical interpretation; and a logical interpretation, in its turn, does not imply any particular linguistic interpretation. In an analogous fashion, generative grammars have established transformation rules for natural languages, quite independently of any questions of truth or falsity. Since the truth-functional calculus has these two degrees of freedom, it can dispense with the notion of a proposition, without damage either to formal logic or to the analysis of natural language. The notion of a proposition, understood in the abstract Fregean way, is not a self-evident *datum* requiring the assimilation of Stoic logic to one of the modern calculi: on the contrary, it is a highly obscure notion which causes vexatious ambiguity and is at best a vehicle for *captatio benevolentiae*.

Truth-functionality makes the modern calculus amenable to an effective decision procedure; and such a procedure has no use for the grammatical and logical structures inherent in the Greek logical tradition. For although they were and remain appropriate to the didactic function and to the pragmatics of natural language,[10] those structures are none the less parasitical from the point of

---

[9] See G. Canguilhen, *Études d'histoire et de philosophie des sciences* (3rd edn., Paris, 1975), 21: 'La complaisance à rechercher, à trouver et à célébrer des précurseurs est le symptôme le plus net d'inaptitude à la critique épistémologique.'

[10] On this see D. Davidson, 'Thought and Talk', in S. Guttenplan, ed., *Mind and Language* (Oxford, 1975), 7–23.

view of the calculus. Greek logic is separated conceptually rather than chronologically from modern logic. Thus the logicians of Port-Royal proved that categorical distinctions were of no relevance within monadic predicate logic (which, as we know, is equivalent to the propositional calculus). The simplification they thereby effected, of course, in no way tells the epistemological function of the categories, as it was refurbished by Kant. Next, the classification of judgements (according to quantity, quality, and modality), and then the very notion of judgement itself, were eliminated by Frege from his successive logical systems. That gradual and piecemeal disintegration of a logical structure built by or borrowed from the Stoics was a necessary preliminary to Frege's formulation of a sentential calculus and to the conception, by Wittgenstein, Post, and Łukasiewicz, of such a calculus as an independent system. To put it in a nutshell: the following pairs of notions characterize—not exhaustively—two distinct logical strategies, between which we must choose:

criterion of truth	: :	truth-functions
category	: :	predicate
deixis	: :	quantification
internal modality	: :	external modality

Those few remarks should lead us to use the adjective 'propositional' in a strictly descriptive sense: unlike Aristotle's logic, which analyses a thesis into its component terms in order to prove it, the Stoic method establishes a conclusion (a) without meddling with its predicative structure, and (b) by resting upon other sentences which are held to derive their truth from associated presentations; and thus the Stoics never leave the discursive or 'propositional' level. Our descriptive use of the term 'propositional' has a certain polemical import. The conclusion of a Stoic syllogism is inferred from other sentences which translate natural signs apprehended in presentations, and which never presuppose the existence of transcendent forms or universals. Presentations form the nerve of the inference and the criterion of truth. Every logical structure rests on the possibility of translating presentations into discursive sequences, and each sequence must exhaust the scientific content latent in its presentation. Inference thus depends on a rhetorical function which maps utterances (*lekta*) on to contents of presentations (*phantasta*).[11] The epistemological aspects of inference lead to the same conclusion. Commentators are often content to illustrate the Stoic rules by stock examples ('If it is day, it is light; it is day . . .'), and then to give analyses of certain more complex schemata which won the admiration of the ancients (e.g. the *consequentia mirabilis*).[12] But they have scarcely even attempted to test Stoic logic against Alexandrian texts, whether or not these bear the stamp of the Stoa. Thus Prantl's conclusion, violently criticized though it has been, is given a seal of approval: Stoic dialectic was only a school exercise, or (better) a method of persuasion, and had no bearing on the sciences of its time. The Stoics themselves were not of that opinion: 'It is by logical investigation (*hē en logois theōria*) that we see everything in the field of natural science, and also everything in the field of ethics' (DL VII 83). That sentence ends Diogenes' exposition of Stoic logic, and indicates its all-embracing epistemological pretensions. Diogenes' concise formula can be compared to the image of the clenching of a fist, by which Zeno illustrates the progress from presentation to knowledge; still more concisely, Epictetus said that we must 'analyse' our presentations. It is logic which describes the method and the 'natural history' behind that precept.[13]

We can see its importance more clearly in a passage where Lucullus explains the powers of perception and presentation, and defends them against the Academics (*Acad.* II 19). The starting-point is the discriminatory capacity of the senses; the goal is the identification of objects and the establishing of their definitions. Progress from starting-point to goal involves two types of act which belong to the intellect but which take their beginning from the most widely possessed of all presentational capacities. The first type of act is apprehension: 'Whatever character belongs to the things we say are perceived by the senses, must belong too to those things which are said to be perceived not by the senses themselves but in a certain way by the senses' (ibid. 21). The second act requires us to link together properties which are

---

[11] For this mapping function, which relies on the structure of Stoic logic and not on any psychological hypothesis, see Imbert [95], 233.

[12] See the analysis of the argument διὰ δύο τροπικῶν in Kneale [43], 172; and that of the argument διὰ τριῶν in Frede [42], 182.

[13] The phrase comes from Schmidt [77], 11: 'aptissime Stoicorum logicam "quandam quasi rationis humanae naturalem historiam" cognominare potueris.'

naturally conjoined, and to capture them in scientific theorem or definitions: 'Then follows the rest of the series, linking together the most important characteristics, which embrace, as it were, a complete comprehension of the objects' (ibid.). These two forms of recognition give presentations their capacity to function as signs—and they thereby solve the problem of scepticism. Ignore them, and you endanger the whole system of the arts and sciences. They also provide the propositional forms which follow upon and bring to expression the silent recognition of whatever is presented.

Lucullus' argument encapsulates four theses:

(1) Presentations, and nothing else, can produce and sustain knowledge; and they do so by virtue of being *signs*. An etymology of Chrysippus' puts the point neatly: '*phantasia*' derives from '*phōs*' ('light'); like light, a *phantasia* enables us to recognize both itself and that which it illuminates (*SVF* II, p. 21.28–p. 22.2). The etymology was inspired by a celebrated passage in Aristotle's *de Anima* (429^a 2–4); but the emendation which Chrysippus makes to Aristotle's remark is more significant than his use of Aristotle as a source: whereas Aristotle simply observes the affinity between presentations and light, Chrysippus adds a *functional* analogy— presentations have the same revelatory power as light; they are plants which will bear fruit once they are fertilized by analysis. Now, as Lucullus' systematic account stresses, analysis proceeds along two lines: it identifies a real object; and it captures the sequence of its properties (*series notionum*) given in the presentation.

(2) Animals have the power of apprehension; but only man has the capacity to construct signs from a perceptual field in which *data* are presented together with their actual or usual properties. Man, according to Sextus, differs from the other animals neither because he can speak a language (animals can imitate that) nor because he has presentations, but rather 'by the fact that man is capable of making transitions and syntheses. Thus man, possessing the notion of consequence, immediately acquires the notion of a sign by way of his experience of consequences (*akolouthia*)' (*M* VIII 288). Thought is identified with 'internal' language, and also with the apprehension of inferential links or signs. The power of constructing or synthesizing a sign is not a passive capacity, as a protreptic argument in Epictetus shows:

The fact that our intellect is so structured that we are not simply passive receivers of impressions from sensible objects, but select and abstract from them and add to them and construct things out of them, and indeed make transitions from some of them to others which have some sort of connection with them—is not all that enough to rouse you, and to encourage you not to forget the Craftsman? (*Diss.* I 6.10)

The capacity to synthesize presentations and to produce new ideas from them works by analogy, transference, composition, contrariety, and transition (*metabasis*) (DL VII 53). (That seems to show that Sextus means to denote the genus (*sunthesis*) by the species name (*metabasis*), *metabasis* being the most remarkable and the most characteristically Stoic form of synthesis.) Now all the procedures which Diogenes lists and illustrates by graphic or mechanical examples, describe in the first place methods of constructing concepts: the procedures extend and amplify the simple notions which we gain 'by experience':

Procedure	*Illustrations*
experience	perceptible objects
similarity	Socrates, from his portrait
analogy	a Cyclops; pygmies; the centre of the earth
transference	eyes in the breast
composition	Centaurs
contrariety	death[14]
transition	place

The same terminology is also used for the conceptual and discursive processes (the identification and the description of an object) which are presupposed by the work of a painter, a geometrical drawing, or the construction of a scale model. Presentation thus introduces into logic a principle of construction which can then be adopted by the discursive processes. We can thus see, in practical examples, that production of speech—both of vocabulary and of grammar—to which pseudo-Longinus parenthetically adverts.

(3) The construction of a sign appropriate to a given presentation, and the transition from an impression to the content of a presentation (*SVF* II 79, 80), require two linking operations: the

[14] See G. E. Lessing, *Wie die Alten den Tod gebildet*, in vol. 5 of his *Werke* (Berlin, 1955)—by way of attributes contrary to those of life: sleep, an inverted torch . . .

first bears on the identification of the object, the second on the grasping of connections among its properties. Those operations determine the two forms of declarative judgement which Stoic logic recognized. Utterances are divided into the simple and the complex (DL VII 68). The class of simple utterances is ordered by reference to 'determinate' propositions (e.g. 'This man is walking'),[15] which translate apprehensions (*katalēpseis*). The second class is ordered about three basic forms: the hypothetical, the conjunctive, and the disjunctive. They translate three ways of grasping connections: implication, non-contradiction, alternation. If we restrict ourselves here to the directly inferential form ('If . . . then—'), we can discern four aspects to its epistemological role:

(a) It is the canonical form for scientific theorems. Chrysippus gives examples from geometry and medicine (Cic. *Fat.* 15):

If two figures are great circles, each bisects the other.
If a man has a high pulse rate, he has fever.

But he refuses to express the conjunctions of the astrologers in a similar form:

It is not the case both that a man is born at the rising of the Dog-star, and that he will die at sea.

(b) It is also the canonical form for definitions, as Lucullus (*Acad.* II 21) implies when he refers to propositions 'which embrace, as it were, a complete comprehension of the objects', e.g.:

If he is a man, he is a mortal animal endowed with reason.

(c) It follows that definitions enjoy no superiority over scientific theorems and to ordinary hypotheticals such as:

If it is day, it is light.
If Dion is walking, Dion is moving.

except in so far as they complete the analytical characterization of their subjects. And that there is a continuous scale from ordinary hypothetical up to definition is shown clearly by the fact that the Stoics also countenanced a sort of 'quasi-definition' (*hupographē*)

---

[15] See the rule reported by Sextus, *M* VIII 98: an indeterminate proposition is true if and only if the corresponding determinate proposition is true.

of an inexact or simple kind (DL VII 60). Definition, description, theorem, scientific implication: these rhetorical forms all elaborate upon the ancient medical notion of a sign or symptom, and they do so in accordance with a single principle: the quality predicated in the antecedent is analysed in the consequent by way of a description which is in some sense more 'objective' and more precise; we start from something immediately perceived and discriminated by the senses, and go on to describe its 'mode of being' or 'how it is' (*pōs echei*), either absolutely or in relation to other things. The epistemological gain consists in glossing the quality in terms of a description which takes it from the context in which it was perceptually discriminated, and inserts it into a more general system—perhaps into a whole cosmology.

(d) The implicational form is hypothetical, and possesses the modality of possibility. It cannot in itself analyse the sign given in the presentation. Its precise formulation requires a complex declarative system, containing two stylistic forms: one fixes the subject (e.g. '*This man* is walking'); the other unpacks the perceived quality, in accordance with the laws of cosmology (or of whatever other system the quality pertains to). The rules for this analytical expansion are given by the sequence of categories: subject, quality, mode of being, relation (*SVF* II 369 f.). The analysis of presentations thus takes us out of the realm of brute impressions; and it consists in identifying the objects which produced them, and unfolding the rich tapestry of nature which those first and relatively crude disciminatory apprehensions tend to disguise. Hence the form of Chrysippus' first indemonstrable:

If the first, the second [universal hypothetical; indeterminate]
The first   [affirmation of the actuality of the antecedent]
Therefore, the second [conclusion, affirming the actuality of the characteristics in the consequent]

(4) The use of categorial predicates in the construction of the theorems and definitions of natural science and theology was remarked upon by de Lacy, in an article which has not received the attention it deserves. It is true that the renewed interest in the theory of predication has thrown doubt both upon Łukasiewicz's idea that Stoic logic is a strictly propositional calculus, and upon the ontological interpretation of the categories proposed by the

Peripatetic commentators and recently revived by Rist, Lloyd, and Graeser.[16] Moreover, the use of the categories is confirmed by the Stoic method of definition. To define something is to give its material substance, its 'proper' qualities, its mode of being, and its relations. (To take another example, consider the definition of voice (*phōnē*): 'voice is body'; it is 'air which has been struck'; and human voice is 'emitted by thought' and is 'the proper object of hearing' (DL VII 55). Sound, the element discriminated in perception, is analysed into a substrate, a physical mode of being, and a set of relations by which it connects transmitter and receiver.)

We are now better able to appreciate the part played by the discursive translation of presentations. Translation analyses a given quality in its physical aspects, and is thereby shown to be a strictly *phenomenological* activity. But the phenomenological description is not limited merely to identifying the *data* of consciousness; rather, it leads consciousness away from sense-impressions, and (like a protreptic argument) enriches them by revealing their capacity to act as signs. Moreover, the discursive activity which enlarges an apprehensive presentation opens up new possibilities for reflection and criticism. Thus human reason becomes self-conscious, and passes in a continuous movement from a simple analysis of presentations to criticism, and even to rejection, of them. 'For what purpose has nature bestowed reason upon us? In order that we may use our presentations as we ought to' (Epict. *Diss.* I 20.5). If ethics can be taught, it must begin by using the categories to gloss and to criticize our human affections and impressions.

We have now seen that rational activity has its scope determined by a 'production' which starts from presentations, and that analysis further defines it as a sort of phenomenology. That two-fold operation constitutes what Philodemus calls the Stoic theory of *sēmeiōsis*; Chrysippus enumerated its five forms, and believed he had exhausted the possibilities (DL VII 79). It would require a systematic study to deduce those modes of inference from the physical and anthropological constraints on presentation, or rather (to come clean), from the *oikeiōsis* which the senses establish between men and nature. I have attempted such a study elsewhere;[17] here I shall look at the weakest link in that deductive chain—I mean its subordination of discursive forms to pre-sentational signs. The 'synchronic' point of view which I shall adopt is suggested by the influence (and the success) of this Stoic doctrine on Alexandrian arts and sciences. Thus we shall be able to see Stoic 'speculative' logic (in the Scholastic and Kantian sense of the term[18]) at work for the men who employed it.

The prologue to *Daphnis and Chloe*, on which I shall shortly focus attention, isolates and examines with exemplary clarity and elegance the way in which discursive thought is subordinated to the enigmatical synthesis of an image treated as a sign.

II

My procedure calls for a word of explanation. I propose, as I have just said, to put systematic treatment to one side and to test the potency of certain Stoic concepts by their effect on the arts and sciences of the time. I need to justify that change of method, my choice of text, and the chronological limits I am setting to the enquiry.

The treatise *On the Sublime* indicates the authority which Stoic logic held over rhetoric and poetics in the century before the second Sophistic movement.[19] Further evidence could readily be amassed by consulting the grammarians, the manuals of logic, and the texts on scientific method.[20] But however numerous those texts were, they could neither explain the durability of the Stoic conceptual system nor—to come closer home—show why discursive thought, in the sense of description or analysis, should be subordinated to signs experienced in or constructed from presentations. Thus I shall ignore all questions of sources and influence, taking my stand on the Kantian maxim that logic is

---

[17] See Imbert, *Logique et langage dans l'ancien stoïcisme* (forthcoming).

[18] On the contrast between 'speculative' and 'critical' see Kant, *Logik* (vol. ix of the Academy edition), Einleitung, Ch. IV.

[19] See Russell, op. cit., Introduction, Part III.

[20] In addition to Barwick [70] and R. H. Robins, *Ancient and Mediaeval Grammatical Theory* (London, 1951), see the recent article by Pinborg [115] (with bibliography). Frede [89] stands somewhat apart from Pinborg's approach. No conclusions can be advanced, I think, until we have a detailed study of Apollonius Dyscolus, *On syntax*. On scientific methodology see Strabo, Book I, and the fragments of Geminus' commentary on Euclid's *Elements* published by Heath (T. L. Heath, *The Thirteen Books of Euclid's Elements* (Cambridge, 1926), Index, s.v. 'Geminus'). Archimedes' treatise *On Method* should also be studied in this connection.

'anonymous':[21] in Wittgenstein's words, logic must look after itself.

A synchronic approach is suggested by the way in which the Greeks themselves created their logical systems: they began from the existence of the sciences and from their didactic aspect. There is no exception to that rule: Plato's 'argument from the sciences' was one argument among others, but it was his most powerful reason for upholding Recollection and the Theory of Forms. At any rate, it is the argument which Aristotle took most pains to refute, and which he thought it most important to correct.[22] Adding the arts to the sciences, the Stoics did not deviate from the general principle, even if they came to somewhat different conclusions. 'What can an art effect if its practitioners have not perceived many things?' (*Acad.* II 22). Instead of hypostatizing Forms or universals, the Stoics reify acts of knowledge. And that is why logic is autonomous: it has the autonomy proper to a mental faculty.

If all Greek logical systems rely on the 'argument from the sciences', they differ from one another in their methods of analysis. Once the methods were determined, they were taught, with varying degrees of success, throughout the Alexandrian period. It follows that, in deciding to pick out a period within which the Stoic analysis predominated, I imply nothing about the evolution or history of Greek logic as a homogeneous cultural unit.

My approach may not enable us to solve the problem of the *history* of logic, which was first posed by Kant, then treated in Kantian fashion by Prantl, and later revived by Scholz and Bochenski;[23] but we can at least look at it from a different point of view. Recent histories of logic have accepted in principle Bochenski's division of the subject into pre-Aristotelian logic, Aristotelian logic, Stoic logic, and—finally—the logic of the commentators.[24] Whatever the heuristic value of that division, the conclusions it leads to must be queried—for their underlying

[21] See Kant, *Logik*, Einleitung, Ch. IX.
[22] See *Metaph.* A 990^b 12, and *Metaph.* M *passim*; also the review of the *Meno* argument in *APo.* A 1.
[23] See Kant, *Logik*, Einleitung, Ch. II, a discussion which throws much light on the position Kant adopts in the Preface to the second edition of the *Critique of Pure Reason* (a passage too often quoted); H. Scholz, *Abriss der Geschichte der Logik* (Berlin, 1931); I. M. Bochenski, *Formale Logik* (Freiburg, 1956).
[24] Bochenski, loc. cit., § 6 B.

principle is questionable. Neither of the two end phases has any
real unity. Plato's logic, as it is put forward in the *Sophist*, stands
in stark opposition to the dialectic of Elea. And if there is an
internal connection between the dialectical logic of Zeno of Elea
and the arguments of Diodorus[25] which are generally regarded
as the 'sources' of Stoic logic, then we must recognize that sometimes a given period divides up and sometimes it overlaps with
another. Note too that the so-called logic of the commentators is
not so much a syncretism as a learned discussion of the different
methods worked out by the Lyceum and the Stoa, leading to the
subtle suggestion that our choice of method should depend on
the type of inference we are analysing.[26] Finally, the principal
distinction, that between Aristotle's Analytics and Stoic logic, is
not really based on a comparison of those two systems: it is
predetermined by the decision to assimilate each system to one
of the two complementary parts of modern logic;[27] and it thus
depends on the unnecessary—and doubtless false—supposition
that there exists, in Husserl's phrase, a *logica perennis* of which
modern formal logic is the canonical representation. The difficulty
arising from Bochenski's chronological division leads to another:
by tying a logic to an author (Aristotle or Chrysippus) or to a
School, the historian seems committed to explaining its characteristics by way of the philosophical system into which it was
born. But in accounting for ancient logics by referring them
extrinsically to some modern calculus, the historian contradicts
that commitment and reduces it to a mere piece of nomenclature.

On the one hand, a logical system belongs initially to the
philosophical school which fathers it; on the other hand, it
comes to enjoy a wide practical diffusion: can we reconcile those
two facts? Stoic principles survived into the Byzantine and
Scholastic periods, in treatises on syntax and rhetoric, long after
the demise of Roman Stoicism. A logical system must seem less
than grateful in thus outliving its parent philosophy. Perhaps we
should adapt the distinction made by Fernand Braudel[28] between

---

[25] See Sedley [24], 84–5.

[26] That is the conclusion of Galen's *Institutio Logica*.

[27] On the mistake of assimilating Aristotle's logic to the predicate calculus and
Stoic logic to the propositional calculus, see Corcoran [85], Frede [88], G. Granger,
La Théorie aristotélicienne de la science (Paris, 1976), Chs. 4–5.

[28] F. Braudel, *La Méditerranée et le monde méditérranéen à l'époque de Philippe II* (Paris,
1949), Preface (reprinted in his *Écrits sur l'histoire* (Paris, 1969), 11–13).

the brief periods into which political history (or philosophy) divides and the longer time-spans of cultural history (or logic)? But that will yield at best an external account of the matter with no explanatory power. For what is the connection between logic and philosophy, given that they have different historical structures? Surely the notion of a strictly *Aristotelian* or *Stoic* logic, narrowly confined within the limits of an esoteric philosophy, is as implausible as the notion of a private language. Rather, we should imagine that a philosophy will put up with its logic to the extent that it explains and reflects its normative intentions. That answer is general and not a little Kantian ('Here the work of the logicians lay before us, finished though not completely free of defects . . .': *Prolegomena*, § 39); and as such it may be suspect. Nevertheless, we must acknowledge that Stoicism shows with particular clarity how a philosophy continually ratifies, elucidates, and explains the canons of rationality which it first derived from the arts and sciences and their didactic procedures.[29] In return, the arts and sciences, without professing Stoicism, peddled those logical structures which the Stoics had analysed and which we today adopt, whether we know it or not, when we do Euclidean geometry or read the Alexandrian historians and geographers. Divorced from its philosophical system and from the pet examples to which that system clung, Stoic logic offers us *in abstracto* a systematic alternative to other formulations—and at the same time a choice of style. And natural language incorporates all logical systems (with the exception of the modern symbolic variety) as so many language-games.

Here it is neither possible nor necessary to give further evidence, beyond the examples already cited, for the diffusion of Stoic logic. After all, multiplication of texts can only go so far in helping us to understand a logic, the difficulty of which arises not so much from the paucity of the doxographical material as from the conceptual distance which separates it from us. The prologue to *Daphnis and Chloe* is an invaluable document; for it provides us with a paradigm, which we may observe, as it were,

---

[29] There is a curious inversion of this argument in Quine, who holds that the methods of language learning and logic must account for scientific theorizing: see 'The Nature of Natural Knowledge', in Guttenplan, op. cit., 79. That simple fact well characterizes the contrast between the speculative logic of the Greeks and modern, post-critical, logics.

under the microscope, of an operation which is supposedly hidden away *in foro interno*—I mean the analytical or discursive interpretation of a presentational sign.[30]

III

(1) In the island of Lesbos, while hunting in a grove sacred to the Nymphs, I saw the most beautiful sight that I have ever seen—a painted picture, a tale of love. The grove itself was charming: wooded, flowery, well watered, a single spring nourishing flowers and trees alike. But the picture was more pleasing, both by its excellent artistry and by its amorous subject; and many men, even foreigners, who had heard tell of it came there to worship the Nymphs and to admire the painting. (2) It depicted women in childbirth, and other swaddling babies; infants exposed, animals suckling them, shepherds carrying them away; young people exchanging vows of love; a pirate attack; an enemy incursion; and many other incidents, all amorous. As I viewed and admired them, I felt a desire to make a written copy of the picture. (3) Having sought out an interpreter of the painting, I composed these four books—an offering to Eros, to the Nymphs, and to Pan; and a pleasant possession for all men, which will cure the sick, console the grief-stricken, refresh the memory of the lover, and instruct those not yet touched by love. (4) For no one has entirely escaped love, and no one will do so as long as beauty exists and there are eyes to see it. May God grant that I remain undisturbed as I describe the passions of others.

In his *Griechische Roman* of 1876 Erwin Rohde saw this passage as an example of *ekphrasis*,[31] and he took it to be a late product of the Second Sophistic. Rohde's fifth-century dating has subsequently been revised, and A.D. 250 is now generally regarded as a *terminus ante quem*.[32] It is not the prologue, but rather the pastoral itself, which is an *ekphrasis*: the prologue in its intro-

---

[30] Quite apart from Plato, this heuristic use of a paradigm was universal in antiquity: see V. Goldschmidt, *Le Paradigme dans la dialectique platonicienne* (Paris, 1947), 98.

[31] The best account of *ekphrasis* is still P. Friedländer, *Johannes von Gaza, Paulus Silentiarius und Prokopios von Gaza—Kunstbeschreibungen justinianischer Zeit* (Berlin, 1912), 1–83. See also D. Schönberger's introduction to his edition of Philostratus' *Imagines* (Munich, 1968), 20–6.

[32] On the approximate date of *Daphnis and Chloe* see B. E. Perry, *The Ancient Greek Romances* (Berkeley, 1967), 350, n. 17; B. P. Reardon, *Courants littéraires grecs des IIème et IIIème siècles après J.C.*(Paris, 1971), 336; M. Mittelstadt, 'Longus: *Daphnis and Chloe*, and Roman Narrative Painting', *Latomus* 26 (1967), 752–61. The dates proposed vary between 150 and 250.

ductory story mirrors the novelist's act of composition. It recounts the occasion of the narrative (the hunt), the method chosen (an interpretative description of the painting), the *motif* (a love story), and the novelist's purpose (cure, consolation, refreshing of the memory, instruction, the production of a thank-offering). At first sight, Longus seems to follow the tradition of the 'living picture', which derives from Homer's description of the shield of Achilles. Long familiar to the Greek and Latin poets, the insertion of such a description within the narrative proper is thoroughly characteristic of the Alexandrian novel.[33] But in transferring the device from the novel itself to the prologue, Longus elevates it into an aesthetic theory. He ties his narrative to the description of a presentation whose rich beauty both evokes the story and supplies its subject matter. The same thing can be found in the first chapter of Philostratus' *Imagines*[34] and in the passage from Longinus which I have already quoted.

In all this, the Stoics may claim priority; for they were the first to associate *ekphrasis* with a theory of prose narrative and with a deontology. Presentations are, by their very nature, 'talkative' (*eklalētikē huparchousa*: DL VII 49). Rhetoric and dialectic merely draw on that primitive chatter: 'Thought expresses in language what it experiences in presentation.' The word *lalia* ordinarily denotes the babblings of a baby, the unarticulated cries of beasts, the sound of a flute, the chat which introduces a dialectical debate (Pl. *Euthd.* 287 d), or even the sugared words of a deceiver (Soph. *Phil.* 110). It is also the term for the introductory part of an *epideixis*, or for a description which, without pretending to argument, outlines and sketches in a thesis without analysing it (cf. Lucian's *Prolaliai*). Education imposes five rhetorical virtues on that *lalia*: Hellenism, clarity, brevity, relevance, structure (DL VII 59). The Suda preserves that Stoic list in preference to the Peripatetic canon (clarity, relevance, purity, ornament), thus sanctioning the intentions of the Stoics and placing correctness of expression above the pleasures of the ear. We find here *apheleia*

---

[33] See e.g. Achilles Tatius, *Leucippe and Clitophon* I 2 (abduction of Europa); III 7–8 (Andromeda and Prometheus); V 3 (rape of Philomela); Philostratus, *Life of Apollonius* (*VA*) I 25 (mythological and historical pieces); Heliodorus, *Ethiopica* I 1 ('Fate had spread a thousand things in a small space').

[34] Philostratus states that his *Imagines* were occasioned by pictures (ἀφορμαὶ τῶν λόγων: 295K 15), that their content is interpretation (ἑρμηνεύειν τὰς γραφάς: 295K 35), and that their purpose is to give a clear *ekphrasis* (σαφῶς φράζοιμι: 296K 4).

or simplicity, to which the Second Sophistic made claim; proper construction, which ties together in one unit the several implications of a subject; brevity, which obliges us to contain the subject's various aspects in a single clause. The art of expression (Epict. *Diss.* II 23.7) transforms *lalia* into *ekphrasis*—a precise account of the sort appropriate to a messenger's speech in tragedy, or such as Hermes required from Prometheus ('Recount each thing to me': Aesch. *Prom.* 950). The rhetorical virtues thus perfect language, giving weight to its appearance, inducing assent, and preparing the way for the application of logical criteria.

The arts supply the rules according to which we are to manage our everyday perceptual experiences. At every point, the world is a sign: in Cicero's neat phrase, it is everywhere 'fit to move our senses'.[35] If one can only interpret it, every individual experience is potentially as rich as those pictures 'fortuitously encountered' by the heroes of a novel or by the novelist himself. But the revelatory points of the world are only distinguished by the quality of whoever grasps and analyses the vision they present: God needs men, says Epictetus, 'as spectators of himself and of his works—and not only as spectators, but as interpreters of them too' (*Diss.* I 6.19). A painting can go proxy for a feeble perception and prepares a commentary suitable for God. Thus a presentational vision (to use Quintilian's phrase) combines the three properties which Plato associates with reflections, mirrors, and eyes. Like a reflection (*Phd.* 99 d), it presents a vision of reality, less rough than that given in sensory contact or simple sense-impression, and containing only the essential differentiating properties (*notae*) of the object. Again, it can synthesize or focus, like a mirror or the polished surface of a shield or the pupil of an eye. Like a mirror (*Sph.* 266 b 9, c 4), it gives a reflected image—yet it is not inhibited by the physical realities of reflection; for thought—like Zeuxis when he painted Helen—composes fictional presentations from the presentations given in perception (DL VII 53), 'hypothesizing by reference to what exists'. Like an eye (*Rep.* 507 cd), it links rays of external light with the inner movements of the soul: cutting through appearances, it identifies its object under the bright light of revelation. And just as an eye gives the philosopher a paradigm of cognitive activity, so a

---

[35] 'Aptior ad sensus commovendos', *ND* II 30; see the edition of C. Appuhn (Paris, n.d.), ad loc. (376 n. 212).

presentation laid out on a *pinax* serves as an adequate model for internal presentation: like such a picture, an internal presentation is not an object but similar to an object. At this point the parallel with Plato ends; for if interpretation brings out the speculative power of a presentation, it also obeys its limits; and the semantic force of a *lekton* is wholly derived from a *phantaston*. Thus the analysis of a presentation will invert the thesis, stated in mythical form in the *Philebus*, that memory, meeting with sensible objects, 'writes sentences in our souls', and that then 'a painter follows the writer and draws pictures corresponding to his words' (39 a 3, b 6). The Stoics held the contrary view: language is a transformation of presentations—a transformation which, admittedly, calls for vigilant interpretation. The masters of the Old Stoa have left us several examples of the interpretative art; and they indicate that in their opinion there is no difference, either in method or in results, between the etymologizing of the names of the gods,[36] the exegesis of mythological pictures, the science of divination, and the humble dialectical interpretation of everyday presentations.

In the second book of the *De finibus*, Cicero reports that Cleanthes taught his pupils that virtue should not subordinate itself to pleasure. His argument began from a picture 'which Cleanthes used to draw so cleverly with words' (*Fin.* II 69). The virtues, kneeling at the feet of an allegorical figure of Pleasure, receive orders from her and pay her homage. The composition recalls that of *Hercules at the Feet of Omphale*, whose moral message the ancients immediately understood.[37] The movement from the virtues to pleasure, and then back again from her to them, is self-contained; and it illustrates how pleasure imposes its own microcosm upon its devotees and makes them careless of the world beyond: 'we have no other business.' The conclusion, that the life of pleasure is insane ('the picture will make you blush'), is inferred *a contrario* from that perversion of nature. Penetrating beyond the narrative sense of the scene, Cleanthes draws his moral by an interpretation *eis ta phusika* (to use the phrase of the

---

[36] See Cleanthes' etymology of 'Apollo': he construes the name as adverting to the successive positions of the sun at its rising (*SVF* I 540).

[37] See Plu. *Comp.Demetr. et Ant.* 3: 'Cleopatra often disarmed Antony, and enchanted him'—as, in the picture, Omphale surreptitiously removes Hercules' club.

Stoic grammarian Chaeremon).[38] We know Chrysippus' commentary on a picture of the Dance of the Graces, which he saw as a model of the mutual interconnection of virtuous acts; 'for the benefit passes in sequence from hand to hand, and comes back in the end to its author' (Sen. *Ben.* I iii 4). We might add Chrysippus' remarks on the *Canon* of Polyclitus,[39] and the title (admittedly enigmatic) of a treatise *pros tas anazōgraphēseis* (DL VII 201). It is possible that the content of the latter was related to those 'physicalist' interpretations of mythological paintings which so angered Chrysippus' readers:

In his book *On the Ancient Scientists* he describes the affair of Zeus and Hera in a disgraceful fashion. . . . They say he tells a most indecent tale; and although he praises it for its scientific meaning, it is more appropriate to whores than to gods, and it is not recorded by any historian of painting. (DL VII 187–8)

In all these cases, the narrative sense and the overt meaning of the painting are ignored, and it is construed as a scale model of 'things natural and divine'. The interpreter attends to the action portrayed rather than to the figures who act it out; he sets more store by the 'modes of being', absolute or relative, of the act than by the colours and perceptual qualities which individuate the agents. The dominant principle of interpretation *eis ta phusika* thus introduces an analogy between Stoic *ekphrasis* and the phenomenological method which, as we have seen, connects the structure of an utterance with the features of a presentation. The analogy was powerful enough to provide not only a notion of individuation but also a *semantic* interpretation of the relations of predication and subordination; and that although the method exhibited a strictly propositional logic of the type first suggested by the discriminatory activity of the senses. Hence, too, the protreptic function of Stoic grammar. The Stoics were well aware that this analogy does not exhaust the rich syntax of natural

---

[38] Grammarian and Egyptologist, contemporary of Cornutus, who taught Nero; he was director of the library of Alexandria: see *Grammatici Graeci* II 1 (2), 248.

[39] Reported by Galen, *Plac. Hipp. Plat.* V 3. Chrysippus inferred by analogy a definition of psychological health: it consists in a harmony among the parts of the living creature, rather than in the absolute quantities of the elements it contains. On the importance of Polyclitus' *Canon* see E. Panofsky, *Meaning in the Visual Arts* (New York, 1955), 64–8: he quotes and analyses the passage from Galen.

language; at any rate, they attempted to derive all the rhetorical forms enumerated by Protagoras from the declarative or statemental form (and from its grammatical analogue, the indicative mood) (DL VII 66 ff.).[40] But it would be rash to undervalue the reliance on paradigms which was typical of the Greek grammarians in general, and of the Stoics in particular; for even today we do not possess any grammar which gives an account of all the utterances of a natural language.

The analogy serves to remind us, even if it was a dogma of Stoic philosophy, how the long Greek experience of painting and tragedy prepared the way for a separation of a presentation from the utterance which assesses and analyses it—and which may break its spell. The mark of the true Athenian is to be a lover of spectacle—that aphorism comes not from Nietzsche but from Heliodorus (*Ethiopica*, III 1).

IV

Longus' prologue contrasts two ways of perceiving the picture he found in the grove of the Nymphs, a picture even 'more pleasing' than the sacred wood itself. Their curiosity aroused by rumour, pilgrims both worship the Nymphs and contemplate the picture (*men . . . de . . .*), without grasping the essential unity of those two acts. Thus they have, as it were, a side view of the picture, their gaze moving from scene to scene across the surface of the canvas; and that way of perceiving the painting gives rise to Longus' first description of it, drawn without art and expressed in the manner of a *lalia*. But the beauty of the picture seems to forbid any superficial interpretation, and Longus, having questioned the priest, elevates the first simple vision into a revelation, its episodes into the play of Fate, the spectators into interpreters, the pilgrims into mystics. For the reader, the narrative will serve as instruction, as an *aide-mémoire*, or as consolation. The moral, which like the picture stands outside time, is directed towards three aspects of consciousness, and aspires to cure their three maladies: regret for the past, ignorance of the future, and present suffering. Longus, for his part, being both historian and panegyrist of love, liberates himself from its amorous bonds by his

---

[40] Cf. DL IX 53. The forms are: prayer, question, answer, command.

understanding of its symptoms and of its purposes.[41] 'As for bodily pleasure, a goal dear to other men, one of the daughters of Memory has led it to its end' (DL VII 30—Athenaeus' epigram on the Stoics).

The four periods into which the prologue divides describe all the phases of love and of liberation from its bondage. First, the pilgrims: their level of apprehension is hardly above that of the beasts: incapable of grasping signs or of propositional language,[42] they are engrossed by the mere identification of objects. In that, they resemble the bird which tried to peck at Zeuxis' painted grapes, or the Athenians who screamed on seeing his *Family of Centaurs*, ignorant of the skill and the accuracy of the composition.[43] For such observers, the picture simply mirrors their own passions. Next come the huntsman, marvelling and astonished; the interpreter-priest; the analytical narrative, published to the world; and finally the healing of the reader by instructing or initiating him into the mysteries of love: such a plan confers on literature some of the nobility of philosophy. 'The Sage alone is a poet'; and the Sage alone is 'sublime, for he participates in all the sublimity that can fall upon an honourable man.'[44] At all events, that is the theory upon which literary composition is founded and by which it seeks to justify itself.

[41] Cf. Epict. *Diss*. II 14.29. Epictetus compares the world to a fair, and its inhabitants to the traders. Only a few men ever stop to *look* at the fair; their wisdom, which the love of money has not destroyed, is characterized by three successive actions: they look; they question themselves about what they see; they give an account of it (τὴν πανήγυριν ἱστορήσαντας).

[42] 'The difference between propositional language and emotional language is the real landmark between the human and the animal world'; 'There does not seem to be a single conclusive proof of the fact that any animal ever made the decisive step from subjective to objective, from affective to propositional language' (E. Cassirer, *An Essay on Man* [New Haven, 1944], 30). That judgement is a fair representation of the Stoic view: they characterized human language in terms of its property of being 'messenger and interpreter'—a property also possessed by the senses, those humblest parts of our psychological equipment (Cic. *ND* II 140). Of course, our descriptions may yet be mere *lalia*.

[43] See Lucian, *Zeux*. 7. Lucian's text implies that the Athenians recognized the strange subject, to which they responded with spontaneous screams (as Alexander's horse neighed on seeing a picture of a horse); but they did not recognize the art or the mode of expression, thereby showing themselves blind to the language of signs.

[44] See Strabo I 2. 3: 'For Eratosthenes says that every poet aims at entertainment (*psuchagōgia*), not instruction. The ancients assert on the contrary that poetry is a sort of elementary philosophy, which introduces us to life. . . . But my school [i.e. Stoicism] actually contends that only the Sage is a poet.' Cf. DL VII 60: 'A poem is

Longus' intention can be summarized in a legal formula: *antigrapsai tēi graphēi,* to pay tribute to the picture by faithfully transcribing it. The possibility of transcription is in fact implicit in the asyndeton of the first sentence: 'I saw ... a painted picture, a tale of love': on what does such an axiom of total translatability rest? It is simply laid down: there is no direct proof of it, no way of demonstrating the existence of that production of speech which is presupposed both by the plan of the prologue and by the structure of Stoic logic, and which is encapsulated in the phrase of pseudo-Longinus. Longus simply offers us the results of his analytical labours, which replace the preliminary description *(lalia)* by an informed *ekphrasis.* And if we ask for an indirect proof, we shall come again to the evidence of common sense, on which Cicero falls back: 'we see his painting, not his poetry.'[45] The cause must thus be judged by its effects: language rests on a revelatory phenomenology. Hence the final equation, in which what is said is identified with what is presented, rests on a postulate: it is only presentations, functioning as signs, which can excite the identifications and heuristic prefigurings about which any system of utterances and of linguistic meanings must be constituted. In just the same way, the theorems of Euclid rest upon certain postulated geometrical constructions.

The priority of the image *qua* sign is revealed again, and with more force, by its enigmatic beauty: parallel to the process of analysis, it discovers a process of initiation which motivates and sustains the analytical task. The picture arouses wonder *(thauma),* and it demands an interpreter and no less than four books to encompass the literary transformation of its content. The movement, if not the method, is Socratic: first, wonder; then interpretation by a master, which involves a detour into things divine; then *ekphrasis,* which brings out the truth behind the appearances. But the master is merely a theologian (or scientist) more skilled than his pupils; and the book is no more than a description of reality. Longus uses the word *'ekponēsamen',* indicating by the aorist tense and the prefix *ek-* the slow labours

a meaningful work, which includes an imitation of things divine and things human.' The moral of the poem is thus both affecting and constrained in the same way as the moral of a picture: a dialectical commentary is needed to explain it. Finally, only the Sage can extract all the sublimity from the presentations he receives *(SVF* I 216).

[45] *Tusc.* V 114, where Cicero refers to Homer.

of analysis. The verbal form—or, rather, its Latin equivalent—is admirably explained by Pliny:

> I should like to be accepted after the fashion of those founders of painting and sculpture, who . . . inscribed their finished works, even the masterpieces which we never cease to admire, with a provisional title, such as: *Worked on by Apelles*, or *Polyclitus*—as though art were a thing always in progress and never completed. (*Nat*. Pref. 26–7)

The writer's modesty fits the majesty of his descriptive duties: all the arts must be measured against the richness and variety of nature, of which they must give a partial and analogical revelation. It is the double role of presentation which alone can justify the 'theory of production' (*gennetikon tou logou*) and reveal its systematic value; for presentation unites indissolubly the heuristic function of a scale model and the instructive or initiatory capacity of a sign. Presentation must be granted a revelatory power if it is to be a reliable map of nature and a ground for definitions and theorems—like Archimedes' sphere, the figure of the three Graces, or the picture of Pleasure enslaving the Virtues. And, vice versa, the heuristic success of scale models—and in general of the arts and sciences—confirms the revelatory powers of those devices, in so far as it implies a cause appropriate to the observed effects. That is no generalization of the sophism of the astrologers, who pretend to confirm the validity of signs by the success of their interpretations; rather, it should be recognized as an example of that form of circular reasoning which no speculative philosophy can avoid.

The picture which gives Longus the matter for his book explicitly assumes the twin functions of scale model and sign. The painting schematizes and prefigures the episodes of the novel, surveying the whole drama which Fortune will play out (*tuchēn erōtikēn echousa*). The novelist thus possesses a synoptic vision; and he communicates it to his readers in the same way as the historian who 'must place before his readers a synoptic vision of the way in which Fortune arranged the consummation of these events' (Polybius I 4). By its very nature, the painting is a repository of speculative activity; for it is unaffected by the delays and the linearity which the temporal ordering of events imposes on discursive consciousness. Indeed, it enjoys a God-like vision of the succession of events: *divinitati omnia praesens*. Anyone who has seen the whole picture knows more than its heroes whom misfortunes have blinded—in the same way, Mauriac (according to Sartre) assumes the position of a clairvoyant god *vis-a-vis* his characters: 'He has chosen divine omniscience and omnipotence.'[46] But Longus has better arguments than Mauriac for his position. Taken in itself, the prologue has a dramatic unity, preparatory to the drama of the narrative. But at the end of the novel we learn that the prelude is in fact the final episode of the main story: the picture which happened to interrupt Longus' hunt was dedicated by the characters of the pastoral: 'They adorned the grotto, and dedicated paintings, and consecrated an altar to Love the Shepherd' (IV 39). In fact, the beginning of the story can be pushed still further back; for the shepherds are the instruments of Eros, as Pan reveals in his diatribe against Chloe's ravishers: 'You have dragged from the altars a young girl about whom Eros wishes to tell a story' (II 27). Thus it is the God of Love who has caused the whole drama and arranged the succession of events as a revelation of his power. He has contrived the lovers, the votive picture, and the narrative itself, acting through human passions and human arts: Longus is merely the narrator of the drama, the picture its symbol. The revelation indicates how properly the scale model was employed.

That too is the source of the two characteristics of the novel, which the Suda and Photius describe as a *logos historikos kai erōtikos*. For the novel both is a history and belongs to that *genre* of initiatory writings exemplified by the *Symposium*. Apart from the artifices of composition which I have just rehearsed, its initiatory function is evident in the connected roles of author, heroes, and readers. Longus, who unveils the painting and then disappears behind his narrative, can be compared to those figures who, in certain Renaissance paintings, stand with their backs to us and introduce us to a gospel scene or a gathering of saints. Correspondingly, the last lines of the prologue require from the reader an act of assent and recognition: he must submit to the trials of love and recognize the power of Eros, now that he has understood his purposes. The same confession is also required from the heroes of the story. For the pastoral is constructed about their incapacity to recognize the signs of incipient love and

---

[46] J. P. Sartre, *Situations* (Paris, 1947), Ch. I: 'M. François Mauriac et la Liberté'.

the obstacles set in its path by ignorance or the ill will of other men. As the dénouement approaches, the scenes of recognition and the contract of marriage represent acts of assent. 'Chloe understood'—those are the closing words of the story: with that, the pastoral, in its scientific and theological sense, ends; and the dedicatory picture is the public confession of that new understanding.[47]

Hellenistic wall-painting provides us with other examples of the double function of images. A fresco, or a picture painted onto a wall with no apparent frame (*embléma*), evinces not an invasion of ordinary space by mythological space, but rather a cultural enrichment of the former and an invitation to construe the room as a temple. The painting both summons up initiatory reflection, and prefigures a thoroughly human situation. That, at least, is suggested by the cycle of paintings in the Villa of the Mysteries which, according to Mittelstadt,[48] is contemporary with Longus' pastoral. We should miss their significance if we saw in them no more than an objective representation of the series of episodes making up the marriage ceremony. The painting shows no more of that ceremony than its first stages, together with their mythological attributes and counterparts. The final, or rather the central, scene—the marriage itself—is not represented. It will actually take place in the alcove whose doorway interrupts the fresco. In a similar fashion, the picture described by Longus does not contain the nuptial scene, because it stands to it in a relation of contiguity or hypallage. The last episode of the 'amorous adventure (*erótiké tuché*)', the *ex voto*, implies the happy consummation of the marriage, for which it is both a thank-offering and a depiction of its antecedent causes. Once we have reconstructed that course of events, the episodes (exposure of

---

[47] The confession (or *recognitio*) is required of the readers no less than of the dramatis personae. See esp. Ach. Tat. I: the author disembarks in the bay of Sidon, goes for a walk, and discovers an *ex voto* picture representing the rape of Europa, which occurred on the very spot in which he finds the picture; after describing the painting, he observes: 'I admired all aspects of the picture, but, being a lover myself, I gazed especially at the depiction of Eros leading the bull; and I said: "Look how a child rules the heavens and the sea and the earth!" And as I spoke, a young man, standing near by, said: "I can attest to that, having myself suffered so greatly at the hands of love."' Later Alexandrian novels explicitly bear the title of 'confessions' (*Confession of St. Cyprian, Confession of pseudo-Clement*). The analogy between the latter and the *Life of Apollonius* is noticed by Perry, op. cit. 295.

[48] Op. cit.

infants, pirate raid, . . .) lose their appearance of chance happenings: in that way human affairs are referred to the divine plan.[49] A presentational sign is both a stimulus and a model (it adumbrates an action). 'On leaving the School, Zeno stumbled and broke his finger. Striking the earth with his hand, he called out in Niobe's words: "I am coming: why do you call?" And immediately he suffocated himself and died' (DL VII 28). The reference to an episode from tragedy turns the incident into a model, supplies it with physico-theological significance, and gives sense to Zeno's reply.

V

If those are the two functions of presentation, its role in the production of speech excludes any empirical or psychological interpretation; for the theory of production implies neither sensationalism nor the priority of mental images. We shall better assess its systematic import if we see how it can account for certain peculiarities of style and logic which are usually passed over in silence. I mean: the use of deixis; the didactic function of narrative; and the paradox of the autonomy of logic.

(1) The preceding remarks support Sextus' evidence about Stoic doctrine: presentation alone is the criterion of truth, by virtue of its revelatory function; and presentation alone can provide language with a synthetic power and the rules of implication (*akolouthia*), by virtue of its function as a scale model.

---

[49] Thus I cannot agree with Heine when, following Hegel, he contrasts romantic (Christian) art with classical (Greek) art and bases his argument on the case of painting. 'The difference consists in the fact that in ancient art plastic forms are wholly identified with what they represent, or with the idea which the artist wanted to represent. For example, the wanderings of Odysseus have no signification beyond the wanderings of the man who was a son of Laertes, the husband of Penelope, and whose name was Odysseus; the Bacchus in the Louvre is nothing but the delightful son of Semele, his eyes full of bold melancholy. . . . With romantic art, things are different: there, the wanderings of a knight have an esoteric meaning' (*Über Deutschland*, Part II, Book 1). The account of the Greek novel implicit in the following sentence from Zola is equally implausible: 'Until that terrible night, the young people had lived a naïvely idyllic life, like many impoverished simpletons from the working class, among whom you may still sometimes find those childish romances familiar from the Greek novels' (*La Fortune des Rougon*, Pléiade edition, 170). The editor notes that Zola had prepared an essay on the Greek novel, in which he refers to *Daphnis and Chloe* as 'an episode of unsurpassable elegance . . . a love story delightfully told'. To say the least, that loses the initiatory force of '*erōtikos*'.

The same remarks explain Sextus' objections to Stoicism—though I shall not pronounce here on their validity. For it is the existence of apprehensive presentations and the grounds of sign-inferences which the sceptical critics chose as their targets.[50]

Sextus overlooks an important benefit which the theory of production confers: it sinks the system of Protagoras. If utterances get their meaning from the presentations which they analyse, then the intentions and the character of the speaker can be suppressed in favour of the presentation which he communicates. A hearer is free to recognize it as an apprehensive presentation, or to reject it; to see it as the basis for an inference, or to ignore it; to give or to withhold his assent. The Second Sophistic found there the method of *ekphrasis*, which protected it from an ignominious reputation, and which gave rise to its philosophical pretensions.[51] Longus stresses that language is subordinate to presentation when he withdraws from his own story after announcing that it will be an interpretative narrative. After the prologue, the author does not reappear. And just because such a withdrawal is so familiar to us, we forget to ask under what conditions it could take place and be accepted by the reader.

The orator Aelius Theon explains the use of *oratio obliqua* in narrative as follows: 'The ancients presented most of their stories in this way, and, as Aristotle observes, they were quite right to do so; for they do not speak *in propria persona*: rather, they refer their tale to some ancient authority, so as to minimize the appearance of telling an impossible story' (*Prog.* 3). The whole narrative must thus be read as one long infinitival construction. The satirists—Lucillus, Petronius, Apuleius, Lucian—wrote in the first person. That custom rests on a tacit convention—'You need not, and indeed you must not, believe me'—which Lucian impudently invokes: 'I decided to lie—but with much more honesty than the rest of them; for there is this one point on which I shall tell the truth: I shall lie' (*VH* I 4). Longus calls on an entirely different principle. He does not assume responsibility for the fiction himself; nor yet does he withdraw in favour of a primary narrator,

---

[50] See e.g. *PH* II 135–60; *M* VII 301–15.

[51] In Book I of *Lives of the Sophists*, Philostratus identifies Sophistic as philosophical rhetoric (480). He claims for his School the heritage of Socrates, so that it is not a 'new' but a 'second' Sophistic movement (481). If the Sophists did not use dialectic, that is because they based their expositions on knowledge and 'a clear apprehension of what exists' (κατάληψιν σαφῆ τοῦ ὄντος) (480).

whose good faith or understanding we would again be at liberty to doubt. Rather, it is the content of the presentation, whose originator, creator, and dedicatee is the God himself, that must alone win our assent. The transition from the first to the second and then to the third person indicates, by style and grammar, this transfer of responsibility. After the first lines of the pastoral, the 'I saw' of the prologue yields to 'you would think you saw' (I 2), and then the function of persuasion is definitively assigned to the captivating charm of the scenery itself. The ebb and flow of the waves which break on the shores of Lesbos murmur with 'enchanting persuasiveness', and at the same time they set the scene and elevate it into a symbol of the pastoral life. Longus lets the things themselves speak (cf. Sen. *Dial*. IX 1. 13).

The fact that this transition is made via the second person reminds us that anyone else in Longus' position would have experienced the same presentation: he, like Longus himself, could be referred to in the dative case (*phainetai moi/soi*). The speaker only assumes responsibility if he makes assertions (*legō*) and judgements (*axioō*), where the first person takes on a performative aspect: 'Anyone who says "It is day" seems to judge that it is day' (DL VII 65). These are 'things which depend on us (*ta eph' hēmin*)'. But judgement has its rules, and so does the making of assertions. In this sense, assertions are in themselves impersonal: any other speaker, given the same presentation and equally instructed in logic, would express himself and give his assent in the same way. A *lekton* carries no trace of a speaker—just as an oracle carries no trace of the soothsayer. A *lekton* is not a *statement* (*apophansis*), understood to include a reference to the act of uttering and to the process of linguistic expression (*hoson eph' hēmin*; or, in Longus' term, *ekponēsamen*); it is *something stated*, which in its grammar and syntax as it were itself bears the responsibility of the assertion (*apophanton hoson eph' hauto*).[52] That definition of a *lekton*, which is ascribed to Chrysippus (DL VII 65), underlines the desire to tie the utterance (*lekton*) to what is presented (*phantaston*), by eliminating the subjective element of the statement (expressed by a personal pronoun in the dative after *phainetai*, or by the first-person subjects of verbs of saying). Thus utterances are given into the keeping of an impersonal art; and the five rhetorical virtues (hellenism, clarity, relevance,

---

[52] The different interpretations of this phrase are discussed in Frede [42], 32–40.

brevity, structure) assure that utterances will enjoy the anonymity of a *lingua caracteristica*.[53] The stylistic strategy of Longus perfectly satisfies those requirements.

But how are we to reconcile the anonymity of utterances with the presence in them of ineliminable deictic elements? Bertrand Russell saw in deixis an egocentricity incompatible with the demands of *lingua caracteristica*.[54] His analysis has been in part confirmed by linguistic studies: deictic elements, or shifters (demonstratives, adverbs of time and place, mood, voice, tense) indicate in the utterance aspects of the actual process of uttering.[55] Hence either Chrysippus' desire will be thwarted (since no natural language can eliminate every trace of the utterer's act from the utterance) or else the grammatical features of acts of uttering, which the Stoics studied in great detail, must be taken to translate elements intrinsic to the presentation itself. Thus the deictic categories are after all phenomenological categories: deixis refers neither to *my* experience, nor to any particular speech-act—that subjective element is eliminated along with the first person; rather, it writes the character of the presentation into the grammar of the utterance, and recalls the conditions in which it was experienced. That fact allows it to serve as a criterion of truth. The speaker is thus simply the interpreter of the presentation he conveys; his identity is lost in his message.

Hellenistic sculpture excellently illustrates the way in which a speaker is thus branded by the content of what he says; Lucian provides an even better illustration: for him, the dancer is, in the last analysis, the best interpreter.[56] But it is enough to restrict ourselves to the definition of rhetoric as 'the order and arrangement of continuous speech'—if that order includes, as Plutarch says it does, modulations of the voice, and expressions or gestures

---

[53] The importance of this notion in Frege's first two logical systems, and its paradoxical consequences, are well known: the Stoic origin of the notion is less familiar—see my 'La sémantique de Frege', in *Les langages, le sens et l'histoire* (Lille, 1976).

[54] B. Russell, *Human Knowledge, its Scope and Limit* (London, 1948), Part II, Ch. 4.

[55] See R. Jakobson, *Shifters, Verbal Categories and the Russian Verb* (Cambridge, Mass., 1957); E. Benveniste, 'L'appareil formel de l'énonciation', in his *Problèmes de linguistique générale* (Paris, 1974), II, Ch. 5.

[56] See *Salt.* 64: Nero entertained a visiting prince from Pontus with a display of dancing; the prince asked for the dancer as a gift, so that he could act as general interpreter in his relations with the neighbouring barbarian kingdoms. Ibid. 65 compares the orator to the dancer.

of the face and hands.[57] For all that mimicry serves the ends of the object presented; it is part of the grammar of the speech, and it belongs to the description not of the orator but of his subject matter.

That defence of the impersonality of language takes care of Plato's objections against indirect speech (*Rep.* 394–6; *Grg.* 502 d): he says that it disguises the inopportune presence of the narrator, and his capacity to create illusions; direct speech is more honest, since it forces the imitator to come into the open—when his interlocutor will conduct him along the 'digression' to the theory of Forms and to the canonical formulation of definitions. In other words, to use a classification suggested by Roman Jakobson, Plato holds that epic and narrative poetry derive their force from the 'conative' and 'emotive' aspects of language. Now by linking a narrative to the *ekphrasis* of a presentation which is, in itself, something public and objective, Longus grounds rhetoric on the 'referential' aspect of language; and in the last lines of the prologue he subordinates the emotive and conative aspects to the didactic.[58]

(2) If indirect speech and prose narrative are freed from any appearance of sophistry, we still have to show that they can fulfil a didactic and probative function.

In contrasting history to tragic poetry, Aristotle indicated three weaknesses of the historian's art: because it deals with individuals, history is less philosophical than tragedy, which deals with 'universal' characters (*Poet.* 1451[b] 6); because it is obliged to narrate a sequence of events defined by some temporal period, it lacks the unity of action proper to tragedy (1459[a] 20 ff.); and finally, even if it ignores the *post hoc ergo propter hoc* fallacy, it can rarely set out the causes of things (1452[a] 22). The theory of production, which makes the narrative depend on the synoptic view of a unitary picture, parries the thrust of those criticisms, and allows political and natural history to make use of the methods of proof. The unitary vision reveals a unity of action, which can be perceived neither by the agents in the story nor by its chroniclers. Like the blueprint for a simple machine, it shows schematically the conflicting forces involved, their tensions and

[57] Plu. *Stoic.rep.* 1047a: κόσμον εἰρομένου λόγου καὶ τάξιν; see Cherniss [5], note ad loc. Compare this definition of rhetorical prose with the definition of poetry at DL VII 60: structure and expressive power replace metre and rhythm.

[58] See R. Jakobson, 'Linguistics and Poetics', in his *Style in Language* (New York, 1960).

their positions of equilibrium. The narrative can thus express the delicate connections of succession (*epeita*) and conjunction (*kai*) between events; it can spend time in naming and describing individuals—for these details illustrate and do not destroy the unitary blueprint. In the same way, the points and lines of a particular figure illustrate and do not destroy the necessity of a geometrical theorem. History deals with sequences of actions in which individuals are the figures, and events the points of intersection. It can be 'demonstrative' (*apodeiktikos*) just because it is, in Hegel's term, 'pragmatical' (Polybius II 37). A unitary vision alone can yield knowledge of true causes, by distinguishing them from the illusion of mere conjunctions: it mirrors the unity of action and the necessity of fate.[59] It thus holds together the demonstrative elements—as the lines of force in the painting described by Cleanthes sustained his ethical proof.

It is true that proofs in political and natural history deal with more complicated objects than those of applied geometry; and that they therefore prefer indirect argument to direct demonstration ('If . . . then—'): they proceed by excluding incompatibilities ('Not both this and that') or by listing the possibilities ('Either . . . or . . . or . . .') and then eliminating all but one of them. But in all three cases, the inference is based on the necessary coherence among all the parts of any totality.[60] By the use of pictures we can apply the properties of geometrical diagrams to physical or political systems without overlooking the mode of apprehension —direct or indirect—which gives access to them. Pictures exorcize the devils of disjointed perceptions—and also of surface grammar and of the logical atomism of the narrative style. Our model, in which the presentation serves as a diagram and the individuals are particular points on it, is supposed to underwrite the continuity of the narrative: and that excludes any distinction between a logical space of facts and a real space of objects. And

[59] Polybius III 6.1 ff. Hegel recognized pragmatical history as a form of reflective history: 'The general conditions and chain of events are no longer, as before, hidden away in particular individual facts, but become a fact themselves: it is no longer the particular but the universal which from now on appears at the surface. It would be foolish to elevate purely individual facts to such a position of universality. But the historian's genius is measured by his capacity to develop to the full the conjunction of facts' (Introduction to *The Philosophy of History*, tr. Nisbet (Cambridge, 1975), 20–1).

[60] The cosmos is the *ratio essendi* of perceived connections, even though they are its *ratio cognoscendi*.

if the logic of the narrative reproduces 'cosmological' connections within the unitary whole it describes, then it can avoid a formal semantics in which the class of individuals and the class of truth-values have no unity. Stoic models are analogical models.

(3) It remains to mention a paradox which appears to be inherent in the logical structure we have so far described: we might well suspect an incompatibility between, on the one hand, the autonomy of human reason and, on the other, the thesis that the discursive modes constitutive of reason have their origin in presentations, visions or intuitions.

The power of presentation suggests the paradox—and also resolves it. 'Things themselves do not touch the soul in the least . . . it alone turns and moves itself' (Marcus Aurelius, V 19). Presentations are wholly involved in the soul's desires to see, to believe, to interpret. And we can no more free ourselves from them than we can give up the *oikeiōsis* or union with nature of which presentation is the instrument. The alternative is philosophical suicide, and a return to the black night of things. Presentation thus gives us the same choice as the banqueter's rule: Either drink or go away (Cic. *Tusc.* V 118). But two types of behaviour are open to us: either our souls will be carried along by the accidental sequence of impressions, always accompanied by fears and hopes; or else they may play off presentation against presentation, and locate each particular experience in the unitary picture presented by the arts and sciences. Just as Archimedes' sphere liberates astronomy from the vulgar interpretation of eclipses as evil omens, so the picture described by Longus liberates love from the hopes and remorse which plague it: it prescribes love's proper course, and describes its scientific and theological aspects—'for it is something divine' (Pl. *Smp.* 206 c 6). The first presentation is overcome by a second, more powerful, one: for who would resist the seduction of that cosmic drama, or refuse the happiness of placing himself in it?

The autonomy of reason consists in its mastery over the presentations which sustain it. By that strategy, it rises above the risky phenomenology of spontaneous *lalia*; and it can provide a cure for the *malaise* of Emma Bovary, or (to stay within the confines of Greek culture) for the madness of Orestes or of Phaedra. As in Bovary's case, the ravings of those tragic figures were first fed by genuine perceptions: Electra and Hippolytus were real, actual objects. But their phenomenology was perverted; 'for what is tragedy but a portrayal in metre of the sufferings of men who stand amazed at external things?' (Epict. *Diss.* I 4.26).

We only free ourselves from one presentation by submitting to another. Longus' pastoral offers us not the insight gained from tragedy, but the tranquillity of the *ex voto*; in place of the passion of the House of Atreus it presents an example, borrowed perhaps from the Stoic Dio Chrysostom,[61] of an initiation into love which knows no discord and no jealousy. The agitation of the lovers is stilled by the course of the seasons; they learn the moral from the flocks committed to their care. The last paragraph lets us see that physical theory has been tested against the pathology of love and 'the games of shepherds'. With the last sentence of the narrative, the initiation comes to an end: the lovers have given the demonstration their seal of approval.

---

[61] See W. Schmid and O. Stählin, *Geschichte der griechischen Literatur* II i (Munich, 1920), 361–7: Dio Chrysostom was a Stoic, a pupil of Musonius, and one of the leading representatives of the Second Sophistic; he composed a *Euboikos*, praising the virtuous simplicity of rustic life.

THE ORIGINAL NOTION OF CAUSE*

Michael Frede

INTRODUCTION

However muddled our notion of a cause may be it is clear that we would have difficulties in using the term 'cause' for the kinds of things Aristotle calls 'causes'. We might even find it misleading to talk of Aristotelian causes and wonder whether in translating the relevant passages in Aristotle we should not avoid the term 'cause' altogether. For an end, a form, or matter do not seem to be the right kinds of items to cause anything, let alone to be causes. It is much less clear what our difficulties are due to. We might think that causes are events. Sometimes this is regarded as almost a truism. And, indeed, philosophers since Hume, who still—at least in his language—is wavering on the matter, have tended to think of causes as events. But I doubt that our difficulty with Aristotelian causes is due to the fact that ends, forms, and matter clearly are not events or anything like events. For apart from the fact that one may have doubts about the general thesis that causes are events, we do not have any difficulty in understanding Kant, e.g., when he talks as if a substance, an object, could be the cause of something in another object (*Critique of Pure Reason* B 111), as if the sun could be said to be the cause of the warming up of the stone or the melting of the butter. And the reason why we do not have any difficulty in understanding this kind of language seems to me to be the following: a physical object like the sun or a billiard-ball can interact with other things, it can affect them and act on them so as to produce an effect in them. Quite generally our use of causal terms seems to be strongly coloured by the notion that in causation there is something which in some sense does something or other so as to produce or bring about an effect. Even if we do think of causes as events the paradigms we tend to

* I would like to thank the members of the conference for their useful comments. I am particularly grateful to Robert Bolton, Myles Burnyeat, Dorothea Frede, Thomas Rosenmeyer, and Richard Sorabji who were kind enough to provide me with written comments which were very helpful in revising this paper.

think of, and certainly the paradigms Hume and Kant thought of, are events in which something does something or other; and we feel that we have to explain that it is only in a very metaphorical sense that an event could be said to produce an effect. Thus, though we may want to get away from such a notion, there is a strong tendency to conceive of causes as somehow active. And it seems that our difficulty with the Aristotelian causes is due to the fact that they cannot even be conceived of in this way. A good part of the unfortunate history of the notion of a final cause has its origin in the assumption that the final cause, as a cause, must act and in the vain attempt to explain how it could do so. It is only with Aristotle's moving cause that we think that we readily understand why it should be called a cause. But it would be a mistake to think that Aristotle with his notion of a moving cause tries to capture our notion of cause or at least a notion we would readily recognize as a notion of cause, though it is significant that people have tended to think that among the Aristotelian causes it is only the moving cause which is a cause really. For Aristotle in more theoretical contexts will tell that it is not the sculptor working on his sculpture who is the moving cause, but the art of sculpture. And with the art of sculpture we have the same problems as with ends, forms, and matter.

Aristotle's notion of cause, then, is quite different from ours. But it is by no means peculiar to Aristotle. The same difficulties we have with Aristotle and the Peripatetics we also have with Plato or Epicurus. Ideas do not seem to be the kind of thing that could cause anything, nor does the void (cf. Epicurus in DL X 44). But how did it come about that people got to think that a cause has to be the kind of item which can do something or other so as to bring about an effect?

From a remark in Sextus Empiricus it is clear that it was already in later antiquity that the notion of a cause had been narrowed down to fit the notion of an active cause. For in his discussion of causality Sextus tells us (PH III 14) that despite all the differences among philosophers concerning causality we still might assume that they all agree on the following general characterization of a cause: the cause is that because of which in virtue of its being active the effect comes about.[1] Sextus, then, claims that it is generally agreed that causes are items which

---

[1] δι' ὃ ἐνεργοῦν γίνεται τὸ ἀποτέλεσμα.

somehow are active and through their activity bring about an effect. This claim would be puzzling, indeed, given what we have said earlier about Plato, Aristotle, and Epicurus, unless it reflected a general shift in the notion of cause. But we have good reason to accept Sextus' claim. First of all Sextus shows himself to be quite aware of the fact that even non-active items get called 'causes'. For in the preceding paragraph he tells us that he now wants to turn to a consideration of the active cause in general (*to energētikon aition*). There would be no point in adding the adjective 'active' if Sextus were not aware that non-active items, too, are called causes. So Sextus must assume that though philosophers go on to call such items as Platonic ideas or Aristotelian causes 'causes', they nevertheless are agreed that, strictly speaking, only active items are causes. Secondly, there is independent evidence that Sextus had good reason to think so. Clement, e.g., tells us (*Strom.* I 17, 82, 3) 'we say . . . that the cause is conceived of as producing, as active, and as doing something'[2] (cf. also *Strom.* VIII 9, 25, 5). As we learn from Simplicius' commentary on the *Categories* (327, 6 ff.), Iamblichus explained a passage in Plato's *Philebus* telling us that it is that which is producing something (*to poioun*) which is, strictly speaking, the cause, whereas matter and form are not causes at all, but auxiliaries (*sunaitia*), and the paradigm and the end only qualifiedly are causes. We find similar remarks throughout the Neoplatonic tradition. Damascius, e.g., tells us that every cause is doing something (*drastērion, in Phileb.* 114, 6 W.). The Peripatetic distinction of kinds of causes is adapted to the shift by claiming that it is the moving cause which is most strictly speaking the cause (*aition to kuriōtaton legomenon*), as we can see from a passage in Simplicius (*in Phys.* 326, 15 ff.). The shift in terminology from 'causa movens' to 'causa efficiens' may be another reflection of the change in notion (cf. e.g. Simpl. *in Phys.* 326, 25). Evidence of this kind is easily multiplied, and thus we have good reason to believe that the notion of a cause by Sextus' time had changed in such a way as to be restricted to items which can do something or other and thus cause something. It also seems to be fairly clear how this change in the notion of a cause did come about. Seneca (*Ep.* LXV 11; cf. 2 ff.) still criticizes Plato for assuming the five kinds of causes we just saw Iamblichus talking about on the grounds that there is just one

---

[2] φαμὲν . . . τὸ αἴτιον ἐν τῷ ποιεῖν καὶ ἐνεργεῖν καὶ δρᾶν νοεῖσθαι.

kind of cause, that which acts so as to produce the effect: 'The Stoics take the view that there is just one cause, that which does something (*facit*)' (LXV 4). In general it is the Stoics who insist that causes are active, and so it seems to be their influence which has brought about the change in question.

But Stoic influence on thought about causes is not restricted to this point. When we look, e.g., at Sextus' discussion of causes in the *Outlines of Pyrrhonism* it turns out that the distinctions of kinds of causes Sextus makes are all of Stoic origin. And hence it might be worth while to review our evidence concerning the Stoic doctrine of causes, not just in order to find out why the Stoics would insist that causes have to be active, but in the hope of getting somewhat clearer on the history of the notion of a cause in general.

Before we go into the details, though, it should be pointed out that the Stoics seem to distinguish at least three uses of 'cause' of increasing narrowness. There is first of all a very general use of 'cause'. It seems to be this use we have to think of when Stobaeus (*Ecl.* I, p. 138, 23) says 'Chrysippus says that a cause is a because of which (*di' ho*).' Just like the English preposition 'because of' and the German '*wegen*' the Greek '*dia*' with the accusative can cover such a variety of explanatory relations that it would rather comfortably accommodate anything that had been called a cause, in ordinary discourse or by philosophers, including the Aristotelian causes (cf. *Phys.* 198ᵇ 5 ff.).

One may, of course, doubt whether Chrysippus' characterization of a cause is supposed to be so generous as to allow us to call all the things causes which actually are called causes. In this case one would have to assume that '*dia*' here is used in a narrower technical sense. But there is evidence that the Stoics were willing to allow for such a generous use of 'cause', though, at the same time, they also insisted on a narrower use. When, then, Clement (VIII 9, 20, 3) says: 'It is the same thing, then, which is a cause and which is productive; and if something is a cause and productive it invariably also is a because of which; but if something is a because of which it is not invariably also a cause' and then goes on to give antecedent causes as examples of things which are because of which, but not causes in this sense, it is natural to assume that he is relying on a contrast between a more general notion of a cause according to which any because of which counts as a cause, and a narrower notion which he wants to adopt, according to which a cause not only has to be a because of which, but also productive. Hence it seems that when Chrysippus characterizes the cause as the because of which he allows for a very general notion of a cause.

Then there is the narrower notion of a cause, which Clement in the passage quoted refers to, according to which causes are restricted to those things which actually do something or other to bring about an effect. It is this notion of an active cause of which Sextus claims that all philosophers are agreed on it. It is not just the because of which, but the because of which through whose activity the effect comes about, to use Sextus' characterization. But even this narrower notion of an active cause covers different kinds of causal relations which the Stoics will distinguish by distinguishing various kinds of causes. And among these kinds they will single out that which is the cause, strictly speaking, namely the perfect (*autoteles*) or containing (*sunektikon*) cause. Since the most general notion of a cause is not specifically Stoic I will in the following discuss first the general Stoic notion of an active cause and then the various kinds of causes distinguished, in particular causes in the narrowest and strictest sense.

THE GENERAL NOTION OF AN ACTIVE CAUSE

We said that one had to explain in what sense Aristotelian causes could be called causes. Ends or forms do not seem to be the right kinds of items to be causes. And, as we have seen, one reason for this may be that they are entities, whereas causes, one might think, are events, facts, things one does, in short, items of the kind I will call propositional items (I take all these items to be propositional items in some very narrow sense, but for our purposes here it will do to take the term in a very generous sense).

Now it is true that at least from the fifth century B.C. onwards such propositional items, too, come to be called causes, *aitia*. But throughout antiquity, as far as I can see, it is non-propositional items like Aristotle's causes which are referred to when causes are discussed systematically. This is not to deny that philosophers when they state the cause of something sometimes refer to propositional items ('The cause of this is that . . .'). In this they just follow the shift in ordinary language mentioned above. Aristotle sometimes even refers to propositional items when he gives examples of his kinds of causes. But in other passages it is clear that when he distinguishes kinds of causes he has entities, non-propositional items in mind. And the later tradition quite definitely treats Aristotelian causes as non-propositional. Similarly Epicurus treats causes as non-propositional when he regards the atoms and the void as the ultimate causes of everything (DL X 44). The same is true of the five causes of the Middle Platonists (Sen. *Ep.* LXV 7–8) and of the six causes of the Neoplatonists (cf. Simp. *in Phys.* 11. 2–3; Olymp. *in Phaed.* 207, 27 ff.; Philop. *De aet. mundi* 159, 5 ff.). And it is certainly true of the Stoics who require a cause to be a being, an entity, a status they deny to propositional items.

The facts of the matter become clearer if we take into account a terminological distinction which Stobaeus attributes to Chrysippus (*Ecl.* I, p. 139, 3 f.W.). This distinction has a basis in the original use of the word 'cause' which distinguished between an *aition* and an *aitia*. But this distinction is not preserved by Aristotle; and as a result it is much less clear than it would otherwise have been whether we are considering propositional or non-propositional items when we talk about causes. Chrysippus' distinction is the following. Having explained that an *aition*, a cause, according to Chrysippus is an entity, Stobaeus goes on to say, 'But an *aitia*, he says, is an account of the *aition*, or the account about the *aition* as *aition*'[3]). We might have doubts as to the precise meaning of this short characterization of an *aitia*, if we did not have a fragment of Diocles of Carystus (frag. 112 Wellmann) preserved by Galen. Diocles discusses aetiology, explanation, in medicine, and in this discussion he uses 'the account about the *aition*' interchangeably with 'the *aitia*' in the sense of 'the reason' or 'the explanation'. Obviously the idea is that the *aitia*, the reason or explanation, is a *logos*, a propositional item of a certain kind, namely a statement or a truth about the *aition*, the cause, or rather the relevant truth about the cause, the truth in virtue of which it is the cause. And this seems to be exactly the characterization of an *aitia* Stobaeus is attributing to Chrysippus.

By Chrysippus' time ordinary usage of '*aition*' and '*aitia*' no longer followed that distinction. But there was some basis for the

³ αἰτίαν δ' εἶναι λόγον αἰτίου, ἢ λόγον τὸν περὶ τοῦ αἰτίου ὡς αἰτίου.

terminological distinction in the original use of these words. *'Aition'* is just the neuter of the adjective *'aitios'* which originally meant 'culpable, responsible, bearing the blame', whereas the *'aitia'* is the accusation, what somebody is charged with having done such that he is responsible for what happened as a result. And if we look at Plato's remarks on explanation in the *Phaedo* we see that such a distinction in use between *'aition'* and *'aitia'* is still preserved. In spite of its ample use both of the adjective and the noun the passage reserves the adjective for entities like Anaxagoras' Nous and Socrates' bones and sinews, whereas an *aitia* throughout seems to be a propositional item, the reason or explanation why something is the way it is. It is true that Aristotle does not preserve the terminological distinction. And Galen in one place tells us explicitly that he uses *'aition'* and *'aitia'* interchangeably (IX 458, 7 K). But even if the terminological distinction was not generally accepted, the distinction itself between causes on the one hand and reasons and explanations, the truths about causes in virtue of which they are causes, on the other, was generally accepted. In fact, for the very reasons for which the Stoics rejected, e.g., Aristotelian final causes as causes, properly speaking, they also had to reject propositional items as causes. Since, on the Stoic view, propositional items are not entities, but only *lekta*, somethings, they are not items of the right kind to cause anything. How would an event go about causing something?

So there would be general agreement that causes are non-propositional items. And there would be general agreement that the notion of a cause is closely tied to the notion of an explanation. For an item is a cause only in so far as something is true of it in virtue of which it is the cause. If Brutus is a cause of Caesar's death he is a cause insofar, e.g., as it is true of him that he stabbed Caesar. And it is exactly these truths about the causes of something which will be regarded as affording an explanation of what the causes are causes of.

It is at this point, though, that the disagreement among ancient philosophers will start. For reasons which will become apparent, the question will arise to which of the two notions, cause or explanation, we should give priority. It seems fairly clear that the opponents of the Stoics give priority to the notion of explanation. They are looking for an account of something and they will just call causes those items which have to be referred to in the account. If it is the presence of the idea of justice which accounts for the fact that something is just, then the idea of justice will be a cause. It is clear that on this view the notion of a cause completely loses its connotation of responsibility. The Stoics, on the other hand, are not so much interested in explanation as they are in responsibility.

Though this is a matter which would need a good deal of elaboration, the following statement by Strabo about Posidonius does seem to me to reflect the Stoic attitude in general well enough: 'With him [sc. Posidonius] we find a lot of aetiology and a lot of Aristotelizing which the members of our school shy away from because of the obscurity of the causes' (II 3, 8). According to Strabo, then, the Stoics in general are hesitant to engage in aetiology because the real causes are so hidden and obscure; Posidonius is an exception, and in this respect he is rather more like a Peripatetic. There is abundant evidence to support Strabo's testimony. Later Stoic physics, presumably under the influence of Posidonius, recognizes aetiology as a separate part of physics (DL VII 132). It in turn is divided into two parts, one whose subject matter the philosopher shares with the physician, namely physiology and psychology, and another part whose subject matter the philosopher shares with the mathematical sciences, namely natural, in particular meteorological, phaenomena. As to the second part of aetiology we not only know how much of an effort Posidonius made to find explanations for particular phaenomena like the tides. The relevant part in Diogenes' exposition of Stoic physics (VII 151, 3–156, 1), e.g., refers again and again to Posidonius. In fact the only other authority that is mentioned in the whole section is Zeno. But we also know from a passage in Seneca (*Ep.* LXXXVIII 26–7) and a precious excerpt from Geminus' Epitome of Posidonius' *Meteorologica* (preserved through Alexander's commentary on the *Physics* by Simplicius, *in Phys.* 291, 21 ff.) that Posidonius held views concerning causation and explanation which would deserve separate treatment. He took, e.g., the view that only the natural philosopher can have knowledge of the true account of the cause of a phaenomenon, whereas the mathematical scientist can only provide us with hypotheses or possible explanations, as Heraclides Ponticus provided us with a possible explanation of the apparent motion of the sun by assuming a somehow stationary sun and a somehow revolving earth (ibid. 292, 20–3). The other part of aetiology which concerns itself with psychology and physiology among other things deals with the passions of the soul (cf. DL VII 158). Of Posidonius' views on this particular topic we are well informed by Galen. Galen in his *De placitis Hippocratis et Platonis* goes to considerable lengths to criticize Chrysippus' views on the matter, and in doing so he relies heavily on Posidonius' criticism of Chrysippus which he also sets out in some detail. It is characteristic that it is a recurring complaint that Chrysippus fails to state the cause or claims that the true explanation is uncertain or too difficult to figure out (cf. 348, 16 ff. Mueller; 395, 12 ff.; 400, 2 ff.; 401, 9 ff.; 439, 4 ff., to just mention the Posidonian passages). It is evidence of this kind which supports Strabo's testimony that Posidonius is an exception and that Stoics in general were hesitant to concern themselves with aetiology, with the explanation of particular phaenomena.

Hence it would seem that the Stoic interest in causes does not arise from an interest in actual explanation. The evidence rather suggests that the Stoic interest in causes arises from their interest in responsibility. For when we look at the actual use to which the Stoics put their theory of causes it always seems to be a matter of allotting and distributing responsibility. For example, whatever things do is determined by fate, but fate is a mere helping cause (*sunergon*). The real cause, the things which really are responsible, are the things themselves; they do what they do out of their own nature or character. Or, the wise man may say what is false. But if, as a result, somebody believes it, it is not the wise man who is the cause, but the person who believes it has only himself to blame. Only dumb and wicked people believe falsehoods. It is in contexts of this sort that the Stoics introduce their doctrine of causes. Moreover, as we will see later, the Stoic distinction of various kinds of causes is a refinement on an ordinary intuitive distinction of various kinds of responsibility.

So for the Stoics the notion of a cause still has a connotation, however tenuous, of responsibility. But for the notion of responsibility to have any content at all that which is responsible must in some sense or other have done something and thus become responsible. It is ultimately for this reason, I take it, that the Stoics insist that causes are active, that they must be the kinds of items that can cause something. But in restricting causes to active items the Stoics seem to loosen the tie between causes and explanation. For to state the causes of something will no longer be a matter of stating all the relevant truths about all the relevant factors which have to enter into a complete explanation, but a matter of referring to just those factors which actively contribute to the effect. And the relevant truths about these will not amount to a complete explanation, or so it would seem. We will see later, though, that the Stoics conceive of the cause in their narrowest sense in such a way that it recaptures the explanatory force causes seem to lose due to their restriction to active causes. Nevertheless it is important to realize that the shift in the notion of a cause threatens the simple and straightforward conceptual link between cause and explanation.

But why should somebody who did not share the Stoics' view that what mattered first of all was the question of responsibility accept the claim that causes, properly speaking, have to be active? The Stoics might argue in the following way: when the question 'What is the *aition*?' was a question of legal, moral, or political responsibility it may have been difficult to come up with the answer in particular cases, but it would have been clear that the person responsible would be a person who had done something or other which he should not have done such that as a result of his doing it something has gone wrong for which he is responsible. (The question of responsibility originally is restricted to cases of blame. It is then extended to all noteworthy cases, including cases in which praise is to be bestowed. It is only then that the question of responsibility gets extended beyond the sphere of human or personal action, which is, of course, facilitated by an unwillingness to determine the limits of personal agency in a narrow way so as to exclude all but human actions. Who knows about the winds and the sea?) When then the use of '*aition*' was extended such that we could ask of anything 'What is its *aition*?' this extension of the use of '*aition*' must have taken place on the assumption that for everything to be explained there is something which plays with reference to it a role analogous to that which the person responsible plays with reference to what has gone wrong; i.e. the extension of the use of '*aition*' across the board is only intelligible on the assumption that with reference to everything there is something which by doing something or other is responsible for it.

This would seem to be a rather questionable assumption. Even in the case of real responsibility we have to construe the notion of doing something quite generously such that forgetting to do something and in general failing to do something which one can be expected to do count as doing something. But if we extend the notion of responsibility across the board we no longer have a set of expectations such that any violation of these expectations counts as a doing. As a result there are considerable difficulties in determining exactly what is to count as doing something and as being active. If columns support a roof this, presumably, counts as a case of doing something, but why? Nevertheless we do have intuitions in this matter which go far beyond, and to some extent correct, the grammatical active–passive distinction. We have a similar difficulty in determining what is to count as the analogue of the thing responsible in a case of real responsibility. In this respect there had been considerable difficulties even when we just had to deal with cases of real responsibility. We had, e.g., to decide that the thing which is responsible has to be a person, rather than an object or an animal. But if the notion of responsibility is to be extended across the board it seems that we need a new set of instructions as to how one finds what is responsible in this extended sense. To the extent, though, that the Stoics will claim that the common notion of a cause does provide us with such instruction and that they will provide us with further instruction, their point may have some weight, after all.

We find another argument to the effect that causes should be conceived of as active in Seneca, *Ep.* LXV. It seems that with the exception of the Epicureans in the case of the swerve all philosophers would have agreed that for any particular thing a complete explanation of that particular thing will involve reference to something which did something or other, i.e. reference to a moving cause in the vulgar sense of 'moving cause'. But once it is agreed that in every case a moving cause is involved why should we extend the notion of cause to also cover whatever other items do enter into our explanation? Why should we not use Plato's distinction in the *Phaedo* between causes and necessary conditions (or rather necessary items, remembering that '*hou*' in the phrase '*aneu hou*' at *Phd.* 99 b does not range over propositional items) and count the other items, e.g. matter, among the necessary conditions? That the presence of something is a necessary

condition does not yet mean that it is a cause. This seems to be the
line Seneca takes in *Ep.* LXV. He claims that there is just one
kind of cause, the active cause, and that if the opponents assume
more kinds of causes it is because they think that the effect would
not obtain if it were not for the presence of certain other kinds of
items in addition to an active cause. In LXV 4–6, e.g. when he
lists and explains Aristotle's four causes, in each of the first three
cases he explains why the presence of each of them is a necessary
condition for obtaining the result. And having explained the
fourth cause he adds the rhetorical question 'or don't you think
that we have to count among the causes of any work brought
about anything such that if that thing had been removed the work
would not have been brought about?' (LXV 6). And again in
LXV 11 he suggests that the reason why Aristotle and Plato posit
a whole bunch of causes ('turba causarum') is that they think that
the presence of items of these various kinds is required for a
result to come about. But if this is the reason why all these things
deserve to be called causes, Seneca argues, the four or five kinds
of causes of the Peripatetics and the Platonists do not suffice in
the least.

Now, apart from the threat of a proliferation of causes, this
argument will only have force if it is already granted that the
moving cause does have a privileged status and is not just another
necessary condition. Hence it does presuppose some other
argument like the one from the basic meaning of '*aition*' presented
above. Another argument to fill the gap left by Seneca's argument
could have been the following. We have to remember that the
various causes supposedly involved in a particular case are not
necessary conditions the conjunction of which is sufficient. They
rather are items the necessary conditions are truths about. What
is it, then, that has to be true of the various causes for the result
to come about? In some sense they will all have to be present.
But this will not be sufficient to account for the result. For in the
case of the moving cause it will not just be its presence which is
required. It will also be necessary that it does or has done something or other. And this does seem to set it off from the other
causes for which we only require their mere presence.

That active causes come to be accorded privileged status may
also be a matter of change of perspective. It may or may not be
the case that Plato and Aristotle had committed themselves to a

position from which it followed that everything is determined by antecedent causes. Even if Aristotle was concerned about determinism, his reflections on the matter seem to have been of little influence on his doctrine in general. Certainly the question had not been a preoccupation of theirs. But with the Stoics' insistence that everything that happens, including our actions, is antecedently determined this problem starts to occupy centre-stage. And the whole technical machinery of explanation gets applied to cases for which it was not really designed, namely to particular events, to find out whether they admitted of an explanation which was compatible with the assumption that not everything is antecedently determined. The problem of determinism makes one look at particular events as the concrete events they are, happening at the particular time they do, rather than just as instances of some general pattern of behaviour. As such they could be accounted for in terms of the nature or form of the thing involved. But if we have to ask why this particular thing behaved in this particular way at this particular time it seems clear that a reference to the general nature of the thing, or its end, or its matter, or its paradigm will not do. In fact, it seems that these, with whatever their presence entails, only form the more or less stable background on which we have to explain the particular event by referring to some particular antecedent change, which, given a stable background, makes the relevant difference. And hence the item involved in that change does seem to be in a privileged position, and, if anything, it seems to be it which deserves to be called the cause.

Once it is admitted that causes have to be active, have to do something or other in order to bring about the effect, it follows easily for the Stoics that causes have to be bodies. For only bodies can do something and can be affected, only bodies can interact. At this point it is important to remember, though, that for the Stoics not just physical objects, but also stuffs and qualities and mixtures thereof are bodies. So a quality could qualify as a cause.

Causes, properly speaking, then, for the Stoics are bodies which do something or other such that the fact that they do what they do is at least an important ingredient in the explanation of whatever it is that the causes are causes of.

But what is it that the causes are supposed to be causes of? We so far have been talking as if it were generally agreed that it is propositional items, facts, events, and the like, that are caused or explained. And this seems to fit the common use of '*aitia*' and '*aition*'. It is true that in common use '*aition*' or '*aitios*', e.g., can be used with a noun in the genitive as in 'the *aitioi* of the murder', i.e. 'those responsible for the murder' (Hdt. IV 200, 1). But it is clear that in such cases the noun is the nominalization of an underlying sentence. It is also true that Aristotle often talks as if causes were causes of entities like a statue, a man, or health. But again, we might be inclined to say that this is just a way of speaking; causes of a statue are cause for there being a statue or for something's being a statue.

Nevertheless there does seem to have been some disagreement. For Clement (*Strom.* VIII 9, 26, 1 = *SVF* II 345) reports that some philosophers assume that causes are causes of bodies. From Sextus (*M* IX 212) we learn more specifically that according to Epicurus the atoms are the causes of their compounds, whereas their incorporeal properties (*sumbebēkota*) are the causes of the incorporeal properties of the corresponding compounds. It is not clear, though, whether we should assume that this reflects a serious disagreement about the notion of a cause, or whether we owe this bit of doxography to somebody who was looking very hard to find somebody on whom he could pin the view that causes can be causes of corporeal items as well as of incorporeal items. After all, even if Epicurus had said what is attributed to him, this way of speaking admits of so many constructions that little can be made of these words, unless one assumes that Epicurus chose this manner of speaking because he had taken a position on the issue. But this is hardly plausible, for it would seem that this is exactly the kind of question which Epicurus would regard as sophistical.

We could leave the matter at that, if we did not have additional evidence which suggests that there actually was a dispute over the question what causes are the causes of. This is a disagreement both Clement and Sextus report on. Sextus (*PH* III 14) distinguishes between what we know to be the Stoic view, namely the view that causes are causes of a predicate's being true of something, and the view that causes are causes of appellations (*prosēgoriai*). Clement (*Strom.* VIII 9, 26, 4) attributes the latter view to Aristotle. Unfortunately it is far from clear what the contrast between the two views is supposed to be, and Sextus' example does not make the matter any clearer. On the first view, according to Sextus, the sun's heat is the cause of the wax's being melted (*tou cheisthai*), whereas on the second view it is the cause of the melting of the wax (*tēs chuseōs*).

It is fairly clear that the contrast is supposed to be indicated by the use of a verb in the first case and a corresponding noun in the second. This would also fit the examples given by Clement who says 'But Aristotle thinks that causes are causes of appellations, i.e. of items of the following sort: a house, a ship, a burning (*kausis*), a cut (*tomē*)', whereas examples of what is caused on the other view seem to be something's being cut (*temnesthai*) or something's coming to be a ship (*gignesthai naun*). Also it would fit the fact that nouns in Greek grammar are called 'appellations' or 'appellatives'; the appellatives in Greek grammar are a word-class which comprises both our nouns and our adjectives. Finally it is presumably relevant that the term we have rendered by 'predicate', namely '*kategorēma*', sometimes is restricted to what is signified by verbs or even is used synonymously with 'verb' (*rhēma*).

Now it is hardly plausible that according to the view in question causes are causes of expressions of whatever kind. To make reasonable sense of the position we have to assume either that what is meant is that causes are causes of something's being properly called something or other or that 'appellation' here does not refer to a certain kind of expression, but to what is signified by an appellative. There is a passage in Stobaeus (*Ecl.* I, p. 137, 5 W) in which 'appellation' is used in the second way, but this may be due to a confusion on Stobaeus' part. Hence it would be preferable if we got by on the assumption that 'appellation' here has its usual meaning as a grammatical term. But what would be the point of saying that a cause is a cause of something's being properly called (an) X where 'X' is a noun or an adjective? Given the lack of evidence the answer has to be quite speculative. It might, e.g., be the case that verbs are associated with processes or coming-into-beings as opposed to the being of something; hence, perhaps, the contrast in Clement between a ship or the being of a ship or something's being a ship and the coming-into-being of a ship or something's coming to be a ship. But if this is the intended contrast we have to assume that the nouns corresponding to the verbs are taken not to signify the process signified by the verbs.

Given the standard ordinary use of these nouns this does not seem to be a plausible assumption. But if we look at Simplicius' commentary on the *Categories* we find that under the category of doing he systematically distinguishes between something's doing something (*poiein*) and a doing (*poiesis*) (301, 29 ff.). And we may assume that Simplicius thinks that a corresponding distinction has to be made for all the verbs associated with the category. Similarly Clement in his discussion of causality refers to a view according to which a cut (*tomē*) has to be distinguished both from something's cutting and something's being cut (*Strom.* VIII 9, 26, 1; '*temnein*' and '*temnesthai*'). The basis for the distinction in Simplicius is that 'a doing' may either refer to an activity or to its effect (301, 33–5). And this suggests that our appellatives in Sextus and Clement are to be taken in the latter way to refer to the effects. There is an obvious difficulty as to what these effects as distinct from the processes and activities are supposed to be. Presumably a (finished) cut is distinct from the thing cut, the process of its being cut and the activity of cutting it, but not from its being (finally) cut. Are we then supposed to say that a house-building (*oikodomēsis*) is distinct from the thing built? Presumably not, for otherwise the activity of building a house will have two effects, a house and a house-building. It is a house, rather than a house-building, which Clement gives as an example parallel to a cut and a burning, and it is a ship, rather than a ship-building, which he contrasts with the coming-into-being of a ship. But this lack of parallel can be explained as being due to the fact that houses and ships, as opposed to cuts and burnings, are substances. Hence a house-building is distinct from the house's being in the process of being built and the activity of building it, but it is not distinct from the house's being (finally) built and hence not distinct from the being of the house. Thus the text can be read as distinguishing coming-into-beings or processes and beings, between the being of a cut or something's being (finally) cut and the cutting of it or its being cut, between the being of a ship or its being (finally) built and the building of it or its being built. But what would be the point of such a distinction? The idea might be that causes are causes of entities, of the being of things, rather than their coming-into-being, and that their coming-into-being has to be understood in terms of their being rather than the other way round. That Peripatetics should conceive of causes as causes of entities is not so surprising given the Aristotelian programme of determining the principles and causes of what there is, where 'what there is' naturally is understood not as referring to all the facts there are, but rather as referring to all the particular entities there are. Really to know all these is to know all that there is to be known (cf. Arist. *Metaph.* M 10 1087ᵃ 15 ff.).

If, on the other hand, one does not focus one's thought about causes on entities and their being, but on particular events because they are what one is mainly concerned with when one is worried about determinism, it seems natural to make causes causes of propositional items, especially since that corresponds to the ordinary use and the original notion of '*aition*'. It also seems natural to make some room for propositional items in one's ontology. This is exactly what the Stoics do when they admit *lekta*, if not as beings (*onta*), at least as somethings (*tina*). In fact, it is not clear to me that the notion of a *lekton* was introduced by the Stoics in the context of their philosophy of language rather than their ontology. For the first Stoic of whom we know that he used the term '*lekton*' is Cleanthes, and he used it precisely to say that causes are causes of *lekta* (Clem. *Strom.* VIII 9, 26).

It seems, though, that the Stoics thought that the canonical representation of the causal relation was not as a two-place relation between a body and a propositional item, but as a three-place relation between a body and another body and a predicate true of that body. Thus a knife is the cause for flesh of being cut, fire is the cause for wood of burning. It is in this sense that the Stoics often are reported as claiming that a cause is a cause of a predicate (*katēgorēma*, cf. Clem. *Strom.* VIII 9, 26, 4). Now it is true that in Greek there is a widespread use of the construction 'a cause of something for something' where the dative represents the person or the object affected and the genitive represents what, as a result, is true of the object affected. And presumably it is also true that we could rewrite all Greek causal statements so as to satisfy this normal form. But of what importance is this for the notion of cause?

Presumably this is supposed to be of relevance in at least three respects. It brings out the fact that for there to be a cause there has to be something which is affected, and since only bodies can be affected this has to be a body. Secondly, whether something does or does not produce a certain effect in something does depend on the nature and state of the thing affected. It has to be the right kind of body. And thirdly, we have to remember that though we want to see how one explains particular facts we also want to have general explanations which tell us what in general causes a certain predicate to be true of something.

The general notion of a cause, properly speaking, according to the Stoics, then, seems to be the following: a cause is a body which does something or other and by doing so brings it about that another body is affected in such a way that something comes to be true of it. It may very well be the case that the Stoics think that this is just a characterization of the common notion of a cause.

KINDS OF CAUSES AND THE CAUSE IN THE STRICT SENSE

The Stoics reject the swarm of causes ('turba causarum', Sen. *Ep.* LXV 11) of their opponents and allow only for an active cause. But within the notion of such an active cause as we have outlined it so far they, too, allow for different kinds of relation between cause and effect and hence for different causes. As Alexander puts it, they have a whole swarm of causes (*smēnos aitiōn, Fat.* 192, 18 = *SVF* II, p. 273, 18).

Unfortunately our sources concerning these various kinds of causes are rather unclear. Hence it may be best to start with what seems to be a quotation from Chrysippus in Cicero's *De fato* 41, in which Chrysippus distinguishes two kinds of causes. Cicero says about Chrysippus: For of causes, he says, some are perfect and principal ('perfectae et principales'), others auxiliary and proximate ('adiuvantes et proximae'). Hence, when we say that everything happens by fate through antecedent causes, we do not want this to be understood as saying 'through perfect and principal causes', but in the sense of 'through auxiliary and proximate causes'.

The point of the distinction, if one looks at the context, would seem to be the following. Chrysippus wants to maintain that everything that happens is fated, is determined by antecedent causes. On the other hand he also wants to maintain that this does not rule out human responsibility, because, though human actions are determined by antecedent causes, it is nevertheless the human beings themselves, rather than the antecedent causes, who are

responsible for these actions. Quite generally, though what a
thing does is determined by an antecedent cause, it is not the
antecedent cause but rather the thing itself or something about
that thing which is responsible for what it does, though, of course,
not necessarily morally responsible; for only with beings of a
certain sort and under certain further conditions is responsibility
moral responsibility.

We are given two kinds of examples to illustrate the point,
one from human behaviour and one from the behaviour of
inanimate objects. Suppose we perceive something and get some
impression (e.g. the impression that there is a piece of cake over
there or the impression that it would be nice to have that piece
of cake now). Now it will depend on us whether we accept or
give assent to this impression. If we do, we will think that there
is a piece of cake over there or that it would be nice to have that
piece of cake now and will feel and act accordingly. And if we do
think so and feel and act accordingly it will have been the impression which brought this about and hence was the antecedent
cause of our action. But the impression by itself does not necessitate that we should think, feel and act that way. Other people
or we ourselves at other times would not accept or give assent
to the same impressions. And hence what decides the matter is
not the impression; it is not the impression, but something about
the person which makes the person accept the impression, though
the person would not accept the impression and act accordingly
if he did not have that impression, and though there is a sense in
which the impression does bring about or cause whatever action
the person takes as a result.

Chrysippus' point about causes, then, as illustrated by this
example is this: everything does have an antecedent cause; our
actions, e.g., have as their antecedent cause an impression. But
these antecedent causes are not the kind of cause that necessitate
the result, they are only 'causae adiuvantes et proximae'. The
'causa perfecta et principalis' which necessitates the result lies in
ourselves, it is that about us which makes us accept the impression
and act accordingly.

The examples from the behaviour of inanimate objects are
motions of a cylinder and a cone or spin-top. 'They could not
start to move unless they received a push. But once that has
happened he thinks that, for the rest, it is by their own nature that

the cylinder rolls and the spin-top turns' (42 *fin.*). The idea here seems to be that the person who gave the cylinder or the column a push is the antecedent cause. Without the push the cylinder would not roll, but the fact that the person gave it a push does not yet account for the fact that it is rolling. What makes it roll is something about the cylinder itself. And it is that which is the perfect and principal cause of its rolling.

It is important that the examples should not be misinterpreted in the following way: we might think that Chrysippus only wants to point out that if one gives an object a push it will depend very much on the kind of object it is how it will be affected, a cylinder will roll one way, a cone another, and a cube will not roll at all. But Cicero does not just say in 42 that the cylinder rolls in virtue of its own peculiar nature ('suapte natura'), he also tells us in 43 that both in the case of human behaviour and the case of the cylinder, once the thing has received an impulse, it will move for the rest 'suapte vi et natura', 'by its own force and nature'. This implies that there are two forces, two *vires* involved,: not just the external *vis* of the antecedent cause, the person who gives a push (cf. 'nulla vi extrinsecus excitata' in 42), but also a *vis* on the inside, and it seems to be that *vis* on the inside which keeps the cylinder rolling once it has gotten its initial impulse. This suggests that there also is something active, something which exerts a force, on the inside of the cylinder when the cylinder is rolling. And given what we said about the general notion of a cause this is not surprising. If causes are active and if in the case of the cylinder two causes are supposed to be involved, there should be two things involved both of which do something or other to bring about the result that the cylinder is rolling.

The picture which we thus get so far is the following: whenever something does something or other there are at least two kinds of active causes involved, an antecedent cause which is classified as an auxiliary and proximate cause and an internal cause which is classified as a 'causa perfecta et principalis'. Though both of them can be said to bring it about that the thing does whatever it does it really is the internal cause which by its activity is responsible for what is done.

This is not to say that whenever something happens to something, say A, there will be two causes involved, one antecedent and one internal to A. A mere passive affection of A does not require the activity of an internal cause. It is clear from the way Cicero sets out his examples that the antecedent causes do have an effect on the object which is not produced by an internal cause. The person who gives the cylinder a push does give the cylinder a beginning of motion, and the external sight or object does produce an impression in us (43) which is not due to an internal cause. It seems that the need for a second cause only comes in when we want to explain what the thing does, how the thing reacts as a result of being affected this way. This in turn suggests that the 'causa perfecta et principalis' is not essentially an internal cause, as we may have thought. For the 'causa perfecta et principalis' of a mere passive affection of an object will lie outside that object in the object which affects it. And this also seems to be required by what we know about 'causae perfectae' from other sources.

There seems to be no doubt that 'causa perfecta' is just Cicero's rendering of *'aition autoteles'*. We do not have a text which claims to give us the Stoic definition of this kind of cause. But we have various texts which distinguish between (i) an *autoteles aition*, (ii) a *sunaition*, and (iii) a *sunergon* (Gal. *Def. med.* XIX, 393 K.; Clem. *Strom.* VIII 9, 33 = *SVF* II, p. 121, 25 ff.). And since we are told in various places that *'autoteles aition'* and *'sunektikon aition'* are used interchangeably (Clem. *Strom.* VIII 9, 33, 2 = *SVF* II, p. 121, 27; VIII 9, 25, 3 = *SVF* II, p. 120, 2 f.) we may also draw on texts like Gal. *Def. med.*, p. 392–3 K.; S.E. *PH* III 15 and Gal. *Hist.phil.* 19 which distinguish (i) a *sunektikon aition*, (ii) a *sunaition*, and (iii) a *sunergon*. Since Sextus tells us that most philosophers agree on this distinction we can be reasonably certain that a consideration of these texts will get us near enough to the Stoic notions of these kinds of causes. In fact, it is almost certain that this is a basically Stoic distinction of Stoic origin. And it is also obviously the right distinction to look at in our context, since the 'causa adiuvans' with which the 'causa perfecta' is contrasted in Cicero clearly is a *sunaition* or a *sunergon*.

What, then, is the distinction? The intuitive idea behind it is fairly simple. It always must have been clear that often the question 'Who or what is responsible for this?' does not admit of a simple straghtforward answer, because there is no single person or thing to be made responsible, but several things have to be referred to, and among them one would often want to divide the responsibility and distinguish among various degrees of it. Hence in ordinary language, but also in more technical discourse, we soon get such terms as *sunaitios, metaitios, sunergos.* If we went by ordinary usage we would guess that the Stoic distinction amounted to the following: whenever there is exactly one thing which is responsible for what happens this is the *autoteles aition.* If there are two or more things which not individually but collectively have brought about the effect, they are *sunaitia.* If something just in some way contributes to an effect, which is brought about, though, by something else, it is a *sunergon.*

The difficulties arise when it comes to the technical definitions of these kinds. For we are told of all three kinds of causes that they bring about the effect (cf. Gal. *Def. med.*). We are also told that the perfect cause *does* bring about the effect by itself (Gal. *Def. med.* XIX, 393 K;[4] cf. 'suapte vi et natura' in Cic. *Fat.* 43.) In fact it seems to be this feature of the perfect cause to which it owes its name: '*autoteles*'. As Clement (*Strom.* VIII 9, 33, 2 = *SVF* II, p. 121, 27 ff.) tells us: they also call it '*autoteles*', since it produces the effect by itself relying on nothing else. Finally, we know from various sources (e.g. Clem. *Strom.* VIII 9, 33 = *SVF* II, p. 121, 35 ff.) that *sunerga* can appear in conjunction with the perfect cause to help to produce the effect. But in this case, it seems, the perfect cause does not bring about the effect by itself; there is also a *sunergon* which can be said to bring about the effect, too. After all, this is why it, too, is called a cause of this effect.

Ultimately, the only way out of the difficulty I can see is the following: we distinguish between a strict sense of producing or bringing about an effect and a weaker sense. It is true of all three kinds of causes that they somehow bring about the effect. If there were no sense in which the impression could be said to bring about our assent and our action, and if there were no sense in which the person who pushed the cylinder could be said to have brought about the cylinder's rolling, these items could not be said to be causes of their respective effects in the first place. But then our consideration of the cylinder case also has shown that there is a stricter, narrower sense of 'bringing about' in which it is not the person who gives the push, but the perfect cause which

---

[4] The way this is put, though, suggests a false etymology: τὸ αὐτὸ καθ' αὑτὸ ποιοῦν τέλος.

brings about the rolling motion of the cylinder 'suapte vi et natura'. Once we make this distinction it is easy to see how we get the threefold classification. Of those things which can be said to bring about an effect in the weaker sense some also can be said to bring about an effect in the narrower sense, namely the perfect causes and the *sunaitia*, whereas in that narrow sense the *sunerga* can only be said to help to bring about the effect. But among those things which bring about an effect in the strict sense, some do bring it about by themselves, namely the perfect causes, whereas others only bring it about in conjunction and cooperation with other causes; these are the *sunaitia*.

What makes a perfect cause perfect or complete, then, is that it does not depend for its causal efficacy on the agency of some other cause outside its control. A potential *sunaition* needs another *sunaition*, a potential *sunergon* needs a perfect cause or *sunaitia* which may or may not be available. This is why the antecedent cause and hence fate by themselves do not necessitate the effect. For whether the antecedent cause does bring about the effect depends on the activity of the perfect cause, and whether the perfect cause does act is outside of the control of the antecedent cause, though it is determined.

So much for the distinction between *autotelē, sunaitia*, and *sunerga*. It rests on an intuitive distinction which divides responsibility. When Chrysippus says that antecedent causes are not *autotelē*, but only *sunerga*, he relies on the fact that intuitively we will understand this as meaning that it is not the antecedent cause which bears the full responsibility. At worst it is something like an accomplice. Given the technical understanding of the distinction Chrysippus' claim amounts to saying that, strictly speaking, it is not the antecedent cause at all which brings about the effect. It is something within the thing itself which produces the effect all by itself.

Given this it is easy to understand why the 'causa perfecta' would be called 'causa perfecta et principalis'. We may assume that the Greek underlying Cicero's 'For of causes some are perfect and principal . . .' is something like this: '. . . of causes some are *autotelē* and *kuria* (or *kuriōtata*)'. It is the perfect cause which is the cause, strictly speaking or in the strictest sense. This also seems to be brought out by the Greek names of these three kinds of causes: '*autoteles aition*', '*sunaition*', and '*sunergon*'. We never get the phrase '*sunergon aition*' (which also might reflect the fact that *sunerga*, as opposed to *aitia* and *sunaitia*, do not bring about the effect, strictly speaking).

Now, before we have a closer look at the nature of this perfect cause, let us briefly turn to the second kind of cause distinguished by Chrysippus according to Cicero: the auxiliary and proximate causes ('causae adiuvantes et proximae'). So far I have been assuming that these are the *sunerga*. But from what has been said it is clear that 'auxiliary cause' could be a translation either of '*sunergon*' or of '*sunaition*'. This ambiguity is apparent in Cicero's classification of causes in the *Topics* (58 ff.), where Cicero refers to the *sunaitia* as those 'which stand in need of help' and to the *sunerga* as 'helping' ('adiuvantia'). Nevertheless it is clear that here we are talking about *sunerga*. For among the causes of something we can either have *sunaitia* or a perfect cause, but not both. Moreover, we know independently that it was a point of Stoic doctrine that fate, the chain of antecedent causes, only provides a *sunergon* for what things do (cf. Cic. *Top.* 58 ff.). And this seems to be exactly what Chrysippus is claiming in our passage when he says that the antecedent causes which somehow constitute fate are not 'causae principales', but 'causae adiuvantes'.

But this raises the question how an antecedent cause can be conceived of as a *sunergon*, if a *sunergon* is the kind of item which helps to bring about the effect by making it easier for the effect to be brought about. The examples Sextus and Clement, e.g., give of a *sunergon* are of little help. If somebody lifts a heavy weight and somebody else comes along and gives a helping hand then the second person is a *sunergon* in so far as he just helps to bring about the effect by making it easier. But the antecedent cause is precisely not the kind of thing which comes in when something is already happening anyway. It is not the case that the cylinder was rolling anyway and that the push just made the rolling easier.

Presumably the idea rather is that the ease with which the cylinder rolls depends on the kind of push it got. The push has to be of a sufficient size for it to be easy enough for the cylinder to roll at all, and any increment in size of the push will make the rolling easier. The difficulty about this is that, to apply generally, this presupposes some general physical theory according to which the antecedent cause contributes something to the force with which the effect is brought about by somehow intensifying that force. But that some such theory of forces and their intensification actually is presupposed seems to be clear enough from our testimonies. Cicero, as we have seen, talks about the external and the internal *vis*, ps.-Galen and Sextus characterize *sunaitia* as each exerting an equal force to bring about the result, whereas the *sunergon* is said only to contribute a minor force. Sextus (*PH* III, 15) talks of the intensification and remission of the perfect cause and a corresponding intensity of the effect. Clement tells us that the *sunergon* helps to intensify the effect (VIII 9, 33, 7; 33, 9). In any case we know independently that fate, i.e. the antecedent cause, is supposed to help in the production of the effect even if it is not the perfect cause (cf. Josephus *BJ* II 163⁵).

Now, the second kind of cause to be distinguished is not just characterized as a helping cause, but also as a proximate cause. 'Causa proxima' could be a rendering of *'aition proseches'*, *'aition proēgoumenon'*, or *'aition prokatarktikon'*. I assume that it renders *'aition prokatarktikon'* and that the *causae antecedentes* are the *aitia proēgoumena*.

If we take the testimony of Sextus, Clement, and others seriously the class of *sunerga* and the class of *aitia prokatarktika* will not coincide, since not all *sunerga* are antecedent causes. But there is also no evidence that the class of *aitia prokatarktika* was arrived at by further subdivision of the class of *sunerga*. This strongly suggests that the distinction of *aitia prokatarktika* is part of a division of causes quite independent of that into *autotelē*, *sunaitia*, and *sunerga*. And this seems to be confirmed by the fact that the *prokatarktika* are usually contrasted with the so-called *sunektika*, a kind of cause to which Cicero in § 44 of the *De fato* refers as the 'causae continentes', and of which we know from Galen that it along with its name was introduced by the Stoics (*De causis cont*. p. 6, 2; IX 458, 11 ff. K.). In fact, ps.-Galen in *Definitiones medicinales* (XIX 392) says that cause is threefold, one is the *prokatarktikon*, the other the *proēgoumenon*, and the third the *sunektikon*. And it is only after definitions of these three kinds that he turns to the distinction into *autotelē*, *sunaitia,* and *sunerga*. Possibly this threefold distinction is of Stoic origin. For Galen in *De causis continentibus* (p. 8, 8 ff.) tells us that Athenaeus, the

---

⁵ καὶ τὸ μὲν πράττειν τὰ δίκαια καὶ μὴ κατὰ τὸ πλεῖστον ἐπὶ τοῖς ἀνθρώποις κεῖσθαι, βοηθεῖν δ᾽ εἰς ἕκαστον καὶ τὴν εἱμαρμένην.

founder of the pneumatic school of medicine, made this distinction and that in this he was influenced by Posidonius (8, 3 ff.). He does not say, though, that Athenaeus got this distinction from Posidonius, and it is clear from our passage in Cicero that the distinction does not go back to Chrysippus, quite apart from the fact that Galen tells us elsewhere that the physicians did not get the notion of *sunektikon* straight (*Adv. Jul.*, XVIII A, 279 f. = *SVF* II, p. 122, 22 ff.; *Synops. de puls.* IX 458 = *SVF* II, p. 122, 38).

If I understand the medical distinction correctly the *prokatarktikon* is the external antecedent cause, the *proēgoumenon* is an internal disposition brought about by the *prokatarktikon* which in turn activates the *sunektikon* which is something like the perfect cause internal to the object in our Cicero passage (Galen, *De causis puls.* IX 2, 11 ff.). But it is exactly this precise distinction between the last external antecedent cause and the first internal antecedent cause which is neglected in our text. For the impression, an internal antecedent cause, is put on a par with the person who gives a push, an external antecedent cause, and this in spite of the fact that the person who gives a push is also compared to the object which brings about the impression. So in Chrysippus we obviously only have the distinction between the *sunektikon* and the *prokatarktikon*. But it is also clear that given the importance of the external–internal distinction for Chrysippus' causal theory the trichotomy easily comes to mind.

Roughly, it seems to me, the two divisions of kinds of causes are related in this way: perfect causes and synhectic causes coincide; *sunerga* may or may not be antecedent causes, but antecedent causes are *sunerga*. Given that antecedent causes and *sunerga* do not coincide, whereas perfect and synhectic causes do, it is not surprising that we sometimes find a list of four kinds of causes: perfect or synhectic causes, *sunaitia, sunerga,* and antecedent causes (cf. Clem. *Strom.* VIII 9, 31, 7; ps.-Galen, *Hist. phil.* 19, p. 611, 9 ff. Diels). Sextus indicates one specific way in which we may arrive at such a list, namely when we distinguish between kinds of causes which are or can be simultaneous with their effects from those which are not or cannot be simultaneous (*PH* III 15–16). But this raises another set of problems which I will not go into here.

Let us, then, consider in detail the distinction between *sunektika* and *prokatarktika*. Though a distinction under these terms was very widespread, though we have many testimonies for it, and though we still have at least translations of monographs by Galen on each of the two kinds of causes, the Stoic doctrine on the matter is far from clear. There are even doubts as to the explanation of the terms 'prokatarktikon'[6] and 'sunektikon'.

As to the term 'sunektikon' Galen tells us in various places that it was the Stoics who introduced the notion and the name 'sunektikon aition' (Synops. de puls. IX 458, 11 ff. K. = SVF II, p. 122, 38 ff.; De causis cont. p. 6, 2 ff.; Adv. Jul. 6 XVIII A, 279, 13 ff. K. = SVF II, p. 122, 21 ff.). And he also repeatedly tells us that this notion is misunderstood and misused by physicians (cf. the passages mentioned above). What they fail to take note of is that for the Stoics a sunektikon is not just a cause of an activity like walking, but the cause of the being of something. And from Galen's De causis continentibus and other sources we learn how this is supposed to be so. There is some fine active substance, a mixture of fire and air, the so-called pneuma which pervades every object, holds its parts together, and thus provides it with unity and form and becomes the cause of the being of the thing. In fact it is the Stoic analogue of an Aristotelian form; in animals it is the soul, in human beings it is an intellectual soul. Since it is a primary function of the sunektikon to hold together the thing it is the form of it seems safe to assume that it is this function to which the sunektikon originally owes its name. But it also seems to be this very same sunektikon which is not just the cause of the being of something, but also of its behaviour.

To explain this in a sense should be no more difficult than to explain how a form, e.g. a soul, accounts both for the being of something and for its behaviour. The explanation would proceed along the same lines. If anything, it should be easier to explain how the pneuma satisfies both functions, since in this case it is a body which makes a body exhibit a certain behaviour. Presumably the pneuma admits of being put into different states and with

---

[6] A clue to the sense of the term 'prokatarktikon' we get from the use of 'κατάρχειν' in passages like this: 'τῶν ἁμαρτημάτων προαίρεσις καὶ ὁρμὴ κατάρχει' (Clem. Strom. I 84, 2), or when Galen says that the ἡγεμονικόν is 'τὸ κατάρχον αἰσθήσεώς τε καὶ τῆς καθ' ὁρμὴν κινήσεως' (Plac. Hipp. Plat. p. 583, 10–11 M.; cf. also the use of καταρχή in a fragment of Chrysippus preserved in Plac. Hipp. p. 216, 13 M). The κατάρχον of something seems to be that in which it has its origin. By contrast, to say of something that it is the προκατάρχον or the προκαταρκτικόν of something would be to deny that the effect has its origin in it and to say that it precedes that which is the real origin and source of the effect.

increasing complexity there will be an increasing number of ranges of such states. Some of these states will be 'active states' such that being in those states the pneuma will act in a certain way. Whether a state is active and how precisely the pneuma will act in such a state will depend on the precise nature of the pneuma, the modifications it has undergone, the dispositions it has acquired, and the other states it is in.

We could, e.g., try to imagine that the pneuma is characterized by a complex set of interdependent tensions in some more or less comfortable equilibrium such that, if certain of these tensions are intensified to a certain degree, we have an active state of the pneuma and a certain kind of action results. Moreover, we might imagine that, if an object is affected, one or more of these tensions are affected and hence, as a result, the whole system of tensions is affected. So we might imagine that if an animal receives a certain impression at least one of these tensions gets intensified. If the whole system of tensions is such that as a result an action producing tension gets sufficiently intensified, this action would be due to the whole system of tensions, but it still might be thought to be literally true that the impression, or more generally the antecedent cause. had contributed some of the force with which the action was executed, in so far as the increased force of the intensified action producing tension in part was the force of the tension intensified by the impression.

But whatever the mechanics of the *aition sunektikon* may have been supposed to be it is clear that most people would not have subscribed to the physical theory underlying it. They might, e.g., deny that the primary active cause for a thing's behaviour was to be found in the thing itself. Even if they accepted the view that the pneuma played an important role in the explanation of the behaviour of things, they might not, as e.g. Galen did not, accept the view that such a pneuma was needed to account for the existence of objects as that which holds them together (cf. *De causis cont*. VI and VII). Nevertheless, they might want to have some kind of cause which on their physical theory in some way or other plays a role analogous to that of the *sunektikon aition* and which they hence would call by the same name. And in this case it would be clear that the name could no longer be interpreted as referring to the fact that this kind of cause is that which holds the object affected together.

And, as a matter of fact, we do find all sorts of non-Stoic uses of 'sunektikon aition'. One of them, in Cicero's De fato 44, seems to have puzzled editors and commentators no end. Von Arnim, e.g., prints a text (SVF II, p. 283, 34 ff.) which makes Chrysippus concede that the antecedent cause is the sunektikon, i.e. the perfect cause. Cicero refers to a doctrine according to which the proximate and containing cause ('proxima illa et continens causa') would be the impression, if somebody gave assent to it. It is clear that here the causa continens is the aition sunektikon. But it is equally clear that this term now is not used in the Stoic sense. For the Stoics specifically deny that the antecedent cause is the containing cause. Moreover the position Cicero describes envisages the possibility that the impression, though it is the containing cause of the assent, also might not have brought about the assent (I take it that the subjunctive of 'moveat' is not just the subjunctive of indirect speech). This again, as we will see shortly, seems to be incompatible with the Stoic notion of a containing cause. Hence it is not surprising that Cicero should go on to say: 'Chrysippus will not admit that the proximate and containing cause of the assent lies in the impression and hence he will also not admit that this cause, i.e. the impression, necessitates the assent.'

Cicero's remarks in De fato 44 very much suggest that Chrysippus thought that if something were the containing cause of something it would necessitate its effect. And this I actually take to be Chrysippus' view. But in what sense could the containing cause be thought to necessitate its effect? In this connection it is presumably relevant to refer to Stobaeus' characterization of Zeno's notion of a cause (Ecl. I, p. 138, 14 ff. W). According to Zeno a cause is such that its presence necessitates the effect. And this principle is illustrated by the following examples: it is wisdom which brings about being wise, the soul which brings about living. This reminds one not just of the unreformed giants of Plato's Sophist (247 b ff.), with whom the Stoics were very much in sympathy (cf. SVF II, p. 123, 16 ff. = Soph. 246 a ff.), but also of Socrates' safe causal accounts in the Phaedo and Aristotle's formal causes.

The connection between wisdom and being wise and soul and being alive might seem to be trivially necessary in so far as it just is with reference to somebody's wisdom that we call him wise.

But this cannot be what Zeno has in mind, for he seems to think of somebody's being wise as an effect produced by wisdom, as if one's wisdom invariably and necessarily brought it about that one is wise. Perhaps the idea is the following. It is true that our common notion of wisdom does not tell us how it is that wisdom makes somebody wise. But if we had a complete technical understanding of what wisdom really is, then we would also understand that wisdom by its very nature brings it about that those who possess it invariably are wise. Looked at in this way the necessity involved still can be regarded as some kind of conceptual necessity. (This is not to attribute to the Stoics a distinction between logical or conceptual and physical or empirical necessity.) Given the correct complete technical notion of wisdom which reflects its nature in all detail, one sees how wisdom cannot fail to produce its characteristic effect. It may be along these lines that the Stoics think that the containing cause necessitates its effects. If one understands the nature of a soul as characterized by wisdom one sees that it cannot fail to produce the effect that somebody is wise. In this case the necessity involved would just be the necessity which characterizes a Chrysippean conditional whose consequent is the statement that the person is wise and whose antecedent is the relevant truth about his soul.

This brings us back to explanation. To simplify matters let us concentrate on cases in which something does something or other, exhibits a certain piece of behaviour. The Stoics assume and argue that nothing happens without a cause. More specifically, they assume that nothing happens without an antecedent cause and argue, e.g., that if things happened without antecedent causes the continuity of the universe would be interrupted. But they also assume that a reference to the antecedent cause is not going to explain why something does something or other. To explain this we have to refer to the *sunektikon*, and we do not have to refer to anything else. For a truth about the *sunektikon* will entail the truth about the object to be explained, whereas no truth about the antecedent cause by itself will be the antecedent of a true Chrysippean conditional with the fact to be explained as the consequent.

These conditionals will be instantiations of universal conditionals of the form 'if the *sunektikon* of x is such-and-such then x is (or does) so-and-so'. We may assume that it is sets of such conditionals which specify the nature of each kind of *sunektikon*, and hence it would be natural to arrange these conditionals according to the kinds of *sunektika*. Since these conditionals are universal and since they can be of any degree of generality we can also draw on them for general explanations.

Now these conditionals will cover what happens within the thing, so to speak. They tell us how a thing, given its kind of nature, the modification of its nature and the states it is in, will behave. But, though this in some sense gives us a complete explanation of what the thing does—for otherwise the corresponding conditional would not be true—we will think that we are missing something if we do not get the antecedent cause into the picture. After all, the thing would not have done what we are trying to explain if there had not been an antecedent cause which in some sense had brought it about that the thing would behave in a certain way. In fact, we are very much tempted to think that the real explanation of what the thing did would be in terms of what the antecedent cause did and some general law which connects what the antecedent cause does with what the object does. And it seems clear that our conditionals do not provide us with such laws. According to Cicero's *De fato* it seems that Chrysippus claims that there can be no true conditionals which connect truths about antecedent causes with facts they are the antecedent causes of. Nevertheless, it seems that for the purpose of explanation we will not need general laws in addition to the conditionals which we already have.

It is true that for other purposes, e.g. divination and prediction, we might want to formulate such general laws. Given his views on cosmic sympathy Chrysippus is not going to deny that events do not occur in isolation of each other, in fact he is going to stress that there is a connection between any two things that happen. He also is not going to deny that by observation we could detect regularities, constant conjunctions, and that it would be worthwhile to formulate and collect corresponding rules or laws for prediction. But he does deny that such rules as 'if somebody is born at the rise of the Dog-star he will die at sea' offer any explanation for somebody's death at sea even if the person was born at the rise of the Dog-star and there in fact is a constant conjunction. For in spite of the fact that he believes in divination in general and does not object to astrological rules as such he rejects their formulation as conditionals (cf. Cic. *Fat.* 15). And the reason for this would seem to be that the antecedents of such rules established by observation do not amount to a sufficient reason for their consequents, that they do not necessitate the consequent in the way in which the principal, but not the antecedent, cause necessitates its effect, even though it invariably may be accompanied by its consequent, and that the antecedents thus do not provide us with an explanation of the consequent. The question, then, is how we can restrict ourselves to Chrysippean conditionals and nevertheless do justice to the role of antecedent causes.

To see how this perhaps could be done we have to take into account that though the antecedent cause is only the antecedent cause of what the object does, it at the same time is the perfect cause of the state of the *sunektikon* which thus affected makes the object do what it does. Though this will hardly do as it stands, we now can look for an explanation along the following lines: we assume that all antecedent causes are antecedent causes of something *p* by being *sunektika* for a *sunektikon s* of a passive affection *q* such that a *sunektikon s* in state *q* is a perfect cause of *p*. In this case it would turn out that the relation between the antecedent cause and the effect can be analysed into at least two relations, each of them between a perfect cause and its effect and hence each of them covered by the laws for containing causes.

So it does seem that the theory of causes, in spite of their restriction to active cause, is after all constructed in such a way that we can fully account for any particular fact in terms of these causes. The fact to be explained can be seen and understood as following with necessity from some truth about the cause once we understand the nature of the *sunektikon* involved in its relevant detail. This nature will be spelled out by universal conditionals which are, so to speak, the laws of their particular nature.

That in this way we account for everything in terms of the nature of the thing involved does not as such seem objectionable. For we ourselves might think that ultimately everything has to be accounted for in terms of its nature. We might, e.g., think that there is just one nature, that of an extended body, say, and that the laws of nature amounted just to the specification of that one nature such that if one really knew what an extended body is one would know and understand that to be an extended body was precisely to satisfy these laws. That according to the Stoics we do have a plurality of natures is an inconvenience with which we may have to live anyway. That the Stoics also assume individual natures, though, will create serious problems. That they themselves do not seem to do anything which could count at least as a start of an attempt to specify these hidden causes, in fact rather shy away from it, does raise further questions.

Nevertheless the Stoic theory of causes may have had a considerable positive effect on actual physical explanation, after all. For, worked out in detail, it presupposes that if an object acts on another object so as to make it react in some way it does so by imparting a force or power to it; there is a transfer of force, an influence into the object affected. For the theory of motion in particular it suggests, as we saw in the case of the rolling cylinder, that we have to work with the notion of an internal force which keeps the body moving and the notion of a force imparted to a body which gets the body moving or increases its motion. It is difficult not to suspect that this may be the ultimate source of Philoponus' theory of imparted forces. It is well known that Philoponus in his discussion of the Aristotelian theory of motion took the position that the motion of a body is caused by an internal force which may be imparted and that it is such an imparted force, rather than the medium, e.g., which accounts for the motion of projectiles. Thus Philoponus has gained a place of honour in the history of science. But in spite of the useful suggestions by Pines, Wolff, and G. E. R. Lloyd,[7] we know little about the historical antecedents of Philoponus' theory of motion. And what tends to be overlooked in this connection is the considerable influence Stoicism had on Philoponus' physics. Hence it does not seem far-fetched at all to suggest that Philoponus' theory of motion has its ultimate origin in the Stoic theory we have been considering. In this case the Stoic theory of causes would not just have had a deep and lasting influence on the history of the notion of cause, it also would have made considerable contribution to science.

---

[7] S. Pines, 'Omne quod movetur necesse est ab aliquo moveri: A Refutation of Galen by Alexander of Aphrodisias and the Theory of Motion', Isis 52 (1961), 21–54; M. Wolff, Fallgesetz und Massebegriff (Berlin, 1971), Part I; G. E. R. Lloyd, Greek Science after Aristotle (London, 1973), 158 ff.

CAUSATION, LAWS, AND NECESSITY

Richard Sorabji

EARLIER TREATMENTS OF CAUSE, LAWS, AND NECESSITY

Modern Anglo-Saxon philosophy tends to link the notions of cause and explanation to the notions of law and necessity. Again, the notions of law and necessity get linked to *each other*. None of these links was considered obvious, I believe, by early Greek philosophy, despite certain tendencies in Aristotle's *Posterior Analytics*, and despite the claims of various modern interpreters.

Let me illustrate these points. In the *Posterior Analytics*, Aristotle discusses the kind of explanation appropriate to universal, necessary truths such as the scientist studies. To explain these, we must show that they are logically necessitated by further universal truths which are themselves necessary (*APo.* I 6, 74ᵇ 26–32). The explanation can be set out in a syllogism.

Aristotle sometimes obtains his necessary premisses for such syllogisms by taking examples of efficient causes which necessitate their effects. One example would be 'Noise accompanies the quenching of fire' (see II 8 93ᵇ 7–14; II 11 94ᵇ 32–3). Another might be 'Leaves fall when the sap coagulates' (see II 16 98ᵇ 36–8). If these premisses are necessary, it is presumably because the effect (noise; fall of leaves) is necessitated by the cause (quenching; coagulation).

So far, this makes Aristotle sound very much in tune, for better or worse, with modern Anglo-Saxon ideas. We are reminded of the dominant theory of explanation, Carl Hempel's,[1] which, in simplified form, says that to explain something is to show that it follows from certain statements of law, coupled with further premisses. We are also reminded of the most discussed account of cause, Donald Davidson's.[2] According to this, a cause necessitates

---

[1] Carl Hempel, *Aspects of Scientific Explanation* (New York and London, 1965).

[2] Donald Davidson, 'Causal Relations', *Journal of Philosophy* 64 (1967), 691–703; 'Mental Events', in *Experience and Theory*, ed. L. Foster and J. W. Swanson (London, 1970), 79–101.

its effect; and whenever a particular cause produces a particular effect, there will be a law relating some description of that cause to some description of that effect, and declaring that when the first description is satisfied, so will be the second.

It is not surprising that a recent account claims that Aristotle is offering very much the same account of explanation as Hempel.[3] But first Aristotle does not regard deduction from universal, necessary truths as *always* supplying an explanation. One cannot explain why vines are broad-leaved by deducing it from the universal necessary truths that vines are deciduous and that deciduous plants are broad-leaved (*APo.* I 13 78ᵃ 29–ᵇ 11; II 16 98ᵇ 4–24). Second, he is not in any case giving an account of *all* explanation, not, for example, of the explanation of particular events. Elsewhere, I believe, he suggests we can give an efficient cause explanation of the event, merely by showing that its cause is of a kind which will *for the most part* produce such an effect.[4] Nor does Aristotle consistently maintain that the efficient cause, coupled with attendant circumstances, makes its effect necessary. For in *GC* II 11, *Ph.* II 9, and *PA* I 1 (639ᵇ 21–640ᵃ and 642ᵃ 1–13), he is tempted to maintain that there is no necessitation of particular events, without showing the slightest tendency to think that particular events lack causes. This implies that there can be causation without necessitation, and if he sometimes deviates from this position, I think he does not deviate as often as has been supposed.[5]

Again, Aristotle does not link necessity and laws to *each other* as firmly as would many modern Anglo-Saxon philosophers. If a

---

[3] Max Hocutt, 'Aristotle's Four Becauses', *Philosophy* 49 (1974), 389.

[4] This has been argued by Christopher Kirwan in connection with *Metaph.* Δ 30, 1025ᵃ 21 (see his *Aristotle's Metaphysics Books Γ, Δ, E* (Oxford, 1971), ad loc.). The same view is to be found at *Poet.* 10 1452ᵃ 19–21, as Myles Burnyeat has pointed out to me.

[5] W. D. Ross ascribes to Aristotle the view that any exceptions to honey-water alleviating fever will themselves fall under a law. Thus although the administration of honey-water does not on its own necessitate alleviation, it presumably does, on Ross' interpretation, when taken with conditions that are not specifiable as exceptional. See W. D. Ross, ad *Metaph.* E 2 1027ᵃ 25, in *Aristotle's Metaphysics* (Oxford, 1924) I, 361. Kirwan ad loc. points out that this view is not in the text. What is more significant is the idea that for every *dunamis* there are conditions in which its exercise is *necessary* (*Metaph.* Θ5 1048ᵃ 6, ᵃ 14). But this is not yet to say that *dunameis* are never exercised *before* the conditions make it necessary. The chapter which above all implies that causes necessitate, I believe, is *Metaph.* E 3. A passage on the *other* side is *APo.* II 11 95ᵃ 3–5, which says that a house or statue never comes into being of necessity; yet it has a cause in the planning (*dianoia*) of the craftsman.

particular event is necessitated, this is normally taken to imply the law that in similar circumstances a similar event would always occur. But this is not what Aristotle finds most obvious about the situation. Certainly, one kind of necessity is closely linked to laws.[6] But he also talks of a stone travelling upwards, when thrown, by a necessity which is *contrary to nature* (e.g. *APo.* II 11 94^b 37–95^a 3). In calling it contrary to nature, part of what he means is that it is contrary to what happens always or for the most part. It is the unusualness, not the lawfulness, which attracts his attention in this case of necessity. Even when a stone falls down with a necessity which is *in accordance with nature*, Aristotle may not mean to associate this necessity with invariable laws. Nature acts the same way always '*or for the most part*',[7] and stones do not always fall: sometimes they are thrown up.

Plato shows no more inclination than Aristotle to link necessity with laws. At *Timaeus* 46 e, he talks of the causes which belong to things that are moved by others and *of necessity* set yet others in motion. These causes, he says, produce *chance* results *without order*; and again necessity is associated with the '*wandering*' cause at 48 a. Plato is not inclined to associate the necessity here with invariable laws. Indeed, there are no such laws available, if we may judge from the statements in *Republic* 530 b and *Statesman* 269 de, that what is bodily cannot always behave in the same way without alteration.

A recent study of the earlier Presocratic philosophers of nature has suggested that they seek to explain everything by reference to certain high-level regularities.[8] Certainly, we find many regularities picked out for attention. But the notion of regularity, I believe, is not nearly so widely applied as that of necessity. Thus for Democritus, every collision and every rebound of every atom (and hence by implication the direction and speed of every rebound) is necessary. Yet it is not clear that he postulates *regularities* to cover every aspect of motion which he regards as necessary. It may be that the move from necessity to regularity was not so obvious to him as to us.

[6] The necessity of the *everlasting*, e.g. *Cael.* I 12 281^b 3–25; *GC* II 11 337^b 35–338^a 3. This has been most fully studied by Jaakko Hintikka, *Time and Necessity* (Oxford, 1973), esp. Ch. 5.

[7] *APr.* 25^b 14; 32^b 4–13; *PA* 663^b 28; *GA* 727^b 29; 770^b 9–13; 772^a 35; 777^a 19–21.

[8] Gregory Vlastos, *Plato's Universe* (Oxford, 1975), Ch. 1.

A word of clarification: I have talked both of laws and of regularities. What is their relation? For Hempel, a law is a special kind of regularity. Some would add, though Hempel would not, that a law must have some *necessity* about it. Apart from this, the legal metaphor in modern talk of laws of nature is virtually dead. In talking of laws, I was therefore concerned with ancient interest in regularities, necessary or otherwise, but not with ancient interest in legal metaphors, although that is a subject that repays study.[9]

THE STOIC INNOVATION IN THE ANALYSIS OF CAUSE

What I want to suggest is that the Stoics made an innovation. It was they who first associated each and every event with exceptionless regularity. They did so by associating regularity with *cause*. Since every event, in their view, had a cause, this linked every event with regularity.

The kind of regularity which concerned them, however, was not like that of earlier Presocratics who said 'like is attracted to like', or of Newton whose third law tells us that, for every action, there is an equal and opposite reaction. These laws had a comparatively specific content, and they were supposed to be instantiated many times a day. It was the dream of Laplace, inspired by Newton's successes, that every event is governed by laws like these. The Stoics, more soberly, postulated a much more abstract kind of law, which might be called a law of causation.

Let us consider the fullest formulation of the Stoic law of causation, which comes in Alexander, *De fato* 22. He says the Stoics postulated many causes. As we know from elsewhere (Clem. *Strom.* VIII 9; see Frede in Chapter 9 above), some were self-sufficient on their own, some were joint causes and only *jointly* sufficient, some merely eased or intensified the effect, some were mere necessary conditions, while some necessary conditions did not *do* anything and so (Sen. *Ep.* LXV 4) were not really causes at all. With regard to each of these causes, Alexander says, the Stoics maintained that when all the circumstances (*peri-*

---

[9] Legal metaphors were applied to nature very early. But the idea of law itself came to be *opposed* to that of nature in the fifth century B.C. For the rather late development of the metaphor of a law of nature, see Klaus Reich, 'Der historische Ursprung des Naturgesetzbegriffs' in *Festschrift Ernst Kapp*, ed. H. Diller and H. Erbse (Hamburg, 1958), 121–34.

estēkota) surrounding the cause and effect were the same, it would be impossible for things to turn out now one way, now another. The word *periestēkota* and its cognates recurs in nearly all the accounts. Judging from this fullest version, what the Stoics envisaged was a repetition of the *totality* of circumstances, both the cause and all its surroundings. Then, they maintained, the effect would be the same.

The point that the same circumstances will have the same outcome is recorded by many sources.[10] And it is incorporated into the very idea of causation. For the Stoics maintained that causation implied the outcome would be the same. If anyone allowed the possibility of an event's happening differently in the same circumstances, he would be denying that event a cause, but there cannot be a causeless event.[11] In this way, both causation and each particular event are associated with regularity.

There was a special reason why the Stoics should think of particular events as connected with exceptionless regularity. For the exact repetition of circumstances was for many of them not an abstract possibility, but something they positively expected. They thought that whatever happens will be exactly repeated in unending cycles (*SVF* I 109; II 596–632). There is an interesting contrast with Aristotle's view. He is prepared to allow that what happens always in unending cycles is necessary, not because of causation, but just on the basis of its happening *always* (*GC* II 11). On the other hand, he does not think, as Zeno and Chrysippus do (*SVF* I 109; II 624), that a particular event can be so repeated. He only allows that certain broadly specified types of event, like eclipse and rainfall, are repeatedly instantiated.[12] He therefore has no incentive for asking, in regard to events like the birth of Mr Smith, what would happen *if* there were an exact repetition of the attendant circumstances.

Later in antiquity, the Stoic view had prevailed sufficiently for one Aristotelian author, Alexander or whoever wrote the

[10] Nemesius, *Nat. hom.* 35; Alex. Aphr. *Fat.* 10 (176, 21–2), 15 (185, 8–9), and 22 (192, 22–3); Plu. *Stoic. rep.* 1045 bc; Alex. Aphr. (?) *Mant.* 171, 20–7; cf. 174, 3–5; and 170, 4–5.

[11] Alex. Aphr. *Fat.* 15 and 22 as in preceding note; Plu. *Stoic. rep.* 1045 bc; cf. Alex. Aphr. (?) *Mant.* 174, 3–5 and 171, 20–7.

[12] But see also his view that inventions are endlessly rediscovered (*Metaph.* Δ 8 1074ᵃ 38–ᵇ 14; *Pol.* II 5 1264ᵃ 1–5; VII 10 1329ᵇ 25–35; *Mete.* I 3 339ᵇ 27). Furthermore, there is a Great Year, with prolonged wintry and summery epochs (*Mete.* I 14).

relevant section of the *De anima mantissa* (171, 20–5), to allow that proper causation is linked with what happens everlastingly and always in the same way. He only pleads that some events have only accidental causes, and concludes that these events at least are not linked with exceptionless regularities.

So far we have noticed that the Stoics linked causation, and hence each particular event, with exceptionless regularity. But did they also make any link between cause and *necessity*? The answer is 'Yes', because all the sources use modal words. If the same circumstances are repeated, it is *necessary* that the same outcome should recur, and it is not *possible* for there to be now one outcome and now another.[13] Moreover, from this is inferred the deterministic conclusion that we *cannot* do otherwise than we do (Alex. Aphr., *Fat.* 15 (185, 9–10)).

ASSESSMENT OF THE STOIC VIEW THAT CAUSE
INVOLVES NECESSITATION AND UNIFORM REGULARITY

I have been arguing that the Stoics made a big stride towards modern accounts of cause, by linking it with exceptionless regularity and necessity. It might seem, then, that I was congratulating them. But, in this instance, I am not sure that the latest is the best. I believe that effects need not always be necessitated or linked to circumstances by exceptionless laws. Various different cases may be possible, and if we want to see what they have in common, we may do better to go back to Aristotle's idea that a cause is what provides a particular kind of *explanation*. According to Aristotle, the efficient cause provides one of four kinds of explanation, namely, the kind which tells us 'whence comes the origin of a change' (*Ph.* II 3 and 7).

Let me provide an illustration of an unnecessitated effect. The case for attending some instructive lecture may seem overwhelming, and nine times out of ten in such circumstances a student may act accordingly and attend the lecture. But when he does so, we may still feel that his action is not necessitated. For what about the tenth time, when (let us suppose) he does not act accordingly, and this not because of any new disincentive or force? There is always *some* disincentive to attending lectures because of the

---

[13] Nemes. *Nat. hom.* 35; Alex. Aphr. *Fat.* 10 (176, 21); 22 (192, 22); Alex. Aphr. (?) *Mant.* 170, 4; 171, 24–5; cf. 174, 5.

effort involved. We need not suppose that the disincentives have grown stronger or more numerous on the tenth occasion. Of course, a determinist will declare that they *must* have done so if the student fails to attend. But this is only an expression of faith on the determinist's part.

But where, it may be asked, does *cause* come in? Surely, on my suggestion, cause is linked to *explanation*, and must it not be admitted that there is no explanation, and hence no cause, of the student's attending on the nine occasions, so long as his attendance is not necessitated?

Not at all: the student's attendance on the nine occasions can be explained by reference to the case, as he saw it, in favour of attending. But explanation, I believe, is relative to the question asked. Often (not always) the question asked, when someone calls for an explanation involves a contrast.[14] Why did the student attend, for example, *in face of the fact that* the lectures were not compulsory? In relation to *this* question, the explanation which cites his interests may be a perfectly complete explanation. Of course, in relation to a *different* question, there may be no explanation at all. For example: why did he go on the nine occasions, *in face of the fact that* he did not on the tenth? In relation to *this* question, his attendance cannot be explained. But then ought we to expect that there will be an explanation available, corresponding to every contrast we care to choose? The important thing is that in relation to many of the most natural questions, there is a wholly adequate explanation of his attendance.[15]

Where does cause come in? I have no objection to saying that the student's interests, desires and beliefs are the cause of his attendance. For by cause I understand something which provides a certain kind of explanation, not something which involves necessitation or laws. On this view, the student's attendance is caused, but is not necessitated, nor is it an instance of uniform regularities.

[14] For this view, see Michael Scriven, 'Explanations, Predictions and Laws', in *Minnesota Studies in the Philosophy of Science* Vol. iii, ed. H. Feigl and G. Maxwell (Minneapolis, 1962), 170–230, and review of E. Nagel's *The Structure of Science* in *Review of Metaphysics* 17 (1963–4), 403–24.

[15] There is even an adequate explanation of his *non-attendance* on the tenth occasion. In relation to the question, 'Why did he not go, seeing that nothing stopped him?', we can reply, 'It is an effort to come in from his lodgings in the suburbs.' What we cannot answer is the *different* question, 'Why did he not go on the tenth occasion, seeing that he did on the other nine?'

There will be objections to this view. What I have been relying on is, first, the link between cause and explanation, and, second, the relativity of explanation to the particular question in view. But the example chosen is a psychological one, and some people would argue that desires, interests, and beliefs are only *reasons*, and that reasons are not causes.[16] Or, again, it has been maintained that psychological causes are causes only in some secondary sense, and that no parallel example could be given in connection with non-psychological causes.[17]

In response to this, I should say that a perfectly good non-psychological example has been given by G. E. M. Anscombe,[18] although to show why I think it good, in spite of criticisms that have been levelled at it, I will have to re-emphasize what I have just said about explanation. Suppose an electron reaches the trigger of an explosive device. Suppose also that the cause and explanation of an electron's reaching the trigger is the fact that a laboratory technician carelessly left out a lump of radioactive material in the room, instead of locking it away in its lead-lined box. The effect in this example, namely, the electron's reaching the trigger, need not be necessitated. For most quantum physicists tell us that the rate and route of radioactive emission is not determined in advance. Perhaps it would be positively *rare* for so small a lump of radioactive material in so short a time to emit an electron in just such a direction. This would not prevent there being a cause and explanation of the electron's reaching the trigger, namely, the material's being left out.

If an impression persists that we have no explanation here, and so no cause, this impression will often arise from one of two things. Either the wrong stage in the process is selected for attention (it is the electron's reaching the trigger that I would pick out as the unnecessitated effect); or it is neglected that explanation is relative to the question asked. Of course, there is no explanation, in relation to the question why the electron reached the trigger in face of the fact that a similar lump in similar circumstances would not always irradiate a similarly placed trigger. But there is a complete and adequate explanation, in relation to the question why an

---

[16] e.g. A. I. Melden, *Free Action* (London, 1961).

[17] Ted Honderich, 'Causes and Causal Circumstances as Necessitating', *Proceedings of the Aristotelian Society* 78 (1977–8), 70–1.

[18] G. E. M. Anscombe, *Causality and Determination* (Inaugural Lecture, Cambridge, 1971).

electron reached the trigger, in face of the fact that most rooms, and this room at other times, have been free from radiation altogether.

This is intended to disarm the determinist's persistent assumption that there is no middle ground between a thing's being completely necessitated and its being completely inexplicable.[19]

All this may seem to take us far away from the Stoics. But I do not think it really does so. For the philosophical point has to be cleared up in order to assess the correctness of their view that, if circumstances are exactly repeated, the same outcome will occur. Tony Long had a distinguished philosophical tradition on his side when he declared that this view was 'true but trivial'.[20] I have been attempting to argue that it is significant, but (hopefully) false. An electron would not always reach the trigger, even if the circumstances were *exactly* similar.

Chrysippus actually discussed an example not so very far removed from that of the student and the lectures, except that he envisaged a person for whom the considerations for and against a course of action were equally balanced. He denied that we could envisage such a case and hold that the person could equally decide either way. Rather, he said, there must be some cause and some difference which leads the person's impulse in one direction rather than the other. And he applied this view equally to the fall of dice or the tipping of a balance (Plu. *Stoic. rep.* 1045 bc). This view is, however, what I have called merely a declaration of faith.

The belief in necessitation appears to be more than a declaration of faith, so long as it can be supported by a certain argument. It is suggested that, if you deny that the man's action, or the tipping of the scales, is necessitated, you will be making what happens *inexplicable*. This is just the charge that certain Stoics pressed, and it has been well documented by Robert Sharples.[21] The Stoics claimed that their opponents were committed to postulating 'causeless motions'.[22] And the claim has been made by modern philosophers too.[23]

[19] For the assumption that there is no middle ground, see e.g. Honderich, op. cit. 68; 76–7.

[20] Long [106], 188.

[21] Sharples [139].

[22] Cic. *Fat.* 19; 23–5; 28; 34–6; 46–8; Alex. Aphr. *Fat.* 8 (173, 13–174, 28); 15 (185, 7–186, 12); 20 (190, 19–26); 22 (192, 8–25); 24 (193, 30–194, 25), Alex. Aphr. (?) *Mant.* (173, 31–175, 32); Plu. *Stoic. rep.* 1045 bc; ps-Plu. *Fat.* 574 e.

[23] Honderich, op. cit. 63–86, esp. 68; 76–7.

The Stoics' opponents sometimes responded, in effect, by looking for ways in which something could be caused without being necessitated. Their methods of doing this were not very successful. They insisted that their unnecessitated events were not causeless, but rather had a special kind of cause. We can distinguish several positions: (a) sometimes they said the causes were *internal*. Faced with the same external circumstances, we may choose the pleasant, the admirable, or the useful aspect of things, and so *we* or our *decisions* are the cause.[24] (b) Sometimes the distinction was made between necessary and sufficient conditions: the father is only a necessary condition of the child.[25] (c) Sometimes there was an appeal to fortuitous or accidental causes of chance phenomena. The lucky discovery of treasure has a merely *accidental* cause in the fact of one's digging in the garden.[26] (d) It was sometimes urged that in the various cases cited there is not an *everlasting* chain of causes.[27]

Although I do not think any of these arguments succeeds, what I have been suggesting is that *in spirit* these arguments are right: cause need not involve necessitation or uniform regularity. All I have been trying to do is to offer a more satisfactory explanation of *how* something can be caused without being necessitated, and without being an instance of an exceptionless regularity.

DID CHRYSIPPUS UNDO THE LINK WITH NECESSITY?

An objection may be raised to my account of the Stoic view. It will perhaps be agreed that the Stoics connected cause with exceptionless regularity: the same circumstances have the same outcome. But how can I claim quite generally that the Stoics linked cause with necessity? For is it not notorious that Chrysippus and others tried to escape from commitment to necessity?[28] For one thing, Chrysippus suggested that certain statements which looked like conditionals were not genuine conditionals, but only

---

[24] Cic. *Fat.* 23–5; Alex. Aphr. *Fat.* 15 (185, 7–186, 12); 20 (190, 19–26); Alex. Aphr. (?) *Mant.* (173, 31–175, 32).

[25] Cic. *Fat.* 36; Alex. Aphr. *Fat.* 24 (193, 30–194, 15).

[26] Cic. *Fat.* 19; 28; Alex. Aphr. *Fat.* 8 (173, 13–174, 28); 24 (194, 15–25).

[27] Cic. *Fat.* 34; Alex. Aphr. (?) *Mant.* 171, 8.

[28] Alex. Aphr. *Fat.* 10; Cic. *Fat.* 12–16; 39–45; August. *City of God* V 9 and 10; Epict. *Diss.* II 19.1–5; Plu. *Stoic. rep.* 1055 de; Plu. *Epitome* I 27 (Aët. *Plac.* I 27 in Diels, *Doxographici Graeci*, p. 322).

negated conjunctions, or, in modern terms, material implications. That is, instead of having the form 'If p, then q', they would have the form, 'Not both (p and not q)'. They would then involve no necessary link between antecedent (p) and consequent (q). Michael Frede and S. Sambursky have both suggested that Chrysippus would view as material implications any statements in which the link between antecedent and consequent was empirical rather than logical.[29] This would place the Stoic law of causation in a new light. We have been construing it as saying that if circumstances (*periestēkota*) are exactly repeated, the same outcome will occur. On the view of Frede and Sambursky, we have a choice: either circumstances and outcome must have a *logical* connection, or the law of causation must be reconstrued as a material implication. It will then read: 'It is not the case both that the same circumstances are repeated and that the same outcome does not occur.' No *necessary* link between circumstances and outcome would then be implied.

In the present volume, Frede has explored the possibility of ascribing to the Stoics a *logical* link between circumstances and effect. Indeed, he has gone further and concentrated on just *one* of the causes distinguished by the Stoics, namely, the one which is indifferently called perfect (*autotelēs, perfecta*) or consolidating (*sunektikē, continens*: in Frede's translation, containing). We are told that these were capable of producing the result self-sufficiently by themselves (*autarkōs di' hautōn poiētika*: Clem. *Strom.* VIII 9). In the case of a cylinder's rolling, or of a man's assenting, Chrysippus would probably distinguish the internal state of the cylinder or of the man as the 'perfect' cause,[30] although perfect causes do not *have* to be internal. If the link between cause and effect is here to be represented as *logical*, perhaps the idea will be that if one understood the internal state sufficiently fully, one would see that the rolling or the assent was *logically* implied. It is, however, only a conjecture that Chrysippus thought in this way. Moreover some examples of perfect causes make one doubt whether Chrysippus can really have meant that every perfect cause on its own necessitated its effect, logically or otherwise. Thus a teacher is a perfect cause of someone's learning, fire of something's burning, and cautery of pain (Clem. loc. cit; and Cic. *Top.* 58–60). In each of these cases, something is required not only

---

[29] Frede [42], 80–93; Sambursky [76], 79.
[30] See Cic. *Fat.* 41–4, where, however, the point is not quite explicit.

of the agent, but also (one would think) of the patient, before an effect can ensue. Sharples has suggested to me that in calling 'perfect' causes *self-sufficient*, the Stoics do not mean that they always necessitate their effects without further preconditions, but only that they rely on no further *causes* for their effects.

The view of Frede and Sambursky allows only two alternatives: either Chrysippus made the link between circumstances and outcome a logical link (which is difficult to show), or he represented it merely by a material implication, and hence not as a necessary link at all. I believe that we need not accept either alternative. For I shall argue below that Chrysippus' use of material implication was not connected with the distinction between the empirical and the logical. None the less, the idea of material implication was used in another context, along with a selection of other devices, for trying to escape from commitment to necessity, and this may suggest that the connection made by the Stoics between cause and necessity is not as firm as I have suggested.

STOIC COMMITMENT TO NECESSITY

I shall maintain that in the end none of these attempts at escape was successful, so that the general picture of the Stoic view which I have been presenting need not be revised. But first, I must substantiate the claim that the Stoics committed themselves to postulating that all events occur of necessity. This was certainly the view of them taken in antiquity. Moreover, their own words make this interpretation virtually inescapable. Chrysippus wrote in the first book of his treatise on Fate that all things are held fast by necessity and fate, though he tried in the second book to deal with some of the difficulties that that created for human conduct.[31] Not only do the words for necessity and necessitated recur in the reports,[32] but the Stoics had a battery of other words for inevitability which they applied to this all-embracing Fate: *aparabatos*,

---

[31] Diogenianus *apud* Eus. *PE* VI 8, 262 a, 265 d. Similar is Plu. *Stoic. rep.* 1049 f; 1050 d; 1056 c; Alex. Aphr. *Fat.* 7 (171, 26); Aul. Gell. VII 2.

[32] *anankē, katēnankasmenon, necessitas, necesse, necessarius*. For reports, some interpreting, some quoting direct, see *SVF* II 913, 914, 916, 918, 923, 926, 937, 939, 942, 943, 963, 975, 997, 1000, and Aul. Gell. XIII 1, 2; M. Aur. 12. 14. 1; Boethius, 2nd commentary on Aristotle's *De Interpretatione*, ed. Meiser, Leipzig, 1877, p. 194; Nemes. *Nat. hom.* 35. It is also the standard interpretation of Alex. Aphr. *Fat.* 1, 7, 8, 9, 11, 13, 14, 15, 22, 28, 30, 31, 34, 36.

atreptos, anekpheuktos, anapodrastos, aniketos, anekbiastos, akolutos, aparallaktos, ametabletos, ametathetos; in Latin: *insuperabilis, indeclinabilis, non posse mutari.*[33] To Zeno and Chrysippus is ascribed a comparison with a dog tied to a cart. If it is willing to follow, it follows, combining its own consent with necessity. But if it is not willing, it will be subjected to necessity anyhow (*SVF* II 975). Nor is any detail exempt from the necessity of Fate.[34]

The necessity which the Stoics postulated arose from causation. In one comparison, fate was conceived as a rope or chain of *causes.*[35]

In view of all this, it is not very surprising that the ancient sources regard as unsuccessful the Stoic attempts to escape from saying that all events happen of necessity.[36] Indeed, for those Stoics who explicitly postulate necessity, the only possible strategy would presumably be to introduce two or more senses in which events can be necessary, and to argue that they are not committed to events being necessary in *every* sense.[37] The task would then be to find a *morally significant* sense in which it can be denied that all events are necessary. By a morally significant sense, I mean one whose invocation will allow us to continue holding people morally responsible, and to continue applying our other moral categories.

THE STOIC RETREAT FROM NECESSITY

I can now turn to the attempts to retreat from necessity. Some of the arguments bear on the related concept of possibility, and are designed to show that there is room for alternative possibilities. This is how Cicero describes Chrysippus' position (*De fato* 13):

But you do not want this at all, Chrysippus, and it is especially on this very point that you have a struggle with Diodorus. For he says that

---

[33] See *SVF* II 202, 528, 913, 914, 917, 918, 923, 924, 1000, and Aul. Gell. XIII 1, 2; M. Aur. 12.14.1; Cornutus, *Theologia Graeca* 13, ed. Lang (Leipzig, 1881), p. 13; Alex. Aphr. *Fat.* 2; 10; Nemes. *Nat. hom.* 35. Sharples has suggested to me that this plethora of words may represent a desire to avoid the naughty word 'necessary'. But for instances of the naughty word and its synonyms, see the preceding two notes.

[34] This is implied by the references in n. 31, p. 261, and by Plu. *Comm. not.* 1076 e.

[35] Cic. *Div.* I 127; Aul. Gell. VII 2.

[36] Cic. *Fat.* 12–16 and 39; Plu. *Stoic. rep.* 1056 c; 1055 de; Alex. Aphr. *Fat.* 10; Aul. Gell. VII 2. 15.

[37] Alexander mentions the denial of necessity in the same breath as he uses one of the words for inevitability (*aparabatos, Fat.* 10).

only that can happen which either is, or will be, true; and that whatever will be must necessarily happen, while that which will not be cannot happen. But you say that things which will not be are also capable of happening. For example, this jewel can be broken, even if it never will be, and it was not necessary that Cypselus should reign at Corinth, although that had been announced a thousand years before by the oracle of Apollo.

We can distinguish no less than eight attempts to escape from necessity. Since I believe they have not been adequately distinguished, it will take some time to disentangle them. Although my conclusion will be that they are unsuccessful, what I do think remarkable is that once again the Stoic arguments look very close to certain modern arguments of the same kind.

The first two attempts: reply to Diodorus' Master Argument

The first four Stoic arguments are defensive. They are intended to rebut certain *particular* attempts to saddle them with a deterministic account of possiblity. Diodorus Cronus, the dialectician, had defined possibility in a way that, suitably interpreted, was deterministic. For he said that nothing else is possible other than that what is or will be (or what is or will be true). Moreover, he produced a famous argument, the Master Argument, in support of this account of possibility. We are told the premisses of the argument by Epictetus.

I shall not here try to explain the argument. My present interest is merely in the fact that Cleanthes and Chrysippus sought to avoid the deterministic conclusion. Cleanthes did so by denying the premiss that what is past and true is necessary; Chrysippus by denying the premiss that the impossible does not follow from the possible (Epict. *Diss.* 2.19 1–5). Cleanthes chose the right point of attack, I believe, provided that Diodorus' argument is construed in the manner that A. Prior has suggested.[38] But Chrysippus who attacked the *other* premiss, chose a strange example in order to do so.[39] If you are talking in Dion's presence, 'Dion is dead' (which is possible) entails 'This man is dead' (which is impossible, since the 'this' would have no reference, if Dion were dead).

[38] Prior [138] and *Past, Present and Future* (Oxford, 1967).
[39] Alex. Aphr. in *APr.* 177.

The third attempt: Cicero De fato *12–14*

At this point, Cicero conducts an imaginary argument with
Chrysippus, which evidently represents earlier debates (*Fat.*
12–16). He doubts whether Chrysippus can succeed in escaping
from Diodorus' determinism. For, first, Chrysippus accepts one
of Diodorus' premisses, namely that the past is irrevocable and
hence necessary. Second, he also accepts divination, and would
therefore have to accept the claims of astrologers. For example:
if Fabius was born at the rising of the Dog-star (antecedent), he
will not die at sea (consequent).

Putting these ingredients together, Cicero argues that what is
mentioned in the antecedent, Fabius' birth at the rising of the
Dog-star, is past and hence necessary. Moreover, the necessity of
the antecedent will spread to the consequent: Fabius will not die
at sea.

Chrysippus' reply is that necessity does not always spread from
antecedent to consequent. Why not? It has been suggested that
he would appeal again to the example concerning Dion. For if we
rearrange the materials of that example, we get a reply relevant to
Cicero's argument. 'This man is not dead' (necessary, because the
'this' requires a living referent) entails 'Dion is not dead' (non-
necessary). Here is an example in which Chrysippus would claim
that the necessity of the antecedent ('This man is not dead') does
not spread to the consequent (Dion is not dead').[40]

I am satisfied with this interpretation. It makes the present
argument into a version of the preceding one. But it would be
challenged by someone who argues, as does Mario Mignucci,[41]
that the Stoics take the necessary to be *always* true. For, if they do,
they cannot view as necessary, 'This man exists', since, as they
see it, the 'this' may sometimes lack a reference, and then the
claim is neither true nor false. In Chrysippus' terminology, the
claim 'perishes', when the word 'this' lacks a reference, and hence
it is not *always* true. (Alex. Aphr. *in APr*, 177, 25–178, 5).

Mignucci's argument is interesting and original. But on the
other side I would urge that it is Diodorus, rather than the
Stoics, who comes close to defining the necessary in terms of what

---

[40] For this interpretation, see Kneale [43], 127, followed by Donini [86], 333–51;
Frede [42], 88.
[41] Mignucci [111].

is *always* true, and even he does not go all the way.[42] Moreover, I doubt whether the Stoics ever transferred their allegiance to the Diodorean definition.[43] The *Stoic* definition of the necessary is that it is that which is true (they do not say: *always* true), and which does not admit of being false, or (a clause not needed for our purposes) which admits of being false, but is prevented from being false by external circumstances (DL VII 75). By the first two tests in this definition, 'This man exists' ought to qualify as necessary. For, said with reference to some man, it is true, and it will 'perish' sooner than admit of being false.[44]

I rest content, then with the orthodox interpretation of the third argument. Before recounting the fourth, Cicero interposes a little sally against Chrysippus, which is left unanswered, but which has some intrinsic interest. He complains that, if there is a natural cause of Fabius' not dying at sea, then it is not possible that he will. He evidently expects Chrysippus to agree, and also to accept that there must be a natural cause. Presumably, he expects the latter because of the view common to himself and the Stoics that things can be foreknown, only if there are natural causes of them.[45]

I shall return to this argument about natural cause below. Can we reconstruct how it went in the original sources from which

---

[42] For convenience, I shall render his definition of 'necessary' as always true, where the nuances do not matter. But in fact, Boethius gives the definition as: 'that which, being true, will not be false', 2nd comm. in *Int.* ed. Meiser, 234.

[43] Mignucci cites two passages in support of the suggestion that the Stoics regard the necessary as *always* true. But in one (Cic. *Fat.* 14), all that need be implied is the Stoic view that what is true and does not admit of being false is necessary. As for the other passage (Alex. Aphr. *Fat.* 10, 177, 7-15), rather than disbelieve our other sources about the Stoics, it is easier to suppose that the argument was devised *ad hominem* by a Stoic against a Diodorean view, and that it incorporates a (slightly loose) rendering of the Diodorean definition of necessity.

[44] A second reason for expecting Chrysippus to treat 'This man *does* exist' as necessary is that he undoubtedly treats as impossible 'This man does *not* exist'. To this second argument Mignucci has a reply, namely, that when we follow out the implications of the Stoic definitions of modal terms, we find that 'not possibly not' does not entail 'necessarily'. This is because calling something necessary is said to carry the implication that it is *true*, while calling its negation impossible is not said to carry a corresponding implication that the negation is *false*. Interesting as this observation is, I am not entirely convinced of its force, since I am not sure that the non-entailment is an *intended* feature. It is not one to which the ancient commentators draw attention, and Frede has suggested that the purpose of adding the implication 'is true' is merely to make clearer the relation of the Stoic definitions to rival ones (Frede [42], 111-13).

[45] Cic. *Div.* I 127; II 15 and 17; II 25. For the Stoic view, see *SVF* II 939-44.

Cicero is drawing? If speculation is allowed, perhaps I may suggest that Cicero has recorded the argument in the wrong order. Chrysippus may first have sought to divest statements about astrological evidence of any necessitarian implications by offering the argument which Cicero postpones until *next*—the argument that such statements are only material implications. Someone may then have reminded him of his view that, where there is an astrological sign, there will also be a cause, and complained that the corresponding *causal* statements could not be treated as mere material implications.

Be that as it may, Cicero leaves Chrysippus without a reply to the argument about natural cause, and goes on to record a *fresh* attempt by him to prevent necessity spreading from antecedent to consequent in the original example about Fabius. This is the attempt that turns on negated conjunction, or material implication.

The fourth attempt: Cicero, De fato 15–16

Instead of saying, 'If someone was born at the rising of the Dog-star, he will not die at sea', the diviners ought merely to use material implication. They ought to say, 'It is not the case both that someone was born at the rising of the Dogstar and that he will not die at sea.' Because the second form of words uses material implication, necessity will not spread from the first clause to the second.

Philo the dialectician had suggested that all conditional statements could be reduced to material implications, and some Stoics followed him. As Frede well argues, Chrysippus probably denied that any could, and maintained instead that in a genuine conditional the denial of the consequent actually 'conflicts' (*machetai*) with the antecedent.[46] Without wishing to commit myself at all on the nature of this 'conflict', I shall for convenience follow a common way of talking, and put the point by saying that

[46] Sextus, *PH* II 110–12 distinguishes four theories, ascribing the first to Philo. Cicero, *Acad.* II 143 tells us that Philo and Chrysippus disagreed. Kneale [43], 129 suggests that Chrysippus' theory was that the denial of the consequent is in conflict with (*machetai*) the antecedent. This would fit with Cicero's use of the notion of conflict (*pugnare*) in reference to Chrysippus (*Fat.* 12), and with Diogenes Laertius' ascription of the conflict view to the Stoics (VII 73). For evidence that some Stoics nonetheless preferred Philo's view, see *PH* II 104–5; *M* VIII 245–7; 447; 449; Simp. *in Ar. Ph.* 1299, 36. Here Sextus seems to ascribe Philo's view quite generally to the Stoics, and he bases one of his criticisms on the assumption that they took it (*PH* II 115–18; *M* VIII 268; 449–51).

antecedent and consequent have a *necessary* connection. In that case, by treating the astrologers' statements as equivalent merely to material implications, he shows that he does not regard them as genuine conditionals. Why not?

It is at this point that Michael Frede, in line with S. Sambursky, offers his alternative. Chrysippus insists on material implication, he suggests, because the link between time of birth, and place of death is *empirical*. Chrysippus, on this interpretation, would have wished to confine genuine conditionals to stating logical, not empirical, connections. The 'conflict' between the antecedent and the denial of the consequent will have been a *logical* one.

Frede is most candid in acknowledging difficulties in this interpretation, and there are a good number of them. One important one is that the distinction between empirical and logical was not a favoured one in antiquity. For another thing, Cicero clearly does not think that material implication was recommended for empirical connections in general, since he implies that Chrysippus did not consider treating as a material implication the connection, which is surely empirical, between a quickened pulse and fever. Indeed, Cicero speaks as if Chrysippus formulated no general principle as to which conditionals were genuine and which not.[47]

Frede acknowledges yet another difficulty. A sign is defined by the Stoics as the antecedent in a certain kind of conditional, the thing signified being the consequent.[48] And we have just seen that the Stoics generally gave the antecedent a *necessary* connection with the consequent in a genuine conditional. Yet the sign and thing signified, which have this necessary connection, appear in several of Sextus' examples to be related *empirically*, or at least not with a logical necessity. Thus milk in the breasts is a sign of having conceived, blushing of shame, sweat of pores in the skin, a viscid bronchial discharge of a wound in the lungs, bodily movements of the presence of soul, smoke of fire, a scar of a wound, and a puncture in the heart of imminent death (*M* VIII 152–5; 173; 252; *PH* II 100; 102; 142).

---

[47] He implies that Chrysippus had not explained why we should not treat as a material implication the (logical) connection between two lines being greatest circles on a sphere and their intersecting each other.

[48] *PH* II 104. *M* VIII 245. I am grateful to Malcolm Schofield for drawing my attention to this.

This evidence that empirical connections may for the Stoics be necessary might be discounted by someone who followed Sextus. For in the very passages which concern us, Sextus defines the Stoic conditional without reference to there being a necessary link between antecedent and consequent (*PH* II 104; *M* VIII 245). But, at the same time, he shows himself aware that the definition was a matter of dispute among the Stoics, and Frede himself has argued convincingly that the normal Stoic definition did postulate a necessary connection.

Frede recognizes the difficulty, and allows that after all there were Stoics who treated some empirical relationships as stateable in genuine conditionals and as involving a necessary connection. His only plea (op. cit. 89) is that these Stoics may have been later than Chrysippus. Part of his evidence is that the distinction between 'indicative' and 'commemorative' signs, which enters into this discussion, may have been a late one. But this evidence is called into question by Jacques Brunschwig, who in the present volume has found very early traces of it.

There is a further difficulty which seems to me still more significant. Cicero has just earlier introduced the idea of a 'natural cause', and he assumes Chrysippus will have to agree that, if there is a natural cause of Fabius' not dying at sea, it is not *possible* that Fabius will die at sea. He does not record Chrysippus as having answered the objection by employing the idea of material implication. Why not? For Chrysippus would be able to escape, if he could argue that we have only a material implication, and not a genuine conditional, in the proposition that if such a natural cause of immunity already exists, then Fabius will not die at sea. In fact, however, Chrysippus is represented as leaving the objection unanswered, and as employing the idea of material implication not in connection with statements about the natural cause of Fabius' immunity, but only in connection with statements about the *astrological evidence* for that immunity.

Chrysippus' silence could be explained away, if it could be made out that, in his view, cause and effect have a *logical* relation. We could then understand why he does not offer to analyse a statement of natural cause by means of material implication. But, as argued above, it is not easy to see how cause and effect could be represented as always having a logical link.

I think that on the whole the evidence is against Frede's suggestion. An alternative has been offered by P. L. Donini.[49] His hypothesis is that time of birth is a mere sign of place of death, and that this is why the two are related only by material implication. On this view, although the Stoics treated the existence of astrological signs as a proof of the existence of necessitating causes, they will not have thought there was any necessary connection involved when one reported the sign, rather than the cause, of the eventual outcome. It might seem to support this interpretation that Aristotle himself, who had earlier cited milk in the breasts as a sign of having conceived, seems to waver on the question of whether a sign can be necessarily linked to the thing signified.[50] But this suggestion runs into the same difficulty as the preceding one. For if a sign is the antecedent in a genuine conditional, it *will* have a necessary connection with the thing signified, and their relationship cannot be represented by material implication. Moreover, it might in any case be doubted that a sign *never* has a necessary link with the thing signified. For one example of a sign is the premisses of a valid and conclusive syllogism (*PH* II 96; 122; 131; 134; *M* VIII 180; 277). And in these the conclusion follows by necessity (*M* VIII 304; *kat' anankēn*).

A modification of Donini's suggestion would exploit the Stoic distinction between two kinds of sign, commemorative (*hupomnēstikon*) and indicative (*endeiktikon*)[51]. The commemorative sign signifies something temporarily non-evident, and works, as its name suggests, by *reminding* us of what it has been observably correlated with in the past. The indicative sign, on the contrary, signifies something which is non-evident by nature, and which cannot therefore have been *observably* correlated with anything encountered in the past. Instead, it makes us *reason* to the existence of the thing signified, not on the basis of memory, but by the

---

[49] Donini [87].

[50] Aristotle normally recognized that there could be a necessary link and gave the example, later used by the Stoics: if she has milk she has conceived (Pl. *Mx.* 237 e; Arist. *APr.* II 27; *Rhe.* I 2; II 25; Sextus *PH* II 106; *M* VIII 252). But at one point, he introduces an uncharacteristically strict criterion for necessity, so that there is necessity only where there is a definitional connection (*APo.* I 4 73ᵃ 34–b 5; I 6 74ᵇ 12; 75ᵃ 20–2; ᵃ 31). And in this context, he seems to imply that sign and thing signified are not linked by ncessity, even if linked invariably (1 6 75ᵃ 31–4).

[51] This was suggested to me by Myles Burnyeat. For the distinction, see *PH* II 99–102; *M* VIII 151–5.

force of its own nature and constitution. To illustrate: if sweat flows through the skin, this is an *indicative* sign of there being invisible pores, but an astrological conjunction must be a *commemorative* sign of the manner of Fabius' future death. The new suggestion would be that Chrysippus postulates material implication because time of birth is a merely *commemorative* sign of mode of death. But this suggestion also violates our evidence; for Sextus clearly intends to place indicative and commemorative signs on the *same* footing, when he says in *PH* II 101 that a sign is the antecedent in a conditional; and he goes on to give a single account (even if not the expected account) of how the Stoics understand conditionals (II 104).

I would suggest tentatively that it is more likely that Cicero is right. On his view, Chrysippus had not worked out when to treat something as a material implication rather than a genuine conditional. Another interesting instance of the resort to material implication comes in the formulation of the Sorites argument: if two is few, three is few; if three is few, four is few; if four is few . . . and so on.[52] The Stoics who related this argument converted it to the form: 'Not both (two is few and three is not few)', perhaps because they felt uncertain about the exact relation between antecedent and consequent, and were confident only that you would not get the first without the second. In other cases, it is hard to discern why material implication is used.[53]

The Stoic arguments considered so far are designed to ward off certain particular difficulties. It remains for Chrysippus to show how his whole treatment of fate can leave room for alternative possibilities.

The fifth attempt: possibility as aptitude in Philo

One argument to allow for alternative possibilities could be based on Philo's definition of the possible. For Philo said that it was possible for a piece of wood at the bottom of the ocean to be burnt, in virtue of the bare *fitness* of the subject (*epitēdeiotēs*), and some Stoics evidently followed him (see p. 266, n. 46). External obstacles to its being burnt are ignored in assessing possibility. By this test of possibility, alternatives would be possible, even if

---

[52] DL VII 82, and see Sedley [24].

[53] Alex. Aphr. *Fat.* 35 and 37, oscillates between the two forms, without any obvious reason, in his report of some Stoic arguments.

fate ensured that obstacles prevented one of the two outcomes from being realized. But it is doubtful that the Stoics can in general avail themselves of this argument. For most sources[54] expressly distinguish their definition of possibility from Philo's, by saying it lays down *two* necessary conditions for possibility, *not only* something corresponding to Philo's 'fitness', *but also* the absence of external obstacles. The possible is that which admits of being true, there not being opposition from external obstacles.

The difference from Philo's definition is easily obscured. The most serious difficulty, though not the only one,[55] is that the grammatical construction in some of the formulations is ambiguous. Is the absence of obstacles meant to be a second prerequisite for *possibility*, as I have claimed, or merely a prerequisite for the possible thing actually being *true*? This makes all the difference.

The ambiguity helps to account for the disagreement among interpreters, several of whom assimilate the Stoic definition to Philo's.[56] One translates the Stoic definition in such a way that the absence of obstacles appears as a prerequisite of truth, not of possibility.[57] Another does the opposite, and attributes both definitions to Philo, construing the absence of obstacles in one account of Philo's definition as a condition of possibility, not of truth.[58] Yet another interpreter suggests that the Stoics recognized two separate senses of each modal term on the grounds that two criteria are cited in the Stoic definition of necessity.[59] But since it is agreed that there is no mention of two senses in the corresponding definition of possibility, it is easier to suppose that in each case there is a single sense defined by *two* necessary conditions.

That the normal Stoic definition was not Philo's is clearly implied by Boethius. That the insistence on absence of external

---

[54] DL VII 75 explicitly refers to the Stoics. Boethius, 2nd commentary on Aristotle's *Int*, ed. Meiser, 234, cites Philo and the Stoics. Three other sources contrast the definitions without attributing them: Simp. *in Ar. Cat.* 195–6; Alex. Aphr. *Quaest.* I 4, p. 9. 5–7; p. 12. 5–12; ps.–Plu. *Fat.* 571 a.

[55] Another difficulty is that one of the two conditions is occasionally cited without the other, something like Philo's condition being attributed by Plutarch to the Stoics (*Stoic. rep.* 1055 df).

[56] So Mates [44], 41; Bochenski [39], 87; Reesor [117].

[57] Reesor [117], 291.

[58] Sambursky [76], 74.

[59] Kneale [43], 122–6.

obstacles is an *additional* precondition of possibility over and above fitness is implied by Alexander, Simplicius and the author of the *De fato* of pseudo-Plutarch.

This finding is amply confirmed by Frede (op. cit. 107–17). In a careful study, he takes the Stoic definitions of four modal terms, as they are recorded by Diogenes Laertius, and he places two constraints on any interpretation. First, the terms (possible, impossible, necessary, non-necessary) should come out as far as possible having the right relation to *each other*. Second, Diogenes' word 'admitting of' (*epidektikon*) should come out having the same sense in each of the definitions where it appears. It emerges that these two reasonable requirements can be conveniently met, only if the absence of external obstacles is taken in the manner suggested above, namely, as an *additional* prerequisite for something's being possible.

We should ask, however, what would have happened if the absence of external obstacles had not been made an extra prerequisite for possibility, and if the normal Stoic definition of possibility had appealed, like Philo's, to mere fitness. Would they then have been able to allow for alternative possibilities in a morally significant sense? I think not; for it is hard to believe that bare fitness to act otherwise than one does would give one a morally significant possibility of acting otherwise. If this fitness is frustrated by external obstacles, could one then be blamed for anything? Nonetheless, there have been comparable arguments in the modern literature, to the effect that we can escape from determinism, by insisting that in something like Philo's sense, we have a capacity or aptitude for acting otherwise than we do.[60]

The sixth attempt: internal causes

A sixth Stoic argument, seems to have been based on a distinction between internal and external causes. But it is hard to be sure what the conclusion of the argument was. Three authors report it in turn: Cicero, Aulus Gellius, and St Augustine, and the last two had both read Cicero's account. According to St Augustine (*City of God* V 10), the aim of the argument was to show that our wills are not subject to necessity at all. The other two accounts are more nuanced, although some phrases in Cicero (*De fato* 39 and 41), taken in isolation, could well have suggested the

[60] See M. Ayers, *The Refutation of Determinism* (London, 1968).

Augustinian interpretation. Thus Chrysippus is said to reject necessity, to aim at escaping necessity while retaining fate, and to side more with those who want the mind to be free from necessity of motion.

In order to decide what the conclusion was, we should first consider the premisses, to see how they drew the distinction between internal and external causes. Zeno had made causes into sufficient conditions, by saying that it was *impossible* (*adunaton*) for a cause to be present and that which it caused to be absent (*SVF* I 89). But Chrysippus drew a distinction between causes.[61] External conditions are only necessary and never sufficient to produce human action. Among the external necessary conditions, one of the most important is the sensory appearance (*phantasia*) which is presented to the agent. From the *external* necessary conditions of action we should distinguish the *internal* efficient causes, some of which produce their results necessarily ('necessario'), some not (Cic. *Top.* 59–60). The most important of these are assent (*sunkatathesis*) and impulse (*hormē*), and we are told by one source that every impulse actually is an assent.[62]

If we move back a stage, and ask what is the cause of assent, we find that the external sensory appearance (*phantasia*) is again merely a necessary condition. The internal cause of assent is the character and quality of our minds. Chrysippus compares a cylinder rolling down a slope. The external necessary condition needed for its rolling is the agent who pushes it, but the internal cause is its own character and nature.[63]

With the distinction of internal and external causes now outlined, I am in a position to distinguish three interpretations of Chrysippus' conclusion. On one view, the distinction of causes is meant to show that our assent is not subject to necessity. That is

---

[61] For the fullest account of Chrysippus' distinctions, see Clem. *Strom.* VIII 9; Cic. *Top.* 58–60. For their application to human conduct, see Cic. *Fat.* 39–45; Alex. Aphr. *Fat.* 13–14; Aul. Gell. VII 2; Origen, extracts in *SVF* II 988 (esp. p. 288, line 23); 989 (esp. p. 289, line 12); Plu. *Stoic. rep.* 47, 1055 f–1056 d.

[62] Stob. *Ecl.* II (=*SVF* III 171). They differ in that the assent is directed to a proposition, the impulse to the action which it mentions. Alex. Aphr. (*de An.* 72.13–73.1) rejects the idea that every assent is an impulse, but not the idea that every impulse is an assent. Plutarch, however, gives us the weaker formulation that an impulse cannot exist without assent (*Stoic. rep.* 1057 a), and other passages the still weaker one that an impulse *culminating in action* cannot exist without assent (*Acad.* II 24; Plu. *Stoic. rep.* 1057 b).

[63] Aul. Gell. VII 2.11; Cic. *Fat.* 42–3.

how St Augustine takes it. It is suggested by some of Cicero's phrases, and we shall see that there were others besides the Stoics who hoped to escape from necessity by relying on *internal* causes. On the other hand, it is baffling how the argument could in fact establish that our assent is not necessitated. Why should it not be necessitated, for example, by our own inner state?

An alternative has been suggested by Donini.[64] According to this, Cicero misunderstood Chrysippus, who was not making a point about necessity at all. Allowing all things to be necessitated by fate, and fate to include all causes, he nonetheless looked for a way in which moral responsibility could be preserved. It can be, in Chrysippus' view, if the distinction between internal and external causes is used in order to define a sense in which things can still be up to us or in our power ('in nostra potestate' will be the Latin translation of *eph' hēmin*: see Cic. *Fat.* 41, 43, 45; Aul. Gell. VII 2.15). Donini takes it that this sort of account is intended by Gellius.

A third interpretation has been suggested to me by Frede. This alternative takes its start from the fact that Cicero says (*De fato* 39) that Chrysippus tried to adopt a *middle* position. He was between those who said that all things happen by fate in such a way that fate exercises the force of necessity, and those who said that our minds move without any fate at all, although he sided more with those who wanted our minds to be free from any necessity of movement. It would be possible to assign Chrysippus a *middle* position, if we do two things. First, we should emphasize that Chrysippus is sometimes described as denying, not necessity (*tout court*), but the necessity of *fate* ('necessitas fati', Cic. *Fat.* 39). Again, he attacks those who attach necessity to *fate* (42), as his opponents are said to do (40). We shall be obliged to reinterpret the references to Chrysippus' denying necessity as elliptical allusions to his denying the necessity of *fate*. Second, we should take fate to consist only of external causes. In denying the necessity of *fate*, he would then not be denying the *existence* of necessity, but only making a point about its source. Necessity would not be derived from fate, i.e. from *external* causes.

But what would be the point of arguing this? It would be to draw a conclusion about what is 'in our power'. Impulse (41) and assent (43) are in our power. For their perfect cause is the

[64] Donini [87].

character and quality of our minds, which may be compared with the inner nature of the rolling cylinder (cf. Aul. Gell. VII 2.7–11). What matters about this perfect cause is that it is *internal*;[65] and, for the purpose of assessing whether something is in our power, Chrysippus simply does not consider whether it is necessitated, but only whether it is necessitated by *external* causes. We shall see that this is exactly the view attributed by Alexander of Aphrodisias to his Stoic opponents.[66]

If either of the last two interpretations is correct, then the present argument does not after all belong with the other ones we have been discussing. For there will be no attempt to deny that everything is necessitated. The strategy will rather be to find room for moral responsibility in spite of necessitation.

A difficulty for the third interpretation is that it makes Chrysippus identify fate, not with the sum total of causes, but only with the external ones. Whether he did so is hard to determine. Cicero believes that he did (*Top.* 59; *Fat.* 41 and 43). Moreover, this is mentioned by Plutarch (*Stoic. rep.* 1056 b) as a possible interpretation of Chrysippus, though not as his explicit contention. Aulus Gellius also speaks at times (VII 2, 7–8 and 11) as if the character of our minds exercised a causal influence independently of fate. A number of modern commentators, therefore, accept that fate is confined to *external* causes. On the other side, however, Plutarch complains that if Chrysippus does mean to confine fate to external causes, he will be contradicting what he says elsewhere. For according to Plutarch (*Stoic. rep.* 1056 b) Chrysippus claims that nothing rests or moves in the slightest degree except in accordance with the reason of Zeus, which is identified with fate, while fate is identified with an inevitable necessity, not with a mere necessary condition which can be overridden. Gellius also reports that for Chrysippus *all* things are compelled by a necessary and principal reason and are bound together by fate. Moreover, he quotes Chrysippus' definition of fate as a natural order of *all* things, following one another in succession from everlasting with an unavoidable interconnection (VII 2.3 and 7). Cicero agrees that, for Chrysippus, *all* things happen by fate (*Fat.* 21). One source records that the

---

[65] Contrast the sensory appearances, which are external. But they do not stop assent from being in our power, because they are not *perfect* causes of assent, but only *auxiliary* causes (*adiuvantes* is the Latin translation of the Greek *sunerga*, 41–2).

[66] *Fat.* 13; 26; cf. *Quaest.* II 4, p. 50, 30.

inner impulse (*hormē*), which is apparently an assent, is given to us by fate in Chrysippus' opinion.[67] Indeed, it was the common view of Stoic theory in general, and of Chrysippus' theory in particular, that the necessity of fate applied to every detail.[68] The third interpretation, then, must saddle Chrysippus with a volte-face about the comprehensiveness of fate.

On any interpretation, the argument does not seem to me a happy one. On the first interpretation, it tries like the others, but fails, to reject necessity. On either the second or the third, it takes a view which I do not myself believe, but which has been popular in modern times, that moral responsibility is compatible with universal necessitation.

Whatever Chrysippus' position in the present argument, it is not the same as the appeal by Philo and certain Stoics to possibility as aptitude in the preceding one. This will be clear enough if Chrysippus is not denying necessity at all. But even if he is denying it, and allowing for alternative possibilities, he still differs from Philo. For unlike Philo he recognizes that external circumstances can restrict possibilities by failing to supply a necessary condition.

The seventh attempt: epistemic possibility

Two final Stoic attempts to escape necessity, and to allow for alternative possibilities, are recorded by Alexander of Aphrodisias, in his *De fato* 10, although he does not himself tell us who devised the arguments. The opening moves of the first argument are best given in a footnote.[69] What matters is that, at a certain point, the

---

[67] Nemes. *Nat. hom.* 35 (=*SVF* II 991). Reesor [117], 287, seeks to disarm this reference by suggesting that what is given us by fate is not impulse, but merely the power of giving or withholding assent. Her evidence is that impulse is elsewhere said to be in our power. But this will not serve as evidence if, as we are told elsewhere, the Stoics were willing to argue that things can be in our power (or up to us) in spite of being fated and necessitated.

[68] All the sources in nn. 31 and 34 above, except Alexander, mention Chrysippus in particular.

[69] The argument starts from the Stoic definition of the possible as what is prevented by nothing from occurring. If this is to be faithful to the Stoics' intentions, Alexander must be referring to prevention whether by intrinsic unfitness, or by external obstacles. The idea is mooted by the Stoics that the opposite of what happens by fate is not actually *prevented* from happening, and is therefore possible. To this the objection is raised that the causes which make one thing happen in accordance with fate equally cause its opposite not to happen; for, on the Stoic view, it is impossible for the same circumstances to be attended by opposite results. At this point, the Stoics try to establish that alternatives are *not* prevented, by means of the epistemic argument cited in the text.

Stoics, who are presumably the authors of the argument, try to establish that alternatives are not prevented, by pleading that we often do not *know* what factors prevent the things which fail to occur. But Alexander protests this cannot be accepted as a proof that they are not prevented. And he adds that, if anyone pressed the plea of ignorance further, and it is not clear that anyone did, he would end up with a merely epistemic sense of possibility. He would be saying that, even if everything happens in accordance with fate, alternatives are still possible as regards the future; and he would mean merely that they are compatible with the limited state of our knowledge.

Certainly this can be a useful way of talking, but in spite of Tony Long's spirited defence of the Stoics,[70] my sympathies lie with Alexander. For a merely epistemic sense of possibility would not help with any of the moral problems that concern the Stoics. If the question is how praise and blame can be appropriate it cannot help to say that there is an *epistemic* sense in which a person has the possibility of acting otherwise than he does.

The eighth attempt: non-necessity as ceasing to be true

In the other argument cited by Alexander, an appeal is made to the definition of a necessary proposition as one which will *always* be true. This looks slightly closer to Diodorus' requirement that a necessary proposition will never be false than to the Stoic requirement that either it does not admit of being false or else it is prevented from being false by external circumstances.[71] If the argument was devised by a Stoic, then it may have been intended as an *ad hominem* argument against Diodorean determinism. But in fact the argument can be adapted so that it applies equally to a Stoic or to a Diodorean definition of necessity.

The argument is that it cannot be a necessary proposition that there will be a sea battle tomorrow. For this proposition, with its future tense, cannot remain true once the battle is over. (Indeed, it might be added, it will then become false.)

At least two doubts should be raised about this argument. First, were the Stoics and Diodorus right to agree, as they did, that a change from truth to falsity would prove a proposition not to be necessary? After all, the proposition that Scipio will die is like the proposition that there will be a sea battle tomorrow, in containing a future tense, which will prevent it from being true after the event. Yet, for all that, Scipio's contemporaries could justifiably regard it as a necessary proposition that he would die.

Then there is the question whether propositions do change from truth to falsity. Diodorus evidently maintained that the proposition that Scipio will die cannot so change (Cic. *Fat.* 17–18). He presumably had not considered the problem created by the future tense 'will'. A modern logician would deal with this problem, by saying that there is not a *single* proposition that Scipio will die, which changes its truth value from true to false. Rather, each time the sentence 'Scipio will die' is used, it expresses a *different* proposition. One speaker expresses the proposition that Scipio's death is later than his utterance; another speaker expresses the different proposition that Scipio's death is later than his quite *different* utterance. Of these two propositions, the first is changelessly true and the second changelessly false. There is not a *single* proposition which changes from true to false.

The Stoics are now confronted with a dilemma. Either their test for necessity prevents it from being a necessary proposition that Scipio will die. Or, if they avail themselves of modern logic, in order to avoid that result, their test will make *all* propositions necessary, even the proposition that there will be a sea battle tomorrow. For *no* propositions will change from true to false.

Résumé

I hope it will have been of some use to distinguish these eight arguments, for they are not always sharply distinguished. The fifth has been assimilated to the sixth[72] the seventh to the fifth,[73] and the third to the fourth.[74] In particular, I would dissent from the view that the Stoics allow *only* an epistemic possibility so that other arguments must be seen as versions of the seventh.[75]

[72] Reesor [117], (endorsed by Long [106], 189 n. 55) ascribes to the Stoics a definition of possibility like Philo's and then relates that definition closely to the fifth argument about internal causes.

[73] The authors of the argument for epistemic possibility (the seventh) quote in their support something like Philo's definition from the fifth.

[74] Donini [86] remarks on this conflation.

[75] Long [106], 176; 189; n. 15; and [104], 248, 256: 'Possibility exists to the extent that, but only to the extent that, men are ignorant of the future.'

My conclusion is that the ancients were right to regard as unsuccessful the various Stoic attempts to escape from commitment to necessity. In that case, my earlier comparison of Stoic with modern views can stand: they did relate causation firmly both to exceptionless regularity and to necessity.

POSITIONS ADOPTED IN THE ANCIENT DEBATE ON CAUSAL DETERMINISM

I have discussed Chrysippus' strategy of trying to retreat from commitment to necessity in the context of the Stoics' innovative treatment of causation. But it is more usually discussed in the context of the ancient debate on causal determinism. And in this connection too, Chrysippus' retreat is of considerable interest. For it can be seen as one of several alternative positions adopted in that debate: I can usefully distinguish five others. In doing so, I have been much helped by the lucid publications of Robert Sharples.[76]

(i) Surprisingly, those Stoics who looked for a sense in which they could deny necessity came close to a certain group of their opponents. Their opponents denied from the start that every event occurred of necessity. But they were then embarrassed, as we have seen, by the charge that changes which occurred not of necessity would be causeless. To escape this charge, we saw some of them insisting that they were not postulating causeless changes, but only changes with a special kind of cause: a fortuitous cause, an internal cause, or a mere necessary condition.

The net result of this manoeuvre was that both parties were looking for a way of showing that something could be caused without being necessitated. The difference between their conclusions would only be that those Stoics who had committed themselves to acknowledging the necessitation of all effects would need to distinguish a sense in which they were necessitated and a sense in which they were not.

(ii) The claim to have found a special kind of cause was not the only line taken against the Stoics. A less common reply to them was that events could occur without a cause. I have argued

---

[76] See his [139], § 4, 'The Problem of Uncaused Motion', 44–6, and his references below relating to 'hard' determinism.

elsewhere[77] that Aristotle has a successful argument in
Metaph. E 3, to show that coincidences lack causes. They lack
causes because they lack explanations. This should help us to
understand some remarks of Alexander of Aphrodisias which
have been found puzzling. Once in the *De fato*, and once in the
Mantissa (if he is the author of the relevant section), Alexander
slips from arguing for a special sort of cause into arguing for no
cause at all.[78] And in this, he need not be devising a fantastical
argument of his own, as has been suggested,[79] but simply following the opinion of Aristotle in *Metaph.* E 3. The best known
attempt, however, to introduce causeless events is that of
Epicurus with his uncaused atomic swerve.[80]

(iii) The Stoics too had more lines of argument. One line no
longer seeks a sense in which necessity can be denied. Indeed,
necessity is asserted,[81] and it is claimed that our ordinary concepts
of morality and conduct are compatible with the necessity of all
things.[82] We have already encountered this as an alternative
interpretation of one of the earlier arguments. The most important
moral concept is that of an action's being up to us (*eph' hēmin*).
It is claimed that an action is up to us, if it is in accordance with
our impulse (*hormē*), and occurs *through* us (*di' hēmōn*). And it is
explicitly denied that an action's being up to us implies the
possibility of alternative actions.[83]

In both respects the argument is reminiscent of modern ones.
The idea that an action's being up to us depends on the occurrence of a mental event has been described and attacked by
Gilbert Ryle.[84] The idea that it does *not* depend on the existence
of alternative possibilities reminds us of Moritz Schlick's account
of freedom. According to Schlick, a man is free so long as he

---

[77] *Necessity, Cause and Blame*, Ch. 1 (see final note).

[78] *Fat.* 8 (174, 3–11): spontaneous events lack causes. *Mant.* 170, 2–171, 27: an accidental cause is not a cause (171, 13–14), and therefore some events lack causes (170, 7–8; 172, 9). See Sharples [139].

[79] Alexander need not be guided by the rather disreputable argument which Long [104], 251, rightly deplores.

[80] Lucr. II 216–93; Cic. *Fat.* 22–3; *Fin.* I 19; *ND* I 69; Diog. Oen. frag. 32 ii–iii (Chilton).

[81] Alex. Aphr. *Fat.* 13; 34; 36; Diogenian. *apud* Eus. *PE* VI 8, 265 d (=*SVF* II 998).

[82] Diogenian. loc. cit. 265 d–267 a; Alex. Aphr. *Fat.* 13–14; 33; 35–8; Nemes. *Nat. Hom.* 35.

[83] Alex. Aphr. *Fat.* 13; 26; cf. *Quaest.* II 4, p. 50, 30.

[84] Gilbert Ryle, *The Concept of Mind* (London, 1949).

does not act under compulsion, where compulsion is defined as the hindrance of natural desires by external factors or by unnatural internal ones.[85] However, Schlick's idea differs from the present one in that he does not admit the necessity of all things.

(iv) In one version, the last line of argument goes over to the offensive. In a style reminiscent of certain modern authors (Hobart, Schlick),[86] it argues that our ordinary conceptions about conduct actually require fate (which Alexander, in his report, still associates with necessity). Without fate, there would be no law, no right or wrong, no virtue or vice, no good or bad, nothing praiseworthy or blameworthy, no honour or punishment, no reward or correction, no wisdom, and no knowledge of right or wrong.

(v) The rarest view in antiquity was that which William James has called *hard* determinism. The hard determinist not only maintains that everything is necessary, *but also* accepts that, because of this, there is no moral responsibility. The first Stoic, Zeno, has an argument with which a hard determinist would agree, though it is unlikely that he himself, with his strong moral views, was a hard determinist. If the thief pleads it was fated that he would steal, we can reply it was fated he would be thrashed (DL VII 1, 23). Where does this argument come from? The earliest instance I know of the same pattern of argument appears in a non-philosophical context. In Aeschylus' *Choephoroe* (909–11), Clytemnestra seeks to excuse herself for the murder of Agamemnon by blaming fate. Orestes replies that fate now has something in store for her. Subsequently, Zeno's contemporary and rival Epicurus anticipated, and objected to, an analogous argument which assigned chance necessity to our admonishing and being admonished.[87] Presumably, Epicurus envisaged a determinist who was faced with the difficulty that necessity would remove the justification for admonishing people, and who replied by saying that, justifiable or not, the practice of admonition was necessitated. There are signs of a similar move in Eusebius,

[85] Moritz Schlick, 'When is a man responsible?', in his *Problems of Ethics,* tr. by David Rynin (New York, 1939).
[86] Alex. Aphr. *Fat.* 35–7. Cf. R. E. Hobart, 'Free Will as Involving Determination and Inconceivable Without It', *Mind* 43 (1934), 1–27; Schlick, op. cit.
[87] Epicurus, *On Nature* (34.27 Arrighetti): 'For if someone assigned *tēn kata to automaton anankēn* to admonishing and being admonished . . .'. I learnt of this passage from David Sedley.

and Robert Sharples has drawn my attention to two other examples in Manilius and Galen.[88] But the strategy is comparatively rare, and in any case does not go quite all the way to denying the existence of moral responsibility, or the justifiability of our moral practices.

To summarize the history of the controversy, as I see it: in Aristotle's time, determinists were not differentiated into the hard, who denied moral responsibility altogether, and the soft, who claimed that it was compatible with determinism. On the contrary, Aristotle addresses himself to undifferentiated determinists, and raises against them objections, to show that determinism is incompatible with normal ways of thinking about conduct. The 'soft' reply, that there is no incompatiblity, did not come until much later, perhaps with Chrysippus, the third head of the Stoic school. The 'hard' reply, that, thanks to determinism, there is indeed no moral responsibility, probably had little appeal. But quite early Zeno, the founder of the Stoic school, and Epicurus, his contemporary, were conscious of an attitude which hard determinists share, namely, that punishment and admonition are inevitable, whether or not justifiable.[89]

---

[88] Eus. *PE* VI 6, 15 (244 a); Manil. *Astron.* IV 106–18; Galen, *Quod. animi mores* 11 init. (IV 815 K).

[89] The material in this paper is drawn from a forthcoming book, *Necessity, Cause and Blame* (London and Ithaca, 1980). Points not exclusively connected with the Stoics are argued more fully there.

I should like to acknowledge my debt to the writings of P. L. Donini, Michael Frede, A. A. Long, Mario Mignucci, and Robert Sharples, and to the comments generously offered me by the last four of these, and by Myles Burnyeat and Malcolm Schofield.

PRECONCEPTION, ARGUMENT, AND GOD

Malcolm Schofield

Cicero reports of Zeno the Stoic that he deemed the senses trustworthy, because he held that a 'grasp' or 'apprehension' (*comprehensio*, Greek *katalepsis*) achieved by the senses is both true and reliable—not in that it grasps all that is in a thing, but inasmuch as it lets slip nothing that could fall within it; and because Nature has given a sort of yardstick (*norma*, Gk. *kanōn*) and starting-point (*principium*, Gk. *archē*) for knowledge of herself —and in consequence there are imprinted subsequently in men's minds notions (*notiones*, Gk. *ennoiai*) of things, which open not merely starting-points but 'latiores quaedam ad rationem inveniendam viae' ('certain broader roads to the discovery of? right reason? the rational order in things') (*Acad.* I 42).

Earlier chapters of this book have been concerned with the idea of unassailable starting-points of knowledge and belief— whether with sceptical doubts of their existence or with the Stoic conviction that reality can be grasped by the senses and the Epicurean doctrine that *all* perception is true. This chapter will consider rather the 'notions subsequently imprinted' and the 'broader roads' of which Cicero speaks. Parts of the territory have, of course, been explored already, in Chapters 6 to 8 (on logic and proof), and in Chapters 9 and 10 (on causation). I shall attempt a rather wider view of it, although like the authors of those chapters I shall confine myself largely to the Stoics, whose position on the issues I want to take up is less clear and has perhaps received less perceptive attention than the familiar Epicurean theory that the secrets of nature will yield themselves to the empiricist enquirer who combines appeal to analogy with recourse to confirmation and disconfirmation in judicious proportions. The evidence which my enquiry ought to review is vaster than the limits equally of this book and of my competence can accommodate. So I shall restrict myself still further to notions and arguments in one particularly important area of Stoic thought, namely theology.

Chrysippus held that the proper order for the philosophical curriculum is to take logic (which included epistemology) first, but to finish with theology (Plu. *Stoic. rep.* 1035 ab; cf. *SVF* II, p. 299, 3–8). We, too, shall begin with the Stoics' epistemological foundations. We shall examine in particular the connection they made between 'apprehension' (i.e. knowledge) and understanding, and the relation between their views on this topic and their conception of the roles of argument and common sense in epistemology. We shall then be in a position to explore the use they made of these and cognate ideas in the great edifice they built upon the foundations.

THE STOIC DEFENCE OF COMMON SENSE

Zeno was the G. E. Moore of Hellenistic philosophy. It is not just that, like Moore, he was fond of using his hands to make a point. Zeno had something like Moore's certainty of the truth of certain sorts of proposition about the world. And in particular he held, as Moore was to argue in his later years, that this certainty derives from the evidence of the senses, i.e. according to him from *phantasia kataleptikē*, 'apprehensive presentation', an impression which is caused by a real external object and accurately represents it (DL VII 45–6, 49, with *M* VII 236, 248, *Acad.* II 18, 77). So far as I know, it is not reliably reported anywhere that Zeno advanced any arguments for the existence of such presentations. Perhaps he did. But whether he did or not, it is very likely that he regarded his position as a matter of common sense. Anyone not infected with philosophy, he might have said, would of course take it to be obvious that our normal waking experience does often satisfy the two criteria of apprehensive presentation mentioned above—unlike, for example, dreams and hallucinations. 'In ordinary life,' says Sandbach, sympathizing with the Stoics, 'every man has no doubt that what "appears to him" is really there, that the sun *is* shining, that those objects are pomegranates, that a waggon and horses are bearing down on him. Only occasionally will he have doubts, so that (if he is a Stoic) he will say that he has a *phantasia akataleptos*. For the most part he will believe without reservation that his presentations give him a grasp of external reality.'

Certainly Zeno's doctrine of apprehensive presentation stands in marked contrast to the epistemological stances of the sceptics and the Epicureans. Ancient scepticism was a philosophy dominated by the question: 'Am I ever justified in affirming that *p* rather than that not-*p*?' (where '*p*' takes as its values propositions about what really is the case). Its whole object—in practice if not always in theory—was to show that, whatever value of '*p*' you might choose, you could never provide sufficient grounds, whether derived from the senses or excogitated, for asserting its truth rather than its falsehood. Epicureanism, on the other hand, was an uncompromisingly dogmatic philosophy, haunted, none the less, by a sceptical fear. For Epicurus' physics and ethics are in intention strictly regulated by what he called canonic (DL X 38; cf. 31); and the epistemology of the canonic rests upon an argument (preserved in the *Sovran Maxims*) for the reliability of all sense perceptions (*aisthēseis*) without exception; and this argument turns on the thought that if you simply reject any one perception you will throw all the rest into confusion and so throw out the criterion (i.e. the epistemological standard) of truth altogether (X 146–7). No doubt Epicurus conceived that whatever reasons we may think we have for rejecting a single sense perception are far outweighed by the reasons we have for treating each sense perception as no more nor less reliable than any other (X 31–2). In thus resisting the threat of scepticism he paid a heavy price. Although the claim that all sense-perceptions are true is meant to sound paradoxically uncontroversial (is not 'perceive' a success verb?), it quickly transpires that this appearance is specious once we realize that dreams and sensory delusions are counted as perceptions (e.g. X 32). And as has often been noticed, the cost of making dreams and delusions true is to devalue the concept of truth when applied to normal perceptions of pomegranates, waggons, and so on—or would be, if Epicurus were consistent (cf. e.g. Plu. *Col.* 1121 a–e).

Imperviousness to the sort of doubts about the reliability of the senses which so impressed the Epicureans and the sceptics need not entail a lack of interest in those doubts on Zeno's part nor a failure to comprehend them. It might even be a result of deciding, after due consideration, that the only way to avoid the thrusts of the sceptic and the desperate foils of the Epicurean was to take an uncomplicated stand on the questions which exercised them and to uphold common sense against the subtleties of dialectic.

Perhaps the very fact that Zeno was prepared to adopt the language of *phantasia*, 'presentation', in articulating his account of apprehension and understanding indicates that at least he shared with the Epicureans a problem: how far are we justified in inferring from how things appear to us to how they are in the world? Compare Moore's allegiance to the vocabulary of 'sense-data', which was one sign that his emancipation from Descartes and Hume was only half complete.

But that is speculation. We are rather better informed about the theory of understanding (*epistēmē*) which Zeno built upon his doctrine of apprehensive presentation (*M* VII 151, *Acad.* I 41–2): and no wonder, for it supplies the basis for his account of the sage, a topic which evidently commanded more of his attention than did the problem of epistemological foundations. The Stoic sage, like the philosopher of the central books of Plato's *Republic*, possesses a perfect understanding of reality, buttressed by the ability to give an account of itself and unshakeable, in consequence, by the dialectic of opponents. Zeno seems to agree with Plato that the central task of epistemology is to explain what such understanding consists in and how, starting from what our senses tell us about the world, we may arrive at it. He does not agree with Plato's thesis that we begin with nothing but *doxa*, opinion, and that to move from opinion to understanding is necessarily to undergo a radical change of view about what truths there are and about what things are real. Zeno concedes that all non-sages are victims of opinions born of incomprehension. But he holds that even fools constantly enjoy apprehensive presentation, and he thinks that understanding is just a form of apprehension—not merely unerring, but (as his famous comparison of the clenched right fist squeezed tightly and forcibly by the left hand illustrates (*Acad.* II 144–5)) firm and unalterable by reason. This seems to entail that the acquisition of understanding involves no more than a reinforcement of the view of the world already achieved by apprehension—an enormously systematic reinforcement, to be sure, whose attainment is supposed to make all the difference between wisdom and folly, virtue and vice. The theory is well matched with Zeno's nominalist material monism, although, as Julia Annas points out, it fits his radically revisionary moral philosophy pretty badly.

Zeno, then, was as interested in the project of establishing the

conditions under which someone may be said to understand that
p as he was in the enterprise, dearer to the hearts of Epicureans
and Sceptics, of establishing the conditions under which one may
be said to be justified in asserting that p. Later the Stoics found
themselves forced to do battle with the sceptics on ground chosen
by the enemy: so much so that one might be tempted to think
that the sceptics' interest in justification was the Stoic's central
concern too. The sceptics began sniping at the Stoics in Zeno's
lifetime, of course; and there is some reason to think that the
final clause in the standard Stoic definition of apprehensive
presentation was added by him in response to criticism from
Arcesilaus. At any rate, Sextus tells us that the words 'such as
could not come to be from a non-existent' (which specify a
further condition beyond the requirements of causation and
representation we have already noticed) were introduced in
order to fend off the complaint of the Academy that indistinguishable presentations may be produced from existents and
non-existents alike (*M* VII 252); and Cicero, who seems to be
aware of this same tradition about the origin of the clause,
acribes the whole definition of which it is a part to Zeno (*Acad.*
II 18, 77). But it was Chrysippus, true to form, who first committed the forces of Stoicism to massive involvement in argument
with the sceptics about the reliability of the senses and the
justification of assent. The evidence for this is too voluminous
even to mention. It will perhaps suffice to recall the six books in
which he collected arguments discrediting the senses—or perhaps,
rather, common sense—entitled 'Against common experience and
usage' (*kata tēs sunētheias*), and the seven (naturally found less
convincing by the Academics) called 'In defence of common
experience and usage' (Plu. *Stoic. rep.* 1036 c, e, 1037 a; *Acad.*
II 75, 87; with DL VII 184, 198, and Cherniss [5] ad *Stoic. rep.*
1036 c). Later Stoics continued the campaign. Antipater, for
example, devoted a great deal of time and effort to the writing of
books against Carneades in particular (cf. *SVF* III, pp. 244, 12–
245, 4). According to Cicero he maintained against the Academics
that consistency required one who asserted that nothing could be
grasped or apprehended to say that that assertion itself at least
could be apprehended (*Acad.* II 28, 109): an argument reminiscent
of some of those charges of self-refutation levelled by Stoics
against sceptics which Burnyeat has recently studied.

No doubt Chrysippus and Antipater wrote on these themes not only in order to keep their students from going over to the opposite camp, but from a growing interest in problems of justification. It was presumably they and other later Stoics who worked out the lines of argument which underlie the defence of the doctrine of apprehensive presentation attributed to Antiochus in Book Two of Cicero's *Academica*. Pride of place must go (as Cicero indicates, 18 *ad fin.*) to the series of transcendental arguments which launch the sequence: if there is no such thing as apprehensive presentation in Zeno's sense, then it would be impossible to perceive anything (18) or remember anything (22) or have technical understanding of anything (22) or discover anything (26) or give credence to a proof (27) or act with the consistency required of the sage (23–5). Notice how readily the Stoics turned to their theory of the conditions of understanding (for all of these items in one way or another constitute such conditions) in order to support their account of what justifies an assertion about the real world. Elsewhere we find them insisting that normal waking experience is just *different* from imagining and dreaming (51–2) and that our very disposition to withhold assent from the presentation which come to us when we know our sensory capacities are at low ebb proves that we are well aware of the fact (52–3). Notice the straightforward appeal to common sense or common experience.

A characteristically Moorean response to the sceptics is attested among some critics of Antipater (who sound more like Epicureans than Stoics, as Professor Sandbach points out to me). Cicero tells us that Antipater was reprehended for spending so much time on controversy with the Academics. It was objected that there is no point in arguing with those who are never convinced by argument; that it is unnecessary to define what knowledge or perception or apprehension is, because it is clear what they are; and—here is the Moorean move—that since nothing (and *a fortiori* no argument) is clearer than *enargeia*, evident presentation or the clear view of things, it is a mistake to try to *argue* that there is something which can be apprehended and perceived (cf. *M* VIII 360). Antipater's supporters (who presumably included Stoics) interestingly replied that they would not have initiated a debate in which they were to speak on behalf of such 'evidence', but that they thought what was said against it should be answered, in case anyone were deceived by the sceptics (*Acad.* II 17).

AN EPISTEMOLOGICAL PROBLEM IN STOIC THEOLOGY

Stoic confidence in the senses, then, was robust, and their assurance of the support of common experience strong. Their principal aim in epistemology was not to justify reliance on apprehensive presentation in the face of sceptic polemic, but to show how from such an assuredly evident starting point the philosophical understanding of the sage could be built up. None the less, the very doctrine of apprehensive presentation was couched in language which seems to acknowledge the force of the sceptic challenge; and increasingly the Stoics found themselves obliged to defend the doctrine and to become immersed in debates about the justification of assent to the presentations of the senses. Their choice of the transcendental argument as principal weapon in their armory was a shrewd one. For its use did not undermine their insistence that the doctrine is just common sense; and it enabled them to elaborate the connection between apprehensive presentation and—what more deeply concerned them—philosophical understanding.

Zeno's sage possesses principally moral and theological understanding. His understanding of God is presumably grounded, like all philosophical understanding, in 'evidence' and common experience. Or are things different in theology? The Stoics seem to have felt much less aversion to argument and to justification in theology than in their theory of apprehensive presentation. Moreover, Stoic epistemology, as we have seen, is at bottom empiricist. But theology is inevitably a metaphysical business. Between assent to individual propositions about particular events or states of affairs in the world accessible to the senses and understanding of God and of his relation to the world there seems an enormous gap. We shall not be surprised to find Stoic efforts to explain how we are entitled to bridge it problematic, although —as will emerge—the enormity of the theological task is not the only reason for their difficulties.

We may begin our examination of these difficulties with a problem raised by Cicero's account of Stoic theology in Book II of *De natura deorum*. He makes Balbus start his exposition by claiming that the existence of the gods seems not to need arguing, on the ground that it is *apertum* and *perspicuum*, plain and evident, to anyone contemplating the sky and the heavenly bodies that they are ruled by a supreme mind (*ND* II 4). A few lines later on we are told that the existence of such a deity is something which we have *cognitum comprehensumque* in our minds—that is, known and grasped (ibid. 5). But, of course, the bulk of the book is occupied by one argument for the existence and providence of God after another. The difficulty is obvious. If we really do have an apprehensive presentation, evident to us, of the existence of God, not only does this truth *seem* not to need arguing; it *does* not need arguing. Yet clearly the Stoics thought the case did need arguing, and at great length. Nor are the arguments they constructed designed merely to rebut the sceptic, like those transcendental and epistemological arguments we noticed at the end of the previous section which, as we saw, left the status of apprehensive presentation as evident undamaged. The theological arguments of *ND* II are in the main inductive and analogical arguments, buttressed by metaphysical presuppositions, which represent *inferences* from physics and biology to the divinity of the universe. Some of them, moreover, are clearly supposed to be strict proofs. And a proof, according to the standard Stoic definition which (as Jacques Brunschwig suggests) may go back to Zeno himself, is 'an argument which, by means of agreed premisses, reveals—by a concludent deduction—an obscure conclusion' (*PH* II 135, 143, *M* VIII 314). When the Stoics worked out proofs (whether conforming to their strict formal criteria of proof or not) for theological propositions, we may presume that they did so on the assumption that only so could the existence and providence of God be *made* evident. This presumption is supported by a doxographical notice from Diogenes Laertius (VII 52): 'According to them [sc. the Stoics] it is by sense perception that we apprehend white and black and rough and smooth, whereas it is by reason that we apprehend things concluded by means of proof, as for example that Gods exist and that they exercise providence.'

At this point one may be inclined to conclude that some of this evidence must be rejected as unsound, or that it must be subjected to a strong amount of interpretation to render it consistent, or that the Stoics were remarkably confused thinkers. We shall have to make a careful examination of their idea of preconception and of its role in theology before we are in a position to decide which alternative, or which permutation of variants of these alternatives, we should choose.

PRECONCEPTIONS

Balbus' speech in *ND* II resembles at least one other Stoic theological treatise in opening with a reference to the 'evident presentation' which we have about God. Plutarch tells us that Antipater began his work 'On the gods' with a brief exposition of the matter: 'we think of God', he said, 'as an animal blessed and imperishable and beneficent towards men' (*Stoic. rep.* 1051 ef). This is a very valuable testimony, for it shows Antipater calling 'evident presentation' what we know the Stoics elsewhere took to be a 'notion' or 'preconception': Chrysippus 'fights especially against Epicurus and against those who do away with providence, basing his attack upon the conceptions which we have of gods in thinking of them as beneficent and humane' (*Stoic. rep.* 1051 de; cf. 1052 b); the Stoics 'make no end of fuss crying woe and shame upon Epicurus for throwing the preconception of the gods into confusion by doing away with providence' (*Comm. not.* 1075 e). What is a preconception, and what role does it play in Stoic philosophy?

Cicero reports that the word *prolēpsis* was first introduced into philosophy in the sense which interests us by Epicurus (*ND* I 44). It will be worth our while to get as clear as we can about his idea of preconception before examining its role in Stoicism. For our evidence we have to turn to the surviving works of Epicurus preserved in Book X of Diogenes Laertius, together with Diogenes' own doxographical notice in the same book and one or two texts in Cicero and Lucretius.

An Epicurean preconcepiton is a concept (*ennoēma*); more precisely, the concept in virtue of which all speakers of a common language understand the basic and commonly accepted meaning of a given word in the language (DL X 37-8 (cf. 33); 123). A preconception is not a proposition, although it may often and perhaps typically be given propositional form: thus because the accepted connotation of the word 'god' is (according to Epicurus) 'imperishable and blessed animal', because we all think of God as an imperishable and blessed animal, the content of our pre-conception can be expressed as: 'God is an imperishable and blessed animal.'

There is little room for doubt about the most prominent function of preconceptions in Epicurus's epistemology. They act as *kanones* or yardsticks against which the views of philosophers and others about general questions are to be tested, and so constitute a criterion of truth (it is only Diogenes, as it happens, who explicitly asserts that preconception is a criterion: X 31). For example, Epicurus bids Menoeceus ascribe to God nothing alien to his blessedness and immortality (X 123); and in the *Letter to Herodotus* belief in the divine administration of the universe and in divine anger and favour is rejected as inconsistent with blessedness (DL X 76-7). Again, if a law is made which turns out not to accord with 'advantage in mutual dealings', then it no longer has the nature of justice; for it does not fit our pre-conception (X 152; *pre*conception because, as David Furley has said, 'we have a conception of what is just *before* we consider the particular instance under discussion').

What is the justification for doing philosophy by inspecting our own preconceptions? We need to grasp what is signified by sounds (sc. preconceptions) 'so that we may be able to refer to them and so judge opinions advanced, questions proposed for enquiry, or difficulties raised; and so that we may not either leave everything undecided by going on proving *ad infinitum*, or else leave sounds empty' (X 37). In other words, justification must come to a stop. Epicurus plainly thought that there was not conceivably any better starting point than preconception. But in his surviving writings there is not much indication what grounds he had for this conviction. Diogenes associates it with his rejection of dialectic, but does not elaborate the point (X 31). There are two features of preconceptions, however, which do very likely account for Epicurus' confidence in using them as criteria. First, Diogenes makes much of the idea that, for the Epicureans, preconceptions are evident or clear (*enargeis*), and indeed connects it with the doctrine just quoted above in Epicurus' own words (X 33). And Epicurus himself writes as if the common thought of gods as blessed and immortal animals derives from clear or evident knowledge of them (X 123). Secondly, Epicurus believed that preconceptions have a healthy causal origin in the deliverances of perception. Diogenes describes preconception (admittedly in Stoicizing terminology) as 'apprehension or right opinion or notion or universal thought stored up (i.e. memory of what has often presented itself externally)—such as "*That* sort of thing is man" ' (X 33). Both Cicero and Lucretius explain the preconception of God as the result of a constant (and therefore presumably reliable) stream of similar images (which are the immediate objects of perception according to the Epicureans); and Cicero stresses that it is imprinted in the minds of men by nature, recording the argument that if all men naturally agree on something, it must be true (*ND* I 43–4, 49, 105; Lucr. V 1169–78).

This Epicurean theory was taken over virtually lock, stock, and barrel by the Stoics. It was presumably Chrysippus who made the appropriation. Zeno, of course, had already taught that from apprehensive presentations there are imprinted in the mind notions, which then constitute the *principia* of *ratio*, as we saw in the quotation at the beginning of this essay (*Acad.* I 42). And Cleanthes, no original nor creative epistemologist, was prepared to invoke common notions in theology (*ND* II 13–15). But the idea of preconception is not attested for either of them, whereas Diogenes explicitly states that Chrysippus held preconception to be a criterion (*DL* VII 54). If he did introduce the idea into Stoicism, this would have been a highly characteristic development. For he it was who worked out in detail, with a plethora of fine distinctions and subdivisions, doctrines left more inchoate by Zeno; and the idea of preconception is an attempt to specify more precisely than Zeno can be shown to have done the exact sort of notion or concept needed in philosophical enquiry. Probably Chrysippus also thought that, if the Stoics were to claim that notions, no less than apprehensive presentations, constitute *principia*, they should say more than Zeno appears to have said to justify reposing so much confidence in them. Such a concern with justification would, as we have seen, again be more characteristic of Chrysippus than of his predecessors. Nor should we by now be surprised to find him tacitly acknowledging that the going in this field had been made not by the Stoic but by another school.

For the Stoics, then, as for Epicurus, preconception is a notion or concept; not any concept, but a general concept (DL VII 54);

not any general concept, but a particularly basic sort of general concept: 'Of concepts some come to be [sc. in an individual person] naturally . . . and without contrivance, but others through our instruction and concern. The latter are called "concepts" only, the former also "preconceptions" ' (*SVF* II, p. 28, 19–22). This account, from Aëtius, does not connect preconceptions explicitly with language. But it does go on to report that 'reason (*logos*), in virtue of which we are called rational, is said to be made up out of preconceptions, the process being completed over the first seven years of life' (ibid. 22–3; cf. Galen, quoting Chrysippus: 'Reason is a collection of certain concepts and preconceptions', ibid., p. 228, 23–4). And the Stoics' belief in the intimate relation between *logos* and language is well known.

A Stoic preconception is not a proposition, any more than an Epicurean preconception is. As a concept, it is a sort of stored or latent thought, which when activated constitutes actual thinking (Plu. *Soll. an.* 961 cd, *Comm. not.* 1085 ab [with Cherniss (5) ad loc.]; cf. Galen, *SVF* II, p. 228, 31–2). But the content of a preconception, as of any rational presentation, will naturally be expressed in propositional form. This explains an apparent ambiguity in the expression *koinē ennoia*, 'common concept', 'common notion'. The Stoics held that many of our preconceptions are common notions (i.e. *concepts* common to all or most men); but often when Plutarch, for example, charges them with doing violence to common notions, he plainly means that they say things at odds with common *beliefs*. The same explanation suffices to account for Epictetus's assumption that possession of a preconception is shown by one's *positing* something; everybody who has a preconception of the good, he says, supposes that it is advantageous and an object of choice and must be sought and pursued in every circumstance (Plu. *Comm. not.* 1073 c etc.; Epict. *Diss.* I 22.1).

Plutarch and Epictetus leave it clear enough what was the most prominent role for preconceptions in Stoic epistemology. They act as *kanones* or yardsticks against which views on general philosophical questions are to be tested (Plu. *Comm. not.* 1083 c, Epict. *Diss.* II 11. 13, etc.). This is what I take to be the doctrine encapsulated in Diogenes Laertius's report that Chrysippus made preconception a criterion (VII 54). Other interpretations of that report are admittedly also current. Thus A. A. Long, for example, writes ([20], 127–8):

The cognitive impression [i.e. apprehensive presentation] by itself [cannot] provide all the information that we need to say 'This is a black dog'. Any statement of such a form also requires the prior acquisition of general concepts. The cognitive impression guarantees that there is some actual object which corresponds precisely to itself. Our general concepts enable the assent to a cognitive impression to be a recognition of *what* its corresponding object is.

And he adds a footnote: 'Hence general concepts are also said to be a criterion of truth.' Long here associates a distinction between what guarantees *that* we are perceiving a real object and what enables us to recognize *what* that object is with the Stoic distinction between apprehensive presentation and preconception. This is an improbable interpretation. On the Stoic view we *experience* apprehensive presentations not merely of sounds, colours, tastes, etc., but of physical objects such as pomegranates (DL VII 177) or Alcestis (*M* VII 254–5). But if I experience an apprehensive presentation of a pomegranate, then it appears to me truly and infallibly that there is a pomegranate. Simply in virtue of having the presentation I recognize what its corresponding object or cause is. Of course, in order to report my presentation and say, 'This is a pomegranate', I need language and so preconceptions. But I do not need any more *information* than is given me already in my presentation. It plainly follows that apprehensive presentations may vary in degree of conceptual richness and syntactical complexity. The Stoics appear to have noticed this consequence. We hear of a distinction, unfortunately obscure, between rational presentations, enjoyed by rational animals, and irrational, enjoyed by the irrational (DL VII 51; cf. *M* VIII 70, 275–6). And Cicero knows of a distinction between purely sensory apprehensive presentations (e.g. of white, sweet, etc.) and presentations which are still in a way sensory but are grasped by the mind (e.g. those expressed in statements like: 'That is white', 'This is sweet', etc.). This latter class are in turn taken to be simpler and more primitive than presentations of physical objects (expressed in statements like: 'That is a horse', 'That is a dog') and presentations which 'as it were embrace a complete grasp of their objects' (expressed in such statements as: 'If it is a man, it is a mortal animal, endowed with reason' (cf. *M* VIII 275–6). Clearly the conceptual component in this last sort of presentation is very large, if indeed it does not exhaust its content.

So it comes as no surprise when Cicero continues: 'From this class notions of things are imprinted on us' (*Acad*. II 21, cf. *M* VII 344–5; I take it that we should stress 'imprinted' here—notions have been in the offing for some while).

It is just possible that the doctrine that preconception is a criterion was meant to point out its role (recognized by the Epicureans, too: DL X 33) in perceptual judgements—to indicate that it is a mental capacity employed in such judgements. That would certainly accord with a familiar use of the word *kritērion* in Greek philosophy. But Hellenistic philosophers were typically concerned with *kritēria* as *guarantees* or *yardsticks* of truth, as Long's own vocabulary betrays. So we do better in this case to follow Gisela Striker's lead and try to construe the doctrine in a way which fits with this more important and interesting use of the expression. She points out ([21] 96–102) that if we consider those passages in our sources which report on the actual employment to which the Stoics put preconceptions and common notions in establishing truth or rejecting falsehood, it transpires that they employed them just as Epicurus had done: as yardsticks. And she infers that this was the sense in which Chrysippus took preconception to be a criterion of truth.

We have already noticed that, just as Epicurus appealed to our preconception of God in order to reject the idea of divine providence, so Chrysippus appealed to it in order to rebut the Epicurean rejection of the idea (a tactic probably already employed, although without use of the term 'preconception', by Cleanthes: *ND* II 13–15). Chrysippus evidently held that any theological proposition which conflicts with our preconception of God must be denied. The same form of argument underlies the Stoic protest that Epicurus 'violates the conceptions by making the velocity of moving bodies equal and denying that any is swifter than any other' (Plu. *Comm. not.* 1082 e), and their objection (characteristic of a general Stoic complaint against sceptics: *Comm. not.* 1059 ab; *M* VIII 157) that the Academics 'annihilate the preconceptions' by their sceptical argument against the notion of growth (*Comm. not.* 1083 ab). Finally, a celebrated passage from Alexander (*Mixt.* 217, 2–9):

He [sc. Chrysippus] tries to establish that these differences in mixture exist by means of the common notions, and in particular he says that we receive these from nature as criteria of truth. At any rate [he points out that] we have one presentation [i.e. of reflection, not of the senses] of bodies composed by juncture, another of bodies confused together and destroyed together, and a third of bodies blended and mutually coextended in this entirety in such a way that each of them preserves its own nature. We would not have this difference of presentations if all bodies which are mixed were [simply] set alongside each other in juncture, whatever the mode of mixing.

Gisela Striker observes that once again Chrysippus invokes pre-conceptions as sufficient ground for *rejecting* a philosophical view which is incompatible with them (in this case, with the very fact of their plurality). As she points out, Alexander begins the passage by suggesting that Chrysippus used the common notions in a *positive* attempt to establish something; but his 'at any rate' (*goun*) looks like conscious backtracking, and in the next chapter he goes on to report a series of *arguments* from sense experience which the Stoics advanced in support of their theory of mixture.

The Stoics seem also to have borrowed from Epicurus the rationale they gave for philosophizing by means of preconceptions. Epicurus himself, as we saw, advanced as his reason for this strategy the claim that we *need* some *basis* for testing opinions and resolving questions and difficulties, since justification cannot go on for ever (DL X 37-8; cf. e.g. Clem. *Strom.* II 4, *M* I 57). Cicero reports the following stretch of reasoning, no doubt Stoic in origin, which is part of an anti-sceptical argument endorsed by Antiochus and runs straight on from a passage we were examining a little while ago (*Acad.* II 21-2; cf. *ND* I 43):

From this class conceptions of things are imprinted upon us, without which there can be no understanding nor enquiry nor debate. But if there were false conceptions (I understand you to call *ennoiai* concep-tions)—well, if these were false or imprinted by presentations of such a king as could not be distinguished from false ones, how could we use them? How could we see what is consistent with each thing and what is consistent?

This passage plainly contains the same defence of preconceptions as we find at the beginning of the *Letter to Herodotus*. Admittedly, as we shall see later, there is more than one way in which the claim that understanding, enquiry and debate are dependent on conceptions can be construed. But the last sentence of our extract shows that it is here intended in the same way as Epicurus intended it: a conception is the yardstick against which we test the truth of propositions put forward in discussion or as object of enquiry.

What special positive marks have preconceptions that we should trust them? The Stoics answered this question, too, as the Epicureans did. Take, first, the idea that preconceptions come to us naturally. One might expect that the Stoics, believing as they did in the pervasive teleology and providential ordering of nature, would make at least as much of this line of argument as the Epicureans. Evidence that they did so is forthcoming not only from Cicero (*Acad.* II 30–1), but from other authors, too—we have already witnessed Alexander reporting Chrysippus as saying that 'we receive [common conceptions] from nature as criteria of truth' (*Mixt.* 217, 3–4). Again, the Stoics appear to have used the argument from the natural *consensus omnium*. Sextus ascribes to the dogmatists the plea that, if the preconception of God as something that exists were false, it would not be shared by nearly all men (*M* IX 61). And Cicero has his Stoic spokesman, Balbus, conclude his explanation of the firmness and permanence of our belief in God with the words: 'The years obliterate the inventions of opinion, but confirm the judgements of nature' (*ND* II 5; cf. 12). Finally, the Stoics, too, appealed to the 'evidence' (*enargeia*) of preconceptions. Plutarch sneers in a single breath at 'these advocates of "evident presentation" and "yardsticks" (*kanones*) of the conceptions' (*Comm. not.* 1083 c). We have already noticed Antipater speaking of our preconception of God as 'evidence'. Despite the silence of our sources, it is likely enough that the ascription of 'evidence' to preconceptions (and, indeed, to apprehensive presentations) goes back to Chrysippus, given that they are to function as *principia*, and given that he introduced so much Epicurean thinking about concepts into the Stoa. It is worth noting that Aristo of Chios, a deviant Stoic contemporary with Zeno and Cleanthes, is supposed to have used the word *enargeia* (in the relevant sense) in cracking a philosophical joke (DL VII 162).

PRECONCEPTION AND THEOLOGICAL ARGUMENT

When Cicero, then, has Balbus speak of the existence of God as something evident and apprehended by the mind, he is following good Stoic practice in drawing our attention at the outset to our preconception of God. As we have seen in the last two or three paragraphs, the Stoics thought that the very existence of such a preconception suffices to guarantee the truth of its content; and they had available to them arguments for defending this belief. Their position here on preconception is directly parallel to their position on the reliability of apprehensive presentation.

How far did Chrysippus attempt to relate his view of preconceptions to the theological proofs which he inherited from his Stoic predecessors and which he worked out himself? With this question we reach the central issue of our enquiry. At first sight the evidence (i.e. principally the theological treatises of Cicero and Sextus, *De natura deorum* and *M* IX 4–194) might suggest that the Stoics kept their appeals to preconceptions pretty well segregated from the physical or metaphysical arguments for the existence and nature of the Gods which they advanced.

Consider, for example, Sextus' account. He tells us (*M* IX 60) that

Those who maintain that gods exist [he evidently has the Stoics principally in mind] try to establish their thesis in four ways, arguing first from the agreement among all men, second from the orderly arrangement of the universe, third from the absurd consequences of rejecting the divine, fourth and last by undermining the opposing arguments.

Whether Chrysippus or any Hellenistic Stoic set out the topic as schematically as this is not known. But the author of the classification presumably felt that his division of the territory corresponded at least roughly with Stoic practice; and although in the sequel it turns out (for example) that Sextus' general characterization of both the first and the second classes of argument was too general, the specimen arguments which he produces do seem to support the propriety of the scheme, even when due allowance is made for the violence done by the scissors-and-paste methods of doxographers to the unity of continuous stretches of philosophical writing. Where, then does argument from preconceptions fit into the classification? Nowhere, on the face of it, in the second class, which consists of positive arguments mostly of a physical or metaphysical sort. It is prominent, however, in the other two classes which are actually discussed by Sextus, i.e. the first and third. Thus under the first division he reports an argument we have already mentioned, that if the preconception of God as something that exists were false, it would not be shared by nearly all men (IX 61). Under the third he records the syllogism (IX 124): 'If gods do not exist, piety is non-existent, as being a sort of justice towards the gods; but according to the common notions and preconceptions of all men piety exists (inasmuch as there is something pious); therefore the divine exists.'

(It is worth pausing for a moment to consider this argument on its own account. Like all the arguments of the section it is formulated in the canonical form of the second Stoic indemonstrable, i.e. *modus tollens* (if *p*, then *q*; but not-*q*; therefore not-*p*)—like all of them, that is, except the Zenonian ontological argument set as a sort of historical appendix at the end of the section (IX 133): 'One may reasonably honour the gods; but those who do not exist one may not reasonably honour; therefore gods exist.' Our syllogism and its predecessor in the text (IX 123) were presumably attempts to represent Zeno's reasoning in the proper Chrysippean style (the discussion in IX 123 makes this very probable). Effectively they say: let the atheist discount proof or preconception of the existence of God if he will; there remains the preconception of piety—and when analysed that proves to involve the preconception of God as existent. Plainly the Stoic who has recourse to this line of argument need not himself concede that the preconception of God is any more or less evident than that of piety.)

A similar segregation of appeals to preconceptions from physical and metaphysical proofs of the existence and nature of God is what we chiefly find in Book II of *De natura deorum*. Here we are not concerned with the rather unsatisfactory formal division of the work (cf. II 3), but with the progress of the argument of the first section (officially concerned with the existence of the gods, but in fact as preoccupied with their nature, the official topic of the second section). We have already seen that the section begins with the claim that the existence of gods is evident and apprehended, a claim which we have linked with Stoic appeals to preconceptions. Much else in chapters 4–12 looks like an appeal to common belief in the gods: of no great philosophical sophistication, to be sure, but doubtless vaguely influenced by an awareness of the Stoic idea of common notions, which are brought into full view at chapters 13–15, where Cicero presents Cleanthes' explanation of the origins of our concept of the gods. But in sketching Cleanthes' fourth reason for our acquisition of the concept, Cicero slips imperceptibly into an analogical proof of the existence of God. And the twenty-nine paragraphs of the section which remain are filled with nothing but proofs, without—it seems—so much as a whisper of preconceptions or common notions at any point.

In Chapter 45, however, at the beginning of the section which supposedly introduces examination of the divine nature, Cicero brings preconception and proof together. He does so in a way which our discussion of Chrysippus' use of preconceptions might have led us to expect:

Since we preconceive by a definite notion of the mind ('certa notione animi praesentiamus') that God is such as to be, first, a living being, and second, unsurpassed in excellence by anything in the whole of nature, I can see nothing which I would rather fit ('accommodem') to this preconception or notion of ours than the first of all candidates: this very universe, which as unsurpassable in excellence I hold to be a living being and God.

Chrysippus used preconceptions as a yardstick by which to rule out as false general philosophical claims that were inconsistent with them. We can scarcely be surprised to find Cicero representing the Stoics as measuring the conclusions of their own arguments against our preconceptions. Balbus here tests his proposition (argued in the preceding section) that the universe is a supremely excellent living being to see whether it 'fits' the preconception of God, and judges that it passes the test with flying colours. This is the same sort of positive use of a preconception as criterion as we find already in Epicurus, when he asserts that if a law fits (*enharmottēi*) our preconception of justice, it is just (DL X 152; cf. Epict. *Diss.* II 11.7–12, 17.6–13).

Although this passage of *De natura deorum* is unique in its explicit application of the theory of preconceptions to the formal proofs for which the Stoics were famous, it is difficult not to look back over the arguments of chapters 15 to 44 and ask the question: is the theory applied *implicitly* there? Consider a syllogism of Chrysippus reproduced by Cicero (II 16):

If there is something in the nature of things which the mind of man and human reason, strength and power cannot produce, that which produces it is assuredly better than man. But the heavenly bodies and all those things whose order is sempiternal cannot be brought about by man. Therefore that through which they are brought about is better than man. But what name could you prefer to give this than 'God'?

It would have been satisfying and appropriate had Chrysippus written a different final sentence: 'But our preconception of God is of a productive agent better than man.' He was content, however, to appeal to our intuitions about the propriety of the use of the word 'god'. Yet that appeal may very easily be read as tantamount to an invitation to consider our preconception of God, particularly in the light of Epicurus' association of pre-conceptions with the commonly accepted meanings of words. And, more generally, all Stoic arguments purporting to prove that the universe or the mind which they take to govern it is divine depend on agreement by language users on what attributes are to *count* as divine. Surely the Stoics will have seen that they must hold that such agreement is the consequence of agreement in our preconceptions?

We are now in a position to grapple with the crucial difficulty about Stoic proofs of the existence of God which we raised earlier: if in advance of argument we can rely upon an evident preconception of God as existent, what room is there for the idea that his existence needs to be made evident by argument? We have simply to make a distinction. In a broad sense it certainly is the case that the Stoics constructed proofs to make evident the existence of God: that is what their numerous arguments for the sentience and rationality of the universe are designed to do. But in a strict sense that is not the aim of these proofs. At any rate on the evidence we have just been reviewing, the Stoics are more accurately interpreted as taking it to be evident that God exists, and as addressing themselves to the man who asks: where in the world can I find the blessed, immortal, sentient, rational, bene-ficent animal which I know God to be? They undertake to prove to this man that, if he will only grant that the rational is better than the non-rational (*M* IX 104; *ND* II 21), or that nothing which lacks soul and reason can produce from itself something animate and possessed of reason (*M* IX 101; *ND* II 22), or that nothing devoid of sensation can have a part of itself that is sentient (*ND* II 22), then he must accept that the world itself is just such a rational, sentient animal. (It is, of course, in these metaphysical assumptions, which were to enjoy magnificent careers in Neoplatonism and beyond, that the chief attractions and the chief epistemological shortcomings of Stoicism lie. I shall speak of the shortcomings a little later. Let us notice here that Zeno's use of the assumptions to argue that man's rationality derives from Nature of which he is a part, and which creates and sustains all his endowments, must have seemed compelling to most of those in the Hellenistic era who were prepared to accept any speculative answer at all to the question of the Xenophontic Socrates (Xen. *Mem.* I 4 8; cf. *M* IX 94, 101, *ND* II 18): 'Where did man get his mind from?'—or as we might rephrase it: 'How does it come about that Nature produces a single rational animal, man?' Certainly the rival Epicurean appeal to the fortuitous clash of atoms seems as inadequate and programmatic as the Stoics complained, lacking as it does any convincing conception of natural selection.)

The Stoics were well aware that their proofs have this structure. At any rate, having shown to their own satisfaction that the world is a sentient, rational animal, they never present any *argument* for the further conclusion that it is divine. That conclusion is simply tacked on at the end of the proof proper, as though acknowledged to be licensed by nothing but our preconception of the divine (e.g. *ND* II 21, 36, 39). The same practice of just adding the inference to divinity at the conclusion is found also, more systematically carried through, in Sextus (e.g. *M* IX 76, 77, 85, 87, 91, 95, 98, 100, etc.).

But Sextus' account creates a difficulty for the interpretation of Stoic theological proofs which I am offering. For although he sometimes puts the concluding inference to divinity in what one might call the pure Ciceronian form: 'So this will be God' (*M* IX 76; cf. 114), he more frequently presents it in a more complex form, which includes the assertion of an existential proposition: e.g. 'It will turn out to be rational, then, and wise, which was [agreed to be the mark] of divine nature. Gods, therefore, exist' (*M* IX 77). This way of putting the point still involves appeal to our preconception of God. But it implies that the mere fact of our possessing such a preconception does not license us to assert his existence; only a proof can establish that the preconception corresponds to something in the real world. It is not possible to determine precisely how the view of preconceptions thus implied differs—as it evidently *does* differ—from the one we attributed to the Stoics on the basis of Cicero's evidence. Perhaps it is just that Sextus is envisaging that our preconception of God is a preconception simply of his nature, whereas Cicero thinks of it as a preconception of his nature *as existent,* or of his nature as *including* his existence. Or perhaps both of them agree in thinking of our preconception as a preconception simply of divine nature, but Cicero takes 'God' in 'God is an immortal, blessed animal, beneficent to men' as a referring expression, whereas Sextus takes it (as a Stoic ought) as a predicate: 'If something is a god, then it is an immortal, blessed animal, etc.' (Notice that the conditional form would suggest that preconceptions grasp the necessary 'connectedness' (*sunartēsis*) of properties.)

It is hard to resist the conclusion that Sextus' report of dogmatic theology is irremediably infected with the epistemological confusion we originally feared that the Stoics were in. His first section (*M* IX 61–74) holds that because we have a preconception of God as existent we are entitled to assert his existence; his second section (*M* IX 75–122) assumes that only proof licenses us to make that assertion. Cicero's account of Stoic theology in his first section, on the other hand, is free of this confusion. It is tempting to surmise that he more accurately represents the position of Chrysippus, who is known to have used the pure Ciceronian form of inference to the divinity of the universe (*ND* II 16; cf. 39). We might then associate the existential form of the conclusion favoured by Sextus with other Stoics (it is explicitly attested for Cleanthes: *M* IX 91). And, finally, we might explain the confusion of Sextus' account as the result of combining Cleanthes' style of argument in his second section with the assertion (which we could connect with Chrysippus but not Cleanthes) that our preconception of God proves that he exists in the first section. But this solution is at once too tidy and too complicated to command credence. The best we can realistically hope is that Chrysippus and his acuter posterity avoided confusion on these issues when writing as accurately and carefully as they could: which the circumspection of the Ciceronian form of theological conclusion gives us reason to hope. Prudence requires us to concede that they may sometimes, for whatever reason, have presented their proofs straightforwardly as proofs of the existence of God—and of his providence, whose defence I have no space to discuss.

In Book II of *De natura deorum* Cicero leads us from appeals to common notions, to explanations of the origins of those notions, to syllogistic proofs of the divinity of the universe, to the elaborate *rationes physicae* of chapters 23–44. We can now see that this sequence is something more than a progressively tougher presentation of Stoic theology, in which disparate chunks of source material are persuasively sewn together by the orator. It reflects Stoic theological strategy. According to that strategy, the philosopher should begin by consulting our common preconception of God, and then inspect the world to find the candidate which best answers to that preconception. Stoic theology not only starts with appeals to the preconception of God; it constitutes nothing but an increasingly profound and elaborate attempt to articulate the structure of rational argument (and so the rational structure of the world) which reinforces confidence in that preconception. Cicero shows us, in short, how, according to the Stoics, 'evidence' (*enargeia*) may be converted into 'understanding' (*epistēmē*).

Preconceptions have a seminal role in this theological strategy. It comes as no surprise, therefore, to find Plutarch reporting the Stoics as claiming that preconceptions supply the seeds from which their system grows (*Comm. not.* 1060 a). Again, in an admittedly somewhat garbled fragment (Plu. *apud* Olymp. *in Phd.* p. 125, 7 Finckh (frag. 215 Sandbach)), he suggests that they introduced 'natural conceptions' in order to solve the *Meno* problem of how enquiry and discovery are possible: either an enquirer knows what he is looking for, and the search is futile, or he does not know, and the search is impossible (an argument perhaps first revived by the Epicureans, as an anti-sceptical dilemma: *M* VIII 337–336 a). Later Stoics give us to understand that philosophy 'articulates' (*diarthroun*) our preconceptions— but that is a story we cannot tell here.

CONCLUSION

Zeno propounded the following argument (*ND* II 22; cf. *M* IX 101): 'Nothing which lacks soul and reason can produce from itself something animate and possessed of reason; but the universe produces things which are animate and possessed of reason; therefore the universe is animate and possessed of reason.' Chrysippus, after putting this syllogism into a canonical form, might have added: 'And these are marks of divinity.'

Now as Jonathan Barnes shows in Chapter 7 of this book, the Stoics misconstrued the epistemological character of proof (and *a fortiori* of theological proof) in taking the pattern of formal deduction to be the ideal way of representing the inferences they were interested in. Their proofs (in theology as elsewhere) are really inductive inferences to the best explanatory hypothesis. This failure of theirs to understand properly what they were about is in a sense immaterial to their success or failure at making inferences to the best explanation. In a sense, however, it is relevant, since their lack of any adequate theory of induction is the natural counterpart to the absence of a proper sense of the limits of induction manifested by the major premiss in Zeno's syllogism. Cicero tells us that Zeno supported his major with an analogy: 'If flutes playing tunes grew on an olive-tree, surely you would not doubt that the olive-tree possessed some knowledge of the flute? What if plane-trees bore well-tuned lyres? You would of course think that there was music in the plane-tree.' We might rather prefer to think that if *that* could happen, anything could happen.

The great defect of Stoic theological argument, however, is the extent and the absoluteness of its reliance on preconceptions—which, to be sure, is not unrelated to its lack of respect for inductive canons. In Zeno's syllogism the whole weight of the inference rests upon a dubious conceptual intuition about causation; and the further inference to the divinity of the universe equally rests on a conceptual intuition about the nature of God. Here is another Moorean element in Stoic thought: what we might call conceptual intuitionism. The weakness of the Stoic position is very similar to the weakness of the appeals made by ordinary language philosophy to 'our' concept of horse or freedom or duty: my intuitions may differ from yours, and there seems no rational way for either of us to persuade the other that he is mistaken, or to win the support of a third party. The Stoics conceived of God as exercising providential care towards men, the Epicureans thought of him as taking no interest in them: you pays your money, and you takes your choice. Each side, of course, gave reasons why preconceptions are reliable guarantees of the truth; but the differences in the content of their preconceptions undermine the reasons given. Thus both sides cited in their support the supposed fact that all or most men agree in their preconception of God. In this instance, however, the Epicureans had to admit that the many contaminate their preconception with false assumptions (DL X 123-4). And on many issues the Stoics were in practice committed to denying the truth of common notions, as Plutarch tirelessly insists. No doubt they, too, pleaded that the common man often takes a false opinion to be a preconception, perhaps because his nature gets warped (so much for the appeal to the naturalness of preconceptions): see e.g. DL VII 89, and in theology *Tusc.* I 30. Yet they had no way of distinguishing between the two that does not beg the question. They might say, for example, that no preconception conflicts with another preconception (Epict. *Diss.* I 22.1), only to have the sceptics flatly (and more plausibly) contradict them (*M* VIII 332 a–333 a). No wonder that some Stoics appear to have settled into a weaker posture, conceding that men differ in their preconceptions of the nature of God, while maintaining that the preconception of his existence is more or less universally shared (*M* IX 61; cf. *ND* II 13). Perhaps we should leave the last word with Sextus (*M* IX 192): 'Different people have different and discordant assumptions about them [sc. the gods], so that neither are all of them to be trusted (because of their inconsistency) nor some of them (because of their equipollence (*isostheneia*)).'

NOTE

This is a shortened version of the paper presented to the Conference in Oxford, considerably revised in the light of criticisms made in the discussion and of my own second thoughts. I am particularly indebted to the conversation and detailed comments of three Cambridge colleagues, Myles Burnyeat, F. H. Sandbach, and David Sedley, whose own writings in the area covered by my essay have been of great help and stimulus to me (especially Burnyeat [55], and his papers 'Examples in Epistemology: Socrates, Theaetetus and G. E. Moore', *Philosophy* 52 (1977), 381–96, and 'Aristotle on Understanding Knowledge', in E. Berti, ed., *Aristotle on Science: the 'Posterior Analytics'* (Atti dell' VIII Symposium Aristotelicum) (Padua and New York, forthcoming), Sandbach [120] and [121], Sedley [24] and [130]. My section entitled 'Preconceptions' develops some ideas of Gisela Striker (see [21]). On the Epicurean side of things see the essay of Long [129] and the monographs of Furley [123], Lemke [124] and Manuwald [125]; on the Stoic side Cherniss's edition of Plutarch's essays [5], Boyancé's article [84], and the relevant sections of the books by Bréhier [30] and Goldschmidt [73]. The valuable article of Goldschmidt [128] was unavailable to me at the time of writing. Of standard works on Hellenistic philosophy I mention those by Bailey [35], Long [20] and Rist [37].

SELECT BIBLIOGRAPHY

The bibliography gives details of all the secondary literature referred to, where this pertains to Hellenistic philosophy or to related aspects of the wider field of ancient philosophy, together with some further useful material.

I. TEXTS AND TRANSLATIONS

The Loeb Classical Library translations of the main sources cited in this volume are:

[1] Hicks, R. D. Diogenes Laertius, *Lives of Eminent Philosophers*, 2 vols. (London and New York, 1925);

[2] Bury, R. G. Sextus Empiricus, 4 vols. (London and Cambridge, Mass., 1933–49). Vol. i contains *PH*, Vol. ii *M* VII–VIII, Vol. iii *M* IX–XI, Vol. iv *M* I–VI (this translation is not always reliable in passages dealing with logic; the best remedy is the collection of passages in translation at the end of Mates [44];

[3] Rackham, H. Cicero, *De Natura Deorum* and *Academica* (London and Cambridge, Mass., 1933).

For the Loeb translation of Plutarch's *Adversus Colotem*, see

[4] Einarson, B., and Lacy, P. H. de Plutarch, *Moralia* Vol. xiv (London and Cambridge, Mass., 1967),

while Plutarch's *De Stoicorum repugnantiis* is in

[5] Cherniss, H. Plutarch, *Moralia* Vol. xiii, Part II (London and Cambridge, Mass., 1976).

A good German translation of *PH*, with interesting introduction, is

[6] Hossenfelder, M. Sextus Empiricus, *Grundriss der pyrrhonischen Skepsis* (Frankfurt am Main, 1968).

Aids to the study of ancient scepticism include the valuable edition of *Acad.*

[7] Reid, J. S. M. Tulli Ciceronis, *Academica* (London, 1885; repr. Hildesheim, 1966), and

[8] Janáček, K. Indices to Sextus Empiricus, in Vol. III or separately as Vol. IV of the Teubner text of Sextus Empiricus, ed. Mutschmann–Mau (Leipzig, 1954, 1962).

The fragments of Timon are collected in

[9] Diels, H. *Poetarum Philosophorum Fragmenta* (Berlin, 1901).

Texts relating to Pyrrhonism and the Empirical school of medicine are collected in

[10] Deichgräber, K. *Die griechische Empirikerschule* (Berlin, 1930).

The largest collection of texts bearing on Stoicism is

[11] Arnim, H. von *Stoicorum Veterum Fragmenta*, 4 vols. (Leipzig, 1903–24); Indices in Vol. iv.

See also

[12] Edelstein, L., and Kidd, I. *Posidonius* Vol. i: *The Fragments* (Cambridge, 1972).

For Epicureanism there are three useful collections:

[13] Usener, H. *Epicurea* (Leipzig, 1887; Rome, 1963). Includes material on the Epicurean School generally.

[14] Bailey, C. *Epicurus, the Extant Remains* (Oxford, 1926). Includes English translation and notes.

[15] Arrighetti, G. *Epicuro, Opere* (2nd edn., Turin, 1973). Includes papyrus fragments of Epicurus, *On Nature*, and Italian translation.

An invaluable aid to study is

[16] Usener, H. *Glossarium Epicureum* (Rome, 1977).

The papyrus text of Philodemus' *On Signs* is edited, with translation and commentary, by

[17] Lacy, P. H. de, and Lacy, E. A. de *Philodemus: On Methods of Inference* (Philadelphia, 1941; 2nd edn. Naples, 1978).

2. GENERAL

General accounts of Hellenistic philosophy may be found in

[18] Zeller, E. *Die Philosophie der Griechen in ihrer geschichtliche Entwicklung*, iii, Abt. 1 and 2: *Die nacharistotelische Philosophie* (4th edn., Leipzig, 1903–9); English translation of the 1st section of iii Abt. 1: Reichel, O. J. Zeller, *The Stoics, Epicureans and Sceptics* (London, 1870); Eng. tr. of the 2nd section of iii Abt. 1: Alleyne, S. F. Zeller, *A History of Eclecticism in Greek Philosophy* (London, 1883).

[19] Hicks, R. D. *Stoic and Epicurean* (New York, 1910; repr. 1962).

[20] Long, A. A. *Hellenistic Philosophy* (London, 1974).

A special study of the notion of a criterion of truth is

[21] Striker, G. Κριτήριον τῆς ἀληθείας (Göttingen, 1974); *Nachrichten der Akademie der Wissenschaften in Göttingen,* Phil.-hist. klasse, 1974, Nr. 2, 47–110.

There is much to be learned about physical and intellectual aspects of ancient schools of philosophy from

[22] Clarke, M. L. 'The Garden of Epicurus', *Phoenix* 27 (1973), 386–7.

[23] Lynch, J. P. *Aristotle's School* (Berkeley, 1972).

[24] Sedley, D. 'Diodorus Cronus and Hellenistic Philosophy', *Proceedings of the Cambridge Philological Society* 203 (N.S. 23) (1977), 74–120.

3. STANDARD WORKS ON SCHOOLS AND TOPICS

(A) *Scepticism*

[25] Brochard, V. *Les Sceptiques grecs* (2nd edn., Paris, 1923; repr. 1969).
[26] Goedeckemeyer, A. *Die Geschichte des griechischen Skeptizismus* (Leipzig, 1905).
[27] Pra, M. dal *Lo scetticismo greco* (2nd edn., Rome–Bari, 1975).
[28] Robin, L. *Pyrrhon et le scepticisme grec* (Paris, 1944).
[29] Stough, C. L. *Greek Skepticism* (Berkeley and Los Angeles, 1969).

(B) *Stoicism*

[30] Bréhier, E. *Chrysippe et l'ancien stoïcisme* (2nd edn., Paris, 1951).
[31] Christensen, J. *An Essay on the Unity of Stoic Philosophy* (Copenhagen, 1962).
[32] Pohlenz, M. *Die Stoa* (2nd edn., Göttingen, 1959).
[33] Rist, J. M. *Stoic Philosophy* (Cambridge, 1969).
[34] Sandbach, F. H. *The Stoics* (London, 1975).

(C) *Epicureanism*

[35] Bailey, C. *The Greek Atomists and Epicurus* (Oxford, 1928).
[36] Farrington, B. *The Faith of Epicurus* (London, 1967).
[37] Rist, J. *Epicurus, An Introduction* (Cambridge, 1972).
[38] Witt, N. W. de *Epicurus and his Philosophy* (Minneapolis, 1954).

(D) *Logic*

[39] Bochenski, I. *Ancient Formal Logic* (Amsterdam, 1951).
[40] Corcoran, J., ed. *Ancient Logic and its Modern Interpretations* (Dordrecht, 1974).
[41] Egli, U. *Zur stoischen Dialektik* (Basel, 1967).
[42] Frede, M. *Die stoische Logik* (Göttingen, 1974).
[43] Kneale, W. and M. *The Development of Logic* (Oxford, 1962).
[44] Mates, B. *Stoic Logic* (2nd edn., Berkeley and Los Angeles, 1961).

4. SCEPTICISM

Books

[45] Burkhard, U. *Die angebliche Heraklit-Nachfolge des skeptikers Aenesidem* (Bonn, 1973).
[46] Dumont, J.-P. *Le Scepticisme et le phénomène* (Paris, 1972).

312   Doubt and Dogmatism

[47] Hartmann, H. *Gewissheit und Wahrheit: der Streit zwischen Stoa und akademischen Skepsis* (Halle, 1927).
[48] Hirzel, R. *Untersuchungen zu Cicero's philosophischen Schriften* iii (Leipzig, 1883; repr. Hildesheim, 1964).
[49] Janáček, K. *Sextus Empiricus' Sceptical Methods* (Prague, 1972).
[50] Naess, A. *Scepticism* (London, 1968).
[51] Natorp, P. *Forschungen zur Geschichte des Erkenntnisproblems im Altertum* (Berlin, 1884).

Collection of articles

[52] Glidden, D., ed. *Riverside Studies in Ancient Scepticism* (forthcoming).

Articles

[53] Arnim, H. von 'Arkesilaos', in Pauly-Wissowa, *Realencyclopädie der classischen Altertumswissenschaft* II 1 (Stuttgart, 1895), 1164–8.
[54]   'Karneades', in Pauly–Wissowa, *Realencyclopädie der classischen Altertumswissenschaft* X 2 (Stuttgart, 1919), 1964–85.
[55] Burnyeat, M. F. 'Protagoras and Self Refutation in Later Greek Philosophy', *Philosophical Review* 85 (1976), 44-69.
[56]   'The Upside-Down Back-to-Front Sceptic of Lucretius IV 472', *Philologus* 122 (1978), 197–206.
[57]   'Tranquillity without a stop: Timon frag. 68', *Classical Quarterly* 72 (N.S. 30) (1980).
[58]   'Carneades Was No Probabilist', in Glidden [52].
[59]   'Idealism and Greek Philosophy: What Descartes Saw and Berkeley Missed', in Vesey, G., ed., *Idealism: Past and Present*, Royal Institute of Philosophy Lectures 13 (Hassocks, 1980).
[60] Couissin, P. 'Le Stoïcisme de la Nouvelle Académie', *Revue d'histoire de la philosophie* 3 (1929), 241–76.
[61]   'L'Origine et l'evolution de l''εποχή' *Revue des études grecques* 42 (1929), 373–97.
[62] Frede, M. Review of Stough [29], *Journal of Philosophy* 70 (1973), 805–10.
[63] 'Des Skeptikers Meinungen', *Neue Hefte für Philosophie* 15/16 (1979), 102–29.
[64] Fritz, K. von 'Pyrrhon', in Pauly–Wissowa, *Realencyclopädie der classischen Altertumswissenschaft* 24 (Stuttgart 1963), 89–106.
[65] Gigon, O. 'Zur Geschichte der sogenannten Neuen Akademie', *Museum Helveticum* 1 (1944) 47–64.
[66] Janáček, K. 'Zur Interpretation des Photios—Abschnittes über Aenesidemos', *Eirene* 14 (1976), 93–100.
[67] Lacy, P. de 'οὐ μᾶλλον and the Antecedents of Ancient Scepticism' *Phronesis* 3 (1958), 59–71.

[68] Long, A. A. 'Timon of Phlius: Pyrrhonist and Satirist', *Proceedings of the Cambridge Philological Society* 204 (N.S. 24) (1978), 68-91.

[69['Sextus Empiricus on the Criterion of Truth', *Bulletin of the Institute of Classical Studies* 25 (1978), 35-49.

5. STOICISM

Books

[70] Barwick, K. *Probleme der stoische Sprachlehre und Rhetorik* (Berlin, 1957).

[71] Bonhöffer, A. *Epiktet und die Stoa* (Stuttgart, 1890).

[72] Brochard, V. *De assensione Stoici quid senserint* (Diss., Paris, 1879).

[73] Goldschmidt, V. *Le Système stoicien et l'idée de temps* (2nd edn., Paris, 1969).

[74] Gould, J. *The Philosophy of Chrysippus* (Leiden, 1970).

[75] Graeser, A. *Zenon von Kition, Positionen und Probleme* (Berlin, 1975).

[76] Sambursky, S. *Physics of the Stoics* (London, 1959).

[77] Schmidt, R. *Stoicorum Grammatica* (Halle, 1839).

[78] Tsekourakis, D. *Studies in the Terminology of Early Stoic Ethics* (*Hermes* Einzelschriften 32, Wiesbaden, 1974).

[79] Voelké, A.-J. *L'Idée de volonté dans le stoicisme* (Paris, 1973).

[80] Watson, G. *The Stoic Theory of Knowledge* (Belfast, 1966).

Collections of articles

[81] Brunschwig, J., ed. *Les Stoïciens et leur logique* (Paris, 1978).

[82] Long, A. A., ed. *Problems in Stoicism* (London, 1971).

[83] Rist, J. M., ed. *The Stoics* (Berkeley, Los Angeles, and London, 1978).

Articles

[84] Boyancé, P. 'Les preuves stoïciennes de l'existence des dieux', *Hermes* 90 (1962), 45-71; repr. in Boyancé, *Études sur l'humanisme cicéronien* (Brussels, 1970), 301-34.

[85] Corcoran, J. 'Remarks on Stoic Deduction', in Corcoran [40], 169-81.

[86] Donini, P. 'Crisippo e la nozione del possibile', *Revista di filologia* 101 (1973), 333-51.

[87] 'Fato de voluntà umana in Crisippo', *Atti dell' Accademia delle Scienze di Torino* 109 (1974/5), 1-44.

[88] Frede, M. 'Stoic vs. Aristotelian Syllogistic', *Archiv für Geschichte der Philosophie* 56 (1974), 1-32.

314   Doubt and Dogmatism

[89]   'The Origins of Traditional Grammar', in Butts, R., and Hintikka, J., edd., *Historical and Philosophical Dimensions of Logic, Methodology and Philosophy of Science* (Dordrecht, 1977), 51–79.

[90]   'Principles of Stoic Grammar', in Rist [83], 27–75.

[91] Görler, W. *'Ασθενὴς συγκατάθεσις*: Zur stoischen Erkenntnistheorie', *Wurzbürger Jahrbücher für die Altertumswissenschaft*, N.F. 3. (1977), 83–92.

[92] Gould, J. B. 'Deduction in Stoic Logic', in Corcoran [40], 151–68.

[93] Goulet, R. 'La classification stoïcienne des propositions simples', in Brunschwig [81], 171–98.

[94] Graeser, A. 'Les catégories stoïciennes', in Brunschwig [81], 199–221.

[95] Imbert, C. 'Théorie de la représentation et doctrine logique', in Brunschwig [81], 223–49.

[96] Kerferd, G. B. 'The Problem of *Synkatathesis* and *Katelēpsis* in Stoic Doctrine', in Brunschwig [81], 251–72.

[97] Kidd, I. G. 'Posidonius and Logic', in Brunschwig [81], 273–83.

[98] Lacy, P. de 'The Stoic Categories as Methodological Principles', *Transactions of the American Philological Association* 76 (1945), 246–63.

[99] Lloyd, A. C. 'Grammar and Metaphysics in the Stoa', in Long [82], 58–74.

[100]   'Activity and Description in Aristotle and the Stoa', *Proceedings of the British Academy* 56 (1970), 227–40.

[101]   'Definite Propositions and the Concept of Reference', in Brunschwig [81], 285–95.

[102] Long, A. A. 'Carneades and the Stoic Telos', *Phronesis* 12 (1967), 59–90.

[103]   'The Stoic Concept of Evil', *Philosophical Quarterly* 18 (1968), 329–43.

[104]   'Stoic Determinism and Alexander of Aphrodisias *De Fato* (i–xiv), *Archiv für Geschichte der Philosophie* 52 (1970), 247–68.

[105]   'The Logical Basis of Stoic Ethics', *Proceedings of the Aristotelian Society* 71 (1970/71), 85–104.

[106]   'Freedom and Determinism in the Stoic Theory of Human Action', in Long [82], 173–99.

[107]   'Language and Thought in Stoicism', in Long [82], 75–113.

[108]   'The Stoic Distinction between Truth and the True', in Brunschwig [81], 297–315.

[109]   'Dialectic and the Stoic Sage', in Rist [83], 101–24.

[110] Mates, B. 'Stoic Logic and the Text of Sextus Empiricus', *American Journal of Philology* 70 (1949), 290–8.

[111] Mignucci, M. 'Sur la logique modale des stoïciens', in Brunschwig [81], 317–46.

[112] Mueller, Ian 'Stoic and Peripatetic Logic', *Archiv für die Geschichte der Philosophie* 51 (1969), 173–87.

[113] Pachet, P. 'La deixis selon Zénon et Chrysippe', *Phronesis* 20 (1975), 241–6.

[114] Pembroke, S. G. 'Oikeiōsis', in Long [82], 114–49.

[115] Pinborg,J. 'Historiography of Linguistics—Classical Antiquity: Greece', *Current Trends in Linguistics* 13 (1975), 69–126.

[116] Pohlenz, M. 'Zenon und Chrysipp', *Nachrichten vonder Akademie der Wissenschaften zu Göttingen*, Phil.-hist. Klasse, N.F. i, 2 (1938), 173–210.

[117] Reesor, M. 'Fate and Possibility on. Early Stoic Philosophy', *Phoenix* 19 (1965), 285–97.

[118] Rist, J. M. 'Categories and Their Uses', in Long [82], 38–57.

[119] 'Zeno and the Origins of Stoic Logic', in Brunschwig [81], 387–400.

[120] Sandbach, F. H. 'Ennoia and Prolēpsis', *Classical Quarterly* 24 (1930), 44–51; repr. with supplementary notes in Long [82],22–37.

[121] 'Phantasia Katalēptikē', in Long [82], 9–21.

[122] Verbeke, G. 'La philosophie du signe chez les stoïciens', in Brunschwig [81], 401–24.

6. EPICUREANISM

Books

[123] Furley, D. J. *Two Studies in the Greek Atomists* (Princeton, 1967).

[124] Lemke, D. *Die Theologie Epikurs* (Munich, 1973).

[125] Manuwald, A. *Die Prolepsislehre Epikurs* (Bonn, 1972).

Articles

[126] Barigazzi, A. 'Épicure et le Scepticisme', *Association Guillaume Budé: Actes due VIIIᵉ Congrès* 1969, 286–92.

[127] Furley, D. J. 'Knowledge of Atoms and Void in Epicureanism' in Anton, J., and Kustas, G., edd., *Essays in Ancient Greek Philosophy* (Albany, 1971), 607–19.

[128] Goldschmidt, V. 'Remarques sur l'origine épicurienne de la prénotion', in Brunschwig [81], 155–69.

[129] Long, A. A. 'Aisthesis, Prolepsis and Linguistic Theory in Epicurus', *Bulletin of the Institute of Classical Studies* 18 (1971), 114–33.

[130] Sedley, D. 'Epicurus, *On Nature*, Book XXVIII', *Cronache ercolanesi* 3 (1973), 5–83.

[131] 'Epicurus and his Professional Rivals', *Cahiers de philologie* 1 (1976), 119–59.

[132] 'Epicurus and the Mathematicians of Cyzicus', *Cronache ercolanesi* 6 (1976), 23–54.

[133] Striker, G. 'Epicurus on the Truth of Sense-Impressions', *Archiv für Geschichte der Philosophie* 59 (1977), 125–42.

[134] Taylor, C. C. W. 'Pleasure, Knowledge and Sensation in Democritus', *Phronesis* 12 (1967), 6–27.

[135] Vlastos, G. 'Zeno of Sidon as a Critic of Euclid', in L. Wallach, ed., *The Classical Tradition: Literary and Historical Studies in honor of Harry Caplan* (Ithaca, 1966), 148–59.

7. MISCELLANEOUS

[136] Barnes, J. 'Aristotle's Theory of Demonstration', *Phronesis* 14 (1969), 123–52; repr. in J. Barnes, M. Schofield, R. Sorabji, edd., *Articles on Aristotle*, vol. 1 (London, 1975), 65–87.

[137] Müller, Iwan von *Über Galens Werk vom wissenschaftlichen Beweis* (Munich, 1895).

[138] Prior, A. 'Diodoran Modalities', *Philosophical Quarterly* 5 (1955), 205–13.

[139] Sharples, R. 'Responsibility, Chance and Not-Being (Alexander of Aphrodisias, *Mantissa* 169–172), *Bulletin of the Institute of Classical Studies* 22 (1975), 37–64.

INDEX LOCORUM*

This index lists all passages from ancient authors which are discussed or cited in the book. Where references are given to a fragmentary work or to a specific edition (e.g. by page and line) of an author, a brief indication of the collection of fragments or the edition in question is supplied. Further information on these collections and editions can in most cases readily be found in Liddell-Scott-Jones, *A Greek-English Lexicon*, or in Hammond and Scullard, *The Oxford Classical Dictionary* (2nd edn., 1970), or in both authorities; see also section I of the select bibliography. Two editions not identifiable by these methods are: Damascius, *Lectures on the Philebus*, edited and translated by L. G. Westerink (Amsterdam, 1959).

Galen, *de Causis continentibus libellus*, edited by C. Kalbfleisch (Marburg, 1904). This edition of the Latin version is re-edited in *Corpus Medicorum Graecorum, Supplementum Orientale* ii (Berlin, 1969), which also contains an edition and English translation of the Arabic version by Malcolm Lyons.

No attempt has been made by the editors of the present volume to collate references to named authors with von Arnim's collection *Stoicorum Veterum Fragmenta* (or *vice versa*). Readers who desire this information should consult Adler's index of sources in Vol. iv of *SVF*.

* Prepared by Elizabeth Schofield, to whom the editors express heartfelt thanks.

Clement of Alexandria

Simplicius

in Categorias (ed. Kalbfleisch)

in Physica (ed. Diels)

Sophocles

Philoctetes

Stephanus

Stobaeus (ed. Wachsmuth and Hense)

Eclogae

INDEX OF GREEK WORDS

This index includes only words which occasion philosophical discussion in this book. Translations are offered for the sake of convenience but at the cost of concealing the complexity or the problematic character of the philosophical use or uses of the words in question.

GENERAL INDEX

approach to ethical questions, 73, 82; sceptical tranquillity, 11, 17, 24–6, 30, 31–3, 37, 40–2, 51–2

Euclid, attacked and defended by Hellenistic philosophers, 162 (with n. 4), 164

evidence (=empirical basis for judgement), and signs in Stoicism, 268–70; Epicurus' doctrine of criterion a theory of evidence, 109–10, 112–13, 120; likewise Zeno's, 284; but the identification more controversial in Carneades' case, 29 n. 16, 70–4 (with n. 42), 81–2; *see* sign (=quality of being evident), *see* evident

evident, defined, 26 n. 9; rational and perceptual evidence, 134; species of non-evident, 132, 177–8; standard example of non-evident, 40 n. 35; dogmatism as involving assent to non-evident, 26, 44, 46; Pyrrhonist abolishes evidence of evident, 46; but younger Stoics hold assent to evident compelled, 75 n. 52; evident presentation as criterion of truth, 95–6, 288–292, 298, 305; signs and non-evident, 139–40, 179–80, 269–70; evident and non-evident in theory of proof, Ch. 6 *passim*, 165, 177–81, 290

explanation, and relation of premisses to conclusion in concludent argument, 168–73; and proof, 134 with n. 23, 177–81, 306; relation to causation in Stoic theory, 222–6, 246–9; contrasting Aristotelian position, 223–4, 255–257; Aristotle's view of relation of explanation and necessity expounded, 250–2; and defended, 255–9

faith, 135–43, 153, 158

fallacies, Stoic classification, 165–6

fate, in Stoic theory of cause and necessity, 225, 234–5, 239, 240, 246, 262, 272–6, 281

force, in Stoics and Philoponus, 236, 240–1, 248–9

Frede, M., on conditionals and necessity, 260–1, 267–8; on Stoic definitions of modal notions, 272; on internal and external causes, 274

Frege, G., his logic compared and contrasted with Stoic logic, 186–7

Galen, attacks Pyrrhonism, 23 n. 4; on proof, 162

gods, sceptical attitude to, 33 n. 26; subject of preconception and demonstrative argument, 289–307; divine prophecy and non-revelatory concludent arguments, 135–43, 153; divine need of interpreters, 200

Gould, J. B., on Stoic criterion of truth, 89

grammar, of the Stoics, 202–3, 212–13

Hempel, C., theory of explanation compared and contrasted with Aristotle's, 250–3

Hirzel, R., on Carneades' scepticism, 55–7

Hume, D., on Pyrrhonism, 20–3, 49, 53; his empiricism contrasted with Epicurus', 119

Iamblichus, on Plato's notion of cause, 219

identification, of objects in Stoic epistemology, 188, 190–1, 192–3, 202 (cf. 204), 295

illusions, Stoic treatment of, 88–90, 284–5, 288; and Epicurean, 111–12, 114–17, 285

inaction, alleged to be consequence of scepticism, 20–3; charge denied, 31–7, 40–2, 63–79

incorrigible acquaintance (of sense contents), and Epicurus' empiricism, 110–11, 117–19, 120–1

indemonstrable arguments, basic textual evidence for, 126 n. 4; form of first, 192; its use in proof, 137; charged with redundancy, 166, 173–5; as are all five, 166, 181; use of second in theology, 299

induction, Stoic incomprehension about, 306

interpretation, Stoic theory, 200–3, 204 n. 42, 212

judgement, attacked by sceptic, 23–7, 77–9

Kirwan, C. A., on definition of redundancy, 172 n. 16

knowledge, not the fundamental target of scepticism, 22, 31–2; but a prime